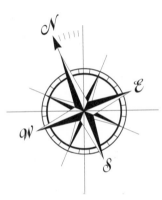

THE TRAVELER'S
ATLAS

A Geographic Handbook

Table of Contents

Legend 7
World Political 8
World Physical 10
World Time Zones 12

Europe 14
British Isles 18
Europe WESTERN 20
Europe NORTH CENTRAL 22
Europe SOUTH CENTRAL-WEST 24
Europe SOUTH CENTRAL-EAST 25
London METRO & DOWNTOWN 26
Paris METRO & DOWNTOWN 28
Amsterdam - The Hague - Rotterdam 30
Antwerp - Brussels 31
Berlin METRO & DOWNTOWN 32
Essen - Dortmund - Düsseldorf 34
Frankfurt / Prague 35
Copenhagen / Stockholm 36
Bern / Zürich 37
Lisbon / Barcelona 38
Madrid 39
Rome / Milan 40
Rome DOWNTOWN 41
Budapest / Vienna 42
Athens / Istanbul 43

Africa and Middle East 44
Tel Aviv - Yafo - Jerusalem / Cairo 50
Pretoria / Tshwane - Johannesburg 51

Northern Asia - Russia 52
Moscow METRO 56
Moscow DOWNTOWN / St. Petersburg 57

Southern Asia 58
Taipei / Manila 62
Bangkok / Singapore 63
Jakarta / Delhi - New Delhi 64
Bombay / Calcutta 65

Far East 66
Tokyo METRO & DOWNTOWN 68
Osaka - Kyoto - Kobe 70
Osaka / Kyoto DOWNTOWN 71
Seoul 72
Beijing 73
Shanghai 74
Hong Kong 75

Australia - New Zealand 76
Sydney 78
Melbourne 79

Pacific 80

Polar Regions 82

South America 84
Lima / Santiago 87
Buenos Aires METRO & DOWNTOWN 88
Caracas / Bogotá 90
Rio de Janeiro 91
São Paulo METRO & DOWNTOWN 92

Caribbean 94

Mexico - Central America 96
Mexico City 98
Guadalajara 99

Canada	100
Toronto	104
Ottawa / Québec	105
Montréal	106
Winnipeg / Vancouver	107
United States	109
New England	114
New York State	116
Middle Atlantic States	118
Southeastern States	120
Florida - Puerto Rico	122
Midwestern States	124
North Central States	126
South Central States	128
Rocky Mountain States	130
California - Nevada	132
Northwestern States	134
Alaska	136
Hawaii	137
Boston METRO & DOWNTOWN	138
New York DOWNTOWN & METRO	141
Philadelphia	144
Pittsburgh	146
Baltimore	147
Washington, D.C. METRO & DOWNTOWN	148
Cleveland	150
Cincinnati	151
Atlanta	152
Orlando	153
Tampa - St. Petersburg	154
Miami - Fort Lauderdale	155
Detroit	156
Milwaukee / Indianapolis	157
Chicago METRO & DOWNTOWN	158
Minneapolis - St. Paul	161
Kansas City / St. Louis	162
New Orleans / San Antonio	163
Dallas - Fort Worth	164
Houston	166
Denver	167
Phoenix	168
San Diego	169
Los Angeles METRO & DOWNTOWN	170
San Francisco DOWNTOWN	173
San Francisco Bay	174
Seattle - Tacoma	176
Portland / Honolulu	177
National Parks & Interstates	178
Yellowstone National Park	180
Grand Teton National Park	181
Yosemite National Park	182
Grand Canyon National Park	183
Cape Cod	184
Acadia National Park	186
Cape Hatteras	187
Florida Keys	188
Appendix	
Traveler's Notes	189
Perpetual Calendar	198
International Travel	201
International Weather	202
U.S. Weather	204
International Air Distances	206
U.S. Road and Air Distances	208
Weights and Measures	210
Country Information	212
Foreign Embassies in the U.S.	213
U.S. & Canadian Area Codes	216
International Dialing Codes	219
Toll-Free Numbers	221
Abbreviations	222
Index	223

Legend

General

———————— International boundary

———————— Internal political boundary

- - - - - - - - Undefined/disputed boundary

- - - - - - - - Boundary in water

⊛ National capital

★ State or provincial capital

• Other city or town.
  City or town type size is an
  indication of the relative size
  or importance of the city
  or town.

Political / Physical

Elevations in meters and feet
above sea level.

Elevation range varies
from map to map.

Regional Maps

———————— Limited access highway

———————— Other main route

UNITED STATES ONLY

- - - - - - - Unpaved road

- - - - - - - - Ferry

Subject states

Non-subject states

Large built-up area

Park

National or state forest

Military reservation

Indian reservation

City Maps

════════ Limited access highway

═ ═ ═ ═ ═ : ...under construction

———————— Other main route

▪ ▪ ▪ ▪ ▪ ▪ Tunnel

- - - - - - - - Ferry

Approximate built-up area

● Point of interest

• City or town.
  Settlements not located with a
  black circle are districts or
  communities that are part of a
  larger city.

Park Maps (United States)

════════ Limited access highway
         (Interstate, toll road etc.)

———————— Other main route

· · · · · · · Scenic Route

- - - - - - - - Trail

Ⓧ Road closed in winter

- - - - - - - - Ferry

National Park

Other park

National or state forest

Military reservation

Indian reservation

▲ Campsite

⚠ Skiing

● Point of interest

7

World POLITICAL

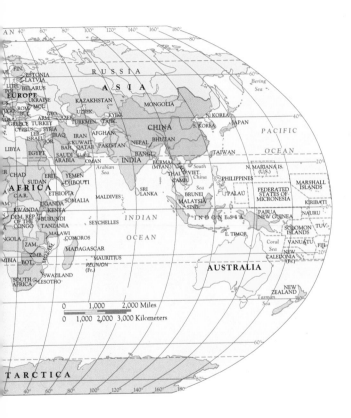

World PHYSICAL

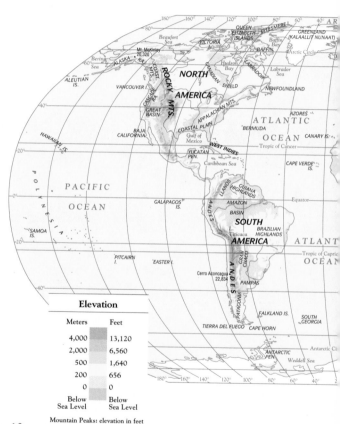

Elevation

Meters	Feet
4,000	13,120
2,000	6,560
500	1,640
200	656
0	0
Below Sea Level	Below Sea Level

Mountain Peaks: elevation in feet

World Time Zones

The World is divided into 24 time zones, beginning at the Prime Meridian, which runs through Greenwich, England. The twelve zones east and twelve zones west of the Prime Meridian meet halfway around the globe at the International Date Line.

Traveling in an easterly direction, the time of day moves ahead one hour for each zone crossed. Traveling west, time falls behind one hour per zone. At the International Date Line a traveler gains one day crossing in an easterly direction, and loses one day traveling west.

The table below the map can be used to quickly compare times of day between places. The vertical columns of the table correspond with the time zones on the map, and are color coordinated with their respective zones. Gray shading is added to the table to mark a change between days of the week ("Monday" is symbolized with gray shading; "Sunday" and "Tuesday" have no shading). By reading horizontally across the table the time of day in each zone can be compared. For example, if it is noon in New York on Monday, it is 5:00 p.m. Monday in London and 2:00 a.m. Tuesday in Tokyo.

Note that times shown are "standard time". Adjustments are necessary when "daylight saving time" is used.

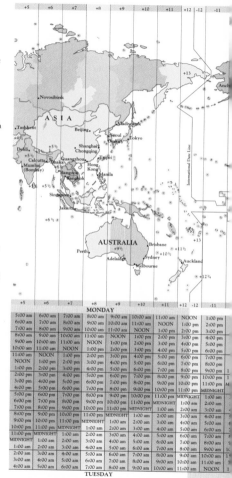

MONDAY

+5	+6	+7	+8	+9	+10	+11	+12	-12	-11
5:00 am	6:00 am	7:00 am	8:00 am	9:00 am	10:00 am	11:00 am	NOON	1:00 pm	
6:00 am	7:00 am	8:00 am	9:00 am	10:00 am	11:00 am	NOON	1:00 pm	2:00 pm	
7:00 am	8:00 am	9:00 am	10:00 am	11:00 am	NOON	1:00 pm	2:00 pm	3:00 pm	
8:00 am	9:00 am	10:00 am	11:00 am	NOON	1:00 pm	2:00 pm	3:00 pm	4:00 pm	
9:00 am	10:00 am	11:00 am	NOON	1:00 pm	2:00 pm	3:00 pm	4:00 pm	5:00 pm	
10:00 am	11:00 am	NOON	1:00 pm	2:00 pm	3:00 pm	4:00 pm	5:00 pm	6:00 pm	
11:00 am	NOON	1:00 pm	2:00 pm	3:00 pm	4:00 pm	5:00 pm	6:00 pm	7:00 pm	
NOON	1:00 pm	2:00 pm	3:00 pm	4:00 pm	5:00 pm	6:00 pm	7:00 pm	8:00 pm	
1:00 pm	2:00 pm	3:00 pm	4:00 pm	5:00 pm	6:00 pm	7:00 pm	8:00 pm	9:00 pm	1
2:00 pm	3:00 pm	4:00 pm	5:00 pm	6:00 pm	7:00 pm	8:00 pm	9:00 pm	10:00 pm	1
3:00 pm	4:00 pm	5:00 pm	6:00 pm	7:00 pm	8:00 pm	9:00 pm	10:00 pm	11:00 pm	M
4:00 pm	5:00 pm	6:00 pm	7:00 pm	8:00 pm	9:00 pm	10:00 pm	11:00 pm	MIDNIGHT	
5:00 pm	6:00 pm	7:00 pm	8:00 pm	9:00 pm	10:00 pm	11:00 pm	MIDNIGHT	1:00 am	
6:00 pm	7:00 pm	8:00 pm	9:00 pm	10:00 pm	11:00 pm	MIDNIGHT	1:00 am	2:00 am	
7:00 pm	8:00 pm	9:00 pm	10:00 pm	11:00 pm	MIDNIGHT	1:00 am	2:00 am	3:00 am	
8:00 pm	9:00 pm	10:00 pm	11:00 pm	MIDNIGHT	1:00 am	2:00 am	3:00 am	4:00 am	
9:00 pm	10:00 pm	11:00 pm	MIDNIGHT	1:00 am	2:00 am	3:00 am	4:00 am	5:00 am	
10:00 pm	11:00 pm	MIDNIGHT	1:00 am	2:00 am	3:00 am	4:00 am	5:00 am	6:00 am	
11:00 pm	MIDNIGHT	1:00 am	2:00 am	3:00 am	4:00 am	5:00 am	6:00 am	7:00 am	
MIDNIGHT	1:00 am	2:00 am	3:00 am	4:00 am	5:00 am	6:00 am	7:00 am	8:00 am	
1:00 am	2:00 am	3:00 am	4:00 am	5:00 am	6:00 am	7:00 am	8:00 am	9:00 am	
2:00 am	3:00 am	4:00 am	5:00 am	6:00 am	7:00 am	8:00 am	9:00 am	10:00 am	1
3:00 am	4:00 am	5:00 am	6:00 am	7:00 am	8:00 am	9:00 am	10:00 am	11:00 am	
4:00 am	5:00 am	6:00 am	7:00 am	8:00 am	9:00 am	10:00 am	11:00 am	NOON	

TUESDAY

World Time Zones

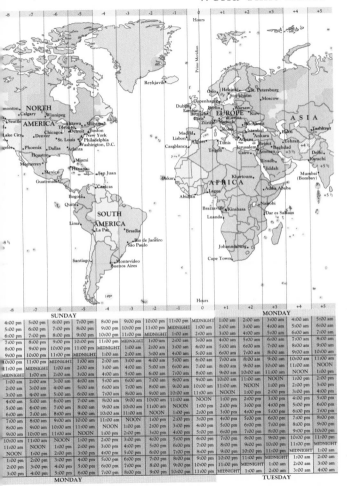

Europe NORTHERN

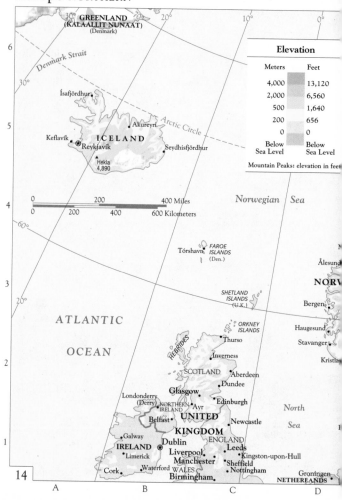

GREENLAND (KALAALLIT NUNAAT) (Denmark)

Denmark Strait

Ísafjördhur

Akureyri

Keflavík Reykjavík
ICELAND
Hekla
4,890
Seydhisfjördhur

Arctic Circle

Norwegian Sea

Elevation	
Meters	Feet
4,000	13,120
2,000	6,560
500	1,640
200	656
0	0
Below Sea Level	Below Sea Level

Mountain Peaks: elevation in feet

0 — 200 — 400 Miles
0 — 200 — 400 — 600 Kilometers

Tórshavn *FAROE ISLANDS* (Den.)

SHETLAND ISLANDS (U.K.)

Ålesund

NORW

Bergen

Haugesund

Stavanger

Kristia

ORKNEY ISLANDS

ATLANTIC

OCEAN

HEBRIDES

Thurso

Inverness

SCOTLAND

Aberdeen

Dundee

Glasgow

Londonderry (Derry) NORTHERN IRELAND Ayr

Edinburgh

Belfast

UNITED

Newcastle

North

Galway

KINGDOM

ENGLAND

IRELAND Dublin

Leeds

Sea

Limerick

Liverpool
Manchester

Kingston-upon-Hull

Sheffield

Nottingham

Cork Waterford WALES

Birmingham

Groningen
NETHERLANDS

14

A   B   C   D

NORTH CAPE

Barents Sea

Hammerfest

Vardø

Murmansk

Tromsø

Ivalo

KOLA PENINSULA

Narvik

L A P L A N D

Apatity

Kiruna

White Sea

Bodø

Arkhangelsk

Rovaniemi

Mo-i-Rana

Kemi

Belomorsk

Luleå

Oulo

FINLAND

Skellefteå

Lake Onega

Umeå

Kokkola

Vassa

Kuopio

Joensuu

Petrozavodsk

Östersund

Jyväskylä

LAKE REGION

Lake Ladoga

Sundsvall

Tampere

Lahti

SWEDEN

Pori

Vyborg

Gulf of Bothnia

Gävle

Turku

Helsinki

Gulf of Finland

St. Petersburg

Borlänge

ÅLAND IS. (Fin.)

Novgorod

RUSSIA

Uppsala

Tallinn

Drammen

Karlstad

Stockholm

ESTONIA

Lake Peipus

Tver

Örebro

Norrköping

Parnu

Tartu

Pskov

Moscow

Vänern

Linköping

Vättern

Jönköping

GOTLAND (Swe.)

Ventspils

Riga

Göteborg

Växjö

LATVIA

ÖLAND

Daugavpils

Vitsyebsk

Smolensk

Århus

Halmstad

Kalmar

Liepaja

LITHUANIA

Helsingborg

Klaipeda

Odense

Malmö

BORNHOLM (Den.)

Kaunas

Vilnius

Mahilyow

Bryansk

DMARK

RUSSIA Kaliningrad

Minsk

Kiel

Gdansk

NORTHERN EUROPEAN PLAIN

BELARUS

Homyel

Rostock

Hamburg

Szczecin

POLAND

Hrodna

GER.

Bydgoszcz

Bialystok

Baltic Sea

Kattegat

Gulf of Riga

15

Europe SOUTHERN

16

*The Former Yugoslav Republic of Macedonia

British Isles

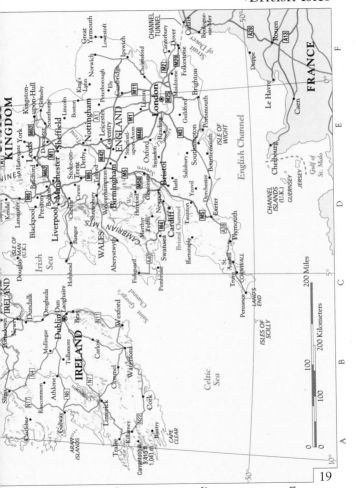

British Isles

Europe WESTERN

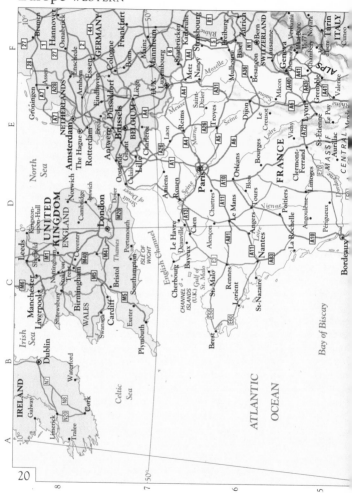

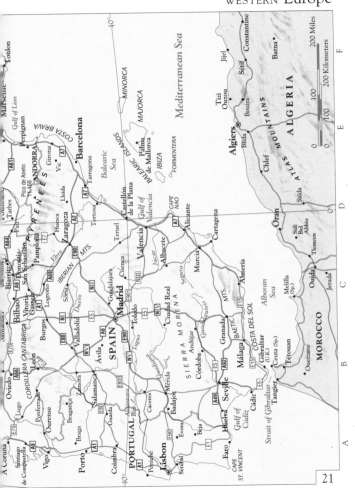

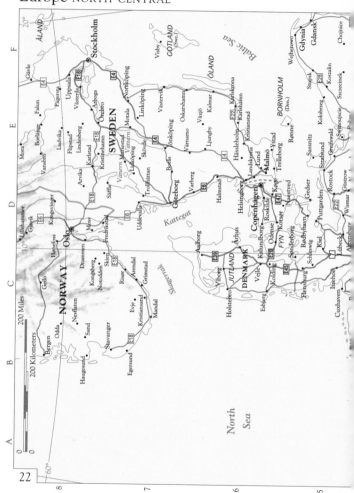

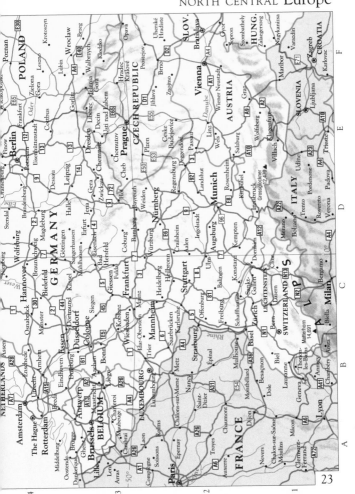

Europe SOUTH CENTRAL - WEST

London UNITED KINGDOM

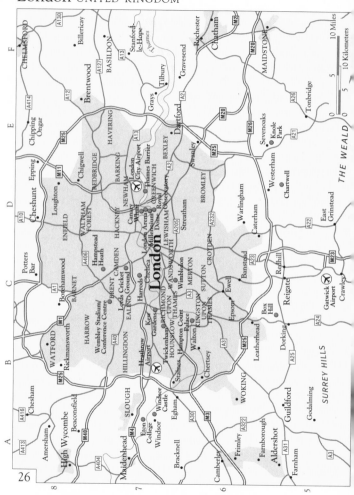

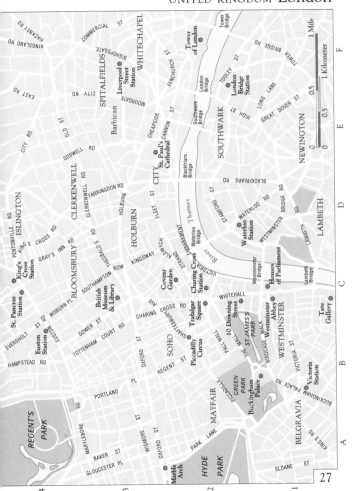

27

Paris FRANCE

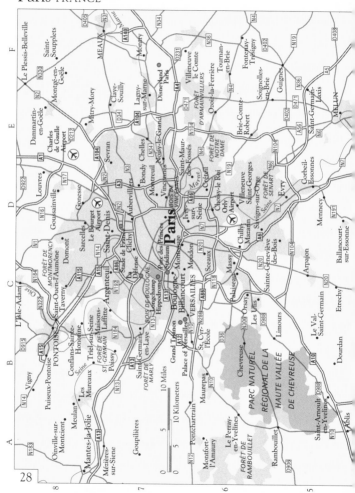

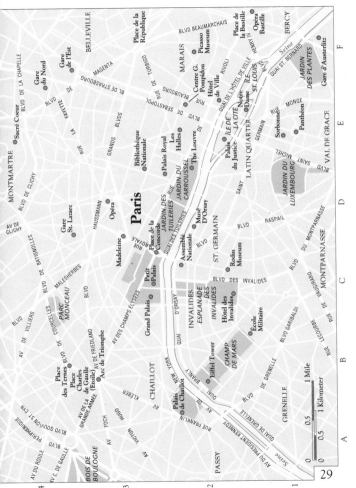

Paris

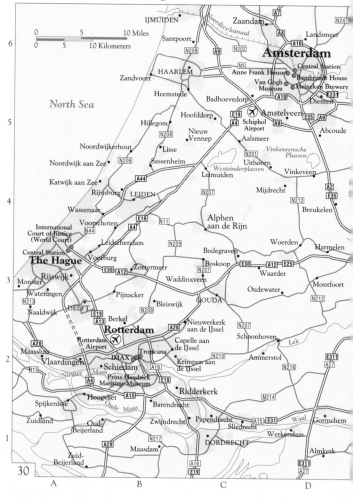

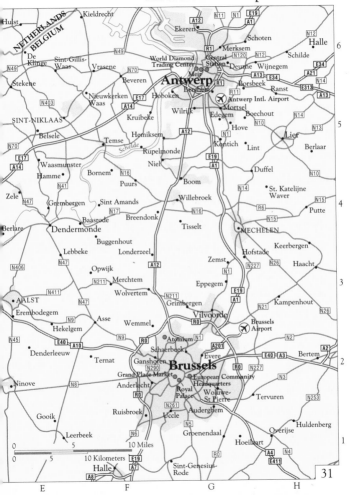

Berlin GERMANY

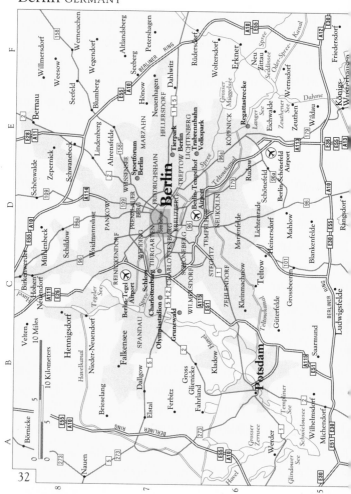

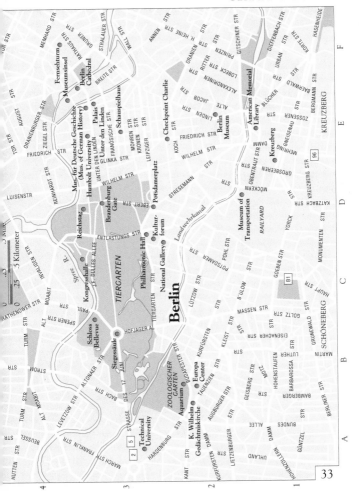

Essen - Dortmund - Düsseldorf GERMANY

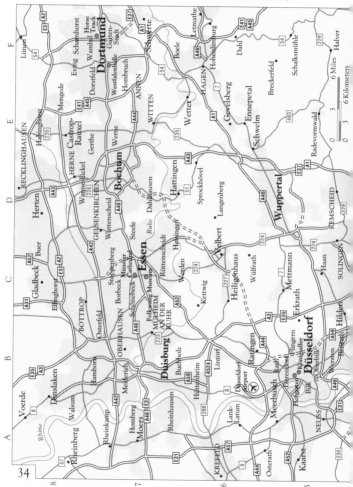

CZECH REPUBLIC Prague (map)

Elbe (Labe)
Kostelec nad Labem
Mratín
Neratovice
Odolena Voda
Vodochody
Libčice nad Vltavou
Kralupy nad Vltavou
Vltava
Husinec
Roztoky
Horoměřice
Velké Přílepy
Tuchoměřice
Ruzyně Airport
Jenec
Jinočany
Rudná
Velen
Libeznice
Zdiby
Kbely
Bohnice
Libeč
Střešovice
Břevnov
Strahov Stadium
Lib, Zoological Garden
Stodůlky
Vinoř
Horní Počernice
Pocernice
Vysočany
Holešovice
Libeň
Military Museum
Prague
Smíchov
St. Apolinaris Church
Podolí
Vršovice
Strašnice
Hostivař
Chodov
Modřany
Běchovice
Uhříněves
Průhonice
Jesenice
Dolní Brezany
Komořany
Radotín
Černošice
Jíloviště
Vrané
Davle
Jílové u Prahy
Kamenice
Mníšek pod Brdy
Řevnice

8 Miles
8 Kilometers

GERMANY Frankfurt (map)

Bad Vilbel
Berkersheim
Bonames
Berkersheim
Niederursel
Eckenheim
Oberursel
Bommersheim
Steinbach
Bommersheim
Eschborn
Nordwest-stadt
Hausen
Rödelheim
Bockenheim
Sossenheim
Höchst
Nied
Schwanheim
Kelsterbach
Frankfurt am Main International Airport
Walldorf
Mörfelden
Bergen-Enkheim
Ginnheim
Grüne-burg Park
Municipal
Bornheim
Zoological Garden
Old Opera House
Kaiser dom Cathedral
Sachsenhausen
Niederrad
Zeppelinheim
Neu-Isenburg
Sprendlingen
Buchschlag
Langen
Egelsbach
Fechenheim
Offenbach
Graben-bruch
Gravenbruch
Steinberg
Heusen-stamm
Dietzenbach
Steinberg
Dreieichenhain
Dreieich
Offenthal
Rödermark

Frankfurt
Main Railroad Station

3 Miles
3 Kilometers

35

Copenhagen DENMARK / Stockholm SWEDEN

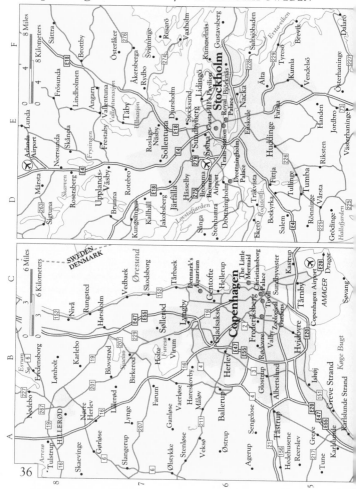

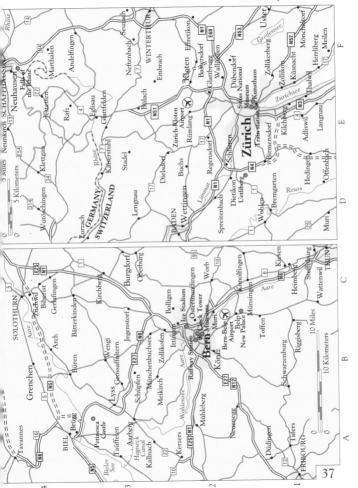

SWITZERLAND

Bern / Zürich

Rhine

Neuhausen
Schaffhausen
Neunkirch
Marthalen
Andelfingen
Seuzach
Winterthur
Uster
Greifensee
Mönchaltorf
Meilen
Herrliberg
Küsnacht
Zollikon
Zollikerberg
Kunsthaus
Museum
Swiss National
Dübendorf
Wallisellen
Glattbrugg
Bassersdorf
Effretikon
Kloten
Nettenbach
Embrach
Bülach
Rafz
Eglisau
Glattfelden
Guntern
Full of the Rhine

Germany
Switzerland
Zurzach
Wurenlingen
Klettgau
Kaiserstuhl
Stadel
Lengnau
Dielsdorf
Buchs
Zürich-Kloten Airport
Rümlang
Regensdorf
Schlieren
Birmensdorf
Baden
Wettingen
Dietikon
Uetliberg
Spreitenbach
Bremgarten
Wohlen
Muri
Hedingen
Offenburg
Reuss
Adliswil
Langnau
Kilchberg
Thalwil
Zürichsee
Zürich
Train-station

Solothurn
Zuchwil
Biberist
Gerlafingen
Burgdorf
Oberburg
Kirchberg
Bätterkinden
Jegenstorf
Bolligen
Ostermundigen
Worb
Konolfingen
Kiesen
Steffisburg
Heimberg
Wattenwil
Thun
Aare
Grenchen
Arch
Büren
Wengi
Münchenbuchsee
Zollikofen
Ittigen
Ice Stadium
Bern
Museum
Clock Tower
Railway Station
Münsingen
Toffen
Schwarzenburg
Riggisberg
Biel
Petinesca Castle
Aarberg
Hagneck Canal
Kallnach
Kerzers
Mühleberg
Neuenegg
Köniz
Bern-Belp Airport
Belp
New Palace
Bieler See
Tavannes
Brügg
Lyss
Grossaffoltern
Schüpfen
Meikirch
Bümpliz
Taters
Düdingen
Fribourg

37

Lisbon PORTUGAL / Barcelona SPAIN

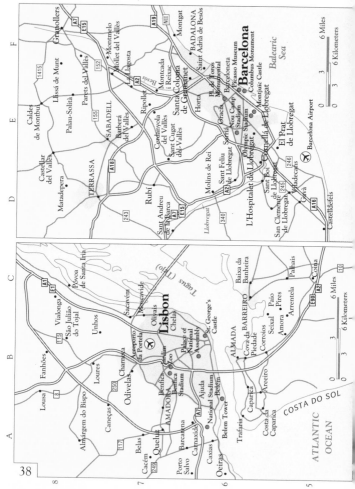

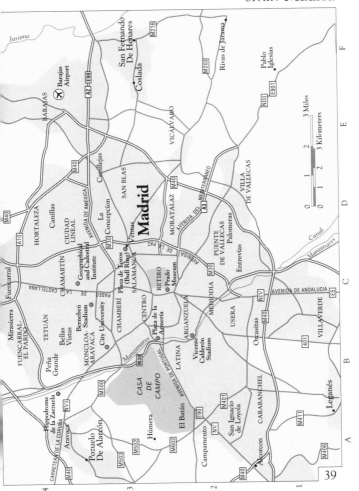

Rome / Milan ITALY

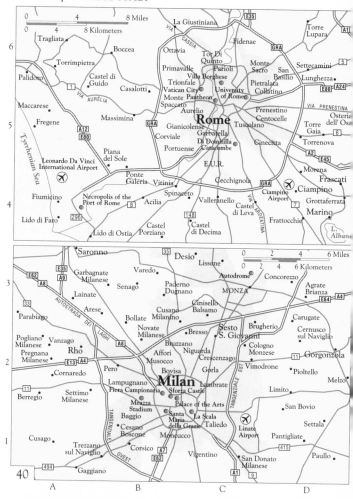

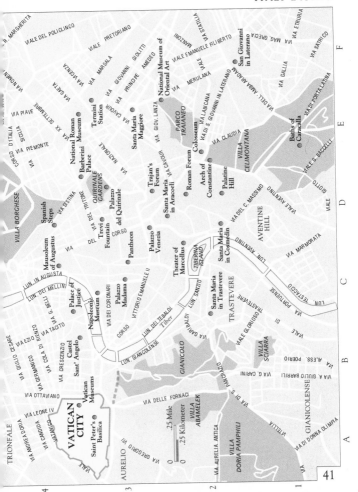

VIALE DEL POLICLINICO

R. MARGHERITA

VIA NOMENTANA

VIA PIAVE

CORSO D'ITALIA

VIA PIEMONTE

VIA SICILIA

VIA XX SETTEMBRE

VIA GAETA

VIALE PRETORIANO

VIA MARSALA

VIA VICENZA

VIA VENEZIA

VIA VOLTURNO

VIA GIOVANNI GIOLITTI

VIALE EMANUELE FILIBERTO

VIA MANZONI

VIA MAG. GRECIA

VIA ETRURIA

VIA SATRICO

VIA GALLIA

VIALE EMANUELE FILIBERTO

MANZONI

VIA MERULANA

VIALE DI S. GIOVANNI IN LATERANO

San Giovanni in Laterano

VIA DELL'AMBA ARADAM

VIA DI PORTA LATINA

VIA SANNIO

VIA DI PORTA LATINA

National Museum of Oriental Art

PARCO TRAIANEO

VIA LABICANA

VIA CLAUDIA

VIA GIOV. LANZA

Santa Maria Maggiore

Termini Station

National Roman Museum

Barberini Palace

QUIRINALE GARDENS

Palazzo del Quirinale

Trajan's Forum

Santa Maria in Aracoeli

Colosseum

Roman Forum

Arch of Constantine

Palatine Hill

Baths of Caracalla

VILLA CELIMONTANA

VIALE G. BACCELLI

GIOTTO

VILLA BORGHESE

Spanish Steps

VIA SISTINA

VIA DEL TRITONE

Trevi Fountain

CORSO

Pantheon

Palazzo Venezia

Theater of Marcellus

TIBERINA ISLAND

Santa Maria in Cosmedin

AVENTINE HILL

VIA DI S. PRISCA

VIA MARMORATA

VIALE AVENTINO

VIA DI C. MASSIMO

Mausoleum of Augustus

LUN. IN AUGUSTA

LUN. DEI MELLINI

Palace of Justice

VIA M. G. BELLI

Napoleonic Museum

VIA DEI CORONARI

Palazzo Madama

VITTORIO EMANUELE II

CORSO

LUN. DEI TEBALDI

LUN. SANZIO

LUN. GIANCOLENSE

Tiber

Santa Maria in Trastevere

TRASTEVERE

VIA GLORIOSO

VILLA SCIARRA

VIA ALESS. POERIO

VIA A. GIULIO BARRILI

VIA G. CARINI

VIA DI S. PANCRAZIO

VIALE DI TRASTEVERE

VIALE GLORIOSO

VIA PORTUENSE

LUN. TESTACCIO

GIANICOLO

VIA GARIBALDI

LUN. GIANCOLENSE

VILLA DORIA PAMPHILI

VIA AURELIA ANTICA

VILLA ABAMELEK

VIA DELLE FORNACI

VATICAN CITY

Vatican Museums

Saint Peter's Basilica

TRIONFALE

VIA ANDREA DORIA

VIA CANDIA

VALTALIO

VIA LEONE IV

VIA OTTAVIANO

VIA GIULIO CESARE

VIA GERMANICO

VIA CRESCENZIO

VIA COLA DI RIENZO

VIA TACITO

VIA EZIO

Castel Sant'Angelo

AURELIO

VIALE

VIA GREGORIO VII

VIA AURELIA ANTICA

VIA DI DONNA OLIMPIA

GIANICOLENSE

VITELLIA

.25 Mile

0

0

.25 Kilometer

41

Budapest HUNGARY / Vienna AUSTRIA

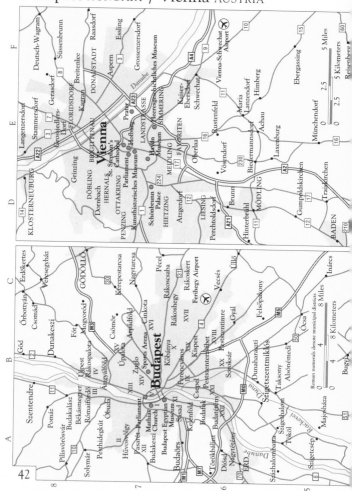

42

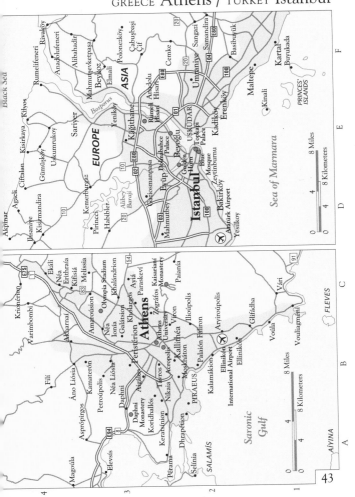

43

Africa NORTHERN

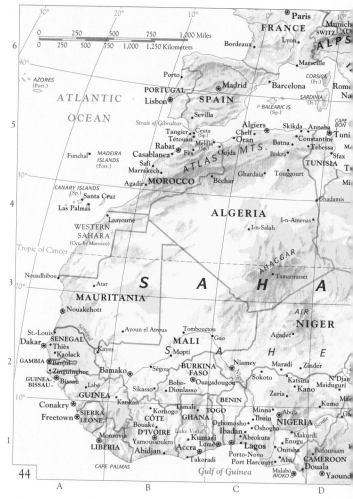

ATLANTIC OCEAN

AZORES (Port.)

MADEIRA ISLANDS (Port.)

Funchal

CANARY ISLANDS (Sp.)
Las Palmas • Santa Cruz

Nouadhibou

Atar

MAURITANIA

Nouakchott

St.-Louis
Dakar ⊛
Thiès • SENEGAL
Kaolack
GAMBIA • Banjul • Kayes
Ziguinchor •
GUINEA- Bissau
BISSAU • Labé
GUINEA • Kankan
Conakry ⊛
Freetown ⊛ SIERRA LEONE
Monrovia ⊛
LIBERIA

Paris ⊛
FRANCE
Bordeaux • Lyon
Marseille

Porto •
PORTUGAL
Lisbon ⊛
Sevilla
SPAIN
Madrid ⊛
Barcelona

Strait of Gibraltar
Tangier • Ceuta (Sp.)
Rabat ⊛ Fès Melilla (Sp.)
Casablanca
Safi
Marrakech •
Agadir • MOROCCO
Laayoune

WESTERN SAHARA (Occ. by Morocco)

Tropic of Cancer

S A H A R A

Ayoun el Atrous •

Tombouctou
MALI Gao
Mopti
Ségou • BURKINA FASO
Bamako
Sikasso • Bobo-Dioulasso
Ouagadougou ⊛
BENIN
Korhogo
CÔTE D'IVOIRE Tamale
Bouaké • GHANA TOGO
Yamoussoukro Kumasi Lomé ⊛
Abidjan Accra ⊛
Takoradi

CAPE PALMAS

Gulf of Guinea

Munich
SWITZ.
ALPS

CORSICA (Fr.)
Rome
SARDINIA (It.) Na
BALEARIC IS. (Sp.)

Algiers ⊛ Skikda • Annaba CAPE BON
Chlef • Constantine • Tuni
Oran Batna • Tebessa TUNISIA
Oujda Biskra • Sfax T
ATLAS MTS. Touggourt
Ghardaia • Ghadamis
Béchar

ALGERIA
I-n-Amenas •
I-n-Salah •

AHAGGAR

Tamanrasset •

A

AIR
NIGER

Agadez •

Niamey Maradi Zinder N'Djan
Sokoto • Katsina Maiduguri
Zaria • Kano
Minna ⊛ Abuja Kumo
Ilorin • NIGERIA Ma
Ogbomosho • Oshogho Makurdi
Ibadan • Abeokuta Enugu
Lagos ⊛ Onitsha Ga
Porto-Novo • Aba Benue
Port Harcourt Bafoussam
Malabo CAMEROON
BIOKO Douala
Yaoundé ⊛

44

Africa SOUTHERN

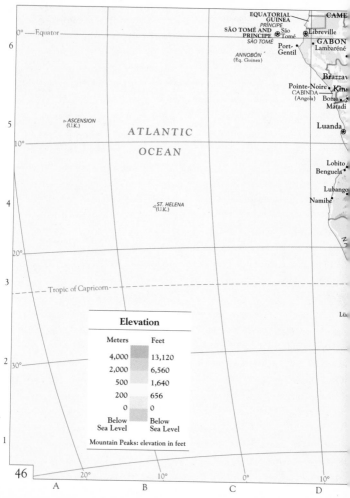

0° — Equator

6

EQUATORIAL GUINEA
CAME

PRÍNCIPE
SÃO TOMÉ AND
PRÍNCIPE
São Tomé
Libreville

SÃO TOMÉ
GABON
Port-
Gentil
Lambaréné

ANNOBÓN
(Eq. Guinea)

Brazzav
Pointe-Noire
Kins
CABINDA
(Angola)
Boma
Matadi

5

ASCENSION
(U.K.)

Luanda

ATLANTIC

10°

OCEAN

Lobito
Benguela

4

ST. HELENA
(U.K.)

Lubango
Namibe

20°

3

Tropic of Capricorn

Lüe

Elevation

Meters	Feet
4,000	13,120
2,000	6,560
500	1,640
200	656
0	0
Below Sea Level	Below Sea Level

Mountain Peaks: elevation in feet

2

30°

1

46

20°   10°   0°   10°

A   B   C   D

CONGO
BASIN
Mbandaka
Bumba
Congo
Lake Albert
Kisangani
Beni
UGANDA
Kampala Jinja
Lake
Victoria
RWANDA
Goma
Bukavu
Kigali
BURUNDI
Bujumbura
Mwanza
Nakuru
SERENGETI
PLAIN
Marsabit
KENYA
Eldoret
Meru
Mt. Kenya 17,057
Nairobi
Machakos
Kilimanjaro
19,340
Arusha
Mogadishu
Marca
SOMALIA
Kismaayo
INDIAN
OCEAN

DEM. REP. OF
THE CONGO
Bandundu
Ilebo
ikwit
Kananga
Tshikapa
Mbuji-Mayi
Kindu
Kabinda
Mwene Ditu
Kalemie
Lake
Mweru
Tabora
Kamina
KATANGA
Dodoma
TANZANIA
Morogoro
Iringa
Zanzibar
PEMBA I.
ZANZIBAR I.
Dar es Salaam
Mombasa
Tanga

NGOLA
Luena
ambo
Menongue
lanje
Kolwezi
Likasi
PLATEAU
Chingola
Kitwe
Lubumbashi
Ndola
Luanshya
Kabwe
ZAMBIA
Lusaka
Mbala
Lake
Tanganyika
RIFT VALLEY
Mbeya
Songea
Chipata
Lake Malawi
Lilongwe
MALAWI
Mtwara
COMOROS
Moroni
Antsiranana

Tsumeb
AMIBIA
Windhoek
Lake Kariba
Livingstone
Zambezi
Harare
Bulawayo
ZIMBABWE
Gweru
Mutare
Tete
Blantyre
MOZAMBIQUE
Chimoio
Beira
Quelimane
Nacala
Nampula
Mozambique
Channel
Mahajanga
Toamasina
Antananarivo
Antsirabe
MADAGASCAR
Fianarantsoa

BOTSWANA
Serowe
Gaborone
Mmabatho
KALAHARI
DESERT
Palapye
Francistown
Messina
Thohoyandou
Limpopo
Xai-Xai
Inhambane
Toliara
Tolanaro

tmanshoop
Orange
Springbok
Upington
Kimberley
SOUTH
AFRICA
Middelburg
Pretoria
Johannesburg
Klerksdorp
Vereeniging
Welkom
Bloemfontein
Maseru
LESOTHO
Orange
Bisho
Mbabane
SWAZILAND
Maputo
Newcastle
Pietermaritzburg
Durban
Umtata

ape
own
PE OF
OD HOPE
CAPE
AGULHAS
Worcester
Middelburg
East London
Port Elizabeth

0   250   500   750   1,000 Miles
0   250   500   750   1,000   1,250 Kilometers

20°   30°   40°   50°

E   F   G   H

6
5
4
3
2
1

0°
6
10°
20°
30°
40°

47

Middle East

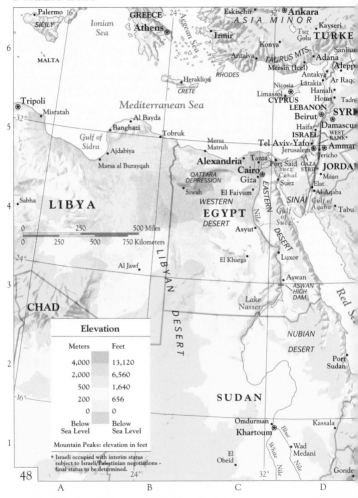

Palermo
SICILY
Ionian Sea
GREECE
Athens ⊕
Eskisehir · 36° **Ankara**
ASIA MINOR · Kayseri
TURKE

MALTA

Aegean Sea
Izmir
Konya · *Tuz Golu*
TAURUS MTS. · Sanliu
Antalya · Adana
Mersin (Icel) · **Alepp**
RHODES · Antakya · Ar Raqq

Heraklion
CRETE
Latakia
Nicosia · Hamah · Tadm
Limassol · **CYPRUS** · Homs
Mediterranean Sea · **LEBANON**
Beirut ⊕ · **SYR**
Tripoli ⊕ · Haifa · Damascu
Misratah
32°
Al Bayda
Banghazi
Tobruk · Mersa · Tel Aviv-Yafo · **ISRAEL** · WEST BANK
Matruh · Jerusalem · GAZA · **Ammar**
Gulf of Sidra · STRIP · **JORDA**
Jericho
Ajdabiya · **Alexandria** · Tanta · Maan
Marsa al Burayqah · *QATTARA DEPRESSION* · Port Said · Suez · Elat
Cairo ⊕ · Canal · Al Aqaba
Siwah · Giza · Suez · *SINAI* · *Gulf of Aqaba* · Tabu
El Faiyum · *WESTERN* · *EASTERN* · *Gulf of Suez*

Sabha
LIBYA
4,000 · *WESTERN DESERT* · **EGYPT** · *DESERT*
DESERT · Asyut

Red Se

Al Jawf
24°

16°

El Kharga · Luxor
Aswan
ASWAN HIGH DAM

CHAD
LIBYAN
Lake Nasser

NUBIAN
DESERT
Port Sudan

Elevation	
Meters	Feet
4,000	13,120
2,000	6,560
500	1,640
200	656
0	0
Below Sea Level	Below Sea Level

DESERT

SUDAN

Mountain Peaks: elevation in feet

* Israeli occupied with interim status
subject to Israeli/Palestinian negotiations -
final status to be determined.

Omdurman · Kassala
Khartoum
Blue
El Obeid · Wad Medani · Gonde
White · *Nile*

0 — 250 — 500 Miles
0 — 250 — 500 — 750 Kilometers

48

6

5

4

3

2

1

A   B   C   D

Erzurum Mt. Ararat 16,853 AZERBAIJAN Caspian Sea TURKMENISTAN 64°
Lake Van AZER. Ardabil Ashgabat KOPET MTS.
l Hasakah Diyarbakir Orumiyeh Lake Urmia Tabriz Rasht Qazvin Sari Gorgan Mashhad Herat
Mosul Kirkuk Arbil Hamadan Tehran ELBURZ MTS. Mt. Damavand 18,606 AFGHANISTAN
Bayji Baqubah Qom Kashan DASHT-E KAVIR Farah 32°
Abu IRAQ Baghdad Kermanshah Khorramabad IRAN Esfahan Birjand Zabol
mal Ar Ramadi Karbala Al Hillah Najaf Ad Diwaniyah Ahvaz Yazd 64°
RIAN An Najaf An Nasiriyah Basra Abadan Kerman Zahedan
SERT Shiraz PAKISTAN
AN NAFUD KUWAIT Kuwait City Persian Gulf Bandar-e Bushehr Bandar-e Abbas Iranshahr 4
Hail AD DAHNA Ad Dammam Al Khasab Strait of Hormuz Jask
Buraydah Manama BAHRAIN Dubai OMAN Bandar Beheshti
Medina Al Mubarraz Doha Abu Dhabi Suhar Muscat 24°
Riyadh Al Hufuf QATAR Al Buraymi Ibri Sur
Harad UNITED ARAB EMIRATES
SAUDI ARABIA JABAL TUWAYQ OMAN 3
ARABIAN MASIRAH
ddah At Taif RUB AL KHALI
ecca Mecca
As Sulayyil Dawkah 2
PENINSULA Arabian Sea 16°
Abha Salalah
RITREA Massawa Sanaa Saywun
smara Al Hudaydah Al Mukalla Sayhut SOCOTRA (Yemen)
YEMEN 1
Taizz Ahwar Aden
Bab el Mandeb
THIOPIA DJIBOUTI Gulf of Aden SOMALIA 56°
40° 48°

E   F   G   H

49

Tel Aviv - Yafo - Jerusalem ISRAEL / Cairo EGYPT

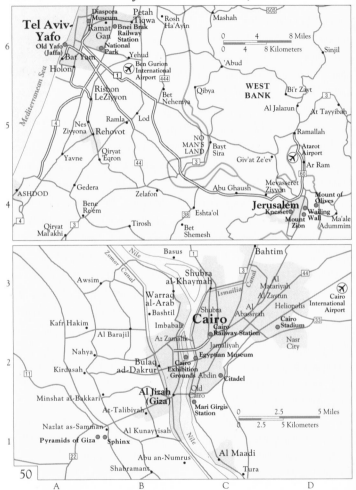

Tel Aviv-Yafo
Diaspora Museum
Petah Tiqwa
Rosh Ha'Ayin
Mashah
505
Ramat Gan
Bnei Brak
Railway Station
National Park
Old Yafo (Jaffa)
Bar Yam
Yehud
'Abud
Sinjil
Holon
Ben Gurion International Airport
444
WEST BANK
Rishon LeZiyyon
Qibya
Bi'r Zayt
3
Mediterranean Sea
Nes Ziyyona
Bet Nehemya
Al Jalazun
At Tayyibah
Rehovot
Ramla
Lod
Ramallah
Yavne
Qiryat 'Eqron
44
NO MAN'S LAND
Bayt Sira
Giv'at Ze'ev
Atarot Airport
Ar Ram
60
ASHDOD
Gedera
Zelafon
Abu Ghaush
Mevasseret Ziyyon
Jerusalem
Mount of Olives
4
Bene Re'em
38
Eshta'ol
Knesset
Wailing Wall
Ma'ale Adummim
Qiryat Mal'akhi
Tirosh
Bet Shemesh
Mount Zion

0   4   8 Miles
0   4   8 Kilometers

6

5

4

Basus
Nile
1
Bahtim
3
Zomzor Canal
Shubra al-Khaymah
3
Al Matariyah
44
Awsim
Warraq al-Arab
Ismailia
Al Zaytun
Heliopolis
Cairo International Airport
Bashtil
Shubra
Al Abassiyah
Kafr Hakim
Imbabah
Cairo
Cairo Stadium
33
Al Barajil
Az Zanatin
Cairo Railway Station
Jamaliyah
Nasr City
Nahya
Kirdasah
Bulaq ad-Dakrur
Egyptian Museum
2
Minshat al-Bakkari
Al Jizah (Giza)
Cairo Exhibition Grounds
Abdin
Citadel
At-Talibiyah
Old Cairo
Nazlat as-Samman
Al Kunayyisah
Mari Girgis Station
Pyramids of Giza
Sphinx
1
22
Abu an-Numrus
Al Maadi
Shabramant
Tura

0   2.5   5 Miles
0   2.5   5 Kilometers

50

A   B   C   D

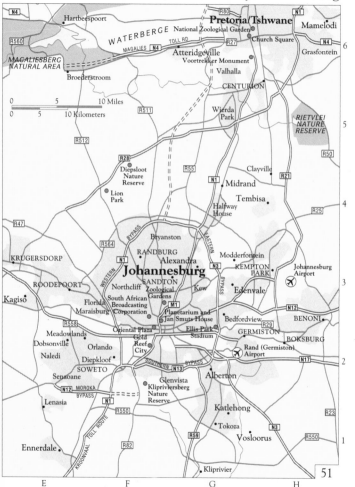

N4
Hartbeespoort

R560

R80
National Zoological Garden
Pretoria/Tshwane
Church Square
N1
Mamelodi

WATERBERGE
MAGALIES N4 TOLL RD
R27
N4
Grasfontein

MAGALIESBERG NATURAL AREA

Atteridgeville
Voortrekker Monument
Valhalla

Broederstroom

CENTURION

6

0   5   10 Miles
0   5   10 Kilometers

R511

Wierda Park

5

R512

R28
Diepsloot Nature Reserve

R55

Clayville

R50

N1
Midrand

R21

Lion Park

Tembisa

R47

Halfway House

R25

4

R564
BYPASS

Bryanston

EASTERN

RANDBURG
Alexandra

Johannesburg

Modderfontein
N3
KEMPTON PARK

Johannesburg Airport

3

KRUGERSDORP
N1
WESTERN

SANDTON
Northcliff
Zoological Gardens

Kew

BYPASS
Edenvale

ROODEPOORT

South African Broadcasting Corporation

M1

Florida
Maraisburg

Planetarium and Jan Smuts House

N12
BENONI

Kagiso

R558
Oriental Plaza

Gold Reef City

Ellis Park Stadium

Bedfordview
R29
GERMISTON
BOKSBURG

Meadowlands
Dobsonville
Orlando
Diepkloof

Rand (Germiston) Airport

N12
SOWETO
SOUTHERN
N13
BYPASS

Alberton

N17

2

Senaoane
MOROKA BYPASS
N1

Glenvista
Klipriviersberg Nature Reserve

Katlehong

N3
R23

Lenasia

Tokoza

R59
Vosloorus
R550

1

Ennerdale

R82

KROONVAAL TOLL ROUTE

R550

Kliprivier

51

E   F   G   H

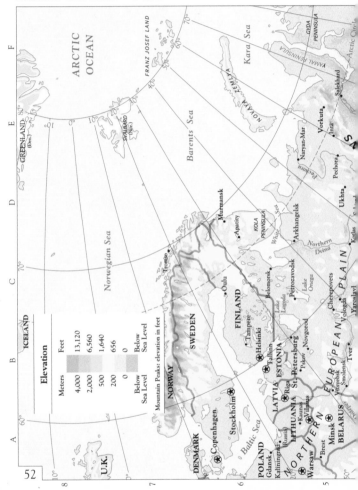

ARCTIC OCEAN

FRANZ JOSEF LAND

Kara Sea

GYDA PENINSULA

YAMAL PENINSULA

Arctic Circle

NOVAYA ZEMLYA

Salekhard

Vorkuta

Inta

SN

GREENLAND (Den.)

SPALBARD (Nor.)

Barents Sea

Naryan-Mar

Pechora

Ukhta

Pechora

Norwegian Sea

Murmansk

Apatity

KOLA PENINSULA

White Sea

Arkhangelsk

Northern Dvina

Kotlas

ICELAND

Tromsø

Oulu

Belomorsk

Petrozavodsk

Lake Onega

Cherepovets

E U R O P E A N   P L A I N

Vologda

Elevation

Meters	Feet
4,000	13,120
2,000	6,560
500	1,640
200	656
0	0
Below Sea Level	Below Sea Level

Mountain Peaks: elevation in feet

FINLAND

Lake Ladoga

Tampere

Helsinki

Tallinn

ESTONIA

St. Petersburg

Novgorod

Pskov

Yaroslavl

Tver

SWEDEN

Stockholm

LATVIA

Riga

LITHUANIA

Kaunas

Vilnius

Smolensk

Vitsyebsk

NORWAY

Baltic Sea

DENMARK

Copenhagen

U.K.

POLAND

Gdansk

Kaliningrad (Russia)

Warsaw

Brest

Minsk

BELARUS

N O R T H E R N

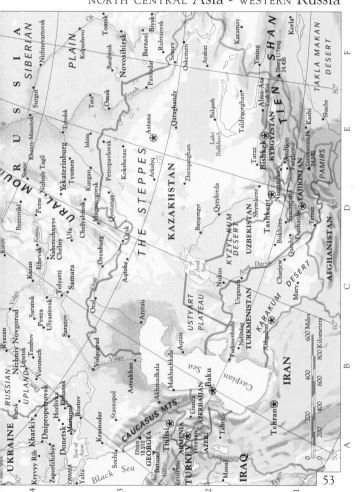

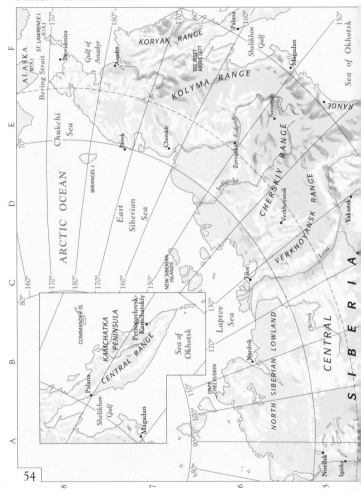

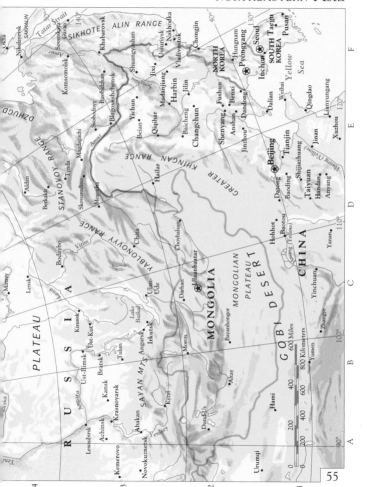

Moscow RUSSIA

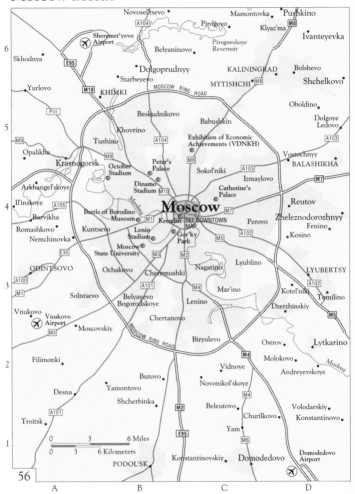

Novosel'tsevo
A104
Pirogovo
Mamontovka
Pushkino
Klyaz'ma
M8
Ivanteyevka

Sheremet'yevo
Airport

Belyaninovo
*Pirogovskoye
Reservoir*

Skhodnya
E95

Dolgoprudnyy
KALININGRAD
Bolshevo
Shchelkovo

Yurlovo
M10
Starbeyevo
MYTISHCHI
M8

KHIMKI
MOSCOW RING ROAD
Oboldino

Beskudnikovo
Babushkin
Dolgoye
Ledovo

PIII
Khovrino
A104
A103

M9
Tushino
Exhibition of Economic
Achievements (VDNKH)
Vostochnyy
BALASHIKHA

Opalikha
M9
Peter's
Palace
M8
Sokol'niki
A103
Izmaylovo
M7

Krasnogorsk
October
Stadium
Dinamo
Stadium
M10
Catherine's
Palace
Reutov

Arkhangel'skoye
A105
M1
Moscow
Kremlin
SEE DOWNTOWN
MAP
M7
Perovo
A102
Zheleznodorozhnyy
Fenino

Il'inskoye
Battle of Borodino
Museum
Gor'ky
Park
Kosino

Barvikha
Kuntsevo
Lenin
Stadium
M5

Romashkovo
Nemchinovka
E30
Moscow
State University
M3
M2
Lyublino
LYUBERTSY

ODINTSOVO
A100
Ochakovo
Cheremushki
Nagatino
A102
Kotel'niki
A102

M1
Solntsevo
A101
Belyayevo
Bogorodskoye
Mar'ino
Dzerzhinskiy
Tomilino
M5

Vnukovo
Vnukovo
Airport
Lenino
Chertanovo
Ostrov
Lytkarino

M3
Moscovskiy
MOSCOW RING ROAD
Biryulevo
Molokovo
Moskva

Filimonki
M4
Vidnoye
Andreyevskoye

Desna
Yamontovo
Butovo
Novonikol'skoye
M4

Shcherbinka
M2
Beleutovo
Volodarskiy

Troitsk
A101
Churilkovo
Konstantinovo

Yam
M6

0   3   6 Miles
0   3   6 Kilometers
Konstantinovskiy
Domodedovo
Domodedovo
Airport

56

PODOL'SK
E95

A   B   C   D

6

5

4

3

2

1

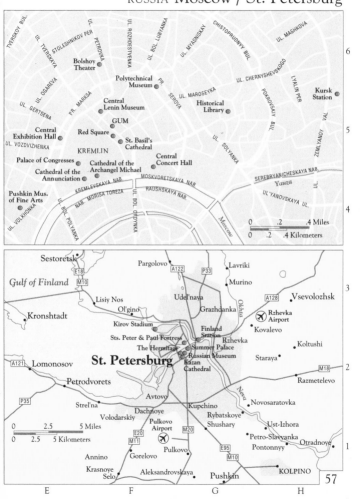

Moscow (top map)

TVERSKOY BUL.
UL. TVERSKAYA
UL. STOLESHNIKOV PER.
UL. OGAREVA
UL. GERTSENA
UL. ROZHDESTVENKA
UL. PETROVKA
PR. MARKSA
UL. BOL. LUBYANKA
UL. MYASNISKAY
CHISTOPRUDNYY BUL.
UL. MASHKOVA
PR. SEROVA
UL. MAROSEYKA
UL. CHERNYSHEVSKOGO
POKROVSKIY BUL.
LYALIN PER.
ZEMLYANOY VAL
UL. SOLYANKA
SEREBRYANICHESKAYA NAB.
Yauza
UL. YANOVSKAYA UL.
MOSKVORETSKAYA NAB.
RAUSHSKAYA NAB.
KREMLEVSKAYA NAB.
NAB. MORISA TOREZA
UL. VOLKHONKA
UL. BOL. POLYANKA
UL. BOL. ORDYNKA
UL. VOZDVIZHENKA

Bolshoy Theater
Polytechnical Museum
Central Lenin Museum
Historical Library
Kursk Station
Central Exhibition Hall
Red Square
GUM
St. Basil's Cathedral
KREMLIN
Central Concert Hall
Palace of Congresses
Cathedral of the Archangel Michael
Cathedral of the Annunciation
Pushkin Mus. of Fine Arts

6
5
4

0   .2   .4 Miles
0   .2   .4 Kilometers

St. Petersburg (bottom map)

Gulf of Finland

Sestoretsk
Pargolovo
Lavriki
Murino
Vsevolozhsk
Lisiy Nos
Ol'gino
Udel'naya
Grazhdanka
Okhta
Rzhevka Airport
Kovalevo
Koltushi
Kronstadt
Kirov Stadium
Finland Station
Rzhevka
Sts. Peter & Paul Fortress
The Hermitage
Summer Palace
Russian Museum
Staraya
St. Petersburg
Kazan Cathedral
Lomonosov
Petrodvorets
Razmetelevo
Strel'na
Avtovo
Kupchino
Novosaratovka
Volodarskiy
Dachnoye
Rybatskoye
Shushary
Ust-Izhora
Pulkovo Airport
Pulkovo
Petro-Slavyanka
Pontonnyy
Otradnoye
Annino
Gorelovo
Krasnoye Selo
Aleksandrovskaya
Pushkin
KOLPINO
Neva

0   2.5   5 Miles
0   2.5   5 Kilometers

E18
M10
A122
P33
A128
A121
P35
E20
M11
M20
M18
E95
M10

3
2
1

E   F   G   H

57

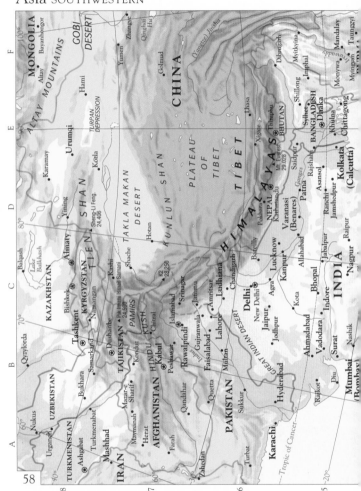

Pyay
Bago
Hinthada
Mawfa-
myine
Rangoon
(Yangon) ✪
Dawei

SUMATRA

Banda Aceh

INDONESIA

NICOBAR
ISLANDS
(India)

ANDAMAN
ISLANDS
(India)

Bay of
Bengal

Bhamapur
Visakhapatnam
Warangal
GHATS
EASTERN
Hyderabad
PLATEAU
Solapur
Vijayawada
Chennai (Madras)
Bangalore
Pondicherry
Mysore
Salem
Tiruchchirappalli
Jaffna
Trincomalee
Madurai
Kandy
Sri Jayawardenepura
Panaji
Hubli
WESTERN GHATS
Coimbatore
Kochi
Thiruvananthapuram
CAPE COMORIN
Colombo ✪
Galle
SRI LANKA

Mangalore

Arabian
Sea

LAKSHADWEEP
(India)

Male ✪

MALDIVES

INDIAN
OCEAN

CHAGOS
ARCHIPELAGO
(U.K.)

Elevation

Meters	Feet
4,000	13,120
2,000	6,560
500	1,640
200	656
0	0
Below Sea Level	Below Sea Level

Mountain Peaks: elevation in feet

500 Miles
0
500 Kilometers
0

−10°
−0°—Equator

70°   80°   90°

A   B   C   D   E   F

4   3   2   1

59

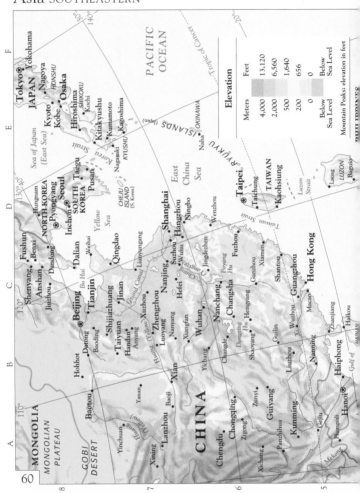

Elevation

Meters	Feet
4,000	13,120
2,000	6,560
500	1,640
200	656
0	0
Below Sea Level	Below Sea Level

Mountain Peaks: elevation in feet

PACIFIC OCEAN

Tropic of Cancer

JAPAN

Tokyo⊛ Yokohama
Nagoya HONSHU
Kyoto Kobe Osaka
Hiroshima SHIKOKU
Kochi
Kitakyushu Kumamoto
Nagasaki KYUSHU Kagoshima
Naha OKINAWA

Sea of Japan (East Sea)

Korea Strait

RYUKYU ISLANDS (Japan)

East China Sea

NORTH KOREA
Hungnam
Pyongyang ⊛
Inchon ⊛ Seoul
SOUTH KOREA
Taegu
Pusan
CHEJU ISLAND (S. Korea)

Taipei ⊛
TAIWAN
Taichung
Kaohsiung

Luzon Strait

LUZON
Laoag
Baguio

Shenyang Fushun
Anshan Benxi
Jinzhou Dandong
Dalian
Weihai
Qingdao

Beijing ⊛ Tianjin
Bo Hai
Shijiazhuang Jinan Lianyungang
Handan Anyang
Taiyuan Xuzhou
Zhengzhou
Luoyang
Nanyang Xiangfan

Yellow Sea

Shanghai
Suzhou Hangzhou
Wuhu Ningbo
Nanjing
Jingdezhen Wenzhou
Hefei
Poyang Hu
Nanchang Fuzhou
Changsha Hengyang Ganzhou
Shaoyang
Dongting Hu Shantou
Changde
Guilin Wuzhou
Liuzhou Guangzhou
Macao Hong Kong
Nanning Zhanjiang
Haikou

Hohhot

Datong
Baoding
Yinchuan
Baotou
Yanan
Baoji Xian
Lanzhou

MONGOLIA
MONGOLIAN PLATEAU
GOBI DESERT

Xining

CHINA

Chengdu
Chongqing
Zigong Zunyi
Guiyang
Xichang Zunyi
Panzhihua Kunming
Guiyang
Geiju

Yichang
Wuhan
Shashi

Grand Canal
Huang (Yellow)
Chang (Yangtze)

HAINAN
Gulf of Tonkin
Haiphong
Hanoi ⊛
Thanh Hóa
Mekong

Taiwan Strait
Xiamen
Quanzhou
Shantou

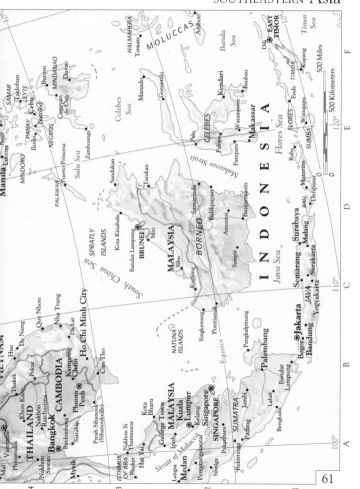

Taipei TAIWAN / Manila PHILIPPINES

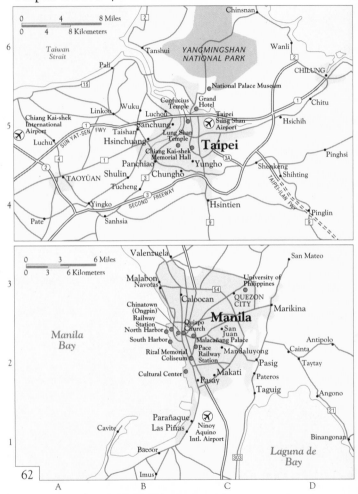

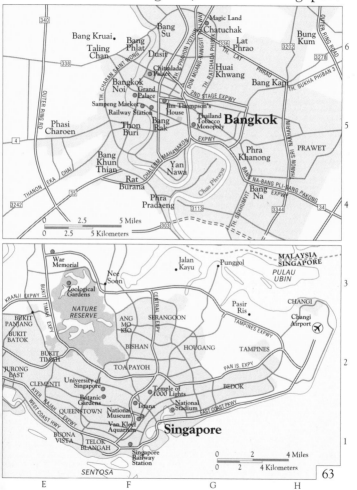

Jakarta INDONESIA / Delhi - New Delhi INDIA

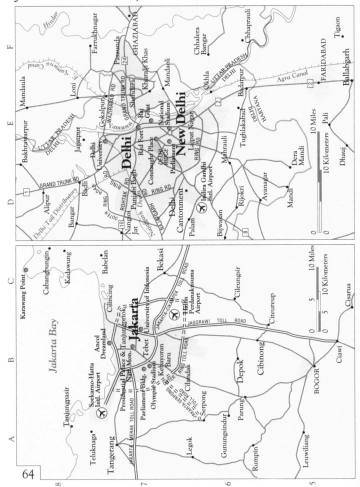

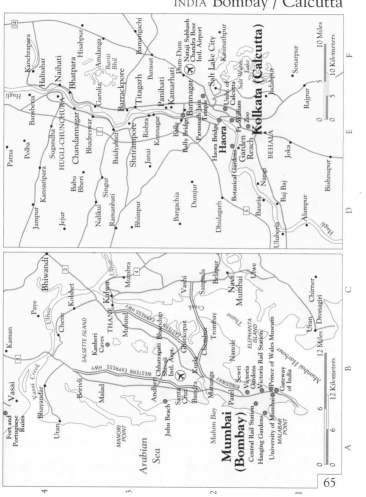

Far East

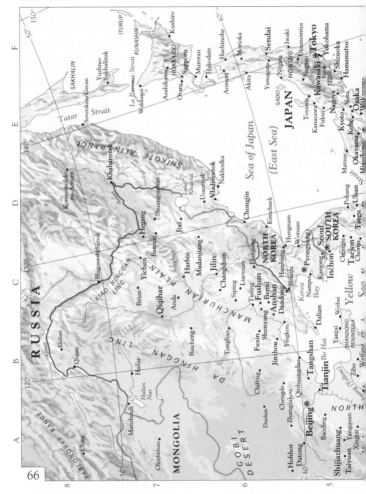

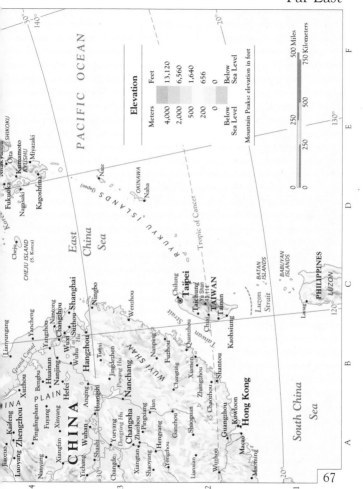

PACIFIC OCEAN

Korea

SHIKOKU

Ota
Kumamoto KYUSHU
Fukuoka
Nagasaki
Miyazaki
Kagoshima

Cheju
CHEJU ISLAND
(S. Korea)

Nare

OKINAWA
Naha

RYUKYU ISLANDS (Japan)

Tropic of Cancer

East
China
Sea

Ningbo
Wenzhou

Chilung
Taipei
Taichung
Yu Shan
13,114
TAIWAN
Chiai
Tainan
Kaohsiung

Taiwan Strait

Lan Yu

BATAN
ISLANDS

BABUYAN
ISLANDS

Luzon
Strait

Laoag

LUZON

PHILIPPINES

Lianyungang
Yancheng
Kaifeng
Zhengzhou
Luoyang
Xuzhou
Nantong
Changzhou
Shanghai
Jiaozuo
Pingdingshan
Benghu
Huainan
Nanjing
Suzhou
Wuxi
Hangzhou
Fuyang
Xinyang
Hefei
Anqing
Tunxi
Nanyang
Xiangfan
Wuhan
Huangshi
Jingdezhen
Shashi
Yichang
Changde
Yueyang
Poyang Hu
Nanchang
CHINA
PLAIN
Grand Canal
Yangzhou
Wuhu
Tai Hu
WUYI SHAN
Nanping
Fuzhou
Changting
Xiamen
Zhangzhou
Quanzhou
Dongting Hu
Changsha
Xiangtan
Zhuzhou
Pingxiang
Jian
Ganzhou
Shaoguan
Chaozhou
Shantou
Hengyang
Yongzhou
Shaoyang
Lianxian
Wuzhou
Guangzhou
Macau
Kowloon
Hong Kong
Maoming

South China Sea

East China Sea

120°

130°

140°

20°

30°

Elevation

Meters	Feet
4,000	13,120
2,000	6,560
500	1,640
200	656
0	0
Below Sea Level	Below Sea Level

Mountain Peaks: elevation in feet

0 250 500 Miles
0 250 500 750 Kilometers

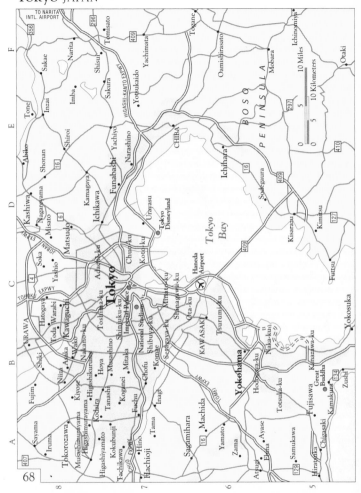

Tokyo JAPAN

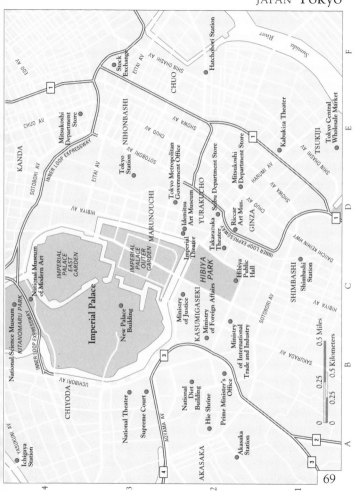

Osaka - Kyoto - Kobe JAPAN

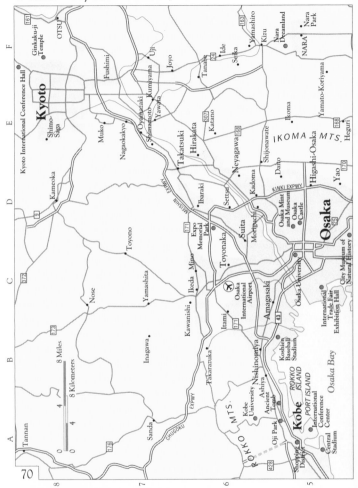

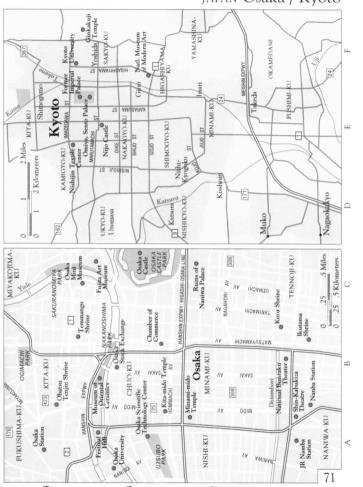

Kyoto

KITA-KU

KAMIGYO-KU

UKYO-KU

Umamasa

NISHIKYO-KU

Katsura

367

Kamo

Takano

Shimogamo

Former Imperial Palace

Kyoto University

Yoshida Temple

Ginkakuji Temple

SAKYO-KU

YAMASHINA-KU

Nat'l. Museum of Modern Art

HIGASHIYAMA-KU

OKAMEDANI

Uji

Gion

Inari

MINAMI-KU

Omiya, Sento Palace

Nijo Castle

Nishijin Textile Center

NAKAGYO-KU

SHIMOGYO-KU

Nishi-Kyogoku

Kisshoin

Katsura

Muko

Nagaokakyo

MEISHIN EXPWY

FUSHIMI-KU

Takeda

IMADEGAWA ST

MARUTAMACHI

KARASUMA ST

HIGASHIYAMA ST

OIKE ST

SHIJO ST

NAKAGYO ST

GOJO ST

NISHIOJI ST

JUJO ST

24

162

9

171

24

2 Miles
0   1   2

2 Kilometers
0   1   2

MIYAKOJIMA-KU

FUKUSHIMA-KU

OGIMACHI PARK

KITA-KU

CHUO-KU

NISHI-KU

NANIWA-KU

MINAMI-KU

TENNOJI-KU

SAKURANOMIYA PARK

NAKANOSHIMA PARK

Osaka Mint Museum

Fujita Art Museum

Osaka Castle

OSAKA CASTLE PARK

Ruins of Naniwa Palace

Tenmangu Shrine

Chamber of Commerce

Kozu Shrine

Ikutama Shrine

Osaka Station

Ohatsu Tenjin Shrine

Festival Hall

Osaka University

Museum of Oriental Ceramics

Osaka Stock Exchange

Osaka Scientific Technology Center

Kita-mido Temple

Minami-mido Temple

Dotombori

National Bunraku Theater

Shin-Kabuki Theatre

Namba Station

JR Namba Station

Osaka

Yodo

HANSHIN EXPWY - HIGASHI-OSAKA LINE

HANSHIN

MIDO

SAKAI AV

NANIWA AV

NANIWA AV

MIDO AV

SAKAI AV

MATSUYAMACHI AV

TANIMACHI AV

UEMACHI AV

NAGAHORI AV

.5 Miles
0   .25   .5

.5 Kilometers
0   .25   .5

176

2

423

25

308

308

Seoul SOUTH KOREA

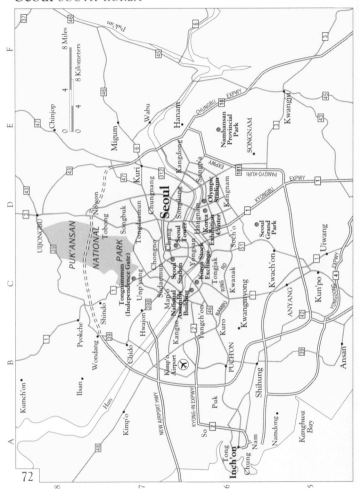

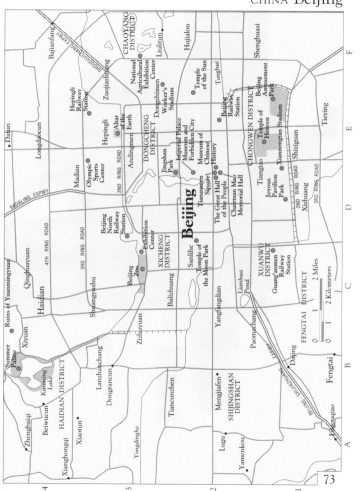

Shanghai CHINA

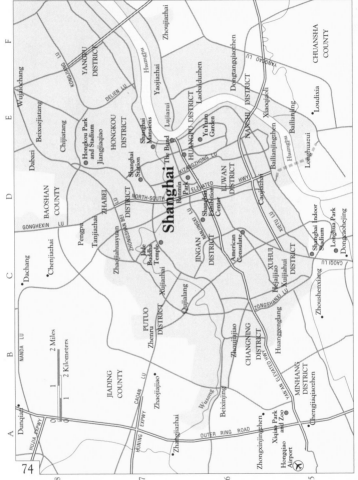

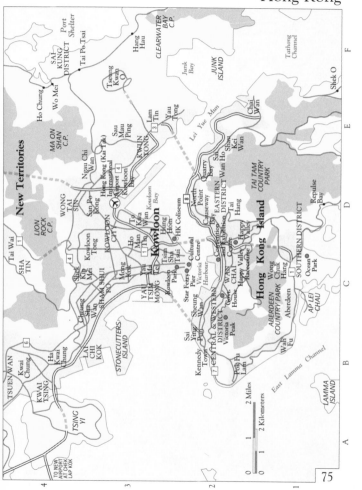

Hong Kong

75

Australia - New Zealand - New Guinea

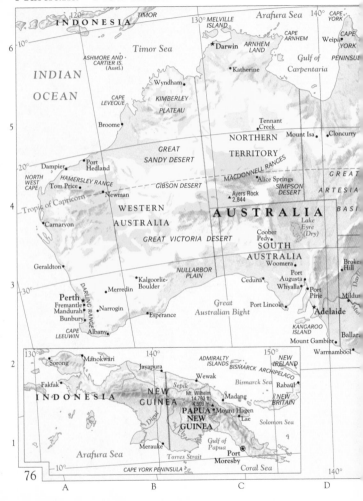

New Guinea - New Zealand - Australia

SOLOMON
ISLANDS

Elevation

Meters	Feet
4,000	13,120
2,000	6,560
500	1,640
200	656
0	0
Below Sea Level	Below Sea Level

Mountain Peaks: elevation in feet

Coral Sea

Townsville

Charters Bowen
Towers
Mackay

Emerald Rockhampton
Gladstone

ngreach

Bundaberg
QUEENSLAND Maryborough
arleville Roma Gympie
Toowoomba Brisbane
Southport

Moree Lismore
Grafton

Bourke Tamworth Armidale
NEW Dubbo Port Macquarie
OUTH Orange Taree
ALES Griffith Newcastle
gga Wagga Sydney
lbury Canberra Wollongong
ndigo AUSTL. CAP. TERR.
CTORIA Mt. Kosciusko
lelbourne 7,310
elong

Tasman
Sea

PACIFIC
OCEAN

NORFOLK
ISLAND
(Australia)

Devonport
Launceston
Queenstown
Hobart
TASMANIA

Whangarei

Auckland

Hamilton Tauranga
NORTH ISLAND Rotorua
New Plymouth
NEW ZEALAND Napier
Cook Gisborne
Strait Palmerston
Nelson North
Greymouth Wellington
SOUTH ISLAND
Mt. Cook Christchurch
12,349
SOUTHERN ALPS Timaru

Dunedin
Invercargill
STEWART ISLAND

| 0 | 250 | 500 | 750 Miles |
| 0 | 250 | 500 | 750 | 1,000 Kilometers |

Sydney AUSTRALIA

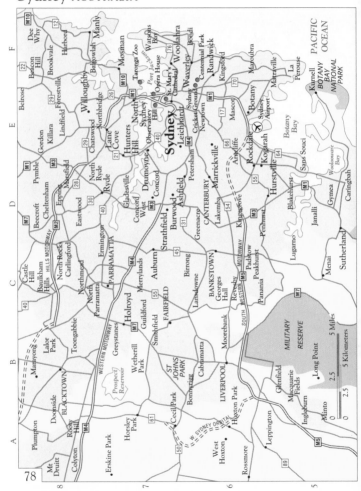

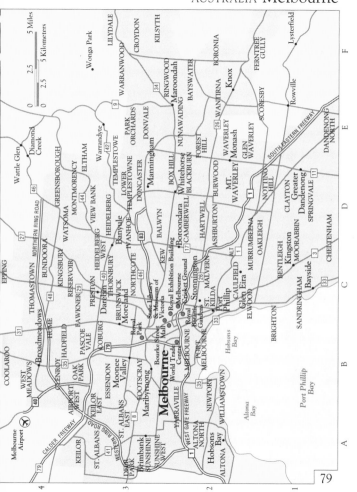

Pacific

Pacific

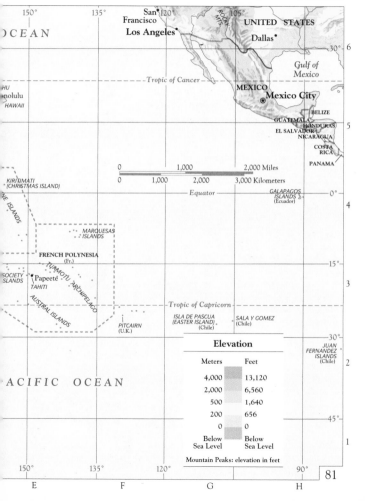

OCEAN

150° 135° 120°

San Francisco
Los Angeles

ROCKY MTS.

UNITED STATES

Dallas

105°

30° 6

Gulf of Mexico

Tropic of Cancer

HU
onolulu
HAWAII

MEXICO Mexico City ⊛

GUATEMALA BELIZE
HONDURAS
EL SALVADOR NICARAGUA
COSTA RICA
PANAMA

5

KIRITIMATI
(CHRISTMAS ISLAND)

E ISLANDS

0 1,000 2,000 Miles

0 1,000 2,000 3,000 Kilometers

Equator

GALAPAGOS ISLANDS
(Ecuador)

0° 4

MARQUESAS
ISLANDS

FRENCH POLYNESIA
(Fr.)

SOCIETY
ISLANDS Papeeté
TAHITI

TUAMOTU ARCHIPELAGO

15° 3

AUSTRAL ISLANDS

Tropic of Capricorn

ISLA DE PASCUA
(EASTER ISLAND)
(Chile)

SALA Y GOMEZ
(Chile)

PITCAIRN
(U.K.)

30°

JUAN FERNANDEZ
ISLANDS
(Chile)

2

PACIFIC OCEAN

Elevation

Meters	Feet
4,000	13,120
2,000	6,560
500	1,640
200	656
0	0
Below Sea Level	Below Sea Level

Mountain Peaks: elevation in feet

45° 1

150° 135° 120° 90°

E F G H

81

Arctic

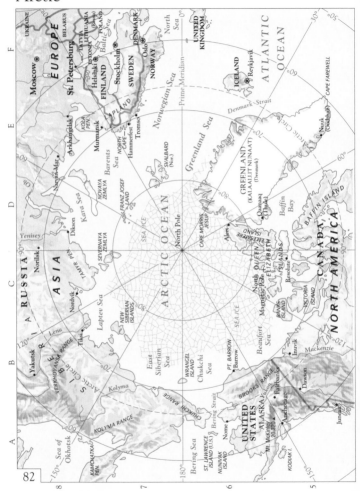

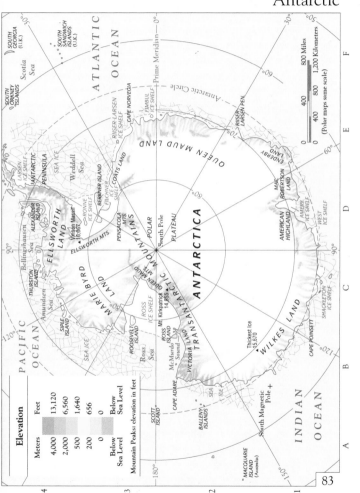

Antarctic

Elevation

Meters	Feet
4,000	13,120
2,000	6,560
500	1,640
200	656
0	0
Below Sea Level	Below Sea Level

Mountain Peaks: elevation in feet

0   400   800 Miles
0   400   800   1,200 Kilometers
(Polar maps same scale)

ATLANTIC OCEAN

SOUTH GEORGIA (U.K.)

SOUTH SANDWICH ISLANDS (U.K.)

Scotia Sea

SOUTH ORKNEY ISLANDS (U.K.)

Antarctic Circle

Prime Meridian

Polar Meridian

RISER-LARSEN ICE SHELF

CAPE NORVEGIA

QUEEN MAUD LAND

FIMBUL ICE SHELF

RISER-LARSEN PEN.

LARSEN ICE SHELF

ANTARCTIC PENINSULA

Weddell Sea

SEA ICE

COATS LAND

ENDERBY LAND

Bellingshausen Sea

ALEXANDER ISLAND

ELLSWORTH LAND

BERKNER ISLAND

FILCHNER ICE SHELF

RONNE ICE SHELF

Vinson Massif 16,067

ELLSWORTH MTS.

PENSACOLA MTS.

POLAR PLATEAU

South Pole

MAC. ROBERTSON LAND

AMERY ICE SHELF

WEST ICE SHELF

AMERICAN HIGHLAND

THURSTON ISLAND

MARIE BYRD LAND

QUEEN MAUD MTS.

TRANSANTARCTIC MOUNTAINS

ANTARCTICA

Amundsen Sea

SIPLE ISLAND

SEA ICE

ROSS ICE SHELF

ROOSEVELT ISLAND

Ross Sea

SEA ICE

McMURDO ISLAND

ROSS ISLAND

Mt Kirkpatrick 14,855

Mt Erebus

VICTORIA LAND

Thickest Ice 15,670

WILKES LAND

SHACKLETON ICE SHELF

CAPE POINSETT

PACIFIC OCEAN

SCOTT ISLAND

CAPE ADARE

BALLENY ISLANDS

South Magnetic Pole

INDIAN OCEAN

MACQUARIE ISLAND (Australia)

PENGUIN

South America NORTHERN

Caribbean Sea

BELIZE
Belmopan
GUATEMALA
HONDURAS
Guatemala City
Tegucigalpa
San Salvador
EL SALVADOR
NICARAGUA
Managua
COSTA RICA
San José
Panama City
PANAMA

PACIFIC OCEAN

GALÁPAGOS ISLANDS (ECUADOR)

Santa Marta
Barranquilla
Cartagena
Sincelejo
Montería
Barrancabermeja
Medellín
Manizales
Pereira
Armenia
Ibagué
Buenaventura
Cali
Popayán
Pasto
Esmeraldas
Quito
Cotopaxi 19,347
Portoviejo
Ambato
ECUADOR
Guayaquil
Cuenca
Machala
Loja
Tumbes
Talara
Sullana
Piura
AGUJA POINT
Chiclayo
Trujillo
Chimbote
Cerro de Pasco
Callao
Lima
Ica
Huancayo
Ayacucho
Cuzco
Juliaca
Arequipa
Tacna
Arica
Iquique
CHILE

Valledupar
Cúcuta
San Cristóbal
Bucaramanga
Tunja
Bogotá
Villavicencio
Palmira
Neiva
Florencia
COLOMBIA
Putumayo
Iquitos
Benjamin Constant
SELVA
Yurimaguas
Marañón
Cajamarca
Pucallpa
Cruzeiro do Sul
Huánuco
LA MONTAÑA
Puerto Maldonado
Cobija
Ribetalta
Trinidad
BOLIVIA
Lake Titicaca
Puno
La Paz
Cochabamba
Oruro
Lake Poopó
Santa Cruz
Sucre
Potosí
ALTIPLANO
ATACAMA DESERT
ANDES

Coro
ARUBA (Neth.)
CURAÇAO (Neth.)
BONAIRE (Neth.)
Maracaibo
Barquisimeto
Caracas
Cumaná
Maracay
Valencia
Cabimas
Mérida
Valera
Lake Maracaibo
San Fernando de Apure
Ciudad Bolí
VENEZUEL
LLANOS
GUIAN
Puerto Ayacucho
Orinoco
AMAZON
BASIN
Negro
Amaz
Juruá
Purús
Rio Branco
Porto Velho
Guajar Mirim
Beni
Negro
Madre

Matu
El Ti
Orinoco

0   250   500   750 Miles
0 250 500 750 1,000 Kilometers

84

90°   80°   70°

6

5

4

0°   Equator

3

2   10°

1

20°

A   B   C   D

DOMINICA

SAINT LUCIA

BARBADOS

ST. VINCENT & THE GRENADINES

GRENADA

TRINIDAD & TOBAGO

ATLANTIC OCEAN

Elevation

Meters	Feet
4,000	13,120
2,000	6,560
500	1,640
200	656
0	0
Below Sea Level	Below Sea Level

Mountain Peaks: elevation in feet

Ciudad Guayana

Georgetown
New Amsterdam
Paramaribo
Kourou
Cayenne

GUYANA

SURINAME

FRENCH GUIANA (Fr.)

HIGHLANDS

Boa Vista

Macapá

MARAJÓ ISLAND

Belém

São Luís

Parnaíba

Fortaleza

Manaus

Santarém

Imperatriz

Teresina

Natal
João Pessoa

Floriano

Juàzeiro do Norte

Campina Grande

BRAZIL

Petrolina

Recife

Maceió

Tapajós

Xingu

Tocantins

São Francisco

Gurupi

Feira de Santana

Aracaju

Salvador

MATO GROSSO

BRAZILIAN

Cuiabá

Vitória da Conquista

Ilhéus

PLATEAU

Araguaia

Anápolis

Brasília

Itabuna

Goiânia

Montes Claros

HIGHLANDS

Jataí

Corumbá

Uberlândia

Teófilo Otoni

Campo Grande

Governador Valadares

PARAGUAY

São José do Rio Prêto

Belo Horizonte

Pico da Bandeira 9,482

Vitória

Paraná

Grande

Ribeirão Prêto

Presidente Prudente

Bauru

Juiz de Fora

Paraguai

Paraná

60° 50° 40°

E F G H

South America SOUTHERN

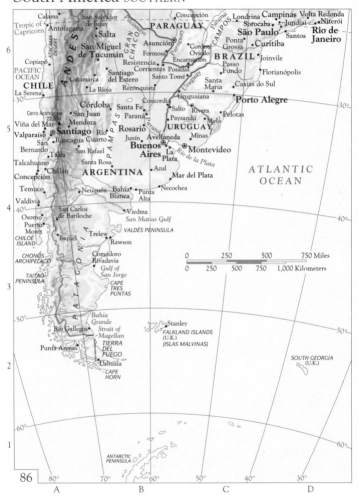

Calama
San Salvador de Jujuy
Tropic of Capricorn
Antofagasta
Salta
PARAGUAY
Concepción
Paraná
Londrina
Campinas
Volta Redonda
Sorocaba
Jundiaí
Niterói
São Paulo
Santos
Río de Janeiro
San Miguel de Tucumán
Asunción
Coronel Oviedo
Curitiba
Copiapó
Catamarca
Resistencia
Formosa
Encarnación
Ponta Grossa
BRAZIL
Joinvile
PACIFIC OCEAN
CHILE
Santiago del Estero
Corrientes
Posadas
Passo Fundo
Florianópolis
La Serena
La Rioja
Reconquista
Santo Tomé
Santa Maria
Caxias do Sul
Córdoba
Santa Fe
Concordia
Uruguaiana
Porto Alegre
Cerro Aconcagua 22,834
San Juan
Mendoza
Paraná
Salto
Rivera
Pelotas
Viña del Mar
Valparaíso
Santiago
Rosario
URUGUAY
San Bernardo
Rancagua
Río Cuarto
Junín
Paysandú
Minas
Talcahuano
Talca
San Rafael
Buenos Aires
Avellaneda
Montevideo
Concepción
Chillán
Santa Rosa
ARGENTINA
La Plata
Río de la Plata
Temuco
Neuquén
Azul
Mar del Plata
ATLANTIC OCEAN
Valdivia
Bahía Blanca
Punta Alta
Necochea
Osorno
Puerto Montt
San Carlos de Bariloche
Viedma
San Matias Gulf
CHILOÉ ISLAND
Esquel
Trelew
VALDÉS PENINSULA
CHONOS ARCHIPELAGO
Rawson
TAITAO PENINSULA
Comodoro Rivadavia
Gulf of San Jorge
CAPE TRES PUNTAS
Bahía Grande
Stanley
Río Gallegos
Strait of Magellan
FALKLAND ISLANDS (U.K.) (ISLAS MALVINAS)
Punta Arenas
TIERRA DEL FUEGO
SOUTH GEORGIA (U.K.)
Ushuaia
CAPE HORN
ANTARCTIC PENINSULA

86

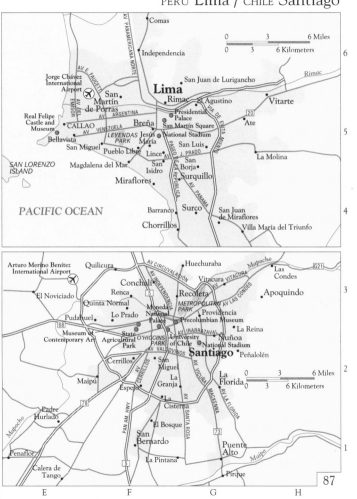

Buenos Aires ARGENTINA

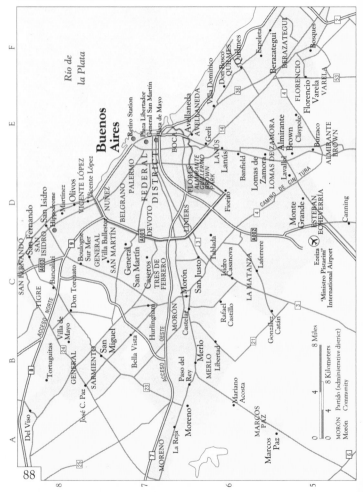

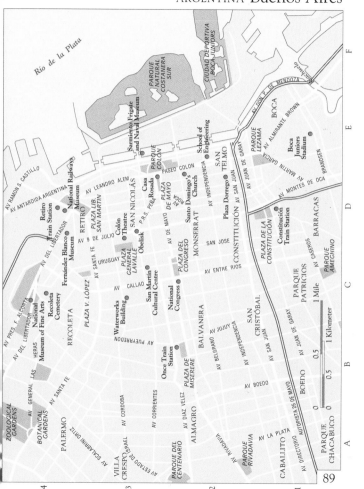

Río de la Plata

PARQUE NATURAL COSTANERA SUR

CIUDAD DEPORTIVA BOCA JUNIORS

Sarmiento Frigate and Naval Museum

PARQUE COLON

School of Engineering

BOCA

PARQUE LEZAMA

Boca Juniors Stadium

AV ALMIRANTE BROWN

AV GDOR. P. DE MENDOZA

AV RAMON S. CASTILLO

AV ANTARDIDA ARGENTINA

AV LEANDRO ALEM

Retiro Train Station

National Railways Museum

PLAZA LIB. SAN MARTIN

PASEO COLON

Casa Rosada

Santo Domingo's Church

SAN TELMO

SAN

P.R.S. PEÑA

PLAZA DE MAYO

Plaza Dorrego

AV INDEPENDENCIA

AV DEL LIBERTADOR

Fernández Blanco Museum

Colón Theatre

RETIRO

AV 9 DE JULIO

SAN MARTIN

Obelisk

SAN NICOLAS

AV DE MAYO

MONSERRAT

AV JUAN DE GARAY

AV MONTES DE OCA

AV MARTIN GARCIA

AV BRANDSEN

BARRACAS

AV PRES. F. ALCORTA

National Museum of Fine Arts

Recoleta Cemetery

RECOLETA

PLAZA V. LÓPEZ

AV SANTA FE

AV URUGUAY

PLAZA GENERAL LAVALLE

San Martín Cultural Centre

PLAZA DEL CONGRESO

National Congress

AV CALLAO

AV ENTRE RIOS

SAN JOSE

CONSTITUCIÓN

Plaza de la Constitución

Constitución Train Station

AV CASEROS

PARQUE PATRICIOS

PARQUE AMEGHINO

AV DEL LIBERTADOR

HERAS

LAS

AV GENERAL

AV SANTA FE

Waterworks Building

AV PUEYRREDON

BALVANERA

AV BELGRANO

SAN CRISTÓBAL

AV JUJUY

AV INDEPENDENCIA

AV SAN JUAN

AV JUAN DE GARAY

1 Mile

ZOOLOGICAL GARDENS

BOTANICAL GARDENS

AV SCALABRINI ORTIZ

PALERMO

AV CORDOBA

AV CORRIENTES

VILLA CRESPO

AV ESTADO DE ISRAEL

ALMAGRO

AV DIAZ VELEZ

Once Train Station

PLAZA DE MISERERE

AV BOEDO

BOEDO

AV JUAN DE GARAY

1 Kilometer

0.5

0

0.5

0

AV CORRIENTES

PARQUE DEL CENTENARIO

AV RIVADAVIA

PARQUE RIVADAVIA

CABALLITO

AV DIRECTORIO

AUTOPISTA 25 DE MAYO

AV LA PLATA

PARQUE CHACABUCO

Caracas VENEZUELA / Bogotá COLOMBIA

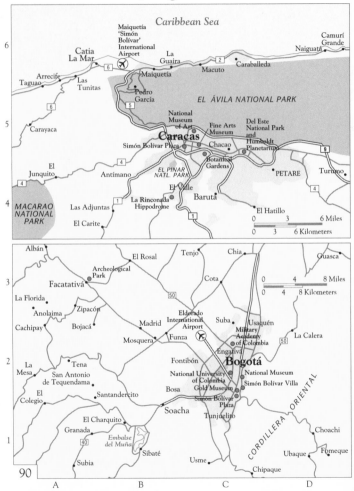

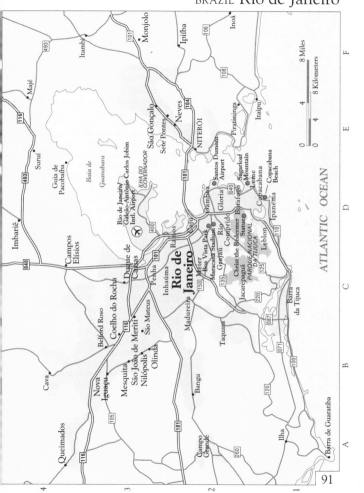

São Paulo BRAZIL

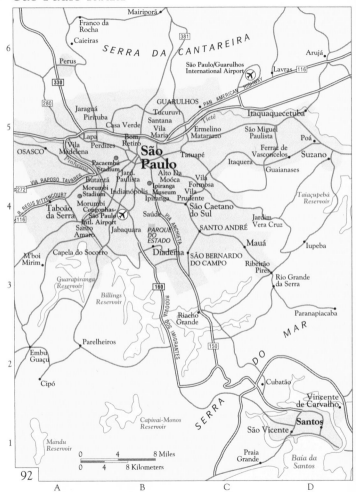

Mairiporã

Franco da
Rocha

Caieiras

SERRA DA CANTAREIRA

Perus

381

Arujá

São Paulo/Guarulhos
International Airport

Lavras

116

330

280

PAN AMERICAN HIGHWAY

Itaquaquecetuba

GUARULHOS

Jaraguá
Pirituba

Tucuruvi

Tietê

Casa Verde

Santana
Vila
Maria

Ermelino
Matarazo

São Miguel
Paulista

Poá

Lapa
Vila
Madalena

Bom
Retiro

Perdizes

São
Paulo

Tatuapé

Itaquera

Ferraz de
Vasconcelos

Suzano

OSASCO

Pinheiros

Pacaembú
Stadium

Jard.
Paulista

Alto Da
Moóca

Vila
Formosa

Guaianases

272

VIA RAPOSO TAVARES

Butantã

Ipiranga
Museum

Vila
Prudente

Taiaçupebá
Reservoir

R. REGIS BITTENCOURT

Morumbi
Stadium

Indianópolis

Ipiranga

São Caetano
do Sul

Taboão
da Serra

Morumbi
Congonhas-
São Paulo
Intl. Airport

Saúde

VIA ANCHIETA

Jardim
Vera Cruz

116

Santo
Amaro

Jabaquara

PARQUE
DO
ESTADO

SANTO ANDRÉ

M'boi
Mirim

Capela do Socorro

Diadema

Mauá

Iupeba

Guarapiranga
Reservoir

SÃO BERNARDO
DO CAMPO

Ribeirão
Pires

Billings
Reservoir

160

Rio Grande
da Serra

Riacho
Grande

RODOVIA DOS IMIGRANTES

Paranapiacaba

MAR

Parelheiros

150

Embu
Guaçu

DO

Cipó

Cubatão

SERRA

Vincente
de Carvalho

Capivai-Monos
Reservoir

São Vicente

Santos

Mandu
Reservoir

Praia
Grande

Baía da
Santos

0   4   8 Miles

0   4   8 Kilometers

A   B   C   D

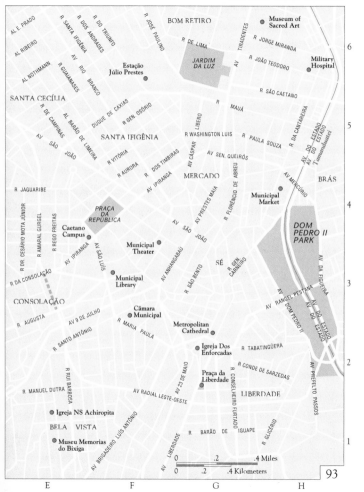

BRAZIL São Paulo

AL E. PRADO
AL RIBEIRO
AL NOTHMANN
R SANTA IFIGÊNIA
R DOS ANDRADES
R DO TRIUNFO
R JOSÉ PAULINO
BOM RETIRO
R DE LIMA
TIRADENTES
R JORGE MIRANDA

Museum of
Sacred Art

Military
Hospital

AV TIRADENTES
AV JOÃO TEODORO
R SÃO CAETANO

R GUAIMASES
AV RIO BRANCO
Estação
Júlio Prestes
JARDIM
DA LUZ

SANTA CECÍLIA
R DE CAMPINAS
AL BARÃO DE LIMEIRA
DUQUE DE CAXIAS
R GEN. OSÓRIO
SANTA IFIGÊNIA
R MAUÁ

AV SÃO JOÃO
R VITÓRIA
R AURORA
R DOS TIMBIRAS
LIBERO
R WASHINGTON LUIS
AV CASPAR
R SEN. QUEIRÓS
R PAULA SOUZA
R DA CANTAREIRA
AV DO ESTADO
AV DO ESTADO

R JAGUARIBE
AV IPIRANGA
MERCADO
R FLORÊNCIO DE ABREU
AV MERCÚRIO
BRÁS

R CESÁRIO MOTA JÚNIOR
R AMARAL GURGEL
PRAÇA
DA
REPÚBLICA
AV PRESTES MAIA
Municipal
Market

R REGO FREITAS
Caetano
Campus
AV IPIRANGA
AV SÃO LUÍS
AV SÃO JOÃO
DOM
PEDRO II
PARK

R DR. CESÁRIO MOTA JÚNIOR
Municipal
Theater
AV ANHANGABAÚ
AV SÃO BENTO
SÉ
R GEN. CARNEIRO
AV DA FIGUEIRA

R DA CONSOLAÇÃO
Municipal
Library

CONSOLAÇÃO
R AUGUSTA
AV 9 DE JULHO
Câmara
Municipal
R MARIA PAULA
AV RANGEL PESTANA
AV DOM PEDRO II
AV DO ESTADO

R SANTO ANTÔNIO
Metropolitan
Cathedral
Igreja Dos
Enforcadas
R TABATINGÜERA
AV PREFEITO PASSOS

R RUI BARBOSA
AV 23 DE MAIO
Praça da
Liberdade
R CONDE DE SARZEDAS
R CONSELHEIRO FURTADO
LIBERDADE

R MANUEL DUTRA
AV RADIAL LESTE-OESTE
R BARÃO DE IGUAPE
R GLICÉRIO

Igreja NS Achiropita
BELA VISTA
Museu Memorias
do Bixiga
AV BRIGADEIRO LUÍS ANTÔNIO
LIBERDADE
0   .2   .4 Miles
0   .2   .4 Kilometers

E   F   G   H

6
5
4
3
2
1

93

Caribbean

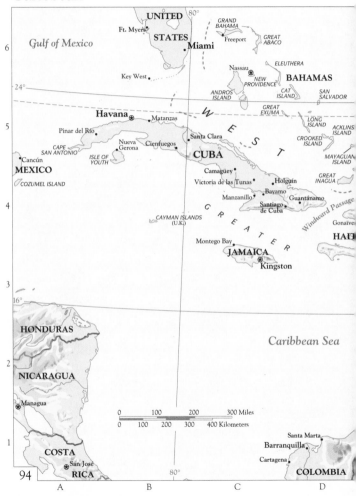

Caribbean

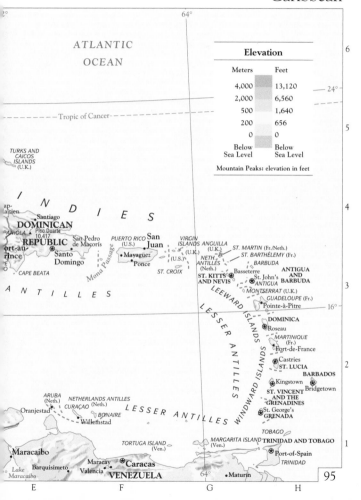

ATLANTIC OCEAN

Tropic of Cancer

I N D I E S

A N T I L L E S

Elevation

Meters	Feet
4,000	13,120
2,000	6,560
500	1,640
200	656
0	0
Below Sea Level	Below Sea Level

Mountain Peaks: elevation in feet

TURKS AND CAICOS ISLANDS (U.K.)

ap-aïtien
Santiago
Pico Duarte
10,417
DOMINICAN REPUBLIC
San Pedro de Macorís
PUERTO RICO (U.S.)
San Juan
VIRGIN ISLANDS (U.K.)
ANGUILLA (U.K.)
ST. MARTIN (Fr./Neth.)
ST. BARTHÉLEMY (Fr.)

PANIOLA
ort-au-rince
'EO
Santo Domingo
Mayagüez
Ponce
ST. CROIX
NETH. ANTILLES (Neth.)
Basseterre
St. John's
ANTIGUA
ANTIGUA AND BARBUDA
BARBUDA
ST. KITTS AND NEVIS
MONTSERRAT (U.K.)
GUADELOUPE (Fr.)
Pointe-à-Pitre

CAPE BEATA
Mona Passage

LEEWARD ISLANDS

DOMINICA
Roseau
MARTINIQUE (Fr.)
Fort-de-France

LESSER ANTILLES

Castries
ST. LUCIA
BARBADOS
Kingstown
Bridgetown
ST. VINCENT AND THE GRENADINES
St. George's
GRENADA

WINDWARD ISLANDS

ARUBA (Neth.)
NETHERLANDS ANTILLES
CURAÇAO (Neth.)
BONAIRE
Oranjestad
Willemstad

LESSER ANTILLES

TORTUGA ISLAND (Ven.)
MARGARITA ISLAND (Ven.)
TOBAGO
TRINIDAD AND TOBAGO
Port-of-Spain
TRINIDAD

Maracaibo
Lake Maracaibo
Barquisimeto
Maracay
Valencia
Caracas
VENEZUELA
Maturín

64°

2°
64°
24°
16°

6
5
4
3
2
1

E   F   G   H

Mexico - Central America

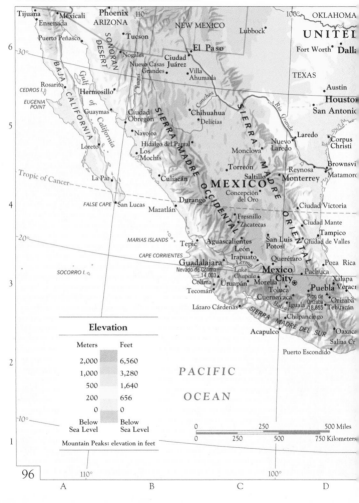

Central America - Mexico

Mexico City MEXICO

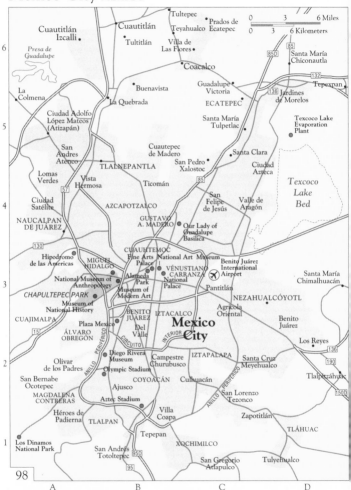

98

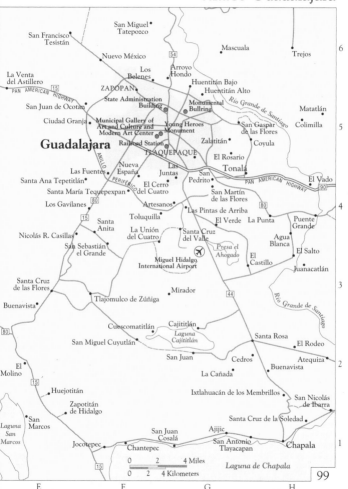

San Francisco
Tesistán

San Miguel
Tatepozco

Mascuala

Trejos

Nuevo México

La Venta
del Astillero

Los
Belenes

Arroyo
Hondo

PAN AMERICAN HIGHWAY

ZAPOPAN

Huentitán Bajo

Huentitán Alto

Río Grande de Santiago

Matatlán

San Juan de Ocotán

State Administration
Building

Monumental
Bullring

Ciudad Granja

Municipal Gallery of
Art and Culture and
Modern Art Center

Young Heroes
Monument

San Gaspar
de las Flores

Colimilla

Guadalajara

Railroad Station

Zalatitán

Coyula

TLAQUEPAQUE

El Rosario

Las Fuentes

Nueva
España

Las
Juntas

Tonalá

El Vado

Santa Ana Tepetitlán

PERIFÉRICO

El Cerro
del Cuatro

San
Pedrito

PAN AMERICAN HIGHWAY

Santa María Tequepexpan

San Martín
de las Flores

Los Gavilanes

Artesanos

Las Pintas de Arriba

Puente
Grande

Santa
Anita

Toluquilla

El Verde

La Punta

Nicolás R. Casillas

La Unión
del Cuatro

Santa Cruz
del Valle

Agua
Blanca

El Salto

San Sebastián
el Grande

Presa el
Ahogado

El
Castillo

Juanacatlán

Santa Cruz
de las Flores

Miguel Hidalgo
International Airport

Mirador

Río Grande de Santiago

Buenavista

Tlajomulco de Zúñiga

Cuescomatitlán

Cajititlán

Santa Rosa

El Rodeo

San Miguel Cuyutlán

Laguna
Cajititlán

San Juan

Cedros

Buenavista

Atequiza

El
Molino

La Cañada

Huejotitán

Ixtlahuacán de los Membrillos

San Nicolás
de Ibarra

Zapotitán
de Hidalgo

Santa Cruz de la Soledad

Laguna
San
Marcos

San
Marcos

San Juan
Cosalá

Ajijic

Jocotepec

Chantepec

San Antonio
Tlayacapan

Chapala

Laguna de Chapala

0   2   4 Miles

0   2   4 Kilometers

6

5

4

3

2

1

E   F   G   H

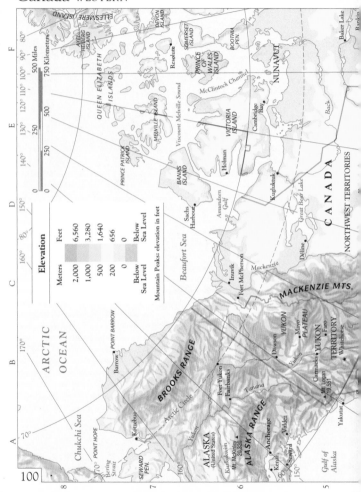

Elevation

Meters	Feet
2,000	6,560
1,000	3,280
500	1,640
200	656
0	0
Below Sea Level	Below Sea Level

Mountain Peaks: elevation in feet

500 Miles

750 Kilometers

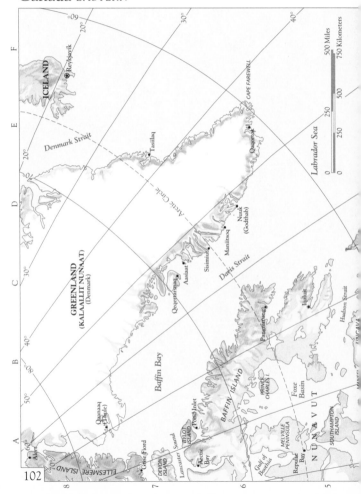

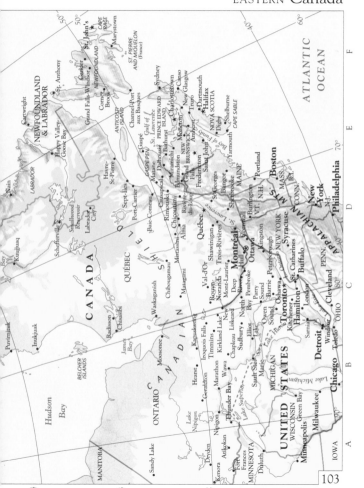

ATLANTIC OCEAN

CAPE RACE
Marystown
St. John's
Gander
ST. PIERRE AND MIQUELON (France)
St. Anthony
Cartwright
NEWFOUNDLAND & LABRADOR
Grand Falls-Windsor
Corner Brook
Channel-Port aux Basques
Sydney
New Glasgow
ANTICOSTI ISLAND
Happy Valley-Goose Bay
Gulf of St. Lawrence
PRINCE EDWARD ISLAND
Charlottetown
NOVA SCOTIA
Dartmouth
Halifax
Shelburne
CAPE SABLE
Digby
Havre-St-Pierre
LABRADOR
Gaspé
GASPÉ PEN.
Matane
Dalhousie
Bathurst
NEW BRUNSWICK
Amherst
Truro
Sept-Îles
Port-Cartier
Carleton
Rimouski
Miramichi
Rivière-du-Loup
Fredericton
Saint John
Bay of Fundy
Yarmouth
Smallwood Reservoir
Labrador City
Baie-Comeau
Chicoutimi
Alma
Edmundston
St. Stephen
St-Georges
Bangor
Portland
Boston
MASS.
CONN.
New York
Philadelphia
N.J.
Schefferville
Nain
QUÉBEC
Mistassini
Québec
Shawinigan
Trois-Rivières
Sherbrooke
Burlington
VT.
N.H.
MAINE
Kuujjuaq
Radisson
Chisasibi
Waskaganish
Chibougamau
Val-d'Or
Rouyn-Noranda
Mont-Laurier
Hull
Montréal
Cornwall
Ottawa
Kingston
Syracuse
NEW YORK
PENN.
St. Lawrence
Puvirnituq
Inukjuak
James Bay
Matagami
Kapuskasing
Moosonee
Deep River
Pembroke
Peterborough
Oshawa
Toronto
St. Catharines
Buffalo
Cleveland
APPALACHIANS
BELCHER ISLANDS
CANADA
Hearst
Geraldton
Timmins
Kirkland Lake
New Liskeard
Parry Sound
Barrie
North Bay
Owen Sound
Hamilton
Kitchener
London
OHIO
Hudson Bay
CANADIAN SHIELD
ONTARIO
Nipigon
Marathon
Thunder Bay
Wawa
Chapleau
Sudbury
Elliot Lake
Sault Ste. Marie
Sarnia
Windsor
Detroit
Toledo
MICHIGAN
Sandy Lake
Lake Nipigon
Lake Superior
MANITOBA
Dryden
Atikokan
Fort Frances
Kenora
Lake Michigan
WISCONSIN
MINNESOTA
IOWA
Duluth
Minneapolis
Milwaukee
Green Bay
Chicago
UNITED STATES

103

Toronto CANADA

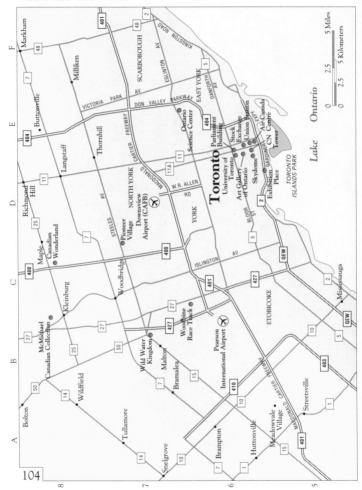

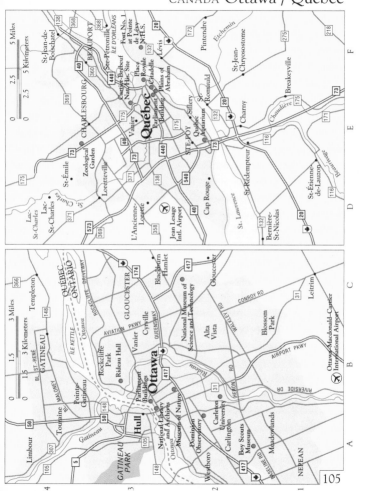

105

Montréal CANADA

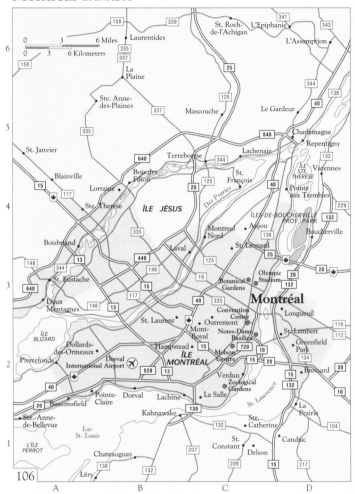

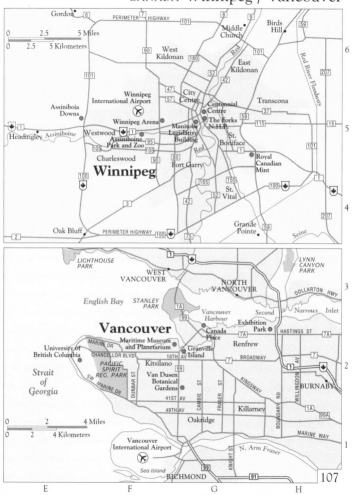

E   F   G   H

UNITED
STATES

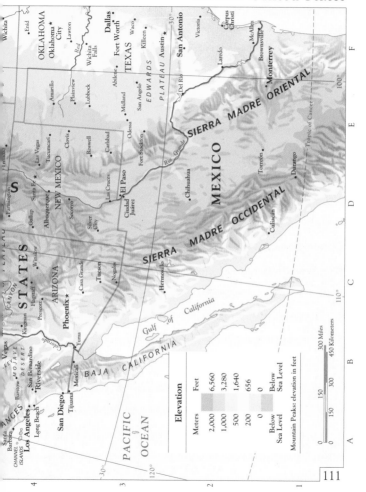

Elevation

Meters	Feet
2,000	6,560
1,000	3,280
500	1,640
200	656
0	0
Below Sea Level	Below Sea Level

Mountain Peaks: elevation in feet

0   150   300 Miles
0   150   300   450 Kilometers

United States EASTERN

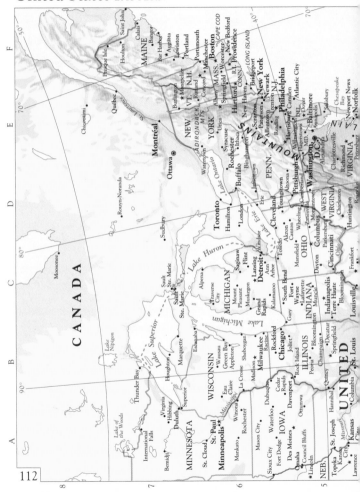

EASTERN United States

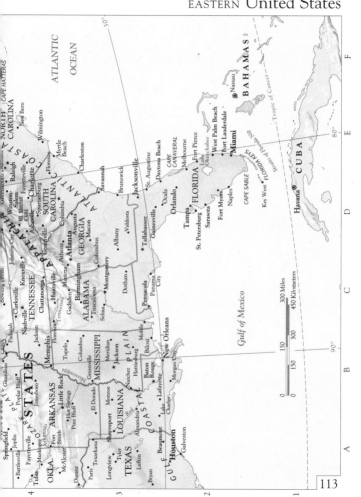

New England

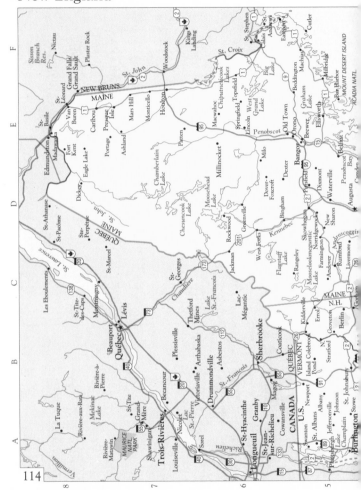

New England

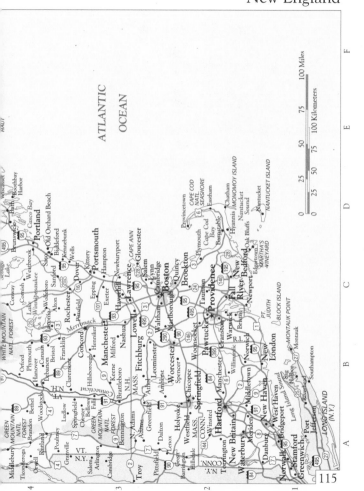

New York State

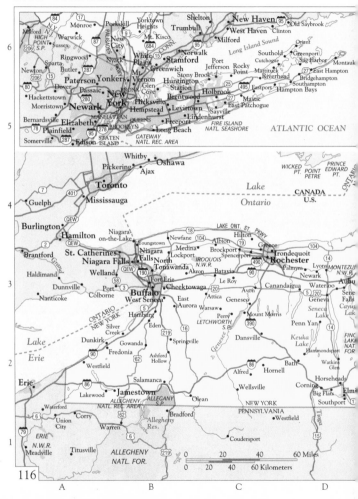

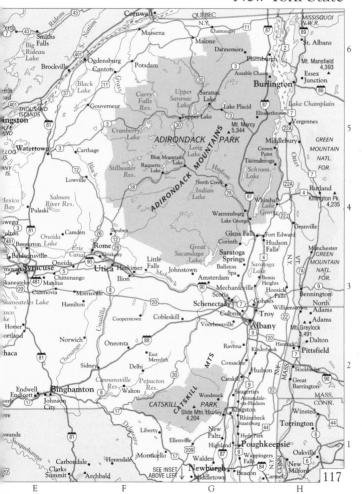

New York State

Middle Atlantic States

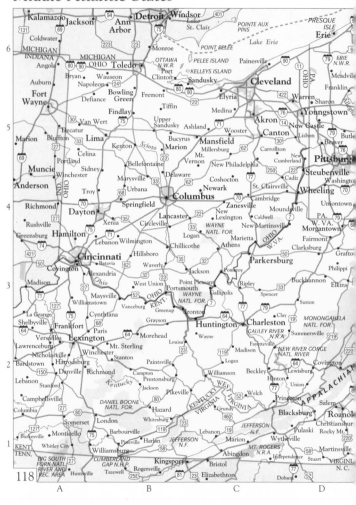

A   B   C   D

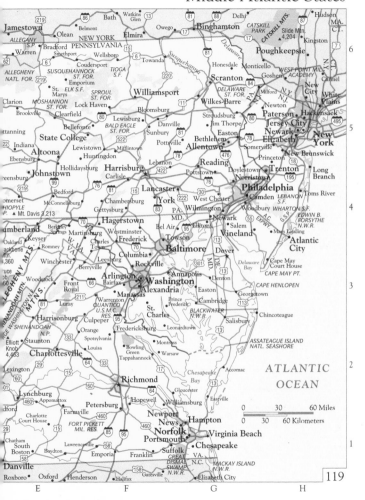

Southeastern States

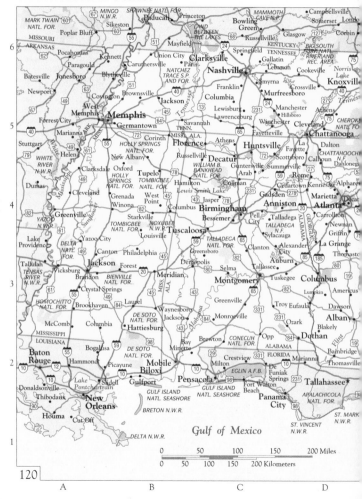

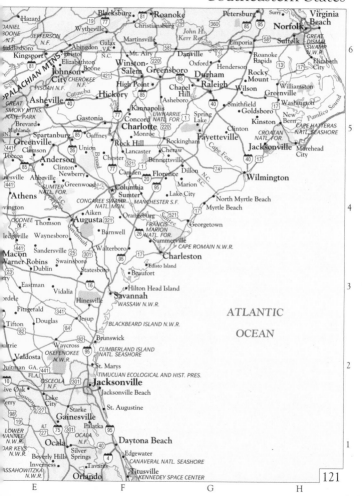

Hazard · Blacksburg · Roanoke · Petersburg · Surry · Virginia
DANIEL · Wytheville · Christiansburg · John H. · Norfolk · Beach
BOONE · JEFFERSON · Kerr Res. · Suffolk · GREAT
N.F. · N.F. · Martinsville · 58 · Emporia · 58 · DISMAL
Middlesboro · Abingdon · Galax · Mt. Airy · Danville · Roanoke · SWAMP
Kingsport · 81 · Bristol · N.C. · 220 · Oxford · Rapids · 13 · N.W.R.
PISCAH N.F. · Elizabethton · Boone · Winston- · Greensboro · Henderson · Rocky · Elizabeth
Johnson · CHEROKEE · Salem · Durham · Mount · City
City · N.F. · 421 · High Point · 85 · Raleigh · Wilson · Williamston
APPALACHIAN MTNS. · Catawba · Chapel · Asheboro · Smithfield · Goldsboro · Washington
Asheville · 40 · Hickory · Hill · Spring · Kinston · New · Pamlico Sound
GREAT · Kannapolis · UWHARRIE · 1 · Lake · Bern · CAPE HATTERAS
SMOKY MTNS. · Gastonia · 77 · Concord · NATL. FOR. · Clinton · Croatan · NATL. SEASHORE
NATL. PARK · Charlotte · 220 · Fayetteville · NATL. FOR.
Brevard · Spartanburg · 85 · Gaffney · Monroe · Rockingham · Jacksonville · Morehead
Highlands · Greenville · Rock Hill · Cheraw · 74 · City
Clemson · Union · Chester · Lancaster · Bennettsville · Dillon · Wilmington
Toccoa · 85 · Anderson · Broad · 77 · Camden · Florence · Marion · N.C.
nesville · Abbeville · Clinton · Newberry · 1 · Lake City · North Myrtle Beach
441 · Greenwood · Columbia · 20 · Myrtle Beach
Athens · SUMTER · Sumter · MANCHESTER S.F. · Georgetown
vington · NATL. FOR. · CONGAREE SWAMP · Lake City
OCONEE · Aiken · NATL. MON. · Orangeburg · 521 · 17
N.F. · Thomson · S.C. · 26 · FRANCIS · CAPE ROMAIN N.W.R.
ledgeville · Waynesboro · Barnwell · MARION · Summerville
Macon · Sandersville · 25 · Walterboro · NATL. FOR. · Charleston
Warner Robins · Swainsboro · 301 · 95
ry · Dublin · 23 · Statesboro · Edisto Island
Eastman · 16 · Beaufort
ordele · Vidalia · Hinesville · Savannah
Fitzgerald · 341 · WASSAW N.W.R. · Hilton Head Island
Tifton · Douglas · 84 · Jesup · BLACKBEARD ISLAND N.W.R. · **ATLANTIC**
82 · 82 · Brunswick
oultrie · Waycross · 95 · CUMBERLAND ISLAND · **OCEAN**
Valdosta · OKEFENOKEE · NATL. SEASHORE
Quitman · GA. · N.W.R. · St. Marys
10 · FLA. · TIMUCUAN ECOLOGICAL AND HIST. PRES.
ive Oak · OSCEOLA · 301 · **Jacksonville**
erry · Lake · N.F. · Jacksonville Beach
98 · 27 · City · St. Augustine
19 · Starke · Palatka
LOWER · **Gainesville**
WANNEE · 75 · 301 · OCALA
N.W.R. · ALT · Ocala · N.F. · 95 · **Daytona Beach**
DAR KEYS · 27 · Beverly Hills · Silver · 40 · Edgewater
N.W.R. · Inverness · Springs · CANAVERAL NATL. SEASHORE
SSAHOWITZKA · Tavares · Titusville
N.W.R. · **Orlando** · KENNEDY SPACE CENTER

6

5

4

3

2

1

E · F · G · H

Florida - Puerto Rico

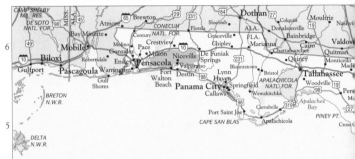

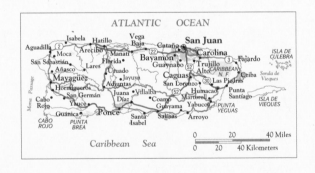

A   B   C   D

ATLANTIC

OCEAN

6

5

4

3

2

1

E   F   G   H

Midwestern States

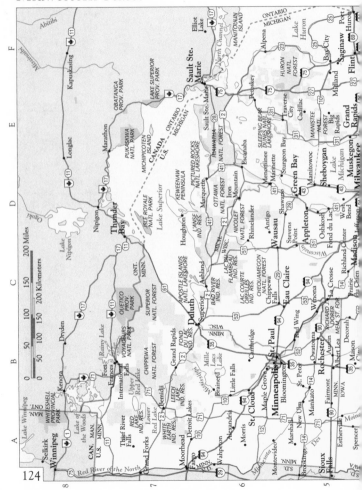

124

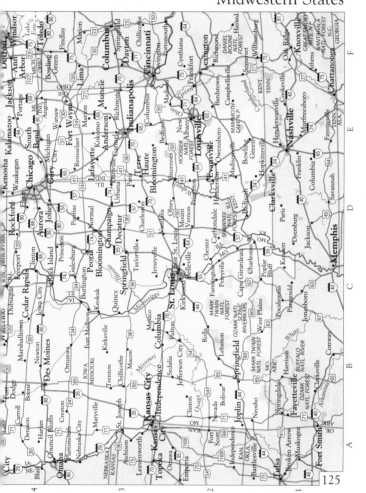

North Central States

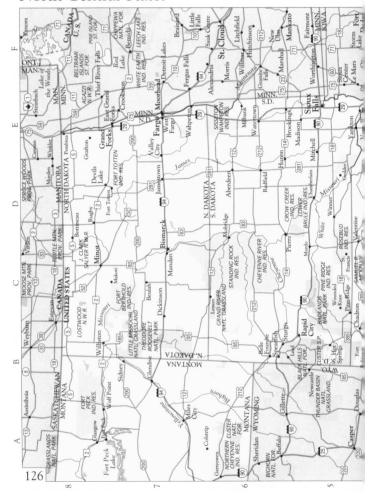

126

North Central States

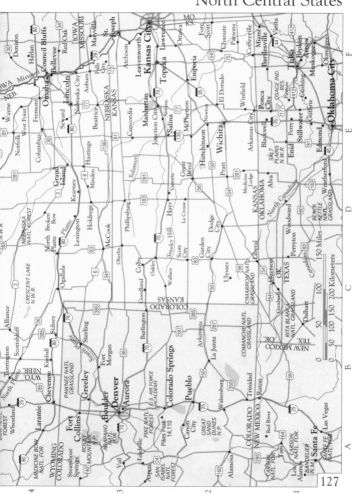

127

South Central States

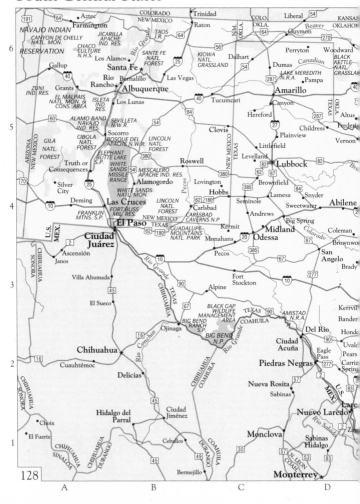

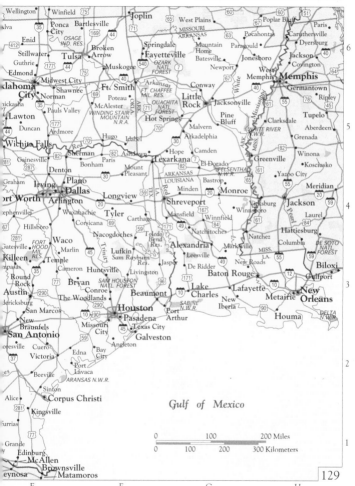

Gulf of Mexico

0   100   200 Miles

0   100   200   300 Kilometers

Rocky Mountain States

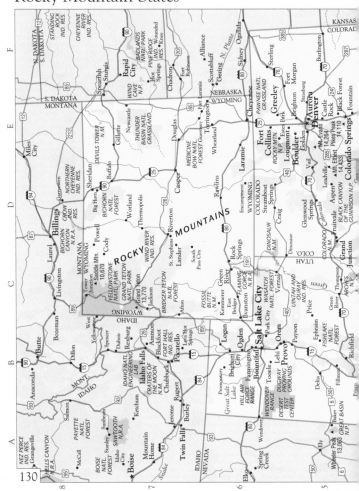

130

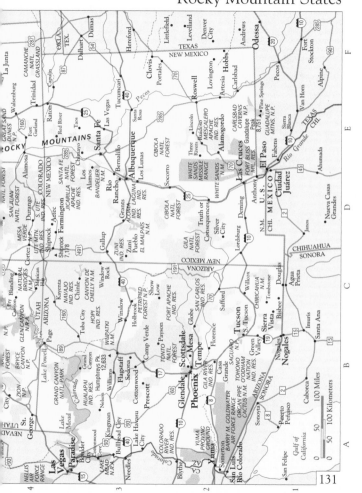

California - Nevada

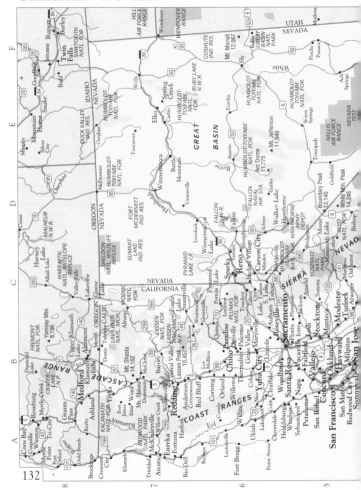

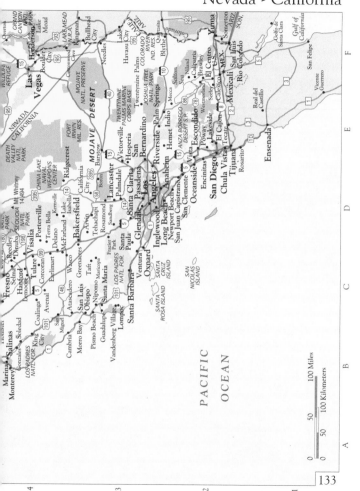

Northwestern States

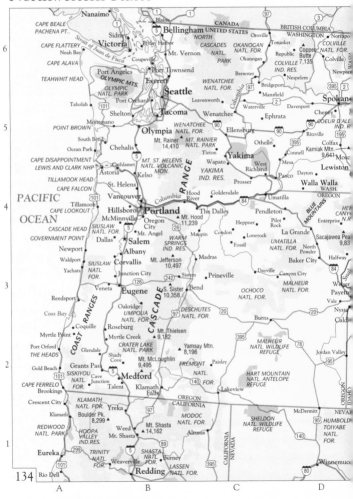

CANADA
UNITED STATES
BRITISH COLUMBIA
WASHINGTON

Nanaimo
Blaine
Oroville
Northport

CAPE BEALE
PACHENA PT.
Sidney
Bellingham
NORTH
OKANOGAN
Tonasket
COLVILLE
NATL. FOR.

CAPE FLATTERY
Neah Bay
Victoria
Friday Harbor
CASCADES
NATL.
PARK
Republic
Coppei
Butte 7,135

CAPE ALAVA
Coupeville
Mt. Vernon
Okanogan
Colville
Newpor

TEAHWHIT HEAD
Port Angeles
OLYMPIC MTS.
Port Townsend
WENATCHEE
Brewster
Nespelem

OLYMPIC
NATL. PARK
Everett
NATL. FOR.
Bridgeport
Mansfield
Spokan

Taholah
Port Orchard
Seattle
Leavenworth
Waterville
Davenport
Cheney

Strait of Juan de Fuca
Shelton
Tacoma
Wenatchee
Ephrata
COEUR D'ALE
IND. R

POINT BROWN
Montesano
Olympia
90
Ellensburg
Othello
90
Ritzville
Colfax
Kamiak Mtn.
9,641

CAPE DISAPPOINTMENT
South Bend
Chehalis
Mt. Rainier
14,410
MT. RAINIER
NATL. PARK
Tieton
395
Connell
Mosc

LEWIS AND CLARK NHP
Ocean Park
Cathlamet
MT. ST. HELENS
Wapato
West
Mesa
Dayton
Lewiston

TILLAMOOK HEAD
Astoria
Kelso
NATL. VOLCANIC
MON.
YAKIMA
IND. RES.
Richland
Pasco
Walla Walla
WASH.

CAPE FALCON
St. Helens
Prosser
Umatilla
OREGON

PACIFIC
Tillamook
Vancouver
Columbia
Goldendale
84
Pendleton
BLUE
HEI
CANY
N.R

OCEAN
CAPE LOOKOUT
Hillsboro
Portland
Mt. Hood
11,239
The Dalles
Heppner
Pilot
Rock
Enterprise

CASCADE HEAD
McMinnville
Oregon
City
26
Maupin
Condon
Lonerock
La Grande
Sacajawea Peak
9,83

GOVERNMENT POINT
Dallas
Mt. Angel
WARM
SPRINGS
IND. RES.
Fossil
UMATILLA
NATL. FOR.
North
Powder
Baker City

Newport
Salem
Madras
Dayville
Halfway
84

Waldport
Albany
Mt. Jefferson
10,497
Canyon City
MALHEUR
NATL. FOR.

Yachats
Corvallis
242
Sisters
Prineville
Welse
Payett

Junction City
126
S. Sister
10,358
Bend
OCHOCO
NATL. FOR.
20
Vale
Nyss

Reedsport
Veneta
Eugene
DESCHUTES
NATL. FOR.
Burns
Cald

Coos Bay
Oakridge
UMPQUA
NATL. FOR.
97
Yamsay Mtn.
8,196
395

Coquille
Roseburg
Mt. Thielsen
9,182
MALHEUR
NATL.
WILDLIFE
REFUGE
78
Jordan Valley

Myrtle Point
Myrtle Creek
CRATER LAKE
NATL. PARK
Paisley
HART MOUNTAIN
NATL. ANTELOPE
REFUGE
95

Port Orford
THE HEADS
Glendale
Shady
Cove
Mt. McLoughlin
9,495
FREMONT
Lakeview

Gold Beach
Grants Pass
SISKIYOU
NATL.
FOR.
NATL.
FOR.
140

CAPE FERRELO
Brookings
Cave
Junction
Talent
Medford
Klamath
Falls
OREGON
CALIFORNIA
McDermitt
NEVA

Crescent City
KLAMATH
NATL. FOR.
Yreka
97
MODOC
NATL. FOR.
SHELDON
NATL. WILDLIFE
REFUGE
95
HUMBOL
TOIYABE
NATL.
FOR.

Klamath
REDWOOD
NATL. PARK
Boulder Pk.
8,299
Weed
Mt. Shasta
14,162
Alturas

HOOPA
VALLEY
IND.RES.
Mt. Shasta
SHASTA
NATL. FOR.
140

Eureka
299
TRINITY
NATL.
FOR.
Weaverville
89
Burney
LASSEN
395
80
Winnemu

Rio Dell
101
Redding
NATL. FOR.

A   B   C   D

Northwestern States

Alaska

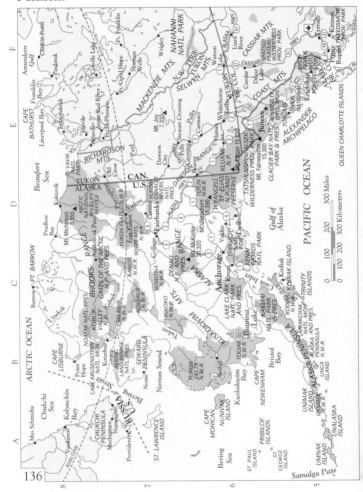

Hawaii

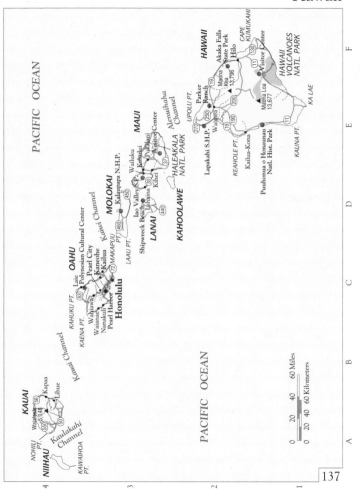

Boston MASSACHUSETTS

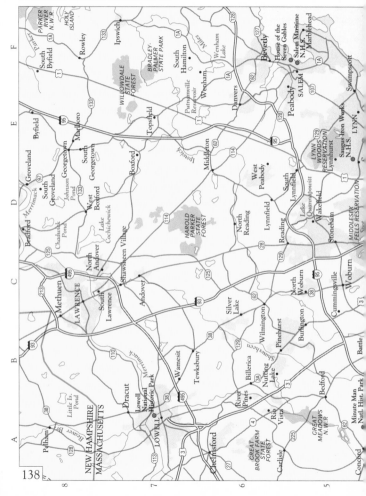

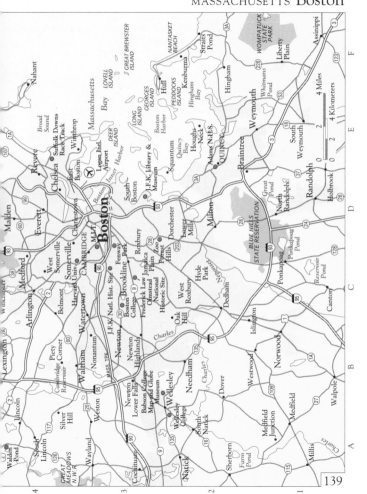

139

Boston MASSACHUSETTS

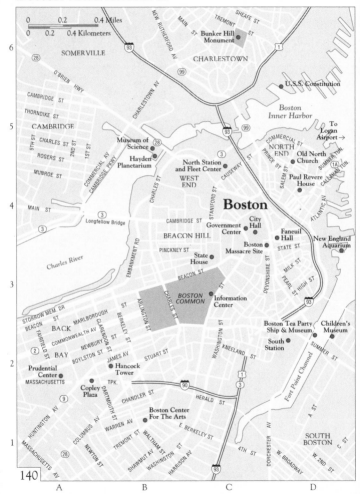

0   0.2   0.4 Miles
0   0.2   0.4 Kilometers

SOMERVILLE

CHARLESTOWN

Bunker Hill Monument

U.S.S. Constitution

Boston Inner Harbor

O'BRIEN HWY

CAMBRIDGE ST

THORNDIKE ST

CAMBRIDGE

CHARLES ST
5TH ST
2ND ST
1ST ST

ROGERS ST

MUNROE ST

CHARLESTOWN AV

COMMERCIAL AV
CAMBRIDGE PKWY

To Logan Airport →

COMMERCIAL ST

Museum of Science

Hayden Planetarium

North Station and Fleet Center

WEST END

NORTH END

Old North Church

PRINCE ST
SALEM ST

Paul Revere House

MAIN ST

Longfellow Bridge

CHARLES ST

STANIFORD ST

CAUSEWAY

Boston

ATLANTIC

Charles River

EMBANKMENT RD

CAMBRIDGE ST

BEACON HILL

Government Center

City Hall

Faneuil Hall

New England Aquarium

PINCKNEY ST

State House

Boston Massacre Site

STATE ST

DEVONSHIRE ST

MILK ST

PEARL ST

HIGH ST

BEACON ST

BOSTON COMMON

Information Center

CHARLES ST

ARLINGTON ST

STORROW MEM. DR

BEACON ST

BACK BAY

MARLBOROUGH ST

COMMONWEALTH AV

BERKELEY ST
CLARENDON ST

NEWBURY ST

BOYLSTON ST

JAMES AV

STUART ST

WASHINGTON ST

KNEELAND ST

Boston Tea Party Ship & Museum

Children's Museum

South Station

SUMMER ST

Fort Point Channel

Prudential Center

MASSACHUSETTS

Hancock Tower

Copley Plaza

DARTMOUTH ST

TPK.

CHANDLER ST

HERALD ST

HUNTINGTON AV

COLUMBUS AV

WARREN ST

TREMONT ST
WALTHAM ST

Boston Center For The Arts

E. BERKELEY ST

4TH ST

DORCHESTER AV

W. BROADWAY

SOUTH BOSTON

W. 2ND ST

C ST

MASSACHUSETTS AV

NEWTON ST

SHAWMUT AV

WASHINGTON ST

HARRISON AV

A ST

140

A   B   C   D

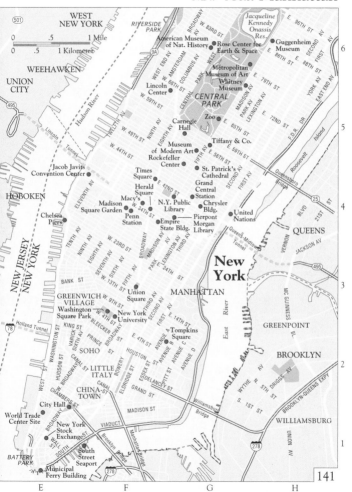

501

WEST
NEW YORK

RIVERSIDE PARK

Jacqueline
Kennedy
Onassis
Res.

WEEHAWKEN

UNION
CITY

American Museum
of Nat. History
Rose Center for
Earth & Space
Guggenheim
Museum

Metropolitan
Museum of Art
Whitney
Museum

Lincoln
Center

CENTRAL
PARK

Hudson River

Lincoln
Tunnel

Carnegie
Hall

Zoo

HOBOKEN

Jacob Javits
Convention Center

Tiffany & Co.

Museum of
Modern Art
Rockefeller
Center

St. Patrick's
Cathedral

Chelsea
Piers

Times
Square

Herald
Square
Macy's

Grand
Central
Station

Chrysler
Bldg.

Madison
Square Garden
Penn
Station

N.Y. Public
Library

Pierpont
Morgan
Library

United
Nations

Empire
State Bldg.

Queensboro
Bridge

Roosevelt
Island

E.O.R. DR.

QUEENS

Queens-Midtown
Tunnel

**New
York**

495

NEW JERSEY
NEW YORK

Union
Square

MANHATTAN

East River

JACKSON AV

GREENPOINT

GREENWICH
VILLAGE
Washington
Square Park
New York
University

Tompkins
Square

MC GUINNESS BLVD

BROOKLYN-QUEENS EXPY

Holland Tunnel

78

SOHO

LITTLE
ITALY

CHINA-
TOWN

Williamsburg
Bridge

BROOKLYN

WILLIAMSBURG

City Hall

MADISON ST

VIADUCT

278

UNION AV

World Trade
Center Site

New York
Stock
Exchange

Brooklyn Bridge

Manhattan Bridge

BATTERY
PARK

South
Street
Seaport

Municipal
Ferry Building

278

E   F   G   H

New York NEW YORK

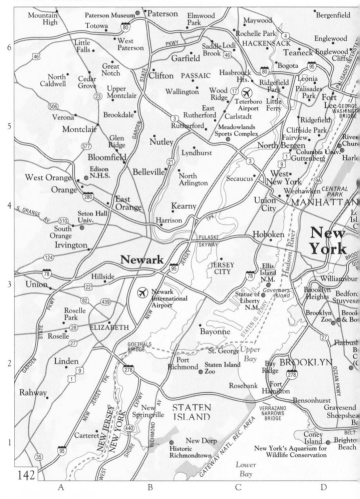

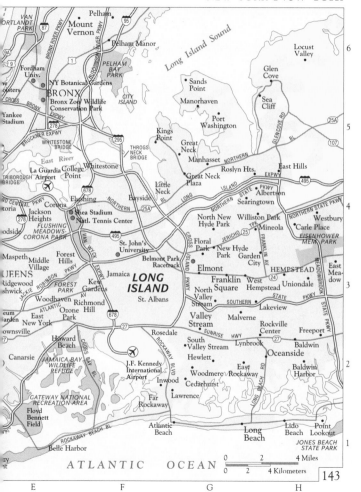

ATLANTIC OCEAN

| 0 | | 2 | | 4 Miles |
| 0 | 2 | | 4 Kilometers |

143

Philadelphia PENNSYLVANIA

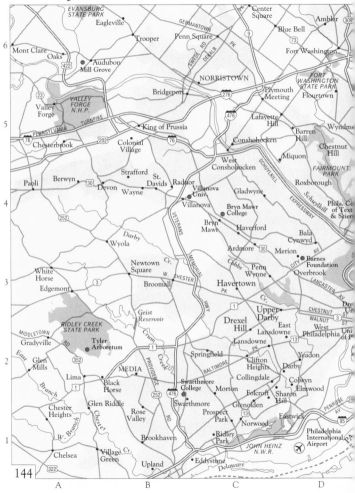

EVANSBURG STATE PARK

Eagleville
Mont Clare
Oaks
Audubon
Mill Grove
Trooper
Penn Square
GERMANTOWN RD
Center Square
Ambler
309
Blue Bell
73
Fort Washington

422

VALLEY FORGE N.H.P.
23
Valley Forge
Bridgeport
NORRISTOWN
276
Plymouth Meeting
FORT WASHINGTON STATE PARK
Flourtown

PENNSYLVANIA TURNPIKE
76
Chesterbrook
King of Prussia
202
Colonial Village
76
Lafayette Hill
476
Conshohocken
West Conshohocken
Barren Hill
Miquon
Wyndm
Chestnut Hill
FAIRMOUNT PARK

Paoli
Berwyn
30
Devon
Wayne
Strafford
St. Davids
Radnor
Villanova Univ.
Villanova
Gladwyne
Roxborough
Phila. C of Text & Scien

252
Darby
Wyola
Bryn Mawr College
Bryn Mawr
Haverford
Ardmore
30
Merion
Bala Cynwyd
Barnes Foundation
Overbrook

White Horse
Edgemont
Newtown Square
Broomall
3
Penn Wynne
Havertown
CITY
LANCASTER AV
Dee Un

RIDLEY CREEK STATE PARK
Geist Reservoir
Upper Darby
Drexel Hill
East Lansdowne
West Philadelphia
Uni of P
CHESTNUT ST
WALNUT ST
3

MIDDLETOWN RD
Gradyville
Tyler Arboretum
1
Lansdowne
Springfield
Yeadon
13

Glen Mills
Lima
Black Horse
352
MEDIA
Clifton Heights
Collingdale
Darby
Colwyn
Elmwood
PENROSE AV
29

Chester Heights
Glen Riddle
Rose Valley
Swarthmore College
476
Swarthmore
Morton
Folcroft
Sharon Hill
Glenolden
Eastwick

Chelsea
Village Green
Brookhaven
Upland
Prospect Park
13
Norwood
Ridley Park
JOHN HEINZ N.W.R.
95
Philadelphia International Airport

322
Eddystone
Delaware

144

A   B   C   D

145

Pittsburgh PENNSYLVANIA

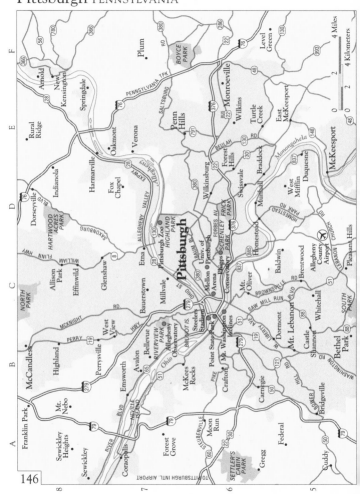

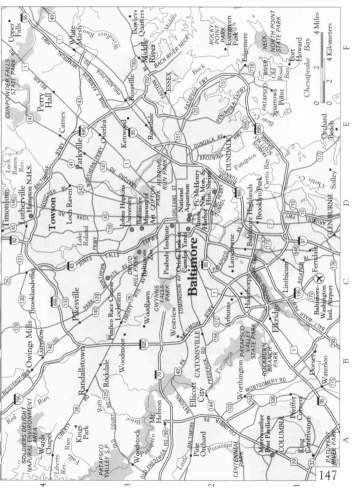

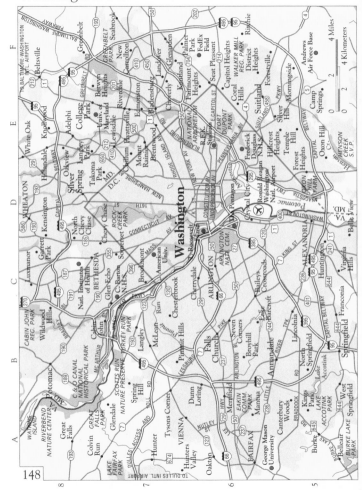

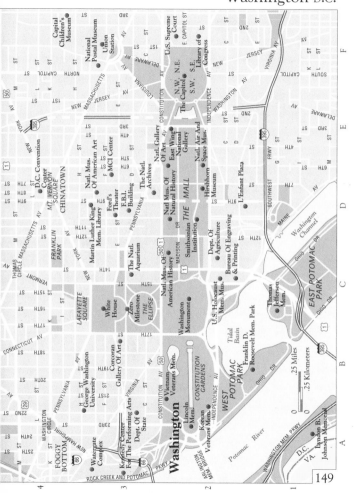

Washington

149

Cleveland OHIO

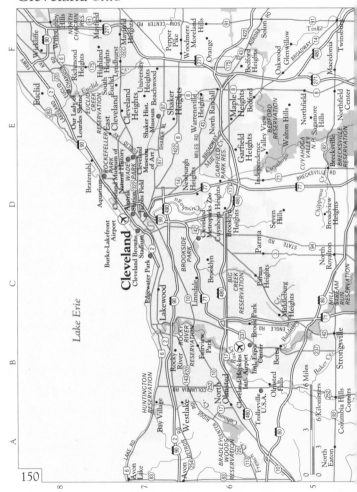

150

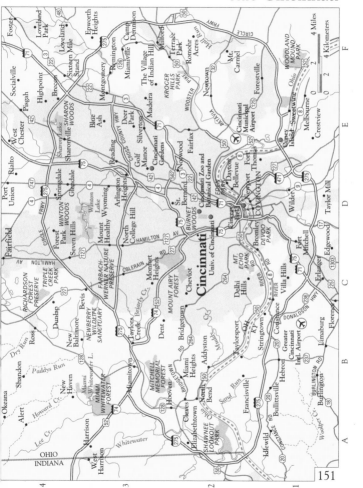

4 Miles

4 Kilometers

OHIO
INDIANA

Atlanta GEORGIA

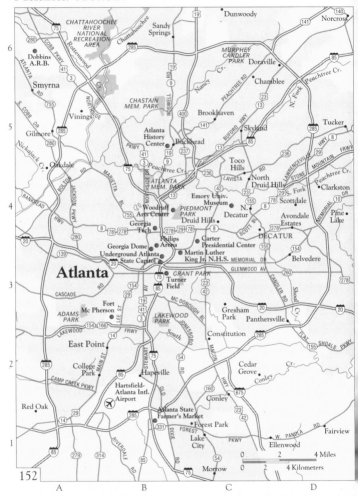

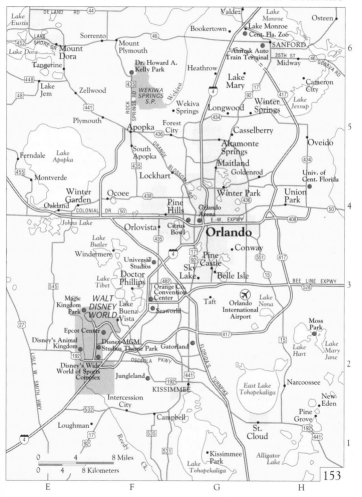

Tampa - St. Petersburg FLORIDA

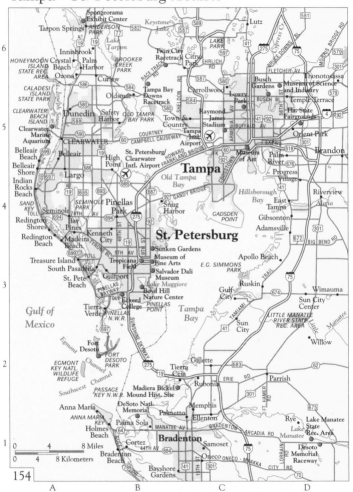

Spongeorama
Exhibit Center
ANDERSON
PARK
Tarpon Springs
Keystone
Lake
Lutz
581
6
Innisbrook
Lake
Tarpon
582
587
275
MORRIS BRIDGE RD
BRUCE B DOWNS BL
HONEYMOON Crystal Palm
ISLAND Beach Harbor
STATE REC. Ozona
AREA
BROOKER
CREEK
PARK
LAKE
PARK
41
597
ERHLICH
RD
FLETCHER AV
579
301
Thonotosassa
CALADESI
ISLAND
STATE PARK
Curlew
586
Tampa Bay
Downs
Racetrack
584
RACE TRACK RD
Twin City
Racetrack
Citrus
Park
587
Carrollwood
580
Lowry
Park
Busch
Gardens
BUSCH BL
Museum of Science
and Industry
Temple Terrace
56TH ST
4
92
CLEARWATER
BEACH
ISLAND
Oldsmar
584
Town &
Country
Raymond
James
Stadium
Fla. State
Fairgrounds
Dunedin
Safety
Harbor
OLD TAMPA
BAY PARK
ARMENIA
BUFFALO
41 92
Orient Park
5
588
590
COURTNEY
CAMPBELL CAUSEWAY
60
Tampa
Int'l.
Airport
JFK 60
Museum
of Art
618
301
Clearwater
Marine
Aquarium
CLEARWATER
High
Point
St. Petersburg/
Clearwater
Int'l. Airport
HOWARD
FRANKLAND
BRIDGE
688
Tampa
Palm
River
676
Brandon
Belleair
Beach 699
Belleair
Belleair
Shore
Largo
686
Old Tampa
Bay
Progress
Village
Indian
Rocks
Beach
ALT
19
695
693
694
687
92 GANDY BRIDGE
Snug
Harbor
Hillsborough
Bay
41
Riverview
East
Tampa
Apollo
4
SAND
KEY
TOLL
Seminole
SEMINOLE
PARK
74TH
AV
Pinellas
Park
GADSDEN
POINT
Adamsville
Redington
Shores
Bay
Pines
275
Gibsonton
301
Redington
Beach
Kenneth
City
19
St. Petersburg
Apollo Beach
672
BIG BEND RD
Madeira
Beach
54TH AV
E.G. SIMMONS
PARK
Treasure Island
(699)
TOLL
Tropicana
Field
Gulf
City
Ruskin
75
Wimauma
South Pasadena
Gulfport
Sunken Gardens
Museum of
Fine Arts
674
Sun City
Center
3
St. Pete
Beach
PINELLAS
BAYWAY
Salvador Dali
Museum
Lake Maggiore
TAMIAMI
TRAIL
Sun
City
301
675
Gulf of
Mexico
Tierra
Verde
TOLL
Eckerd
College
PINELLAS
N.W.R.
Boyd Hill
Nature Center
PINELLAS
POINT
Tampa
Bay
LITTLE MANATEE
RIVER STATE
REC. AREA
Willow
41
Fort
Desoto
FORT
DESOTO
PARK
SUNSHINE SKYWAY
683
ERIE
RD
62
2
EGMONT
KEY NATL.
WILDLIFE
REFUGE
Channel
275
Gillette
Parrish
FT HAMER RD
Tierra
Ceia
19
Rubonia
301
ARCADIA RD
675
PASSAGE
KEY N.W.R.
Southwest
Channel
Madiera Bickel
Mound Hist. Site
Memphis
Rye
Lake
Manatee
State
Rec. Area
DeSoto Nath.
Memorial
Palmetto
Ellenton
BRADENTON
Lake
Manatee
Anna Maria
ANNA
MARIA
KEY
Holmes
Beach
Palma Sola
MANATEE AV
Desoto
Memorial
Raceway
1
0   4   8 Miles
0 4 8 Kilometers
154
Bradenton
Beach
789
Cortez
44TH AV
64
684
Bradenton
Samoset
41 301
13TH
ST
ONECO
MYAKKA
CITY
Oneco
LORRAIN RD
70
Bayshore
Gardens

A   B   C   D

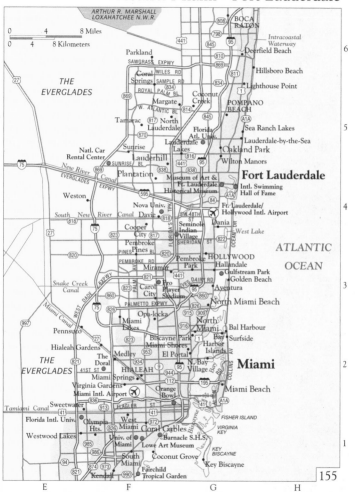

ARTHUR R. MARSHALL
LOXAHATCHEE N.W.R.

BOCA
RATON

0   4   8 Miles
0   4   8 Kilometers

Intracoastal
Waterway

Deerfield Beach

6

THE
EVERGLADES

Parkland

SAWGRASS EXPWY

WILES RD

Hillsboro Beach

SAMPLE RD

Coral
Springs

ROYAL PALM BL

Lighthouse Point

Coconut
Creek

Margate

POMPANO
BEACH

W. ATLANTIC BL

North
Lauderdale

Sea Ranch Lakes

5

Tamarac

Florida
Atl. Univ.

Lauderdale-by-the-Sea

Sunrise

Lauderdale
Lakes

Oakland Park

Natl. Car
Rental Center

Wilton Manors

Lauderhill

Plantation

SUNRISE BL

New River

Fort Lauderdale

EVERGLADES

Museum of Art &
Ft. Lauderdale
Historical Museum

Intl. Swimming
Hall of Fame

4

Weston

Nova Univ.

Davie

SW 48TH
ST

Ft. Lauderdale/
Hollywood Intl. Airport

South New River Canal

Cooper
City

Seminole
Indian
Village

Dania

West Lake

ATLANTIC

Pembroke
Pines

SHERIDAN
ST

OCEAN

Pembroke
Park

HOLLYWOOD

Miramar

Hallandale

Gulfstream Park

Carol
City

Pro
Player
Stadium

Golden Beach

Snake Creek
Canal

DAIRY RD

Aventura

North Miami Beach

3

Opa-locka

Miami Canal

Miami
Lakes

North
Miami

Bal Harbour

Pennsuco

Surfside

Hialeah Gardens

Biscayne Park
Miami Shores

Bay
Harbor
Islands

The
Doral

El Portal

Miami

Medley

2

THE
EVERGLADES

HIALEAH

N. Bay
Village

41ST ST

Miami Springs

Orange
Bowl

Miami Beach

Virginia
Gardens

Miami Intl. Airport

FLAGLER
ST

Tamiami Canal

Sweetwater

FISHER ISLAND

Florida Intl. Univ.

Olympia
Hts.

West
Miami

VIRGINIA
KEY

Coral Gables

Barnacle S.H.S.

KEY
BISCAYNE

Westwood Lakes

Univ. of
Miami

Lowe Art Museum

South
Miami

Coconut Grove

Key Biscayne

1

Kendall

Fairchild
Tropical Garden

155

E   F   G   H

Detroit MICHIGAN

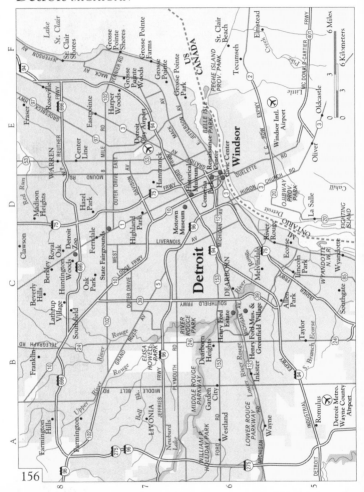

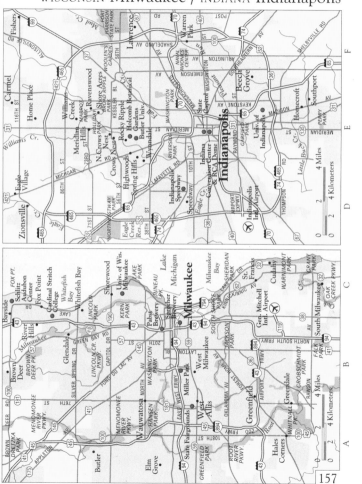

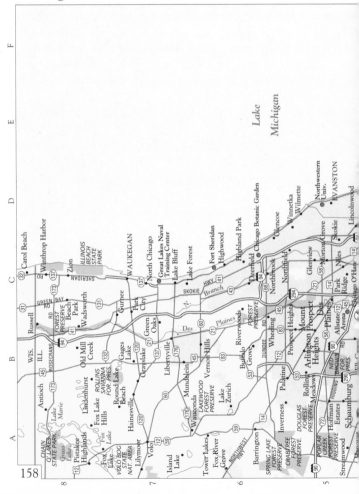

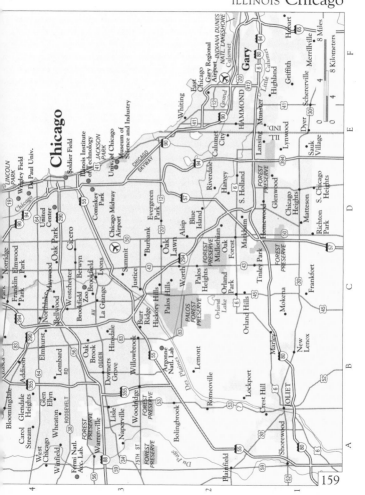

159

Chicago ILLINOIS

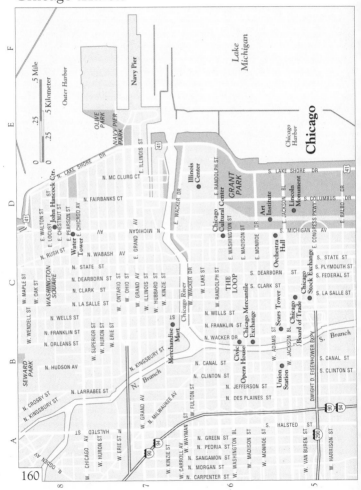

160

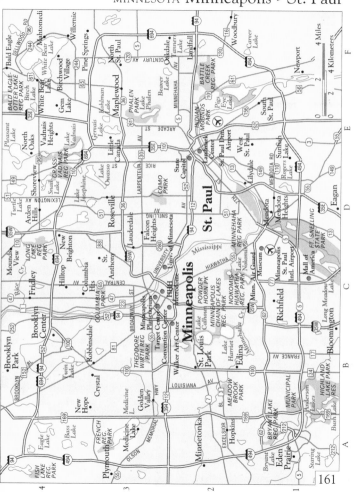

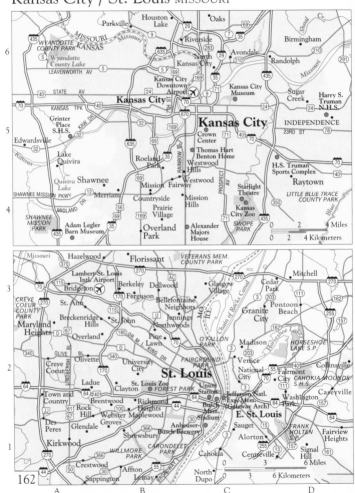

Kansas City

Parkville • Houston Lake • Oaks • Shoal Cr

435 WYANDOTTE COUNTY PARK • WYANDOTTE KANSAS • MISSOURI

Wyandotte County Lake • LEAVENWORTH AV

69 Riverside 283 Avondale • Birmingham 291

North Kansas City 29 210 • Randolph 210

635 5 169 35 • Kansas City 435

STATE AV • Kansas City Downtown Airport 24 9 • Kansas City Museum • Sugar Creek • Harry S. Truman N.H.S.

40 KANSAS TPK • KANSAS STATE AV 40 • **Kansas City** • 24

Grinter Place S.H.S. 32 • **Kansas City** 670 • INDEPENDENCE 23RD ST 78

Edwardsville • 32 • 635 • 169 • Crown Center 40 • 70

Lake Quivira • Roeland Park 35 • Thomas Hart Benton Home • H.S. Truman Sports Complex 70

Quivira Lake • Westwood Hills • Westwood • Raytown

Shawnee • 69 Mission Fairway • PROSPECT AV • Starlight Theatre • LITTLE BLUE TRACE COUNTY PARK

SHAWNEE MISSION PKWY • 12 Merriam • 56 Countryside • Mission Hills • Kansas City Zoo 350 Blue

SHAWNEE MISSION PARK • MIDLAND DR • 69 Prairie Village 169 • SWOPE PARK 435

Adam Legler Barn Museum 435 35 • **Overland Park** • Alexander Majors House

0 2 4 Miles
0 2 4 Kilometers

St. Louis

Missouri • Hazelwood • Florissant • VETERANS MEM. COUNTY PARK

370 • 270 AC • • Mitchell 270

Lambert-St. Louis Intl. Airport • Berkeley • Dellwood • Glasgow Village • Cedar Park 203

70 115 • Bridgeton • 170 • Ferguson • Bellefontaine Neighbors 111 • Pontoon Beach 162 255

CREVE COEUR COUNTY PARK 270 • St. Ann • 115 • Jennings Northwoods • Granite City 162 157

Maryland Heights • Breckenridge Hills • St. John • Pine Lawn • O'FALLON PARK • Madison 203 • HORSESHOE LAKE S.P.

340 • Overland • 180 DR M.L. KING DR • Venice • National City 55 • Fairmont City

OLIVE BL • Olivette • University City • FAIRGROUND PARK • 70 • CAHOKIA MOUNDS S.H.S. • Collinsville

Creve Coeur • 170 • **St. Louis** • Union Station 64 • 111 • Washington Park 157 • Caseyville

64 • Ladue • Clayton • St. Louis Zoo FOREST PARK • Jefferson Natl. Exp. Mem. (Gateway Arch) 64

Town and Country • 64 40 • Brentwood • Richmond Heights • Busch Mem. Stadium • E. St. Louis 157

JJ 61 • Rock Hill • 100 Webster Maplewood Groves • 366 • Anheuser-Busch Brewery • Sauget • FRANK HOLTEN S.P. 64 • Fairview Heights

Des Peres • Glendale • Shrewsbury • Alorton 15 • Signal Hill 161

Kirkwood • WILLMORE PARK • CARONDELET PARK • Cahokia • 255 157 13 • Centreville

270 • 366 • 55 BROADWAY • Mississippi • North Dupo

44 • 50 Crestwood • Affton • Lemay

Sappington

0 3 6 Miles
0 3 6 Kilometers

A B C D

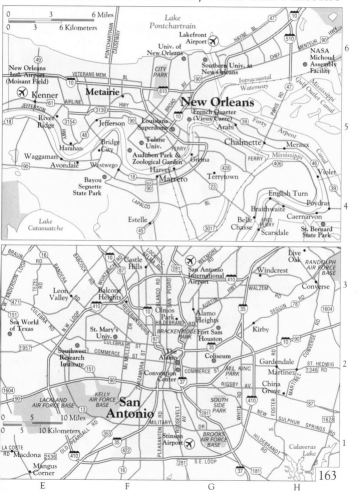

Dallas - Fort Worth TEXAS

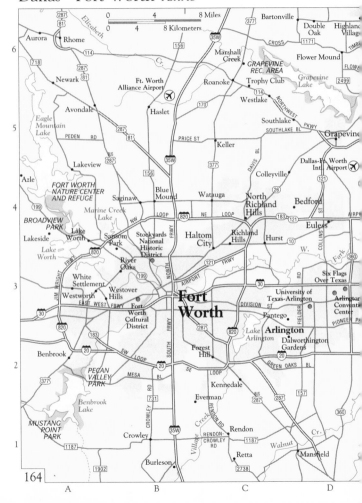

164

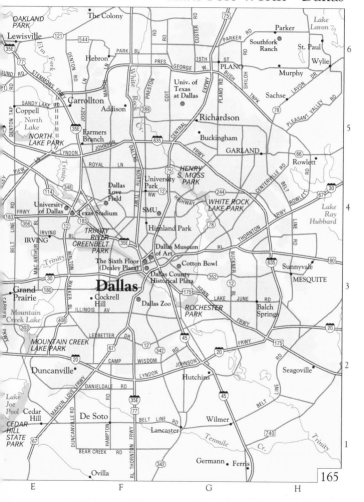

OAKLAND PARK

The Colony

Lewisville

Lake Lavon

Parker

Southfork Ranch

St. Paul

Wylie

Hebron

PLANO

Murphy

Sachse

Carrollton

Coppell

North Lake

Addison

Univ. of Texas at Dallas

Richardson

Sachse

Farmers Branch

Buckingham

GARLAND

NORTH LAKE PARK

Rowlett

Dallas Love Field

HENRY S. MOSS PARK

University Park

WHITE ROCK LAKE PARK

University of Dallas

Texas Stadium

SMU

Lake Ray Hubbard

IRVING

TRINITY RIVER GREENBELT PARK

Highland Park

Dallas Museum of Art

Cotton Bowl

Sunnyvale

MESQUITE

The Sixth Floor (Dealey Plaza)

Dallas County Historical Plaza

Dallas

Grand Prairie

Cockrell Hill

Dallas Zoo

ROCHESTER PARK

Balch Springs

Mountain Creek Lake

MOUNTAIN CREEK LAKE PARK

Duncanville

Hutchins

Seagoville

Lake Joe Pool

Cedar Hill

De Soto

Wilmer

CEDAR HILL STATE PARK

Lancaster

Tenmile Cr.

Trinity

Germann

Ferris

Ovilla

165

E   F   G   H

Houston TEXAS

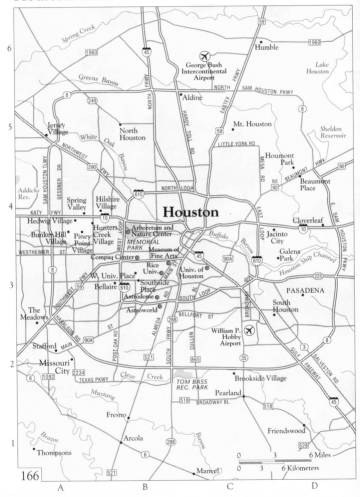

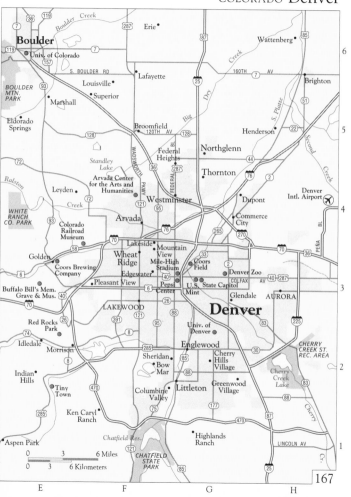

6

5

4

3

2

1

Boulder Creek
36 119
7
287 Erie
Wattenberg 85
119
Boulder
Univ. of Colorado 157
7 160TH AV
S. BOULDER RD Lafayette 25 7 Brighton 51
Louisville Dry
BOULDER
MTN.
PARK 93 Marshall Superior
Eldorado
Springs 72 128 Broomfield 120TH AV 128 Henderson 22 Second
Standley
Lake 36 Federal Heights Northglenn S. Platte Creek
WADSWORTH 287 Thornton 44
Leyden Arvada Center
for the Arts and
Humanities 121 **Westminster** 76 2 Denver
Intl. Airport ✈
WHITE
RANCH
CO. PARK 93 Creek 95 Dupont Commerce
City 270 70 36 PENA BL
Colorado
Railroad
Museum Lakeside Mountain
View 265
Golden 58 Wheat
Ridge Mile-High
Stadium 33 Coors
Field Denver Zoo
6 Coors Brewing
Company Edgewater Pepsi COLFAX
Buffalo Bill's Mem.
Grave & Mus. 40 Pleasant View 6 Center U.S. State Capitol 40 287
70 Mint Glendale **AURORA** 225
Red Rocks
Park 26 **LAKEWOOD** 391 121 **Denver** 83
74 8
Idledale 285 88 Univ. of
Denver 30 CHERRY
CREEK ST.
REC. AREA
Morrison 8 **Englewood**
Indian
Hills Sheridan Cherry
Hills
Village Cherry
Creek
Lake 83
Tiny
Town 470 Bow
Mar 85 Greenwood
Village 88 Cherry
Ken Caryl
Ranch Columbine
Valley **Littleton** 177 87
285 75 470
Aspen Park Highlands
Ranch LINCOLN AV
0   3   6 Miles 121 CHATFIELD
STATE
PARK 25
0   3   6 Kilometers 85

167

E   F   G   H

Phoenix ARIZONA

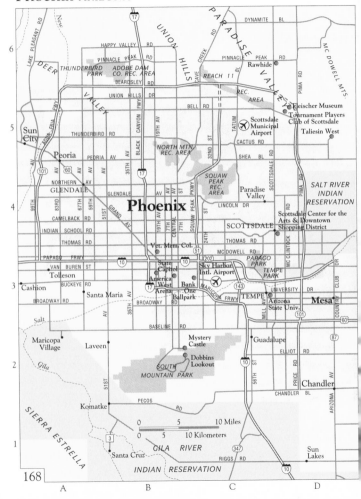

168

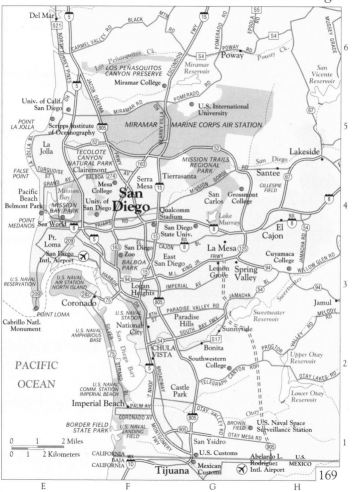

Del Mar

CARMEL VALLEY RD

BLACK MTN RD

Los Peñasquitos Ck.

POMERADO RD

EPSOLA

MUSSEY GRADE RD

NORTH TORREY PINES RD

JACOB DEKEMA

ESCONDIDO FWY

POMERADO RD

POWAY RD

Poway

Poway Ck.

San Vicente Reservoir

LOS PEÑASQUITOS CANYON PRESERVE

Miramar College

Miramar Reservoir

POINT LA JOLLA

Univ. of Calif. San Diego

Scripps Institute of Oceanography

MIRAMAR RD

KEARNY VILLA RD

POMERADO RD

U.S. International University

U.S. MARINE CORPS AIR STATION

MIRAMAR

La Jolla

TORREY PINES RD

FALSE POINT

TURQUOISE ST

TECOLOTE CANYON NATURAL PARK

Clairemont

San Diego R.

Lakeside

MISSION TRAILS REGIONAL PARK

MISSION GORGE RD

Santee

GILLESPIE FIELD

LA JOLLA BL

GRAND AV

Mesa College

Serra Mesa

Tierrasanta

Pacific Beach

Belmont Park

Mission Bay

MISSION BAY PARK

Univ. of San Diego

San Diego

San Carlos

Grossmont College

Lake Murray

El Cajon

POINT MEDANOS

Sea World

Qualcomm Stadium

La Mesa

PRIARS RD

San Diego State Univ.

EL CAJON BL

M.L. KING JR. FRWY

Cuyamaca College

Pt. Loma

San Diego Intl. Airport

San Diego Zoo

BALBOA PARK

East San Diego

WILLOW GLEN RD

U.S. NAVAL RESERVATION

HARBOR

Logan Heights

IMPERIAL AV

Lemon Grove

Spring Valley

JAMACHA RD

Cabrillo Natl. Monument

POINT LOMA

Coronado

U.S. NAVAL STATION

8TH ST

PARADISE VALLEY RD

Jamul

MELODY RD

San Diego Bay

U.S. NAVAL AMPHIBIOUS BASE

National City

Paradise Hills

SOUTH BAY FWY

Sunnyside

Sweetwater Reservoir

PROCTOR VALLEY RD

PACIFIC OCEAN

SILVER STRAND

San Diego Strand

CHULA VISTA

BROADWAY

Bonita

Southwestern College

Upper Otay Reservoir

OTAY LAKES RD

U.S. NAVAL COMM. STATION IMPERIAL BEACH

JOHN ST

Castle Park

TELEGRAPH CANYON RD

Lower Otay Reservoir

Imperial Beach

PALM AV

CORONADO AV

MONTGOMERY FWY

OTAY VALLEY RD

BROWN FIELD

U.S. Naval Space Surveillance Station

BORDER FIELD STATE PARK

U.S. NAVAL LANDING FIELD

San Ysidro

OTAY MESA RD

0   1   2 Miles

0   1   2 Kilometers

CALIFORNIA

BAJA CALIFORNIA

Tijuana

U.S. Customs

Mexican Customs

Abelardo L. Rodriguez Intl. Airport

U.S. MEXICO

E   F   G   H

6

5

4

3

2

1

Los Angeles CALIFORNIA

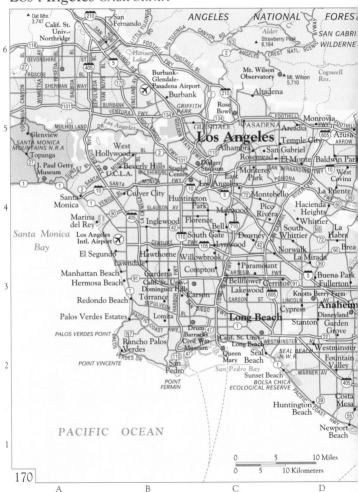

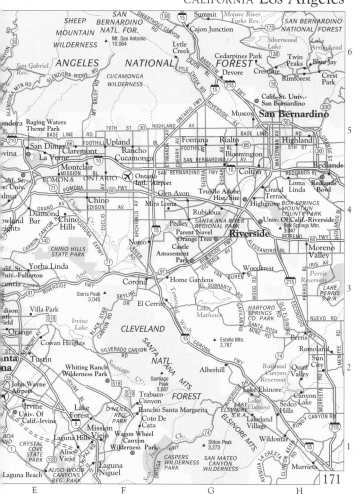

SHEEP MOUNTAIN WILDERNESS

SAN BERNARDINO NATL. FOR.

SWARTHOUT CANYON

Summit

(138) (15)

Cajon Junction

Mojave River Forks Res.

SAN BERNARDINO NATIONAL FOREST

(173)

Silverwood Lake

Lake Arrowhead

Mt. San Antonio 10,064

ANGELES NATIONAL FOREST

CUCAMONGA WILDERNESS

GLENDORA RIDGE RD

MT BALDY RD

Lytle Creek

Cedarpines Park

Devore

(138)

Twin Peaks

Blue Jay

Crestline

Rimforest

Crest Park

(18)

(330)

Calif. St. Univ.- San Bernardino

Muscoy

San Bernardino

(210)

Raging Waters Theme Park

San Dimas

(66)

Upland

19TH ST

(30)

HIGHLAND

AV

Fontana

Rialto

BASE LINE

FOOTHILL RD

La Verne

Claremont

Rancho Cucamonga

FOOTHILL

BL

SAN BERNARDINO

Bloomington

AV

Highland

(66)

5TH ST

(30)

ORANGE ST

Redlands

Montclair

MISSION BL

POMONA

ONTARIO

(60) FWY

Ontario Intl. Airport

SAN BERNARDINO FWY

(10)

Colton

REDLANDS BL

Calif. St. Univ.-Fullerton

Chino

EDISON AV

Glen Avon

Trujillo Adobe Hist. Site

Grand Terrace

Loma Linda

Redlands Bowl

Diamond Bar

Chino Hills

Mira Loma

Rubidoux

Highgrove

Univ. of Calif.-Riverside

BOX SPRINGS MOUNTAIN COUNTY PARK

CHINO HILLS STATE PARK

Pedley

Parent Navel

SANTA ANA RIVER REGIONAL PARK

Box Springs Mtn. 3,047

MORENO

(60)

Yorba Linda

Norco

Orange Tree

Riverside

Castle Amusement Park

Wooderest

Moreno Valley

Perris Reservoir

Corona

Home Gardens

EL SOBRANTE

VAN BUREN BL

LAKE PERRIS S.R.A.

Sierra Peak 3,045

El Cerrito

(91)

RIVERSIDE AV

VICTORIA AV

Alessandro

(215)

IRIS AV

CLEVELAND

Lake Mathews

HARFORD SPRINGS CO. PARK

Perris

Romoland

Sun City

Santiago Peak 5,687

Alberhill

Estelle Mtn. 2,767

Quail Valley

Canyon Lake

Whiting Ranch Wilderness Park

(S18)

Trabuco Canyon

Lake Elsinore

Sedco Hills

Irvine Lake

Rancho Santa Margarita

Coto De Caza

ELSINORE

Lake Elsinore

Lakeland Village

Mission Viejo

O'NEILL REG. PARK

Wagon Wheel Canyon Wilderness Park

(74)

Sitton Peak 3,273

Wildomar

CRYSTAL COVE STATE PARK

Aliso Viejo

Laguna Niguel

CASPERS WILDERNESS PARK

SAN MATEO CANYON WILDERNESS

Murrieta

ALISO-WOOD CANYONS REG. PARK

171

Los Angeles CALIFORNIA

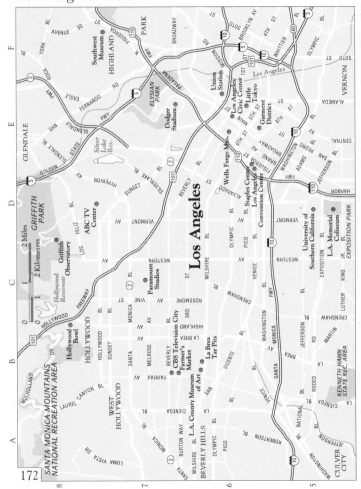

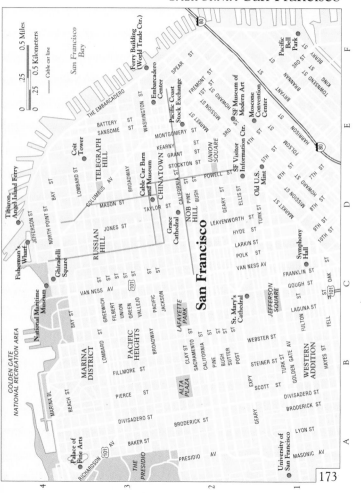

San Francisco Bay

0.5 Miles

0.5 Kilometers

Cable car line

San Francisco

Ferry Building (World Trade Ctr.)

THE EMBARCADERO

Embarcadero Center

Pacific Coast Stock Exchange

SPEAR ST

FREMONT ST

FIRST ST

HOWARD ST

SF Museum of Modern Art

Moscone Convention Center

BEALE ST

MAIN ST

SPEAR ST

BRYANT

Pacific Bell Park

KING

TOWNSEND ST

3RD ST

BERRY

80

Tiburon, Angel Island Ferry

Fisherman's Wharf

Ghirardelli Square

National Maritime Museum

Coit Tower

TELEGRAPH HILL

BATTERY ST

SANSOME ST

WASHINGTON ST

MONTGOMERY

KEARNY

GRANT

STOCKTON

POWELL

CHINATOWN

CALIFORNIA ST

UNION SQUARE

MARKET ST

SF Visitor Information Ctr.

MISSION ST

3RD

4TH ST

5TH ST

6TH ST

HOWARD ST

FOLSOM ST

HARRISON

80

Cable Car Barn and Museum

Grace Cathedral

NOB HILL

BUSH

GEARY

ELLIS ST

Old U.S. Mint

7TH ST

8TH ST

9TH ST

10TH ST

MARKET ST

COLUMBUS AV

LOMBARD ST

BROADWAY

MASON ST

TAYLOR

JONES ST

HYDE ST

LEAVENWORTH

LARKIN ST

POLK ST

VAN NESS AV

FRANKLIN ST

Symphony Hall

GOUGH ST

101

OAK

BAY ST

NORTH POINT ST

JEFFERSON ST

RUSSIAN HILL

VAN NESS AV

GREENWICH

FILBERT ST

UNION ST

GREEN

VALLEJO

PACIFIC

JACKSON

LAFAYETTE PARK

CLAY ST

SACRAMENTO

CALIFORNIA

PINE

BUSH

SUTTER

POST

St. Mary's Cathedral

JEFFERSON SQUARE

LAGUNA ST

FULTON

FELL

101

GOLDEN GATE NATIONAL RECREATION AREA

MARINA BL

BEACH ST

Palace of Fine Arts

MARINA DISTRICT

PACIFIC HEIGHTS

LOMBARD ST

FILLMORE ST

PIERCE ST

DIVISADERO ST

BROADERICK ST

ALTA PLAZA

WEBSTER ST

STEINER ST

EXPY

SCOTT

TURK ST

GOLDEN GATE AV

HAYES ST

GEARY

WESTERN ADDITION

DIVISADERO ST

BRODERICK ST

LYON ST

BAKER ST

THE PRESIDIO

RICHARDSON

101

AV

PRESIDIO AV

University of San Francisco

MASONIC AV

173

San Francisco Bay CALIFORNIA

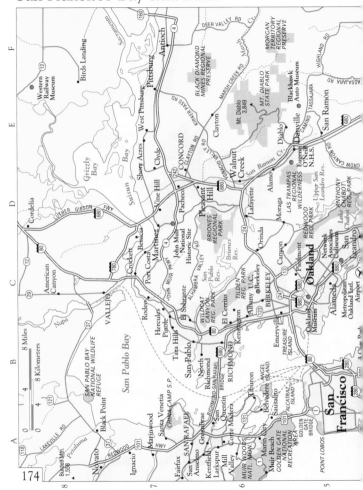

174

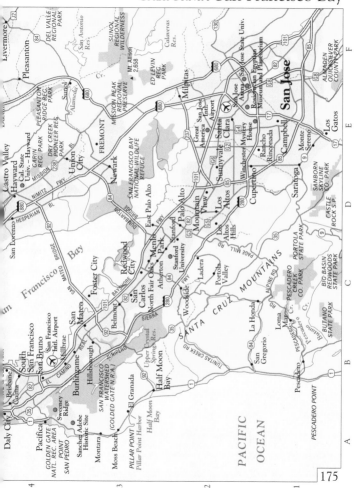

Seattle - Tacoma WASHINGTON

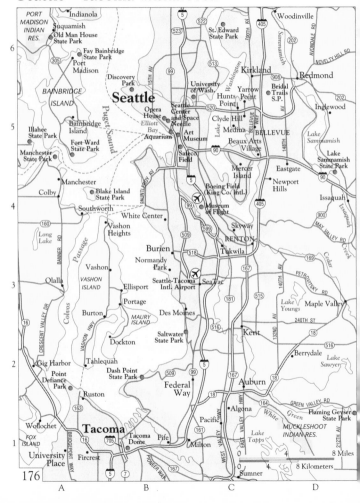

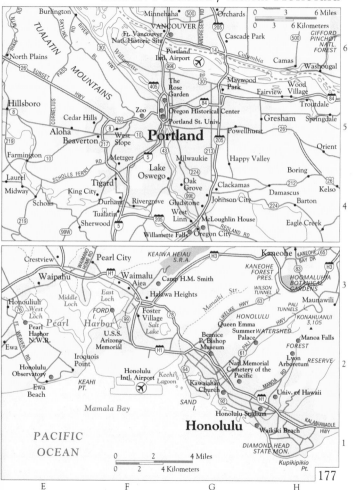

OREGON Portland

Burlington
Minnehaha
Orchards
500
6 Miles
6 Kilometers
VANCOUVER
Cascade Park
205
GIFFORD PINCHOT NATL. FOREST
TUALATIN
Ft. Vancouver Natl. Historic Site
SKYLINE RD
RIVER RD
ANDRESEN RD
Columbia
Camas
Washougal
500
North Plains
30
Portland Intl. Airport
14
99E
Maywood Park
BYP 30
Fairview
Wood Village
MOUNTAINS
SUNSET HWY
26
405
The Rose Garden
84
Troutdale
84
Hillsboro
8
Zoo
CORNELIUS
26
Oregon Historical Center
Portland St. Univ.
Gresham
26
Springdale
Cedar Hills
Portland
Powellhurst
Orient
Aloha
Beaverton
8
217
West Slope
205
Happy Valley
Farmington
10
Metzger
5
43
Milwaukie
213
Boring
Laurel
SCHOLLS FERRY RD
Tigard
King City
224
Lake Oswego
Oak Grove
Clackamas
212
Kelso
26
Midway
Scholls
Durham
Rivergrove
99E
Johnson City
Damascus
Barton
219
Tualatin
5
Gladstone
West Linn
224
Eagle Creek
Sherwood
205
McLoughlin House
REDLAND RD
99W
Willamette Falls
Oregon City

HAWAII Honolulu

Crestview
Pearl City
KEAIWA HEIAU S.R.A.
H3
Kaneohe
KANEOHE BAY DR
65
WAIMANO HOME RD
H1
Waimalu
KANEOHE FOREST PRES.
83
H3
Waipahu
Aiea
Camp H.M. Smith
WILSON TUNNEL
HOOMALUHIA BOTANICAL GARDENS
Honouliuli
76
Middle Loch
East Loch
Halawa Heights
Mamaki Str.
63
Maunawili
West Loch
FORD I.
Foster Village
99
78
IKELIKE HWY
PALI TUNNELS
KONAHUANUI 3,105
Pearl Harbor
Salt Lake
Queen Emma Summer Palace
PALI HWY
WATERSHED
Pearl Harbor N.W.R.
U.S.S. Arizona Memorial
Bernice P. Bishop Museum
61
Manoa Falls
Ewa
Iroquois Point
H1
Natl. Memorial Cemetery of the Pacific
Lyon Arboretum
FOREST RESERVE
Honolulu Observatory
KEAHI PT.
Honolulu Intl. Airport
Keehi Lagoon
64
Kawaiahao Church
MANOA RD
Ewa Beach
92
Univ. of Hawaii
KALANIANAOLE HWY
Mamala Bay
SAND I.
Honolulu Stadium
H1
Waikiki Beach

PACIFIC OCEAN

Honolulu

DIAMOND HEAD STATE MON.
0   2   4 Miles
0   2   4 Kilometers
Kupikipikio Pt.

177

E   F   G   H

National Parks and Interstates

Interstates and National Parks

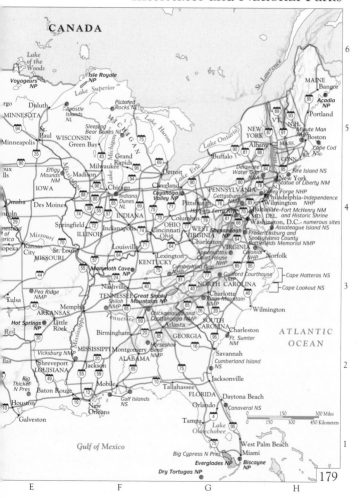

Yellowstone National Park WYOMING

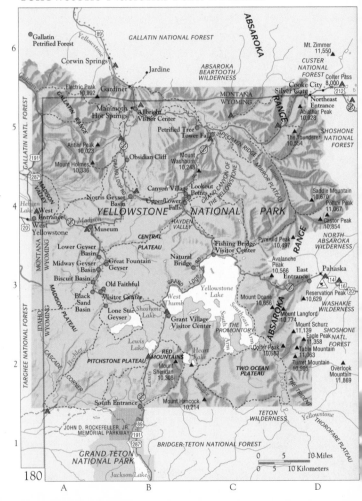

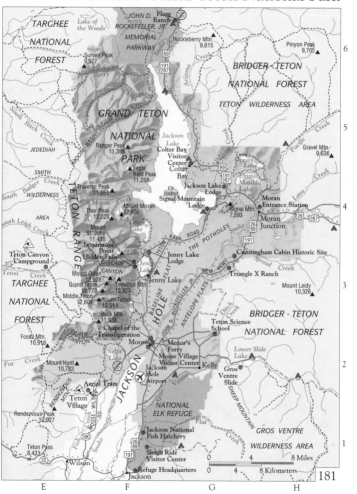

TARGHEE

NATIONAL

FOREST

Lake of
the Woods

JOHN D.
ROCKEFELLER, JR.

Flagg
Ranch

Huckleberry Mtn.
9,615

Pinyon Peak
9,705

6

MEMORIAL

PARKWAY

Survey Peak
9,277

BRIDGER - TETON

NATIONAL FOREST

TETON WILDERNESS AREA

GRAND TETON

South Bitch Creek

JEDEDIAH

NATIONAL

Jackson
Lake

Pacific Creek

5

SMITH

PARK

Ranger Peak
11,355

Colter Bay
Visitor
Center

Gravel Mtn.
9,636

Badger Creek

WILDERNESS

Eagle
Rest Peak
11,258

Colter
Bay

Jackson Lake
Lodge

Ocean Lake

Emma
Matilda
Lake

South Leigh Creek

AREA

Traverse Peak
11,051

Elk
Island

Signal Mtn.
7,593

Moran
Entrance Station

4

TETON

Thor Peak
12,028

Mount Moran
12,605

Signal Mountain
Lodge

Moran
Junction

Mount
St. John
11,430

Leigh
Lake

TETON PARK ROAD

THE POTHOLES

RANGE

Inspiration
Point

String
Lake

Jenny Lake
Lodge

Cunningham Cabin Historic Site

Teton Canyon
Campground

Hidden Falls

CASCADE
CANYON

Jenny
Lake

Triangle X Ranch

3

Mount Owen
12,928

Jenny Lake

BASELINE FLATS

Mount Leidy
10,326

Grand Teton
13,770

Teewinot Mtn.
12,325

ANTELOPE FLATS

Middle Teton
12,804

South Teton
12,514

JOHN D. ROCKEFELLER, JR. MEM. PKWY.

Spread Creek

BRIDGER - TETON

TARGHEE

Buck Mtn.
11,938

Teton Science
School

NATIONAL FOREST

NATIONAL

DEATH
CANYON

Chapel of the
Transfiguration

JACKSON

FOREST

Fossil Mtn.
10,916

Phelps
Lake

Moose

Menor's
Ferry

HOLE

Kelly

Lower Slide
Lake

2

Fox Creek

Mount Hunt
10,783

Moose Village
Visitor Center

Gros
Ventre
Slide

Aerial Tram

Jackson
Hole
Airport

NATIONAL

SHEEP MOUNTAIN

RENDEZVOUS MTNS.

Teton
Village

Gros Ventre

GROS VENTRE

Rendezvous Peak
10,927

ELK REFUGE

Flat Creek

WILDERNESS AREA

1

Teton Pass
8,431

MOOSE-WILSON RD.

Snake River

Fish Creek

390

Jackson National
Fish Hatchery

22

Ditch Creek

Wilson

191
26
89

Sleigh Ride
Visitor Center

0   4   8 Miles

Refuge Headquarters

0   4   8 Kilometers

181

Jackson

E   F   G   H

Yosemite National Park CALIFORNIA

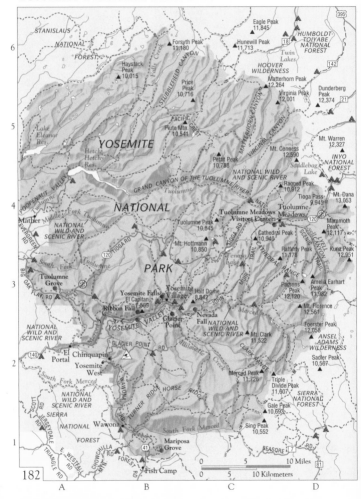

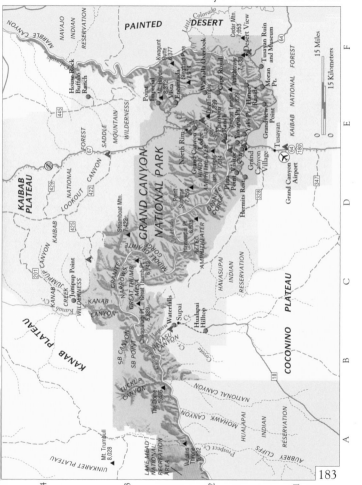

ARIZONA Grand Canyon National Park

183

Cape Cod MASSACHUSETTS

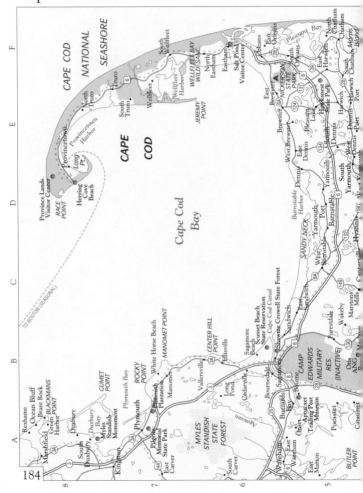

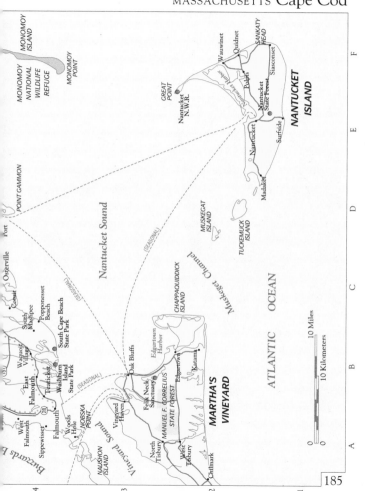

MONOMOY ISLAND

MONOMOY NATIONAL WILDLIFE REFUGE

MONOMOY POINT

Wauwinet

Quidnet

SANKATY HEAD

Polpis

Siasconset

Nantucket Harbor

GREAT POINT

Nantucket N.W.R.

NANTUCKET ISLAND

Nantucket State Forest

Nantucket

Surfside

Madaket

Nantucket Sound

POINT GAMMON

Osterville

Cotuit

Port

(SEASONAL)

MUSKEGET ISLAND

Muskeget Channel

TUCKEMUCK ISLAND

South Mashpee

Ponponesset Beach

South Cape Beach State Park

Waquoit Village

East Falmouth

Teaticket

Washburn Island State Park

(US) 28

Falmouth

West Falmouth

Sippewisset

Woods Hole

NOBSKA POINT

NAUSHON ISLAND

Buzzards B

Vineyard Sound

North Tisbury

West Tisbury

Chilmark

MANUEL F. CORRELIUS STATE FOREST

Vineyard Haven

Felix Neck Sanctuary

Oak Bluffs

Edgartown Harbor

CHAPPAQUIDDICK ISLAND

Edgartown

Katama

MARTHA'S VINEYARD

ATLANTIC OCEAN

10 Miles

10 Kilometers

0

Acadia National Park MAINE

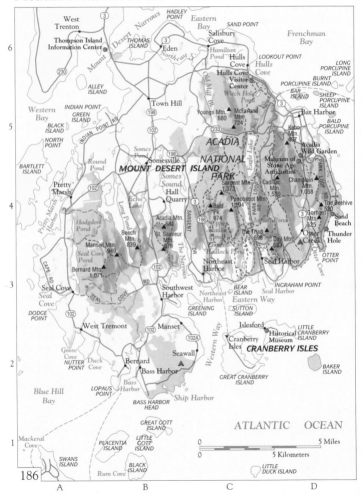

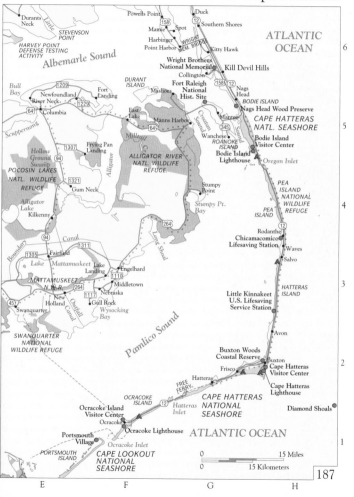

Durants
Neck
STEVENSON
POINT

Powells Point
Duck
Southern Shores
Mamie
Spot
158
12
Harbinger
Point Harbor
Kitty Hawk

HARVEY POINT
DEFENSE TESTING
ACTIVITY

ATLANTIC
OCEAN

Albemarle Sound

6

Wright Brothers
National Memorial
Kill Devil Hills
Collington
158
12

DURANT
ISLAND

Fort Raleigh
National
Hist. Site
Nags
Head

Bull
Bay
1209
Fort
Landing
Mashoes
BODIE ISLAND
Nags Head Wood Preserve

Newfoundland
River Neck
64
1229
Columbia

East
Lake
Manns Harbor
64
Manteo
345
CAPE HATTERAS
NATL. SEASHORE

5

Scuppernong

1307
Frying Pan
Landing
Milltail

Wanchese
ROANOKE
ISLAND
Bodie Island
Visitor Center

Hollow
Ground
Swamp
POCOSIN LAKES
NATL. WILDLIFE
REFUGE

Bodie Island
Lighthouse
Oregon Inlet

1321
Gum Neck

ALLIGATOR
RIVER
NATL. WILDLIFE
REFUGE

PEA
ISLAND
NATIONAL
WILDLIFE
REFUGE

Alligator
Lake
Kilkenny
94

Stumpy
Point

4

Stumpy Pt.
Bay
PEA
ISLAND

Canal
264
12
Rodanthe

94
Fairfield
1305
1311

Chicamacomico
Lifesaving Station
Waves

Boundary
Lake
Mattamuskeet
Lake
Landing
Engelhard
Salvo

1110
MATTAMUSKEET
N.W.R.
264
Middletown
HATTERAS
ISLAND

New
Holland
1117
Nebraska
Gull Rock

45
Swanquarter
Wysocking
Bay

Little Kinnakeet
U.S. Lifesaving
Service Station

3

SWANQUARTER
NATIONAL
WILDLIFE
REFUGE

Pamlico Sound

Avon

Buxton Woods
Coastal Reserve
Buxton

Frisco
Cape Hatteras
Visitor Center

2

FREE
FERRY
Hatteras
Cape Hatteras
Lighthouse

OCRACOKE
ISLAND
CAPE HATTERAS
NATIONAL
SEASHORE

Ocracoke Island
Visitor Center
12
Hatteras
Inlet
Diamond Shoals

Ocracoke
Ocracoke Lighthouse
ATLANTIC OCEAN

Portsmouth
Village
Ocracoke Inlet

1

PORTSMOUTH
ISLAND
CAPE LOOKOUT
NATIONAL
SEASHORE

0
15 Miles
0
15 Kilometers

E
F
G
H

Florida Keys FLORIDA

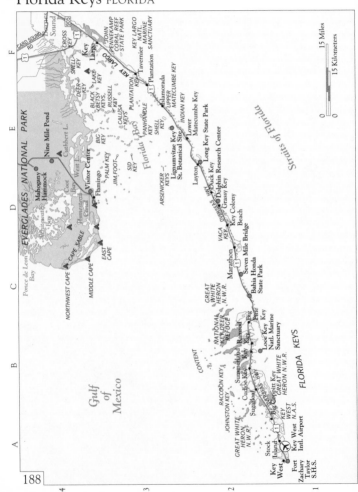

188

Traveler's Notes

Perpetual Calendar

1

SUN	MON	TUE	WED	THU	FRI	SAT
1	2	3	4	5	6	7
8	9	10	11	12	13	14
15	16	17	18	19	20	21
22	23	24	25	26	27	28
29	30	31				

1A

SUN	MON	TUE	WED	THU	FRI	SAT
1	2	3	4	5	6	7
8	9	10	11	12	13	14
15	16	17	18	19	20	21
22	23	24	25	26	27	28
29	30					

2

SUN	MON	TUE	WED	THU	FRI	SAT
	1	2	3	4	5	6
7	8	9	10	11	12	13
14	15	16	17	18	19	20
21	22	23	24	25	26	27
28	29	30	31			

2A

SUN	MON	TUE	WED	THU	FRI	SAT
	1	2	3	4	5	6
7	8	9	10	11	12	13
14	15	16	17	18	19	20
21	22	23	24	25	26	27
28	29	30				

3

SUN	MON	TUE	WED	THU	FRI	SAT
		1	2	3	4	5
6	7	8	9	10	11	12
13	14	15	16	17	18	19
20	21	22	23	24	25	26
27	28	29	30	31		

3A

SUN	MON	TUE	WED	THU	FRI	SAT
		1	2	3	4	5
6	7	8	9	10	11	12
13	14	15	16	17	18	19
20	21	22	23	24	25	26
27	28	29	30			

4

SUN	MON	TUE	WED	THU	FRI	SAT
			1	2	3	4
5	6	7	8	9	10	11
12	13	14	15	16	17	18
19	20	21	22	23	24	25
26	27	28	29	30	31	

4A

SUN	MON	TUE	WED	THU	FRI	SAT
			1	2	3	4
5	6	7	8	9	10	11
12	13	14	15	16	17	18
19	20	21	22	23	24	25
26	27	28	29	30		

5

SUN	MON	TUE	WED	THU	FRI	SAT
				1	2	3
4	5	6	7	8	9	10
11	12	13	14	15	16	17
18	19	20	21	22	23	24
25	26	27	28	29	30	31

5A

SUN	MON	TUE	WED	THU	FRI	SAT
				1	2	3
4	5	6	7	8	9	10
11	12	13	14	15	16	17
18	19	20	21	22	23	24
25	26	27	28	29	30	

6

SUN	MON	TUE	WED	THU	FRI	SAT
					1	2
3	4	5	6	7	8	9
10	11	12	13	14	15	16
17	18	19	20	21	22	23
24/31	25	26	27	28	29	30

6A

SUN	MON	TUE	WED	THU	FRI	SAT
					1	2
3	4	5	6	7	8	9
10	11	12	13	14	15	16
17	18	19	20	21	22	23
24	25	26	27	28	29	30

7

SUN	MON	TUE	WED	THU	FRI	SAT
						1
2	3	4	5	6	7	8
9	10	11	12	13	14	15
16	17	18	19	20	21	22
23/30	24/31	25	26	27	28	29

7A

SUN	MON	TUE	WED	THU	FRI	SAT
						1
2	3	4	5	6	7	8
9	10	11	12	13	14	15
16	17	18	19	20	21	22
23/30	24	25	26	27	28	29

8

SUN	MON	TUE	WED	THU	FRI	SAT
						1
2	3	4	5	6	7	8
9	10	11	12	13	14	15
16	17	18	19	20	21	22
23	24	25	26	27	28	29

Every possible monthly calendar is represented above. In the tables on the following pages you will find the years 1976 through 2025; leap years, having 29 days in February, are in the bold type. On the lines with each year, under the month, is the reference number for the applicable calendar month above. For example, to find the day of the week for April 24, 1989, locate 1989 in the year column; looking across that line, under the **Apr.** column, you will find the reference number 7A; in that numbered calendar month above you will note that April 24, 1989 was a Monday.

Year	Jan.	Feb.	Mar.	Apr.	May	June	July	Aug.	Sept.	Oct.	Nov.	Dec.
1976	5	1_A	2	5_A	7	3_A	5	1	4_A	6	2_A	4
1977	7	3_A	3	6_A	1	4_A	6	2	5_A	7	3_A	5
1978	1	4_A	4	7_A	2	5_A	7	3	6_A	1	4_A	6
1979	2	5_A	5	1_A	3	6_A	1	4	7_A	2	5_A	7
1980	3	6_A	7	3_A	5	1_A	3	6	2_A	4	7_A	2
1981	5	1_A	1	4_A	6	2_A	4	7	3_A	5	1_A	3
1982	6	2_A	2	5_A	7	3_A	5	1	4_A	6	2_A	4
1983	7	3_A	3	6_A	1	4_A	6	2	5_A	7	3_A	5
1984	1	4_A	5	1_A	3	6_A	1	4	7_A	2	5_A	7
1985	3	6_A	6	2_A	4	7_A	2	5	1_A	3	6_A	1
1986	4	8	7	3_A	5	1_A	3	6	2_A	4	7_A	2
1987	5	1_A	1	4_A	6	2_A	4	7	3_A	5	1_A	3
1988	6	2_A	3	6_A	1	4_A	6	2	5_A	7	3_A	5
1989	1	4_A	4	7_A	2	5_A	7	3	6_A	1	4_A	6
1990	2	5_A	5	1_A	3	6_A	1	4	7_A	2	5_A	7
1991	3	6_A	6	2_A	4	7_A	2	5	1_A	3	6_A	1
1992	4	8	1	4_A	6	2_A	4	7	3_A	5	1_A	3
1993	6	2_A	2	5_A	7	3_A	5	1	4_A	6	2_A	4
1994	7	3_A	3	6_A	1	4_A	6	2	5_A	7	3_A	5
1995	1	4_A	4	7_A	2	5_A	7	3	6_A	1	4_A	6
1996	2	5_A	6	2_A	4	7_A	2	5	1_A	3	6_A	1
1997	4	8	7	3_A	5	1_A	3	6	2_A	4	7_A	2
1998	5	1_A	1	4_A	6	2_A	4	7	3_A	5	1_A	3
1999	6	2_A	2	5_A	7	3_A	5	1	4_A	6	2_A	4
2000	7	3_A	4	7_A	2	5_A	7	3	6_A	1	4_A	6

Year	Jan.	Feb.	Mar.	Apr.	May	June	July	Aug.	Sept.	Oct.	Nov.	Dec.
2001	2	5_A	5	1_A	3	6_A	1	4	7_A	2	5_A	7
2002	3	6_A	6	2_A	4	7_A	2	5	1_A	3	6_A	1
2003	4	8	7	3_A	5	1_A	3	6	2_A	4	7_A	2
2004	5	1_A	2	5_A	7	3_A	5	1	4_A	6	2_A	4
2005	7	3_A	3	6_A	1	4_A	6	2	5_A	7	3_A	5
2006	1	4_A	4	7_A	2	5_A	7	3	6_A	1	4_A	6
2007	2	5_A	5	1_A	3	6_A	1	4	7_A	2	5_A	7
2008	3	6_A	7	3_A	5	1_A	3	6	2_A	4	7_A	2
2009	5	1_A	1	4_A	6	2_A	4	7	3_A	5	1_A	3
2010	6	2_A	2	5_A	7	3_A	5	1	4_A	6	2_A	4
2011	7	3_A	3	6_A	1	4_A	6	2	5_A	7	3_A	5
2012	1	4_A	5	1_A	3	6_A	1	4	7_A	2	5_A	7
2013	3	6_A	6	2_A	4	7_A	2	5	1_A	3	6_A	1
2014	4	8	7	3_A	5	1_A	3	6	2_A	4	7_A	2
2015	5	1_A	1	4_A	6	2_A	4	7	3_A	5	1_A	3
2016	6	2_A	3	6_A	1	4_A	6	2	5_A	7	3_A	5
2017	1	4_A	4	7_A	2	5_A	7	3	6_A	1	4_A	6
2018	2	5_A	5	1_A	3	6_A	1	4	7_A	2	5_A	7
2019	3	6_A	6	2_A	4	7_A	2	5	1_A	3	6_A	1
2020	4	8	1	4_A	6	2_A	4	7	3_A	5	1_A	3
2021	6	2_A	2	5_A	7	3_A	5	1	4_A	6	2_A	4
2022	7	3_A	3	6_A	1	4_A	6	2	5_A	7	3_A	5
2023	1	4_A	4	7_A	2	5_A	7	3	6_A	1	4_A	6
2024	2	5_A	6	2_A	4	7_A	2	5	1_A	3	6_A	1
2025	4	8	7	3_A	5	1_A	3	6	2_A	4	7_A	2

International Travel

Passports usually take two weeks or longer to be issued. They are often required for identification and should be carried at all times when traveling abroad. Canada, Mexico, and some Caribbean Islands do not require passports.

Places of Issuance: Passport agencies located in major cities; office of a clerk of any Federal court or State court of record, or a judge or clerk of any probate court accepting applications; selected post offices.

Requirements: Applicants of all ages must apply in person and submit: **1)** Proof of citizenship: old passport or birth certificate; if not available, a notice from the registrar stating that no birth record exists, accompanied by a baptismal or synagogue certificate, hospital birth record, affidavits of persons having knowledge of the facts of birth, or other documentary evidence; citizens not born in the United States must submit certificate of naturalization or citizenship. **2)** Two recent identical photographs, measuring 2" x 2" with image from bottom of chin to top of head not less than 1" nor more than 1⅜", and signed on the back in the center. **3)** Fees totaling $97 for adults 16 years and older, $82 for children. **4)** Proof of identity that contains your signature and readily identifies you by physical description or photograph.

Validity: Adult passports are valid 10 years, children's five years, from the date of issue.

Lost Passport: If in the United States, notify the Passport Office of the Department of State, Washington, D.C. 20520. If you are out of the country, notify the nearest United States Consul and the local police authorities.

Visas: You should obtain necessary visas before you leave the United States. Apply directly to the embassies or consulates of the countries you wish to visit or consult with a travel agent. The process may take several weeks for each visa.

Customs: All articles acquired abroad and in your possession at the time of your return must be declared. There is a $800 duty exemption on articles for personal or household use (gifts are considered for personal use) for residents who have stayed abroad 48 hours or more (no minimum from Mexico or the U.S. Virgin Islands); this exemption is allowed once in 30 days. The next $1,000 worth of merchandise is charged at a flat 10% rate; above $1,400, at the various rates of duty applicable to the articles. When returning from the U.S. Virgin Islands, American Samoa, or Guam, the exemption is $800 and the flat rate of duty is 5% for the next $1,000 worth of merchandise. A written declaration must be presented when the total value exceeds your personal exemption. It is a good idea to save sales slips of all merchandise bought abroad; they will help speed up the process of going through Customs when re-entering the United States.

Antiques are free of duty if proof that they are over 100 years old is provided. **Gifts** shipped to the United States are duty-free if the retail value of not more than $50 is received by one person in one day. **Personal items** acquired abroad and shipped home are not exempt from duty. **Money,** in excess of $5,000, sent out, brought in, or received by mail or any other means requires the filing of Customs form 4790, available from a Customs officer. This amount includes U.S. or foreign currency, traveler's checks, money orders, and negotiable instruments or investment securities in bearer form.

Health: No vaccinations are required to return to the United States from any country. Some countries, however, may require certain immunizations and International Certificates of Vaccination documenting the dates of your inoculations. The booklet "Health Information for International Travel," available from the Superintendent of Documents, U.S. Government Printing Office, Washington, D.C. 20402, provides pertinent information.

An international driving license is required in some countries which do not recognize a U.S. driver's license. Check with the embassy or consulate of the countries in which you plan to drive. It can be obtained at an established automobile club. You will need two passport-size photographs and your valid U.S. license.

Insurance policies should be checked before leaving home to be sure they provide coverage while abroad.

Electrical converters may be necessary for the appliances you bring with you. U.S. appliances operate on 110 volts while 90% of the world operates on 220 volts.

International Weather*

Country / City	Jan.			Feb.			Mar.			Apr.			May			June		
Argentina, Buenos Aires	85°	63°	7	83°	63°	6	79°	60°	7	72°	53°	8	64°	47°	7	57°	41°	7
Australia, Sydney	78	65	14	78	65	13	76	63	14	71	58	14	66	52	13	61	48	12
Austria, Vienna	34	25	15	38	28	14	47	30	13	58	42	13	67	50	13	73	56	14
Bahamas, Nassau	77	65	6	77	64	5	79	66	5	81	69	6	84	71	9	87	74	12
Belgium, Brussels	40	30	21	44	32	17	51	36	17	58	41	18	65	46	16	72	52	15
Brazil, Rio de Janeiro	84	73	13	85	73	11	83	72	12	80	69	10	77	66	10	76	64	7
Canada, Toronto	30	16	16	30	15	12	37	23	13	50	34	12	63	44	13	73	54	11
Canada, Vancouver	41	32	20	44	34	17	50	37	17	58	40	14	64	46	12	69	52	11
China, Beijing	34	14	3	39	18	3	52	30	3	70	45	4	81	55	6	88	64	8
China, Hong Kong	64	56	4	63	55	5	67	60	7	75	67	8	82	74	13	85	78	18
Denmark, Copenhagen	36	28	17	36	28	13	41	31	12	51	38	13	61	46	11	67	52	13
Egypt, Cairo	65	47	1	69	48	1	75	52	8	83	57	4	91	63	2	95	68	0
England, London	43	36	15	44	36	13	50	38	11	56	42	12	62	47	12	69	53	11
France, Paris	43	34	17	45	34	14	54	39	12	60	43	13	68	49	12	73	55	12
Germany, Berlin	35	26	17	37	26	15	46	31	12	56	39	13	66	47	12	72	53	13
Greece, Athens	55	44	16	57	44	11	60	46	11	68	52	9	77	61	8	86	68	4
India, New Delhi	70	44	2	75	49	2	87	58	1	97	68	1	105	79	2	102	83	4
Ireland, Dublin	46	34	13	47	35	10	51	37	10	55	39	11	60	43	10	65	48	11
Israel, Jerusalem	55	41	9	56	42	11	65	46	3	73	50	3	81	57	6	85	60	.1
Italy, Rome	52	40	8	55	42	9	59	45	8	66	50	6	74	56	5	82	63	4
Japan, Tokyo	47	29	5	48	31	6	54	36	10	63	46	10	71	54	10	76	63	12
Kenya, Nairobi	77	54	5	79	55	6	77	57	11	75	58	16	72	56	17	70	53	9
Korea, Seoul	32	15	8	37	20	6	47	29	7	62	41	8	72	51	10	80	61	10
Mexico, Acapulco	88	72	1	88	72	0	88	72	0	90	73	0	90	77	3	91	77	13
Mexico, Mexico City	66	42	4	69	43	5	75	47	9	77	51	14	78	54	17	76	55	21
Monaco, Monte Carlo	54	47	5	55	47	5	57	50	7	61	54	5	66	59	5	73	66	4
Morocco, Marrakech	65	40	7	68	43	5	74	48	6	79	52	6	84	57	2	92	62	1
Netherlands, Amsterdam	40	31	22	42	31	19	49	34	16	56	40	16	64	46	14	70	51	14
Norway, Oslo	28	19	15	30	19	12	39	25	9	50	34	11	61	43	10	68	50	13
Philippines, Manila	86	69	6	88	69	3	91	71	4	93	73	4	93	75	12	91	75	17
Portugal, Lisbon	57	46	15	59	47	12	63	50	14	67	53	10	71	55	10	77	60	5
Russia, Moscow	15	3	18	22	8	15	32	18	15	50	34	13	66	46	13	70	51	12
Saudi Arabia, Riyadh	70	46	1	73	48	1	82	56	3	89	64	4	100	72	1	107	77	0
Singapore	86	73	17	88	73	11	88	75	14	88	75	15	89	75	15	88	75	13
Spain, Madrid	47	35	8	52	36	7	59	41	10	65	45	9	70	50	10	80	58	5
Sweden, Stockholm	30	23	16	30	22	14	37	26	10	47	34	11	58	43	11	67	51	13
Switzerland, Geneva	38	29	11	42	30	9	51	36	9	59	42	9	66	49	11	73	55	11
Taiwan, Taipei	66	54	9	65	53	13	70	57	12	77	63	14	83	69	12	89	73	13
Turkey, Istanbul	46	37	18	47	36	14	51	38	14	60	45	9	69	53	8	77	60	6
Venezuela, Caracas	75	56	6	77	56	2	79	58	3	81	60	4	80	62	9	78	62	14

*Average maximum and minimum temperatures and days with 0.04 inches of precipitation.

International Weather*

July			Aug.			Sept.			Oct.			Nov.			Dec.			Country / City
57°	42°	8	60°	43°	9	64°	46°	8	69°	50°	9	76°	56°	9	82°	61°	8	Argentina, Buenos Aires
60	46	12	63	48	11	67	51	12	71	56	12	74	60	12	77	63	13	Australia, Sydney
76	60	13	75	59	13	68	53	10	56	44	13	45	37	14	37	30	15	Austria, Vienna
88	75	14	89	76	14	88	75	15	85	73	13	81	70	9	79	67	6	Bahamas, Nassau
73	54	17	72	54	18	69	51	13	60	45	17	48	38	20	42	32	19	Belgium, Brussels
75	63	7	76	64	7	75	65	11	77	66	13	79	68	13	82	71	14	Brazil, Rio de Janeiro
79	59	10	77	58	9	69	51	12	56	40	11	43	31	13	33	21	13	Canada, Toronto
74	54	7	73	54	8	65	49	9	57	44	16	48	39	19	43	35	22	Canada, Vancouver
88	70	13	86	68	11	79	57	7	68	43	3	48	28	3	37	18	2	China, Beijing
87	78	17	87	78	15	85	77	12	81	73	6	74	65	2	68	59	3	China, Hong Kong
71	57	14	70	56	14	64	51	15	54	44	16	45	38	16	40	34	17	Denmark, Copenhagen
96	70	0	95	71	0	90	68	0	86	65	.3	78	58	.8	68	50	.1	Egypt, Cairo
71	56	12	71	56	11	65	52	13	58	46	13	50	42	15	45	38	15	England, London
76	58	12	75	58	13	70	53	13	60	46	13	50	40	15	44	36	16	France, Paris
75	57	14	74	56	14	68	50	12	56	42	14	45	36	16	38	29	15	Germany, Berlin
92	73	2	92	73	3	84	67	4	75	60	8	66	53	12	58	47	15	Greece, Athens
96	81	8	93	79	8	93	75	4	93	65	1	84	52	.2	73	46	1	India, New Delhi
67	52	13	67	51	12	63	48	12	57	43	11	51	39	12	47	37	14	Ireland, Dublin
87	63	0	87	64	0	85	62	.1	81	59	1	70	53	4	59	45	7	Israel, Jerusalem
87	67	1	86	67	2	79	62	5	71	55	8	61	49	11	55	44	10	Italy, Rome
83	70	10	86	72	9	79	66	12	69	55	11	60	43	7	52	33	5	Japan, Tokyo
69	51	6	70	52	7	75	52	6	76	55	8	74	56	15	74	55	11	Kenya, Nairobi
84	70	16	87	71	13	78	59	9	67	45	7	51	32	9	37	20	9	Korea, Seoul
90	77	14	91	77	13	90	75	16	90	75	9	90	73	2	88	72	1	Mexico, Acapulco
73	53	27	73	54	27	74	53	23	70	50	13	68	46	6	66	43	4	Mexico, Mexico City
78	71	1	78	71	2	74	67	4	68	61	7	61	54	7	56	49	6	Monaco, Monte Carlo
101	67	1	100	68	1	92	63	3	83	57	4	73	49	3	66	42	7	Morocco, Marrakesh
72	55	17	71	55	18	67	50	19	57	44	20	48	38	21	42	33	21	Netherlands, Amsterdam
72	55	15	70	53	14	60	46	14	48	38	14	38	31	16	32	25	17	Norway, Oslo
88	75	24	87	75	23	88	75	22	88	74	19	87	72	14	86	70	11	Philippines, Manila
81	63	2	82	63	2	79	62	6	72	58	9	63	52	13	58	47	15	Portugal, Lisbon
73	55	15	72	53	14	61	45	13	48	37	15	35	26	15	24	15	23	Russia, Moscow
107	78	0	107	75	0	102	72	0	94	61	0	84	55	0	70	49	0	Saudi Arabia, Riyadh
88	75	13	87	75	14	87	75	14	87	74	16	87	74	18	87	74	19	Singapore
87	63	2	85	63	3	77	57	6	65	49	8	55	42	9	48	36	10	Spain, Madrid
71	57	13	68	56	14	60	49	14	49	41	15	40	34	16	35	29	17	Sweden, Stockholm
77	58	9	76	58	11	69	53	10	58	44	10	47	37	11	40	31	10	Switzerland, Geneva
92	76	10	91	75	12	88	73	10	81	67	9	75	62	7	69	57	8	Taiwan, Taipei
82	65	4	82	66	4	76	61	7	68	55	11	59	48	14	51	41	18	Turkey, Istanbul
78	61	15	79	61	15	80	61	13	79	61	12	77	60	13	78	58	10	Venezuela, Caracas

*To convert degrees Fahrenheit to degrees Celsius, subtract 32, multiply by 5, and divide by 9.

United States Weather

City	Average Monthly Temperatures (Fahrenheit Degrees) and *Average Number of Rain Days*										
	Jan.		Feb.		Mar.		Apr.		May		June
Albuquerque, NM	34°	4	40°	4	47°	5	55°	3	64°	5	74°	4
Atlanta, GA	41	11	45	10	54	11	62	9	69	9	76	10
Bismarck, ND	9	10	16	10	28	10	43	9	55	10	64	9
Boise, ID	29	12	36	10	42	10	49	8	58	8	67	6
Boston, MA	29	11	30	10	39	12	48	11	58	12	68	11
Buffalo, NY	24	20	25	17	34	16	45	14	57	12	66	10
Charleston, WV	32	15	36	14	46	15	55	14	64	13	71	11
Charlotte, NC	39	10	43	10	51	11	59	9	67	10	76	10
Chicago, IL	21	11	25	9	37	12	49	13	59	11	69	10
Cleveland, OH	25	16	27	14	37	15	48	14	58	13	68	11
Columbia, SC	44	10	47	10	55	10	63	8	71	9	77	10
Concord, NH	19	11	22	10	32	11	44	12	55	12	64	11
Dallas, TX	43	7	48	6	57	7	66	8	73	9	81	7
Denver, CO	30	6	33	6	39	9	48	9	57	11	67	9
Des Moines, IA	19	7	25	7	37	10	51	11	62	11	72	11
Detroit, MI	23	13	25	11	36	13	47	13	58	11	68	10
Honolulu, HI	73	10	73	9	74	9	76	9	78	7	79	6
Indianapolis, IN	26	12	30	10	41	13	52	12	63	12	72	10
Juneau, AK	24	18	28	17	33	18	40	17	47	17	53	15
Los Angeles, CA	57	6	58	6	58	6	60	3	63	1	66	–
Miami, FL	67	7	69	6	72	6	76	6	79	10	81	15
Milwaukee, WI	19	11	23	10	33	12	44	12	55	12	65	11
Minneapolis, MN	12	9	18	7	31	10	46	10	59	11	68	12
Nashville, TN	36	11	40	11	50	12	59	11	68	11	76	9
New Orleans, LA	51	10	54	9	62	9	69	7	75	8	80	11
New York, NY[1]	32	11	34	10	42	11	53	11	63	11	72	10
Oklahoma City, OK	36	5	41	6	50	7	60	8	68	10	77	9
Phoenix, AZ	54	4	58	4	62	4	70	2	79	1	88	1
Pittsburgh, PA	26	16	29	14	39	16	50	14	60	13	68	11
Portland, ME	21	11	23	10	33	11	43	12	53	12	62	11
Portland, OR	40	18	44	16	47	17	51	14	57	12	64	9
St. Louis, MO	30	8	34	8	45	11	57	11	66	11	75	9
Salt Lake City, UT	28	10	34	9	42	10	50	9	59	8	69	5
San Francisco, CA	49	11	52	10	53	10	56	6	58	3	62	1
Seattle, WA	40	19	44	16	46	17	49	14	55	10	61	9
Washington, DC	35	10	38	9	47	11	57	10	66	11	76	9

Airport data except as noted. Temperature is based on standard 30-year period, 1961-1990.
Precipitation is based on average number of days with 0.01 inch or more.

United States Weather

Average Monthly Temperatures (Fahrenheit Degrees) and *Average Number of Rain Days*

July		Aug.		Sept.		Oct.		Nov.		Dec.		City
79°	9	76°	9	69°	6	57°	5	44°	3	35°	4	Albuquerque, NM
79	12	78	10	73	8	62	6	53	8	45	10	Atlanta, GA
70	11	68	10	57	8	46	7	29	8	14	9	Bismarck, ND
74	2	73	3	63	4	52	6	40	10	31	11	Boise, ID
74	9	72	10	65	9	55	9	45	11	34	12	Boston, MA
71	10	69	11	62	11	51	12	41	16	29	20	Buffalo, NY
76	13	74	11	68	10	56	9	47	12	37	14	Charleston, WV
79	11	78	10	72	7	61	7	52	8	43	10	Charlotte, NC
73	10	72	9	64	10	53	9	40	11	27	11	Chicago, IL
72	10	70	10	64	10	53	11	43	15	31	16	Cleveland, OH
81	12	80	11	74	8	63	6	55	7	47	9	Columbia, SC
70	10	67	10	59	9	48	9	37	11	24	11	Concord, NH
85	5	85	5	77	7	67	6	56	6	47	7	Dallas, TX
74	9	71	9	62	6	51	5	39	6	31	5	Denver, CO
77	9	74	9	65	9	54	9	39	7	24	8	Des Moines, IA
72	9	71	9	63	10	51	10	40	12	28	14	Detroit, MI
81	7	81	6	81	7	80	9	77	9	74	10	Honolulu, HI
75	10	73	9	67	8	55	8	43	10	31	12	Indianapolis, IN
56	17	55	18	49	20	42	23	32	20	27	21	Juneau, AK
69	1	71	–	70	1	67	2	62	3	57	5	Los Angeles, CA
83	16	83	17	82	17	78	14	74	9	69	6	Miami, FL
71	10	69	9	62	9	50	9	38	11	24	11	Milwaukee, WI
74	10	71	10	61	10	49	8	33	9	18	9	Minneapolis, MN
79	10	78	9	72	8	60	7	50	8	41	11	Nashville, TN
82	15	82	13	78	10	69	6	61	7	55	10	New Orleans, LA
77	11	76	10	68	8	58	8	48	9	37	10	New York, NY[1]
82	6	81	7	73	7	62	6	50	5	39	6	Oklahoma City, OK
94	4	92	5	86	3	75	3	62	3	54	4	Phoenix, AZ
72	11	71	10	64	9	52	10	42	13	32	16	Pittsburgh, PA
69	10	67	10	59	8	49	9	39	12	27	11	Portland, ME
68	4	69	5	63	8	55	12	46	18	40	19	Portland, OR
80	9	78	8	70	8	58	8	46	10	34	9	St. Louis, MO
78	5	76	6	65	5	53	6	41	8	30	9	Salt Lake City, UT
63	–	64	–	65	1	61	4	55	7	49	10	San Francisco, CA
65	5	66	6	61	9	53	13	45	18	41	19	Seattle, WA
80	10	79	9	71	8	60	7	50	9	39	9	Washington, DC

[1]City office data. – Less than half a day.

Source: U. S. Bureau of the Census, *Statistical Abstract of the United States: 1994*

International Air Distances

Major Cities	Athens	Bangkok	Berlin	Bombay	Buenos Aires	Cape Town	Frankfurt	Hong Kong	Honolulu	London	Madrid	Melbourne
Amsterdam	1349	5707	360	4258	7117	5997	227	5772	7238	222	921	10286
Athens		4930	1121	3209	7269	4957	1123	5316	8337	1488	1474	9297
Bangkok	4930		5351	1870	10490	6301	5305	1076	6610	5929	6334	4579
Beijing	4734	2027	4600	2960	11968	8034	4836	1195	5049	5089	5759	5632
Beirut	719	4272	1689	2527	7695	4794	1762	4756	8520	2151	2190	8579
Berlin	1114	5351		3915	7395	5958	345	5443	7323	580	1162	9929
Bombay	3209	1870	3915		9275	5103	4078	2679	8024	4478	4689	6101
Buenos Aires	7269	10490	7395	9275		4285	7142	11478	7558	6907	6236	7219
Cairo	694	4521	1768	2706	7341	4510	1823	5057	8838	2158	2069	8700
Cape Town	4957	6301	5958	5103	4285		1730	7377	11534	5988	5306	6428
Caracas	5805	10558	5242	9024	3167	6361	5015	10171	6009	4662	4351	9703
Copenhagen	1327	5361	222	3990	7498	6179	421	5392	7088	595	1289	9936
Frankfurt	1123	5305	345	4078	7142	1730		5403	7432	442	1106	9882
Helsinki	1549	4903	689	3686	8061	6490	955	4867	6788	1135	1835	9448
Hong Kong	5316	1076	5443	2679	11478	7377	5403		5557	5986	6556	4605
Honolulu	8337	6610	7323	8024	7558	11534	7432	5557		7241	7874	5501
Istanbul	346	4648	1075	2992	7611	5204	1156	4989	8104	1551	1701	9100
Lima	7309	12241	6893	10389	1958	6074	6659		5938	6315	5907	8052
Lisbon	1771	6651	1442	4982	5964	5201	1164	6862	7821	989	317	11049
London	1488	5929	580	4478	6907	5988	442	5986	7241		786	10508
Madrid	1474	6334	1162	4689	6236	5306	1106	6556	7874	786		10766
Melbourne	9297	4579	9929	6101	7219	6428	9882	4605	5501	10508	10766	
Mexico City	7006	9793	6054	9782	4591	8516	5931	8789	3781	5558	5642	8420
Montréal	4736	8337	3740	7499	5642	7920	3638	7736	4886	3256	3449	10390
Moscow	1387	4394	1001	3132	8369	6277	961	4443	7049	1556	2140	8965
Nairobi	2836	4481	3947	2816	6463	2543	3922	5447	10739	4229	3840	7159
New Delhi	3107	1812	3598	708	9809	5769	3801	2339	7398	4178	4528	6340
New York	4938	8669	3980	7811	5279	7801	4028	8061	4969	3473	3596	10352
Oslo	1625	5395	523	4130	7618	6477	686	5342	6782	718	1485	9934
Paris	1305	5877	549	4367	6857	5782	353	5992	7452	215	652	10442
Rio de Janeiro	6030	9987	6207	8334	6857	3773	6237	11002	8295	5751	5045	8218
Rome	665	5493	735	3837	6929	5231	594	5773	8026	892	849	9940
San Francisco	6792	7930	5673	8406	6455	10248	5709	6904	2397	5369	5806	7850
Shanghai	5301	1797	5231	3117	12197	8062	4406	760	4947	5728	6386	4991
Singapore	5629	887	6167	2427	9870	6007	6119	1608	6728	6747	7079	3767
Stockholm	1524	5141	505	3880	7823	6422	759	5115	6832	892	1613	9693
Tokyo	5924	2865	5557	4196	11411		5533	1782	3860	5956	6706	5070
Vienna	793	5252	323	3701	7353	5656	386	5432	7621	767	1124	9802
Warsaw	994	5032	322	3589	7656	5934	557	5147	7353	901	1425	9609
Zurich	1014	5605	410	4060	7028	6018	177	5775	7605	489	770	10370

All distances in statute miles. To convert to kilometers, multiply by 1.6

International Air Distances

Mexico City	Montréal	Moscow	New York	Paris	Rio de Janeiro	Rome	San Francisco	Singapore	Stockholm	Tokyo	Warsaw	Major Cities
5717	3420	1337	3654	271	5983	804	5465	6526	716	5788	684	Amsterdam
7006	4736	1387	4938	1305	6030	665	6792	5629	1524	5924	994	Athens
9793	8337	4394	8669	5877	9987	5493	7930	887	5141	2865	5032	Bangkok
7722	6470	3627	6867	5138	10778	5059	5934	2754	4156	1305	4041	Beijing
7690	5400	1514	5622	1987	6478	1377	7302	4935	1954	5598	1458	Beirut
6054	3740	1001	3980	549	6207	735	5673	6167	505	5557	322	Berlin
9728	7499	3132	7811	4367	8334	3837	8406	2427	3880	4196	3589	Bombay
4591	5642	8369	5279	6857	1231	6929	6455	9870	7823	11411	7656	Buenos Aires
7687	5424	1770	5598	1973	6153	1325	7436	5143	2135	5937	1614	Cairo
8516	7920	6277	7801	5782	3773	5231	10248	6007	6422	9155	5934	Cape Town
2228	2458	6176	2124	4735	2805	5196	3908	11408	5406	8813	5551	Caracas
5912	3602	971	3857	642	6321	951	5473	6195	340	5415	413	Copenhagen
5931	3638	961	4028	353	6237	594	5709	6119	759	5533	557	Frankfurt
6105	3827	554	4126	1192	6872	1386	5435	5759	248	4872	583	Helsinki
8789	7736	4443	8061	5992	11002	5773	6904	1608	5115	1792	5147	Hong Kong
3781	4886	7049	4969	7452	8295	8026	2397	6728	6832	3860	7353	Honolulu
7087	4792	1087	5022	1400	6378	859	6711	5379	1371	5574	856	Istanbul
2635	3989	7855	3635	6367	2351	6733	4516	11689	7109	9628	7209	Lima
5391	3261	2433	3377	904	4777	1157	5679	7393	1862	6943	1708	Lisbon
5558	3256	1556	3473	215	5751	892	5369	6747	892	5956	901	London
5642	3449	2140	3596	652	5045	849	5806	7079	1613	6704	1425	Madrid
8420	10390	8965	10352	10442	8218	9940	7850	3767	9693	5070	9609	Melbourne
	2305	6671	2086	5723	4769	6365	1889	10331	5932	7036	6335	Mexico City
2305		4397	333	3432	5082	4093	2544	9207	3642	6470	4015	Montréal
6671	4397		4680	1550	7162	1477	5884	5236	764	4663	716	Moscow
9207	7281	3928	7365	4020	5556	3350	9598	4636	4333	6996	3809	Nairobi
9104	6992	2703	7391	4103	8747	3684	7691	2574	3467	3638	3268	New Delhi
2086	333	4680		3638	4805	4293	2574	9539	3939	6757	4271	New York
5703	3406	1024	3686	838	6462	1251	5196	6249	254	5238	665	Oslo
5723	3432	1550	3638		5681	688	5579	6676	964	6054	853	Paris
4769	5082	7162	4805	5681		5704	6621	9776	6638	11535	6453	Rio de Janeiro
6365	4093	1477	4293	688	5704		6259	6231	1255	6140	823	Rome
1889	2544	5884	2574	5579	6621	6259		8449	5372	5148	5854	San Francisco
7067		4248	7384	5772	1139	5671	6150	2363	4837	1097	4963	Shanghai
10331	9207	5236	9539	6676	9776	6231	8449		5993	3304	5846	Singapore
5932	3642	764	3939	964	6638	1255	5372	5993		5091	530	Stockholm
7036	6470	4663	6757	6054	11535	6140	5148	3304	5091		5346	Tokyo
6316	4014	1039	4233	643	6124	483	5992	6039	798	5689	341	Vienna
6335	4015	716	4271	853	6453	823	5854	5846	530	5346		Warsaw
5692	3727	1355	3919	296	5820	430	5810	6502	923	5960	643	Zurich

United States Road and Air Distances

Major Cities	Atlanta	Boston	Chicago	Cleveland	Dallas	Denver	Houston	Indianapolis	Kansas City	Los Angeles	Louisville	Miami
Atlanta, GA		1037 / 946	674 / 606	672 / 554	795 / 731	1398 / 1208	789 / 689	493 / 432	798 / 693	2182 / 1946	382 / 321	655 / 595
Boston, MA	1037 / 946		963 / 867	628 / 563	1748 / 1561	1949 / 1767	1804 / 1597	906 / 817	1391 / 1257	2779 / 2611	941 / 829	1504 / 1258
Chicago, IL	674 / 606	963 / 867		335 / 316	917 / 802	996 / 901	1067 / 925	181 / 177	499 / 403	2054 / 1745	292 / 286	1329 / 1197
Cleveland, OH	672 / 554	628 / 563	335 / 316		1159 / 1021	1321 / 1213	1273 / 1091	294 / 261	779 / 695	2367 / 2053	345 / 304	1264 / 1080
Dallas, TX	795 / 731	1748 / 1561	917 / 802	1159 / 1021		781 / 645	243 / 224	865 / 762	489 / 460	1387 / 1235	819 / 732	1300 / 1121
Denver, CO	1398 / 1208	1949 / 1767	996 / 901	1321 / 1213	781 / 645		1019 / 864	1058 / 989	600 / 543	1059 / 849	1120 / 1035	2037 / 1716
Detroit, MI	699 / 595	695 / 632	266 / 235	170 / 95	1143 / 987	1253 / 1135	1265 / 1076	278 / 230	743 / 630	2311 / 1979	360 / 306	1352 / 1146
Indianapolis, IN	493 / 432	906 / 817	181 / 177	294 / 261	865 / 762	1058 / 989	987 / 845		485 / 452	2073 / 1815	111 / 111	1148 / 1021
Los Angeles, CA	2182 / 1946	2779 / 2611	2054 / 1745	2367 / 2053	1387 / 1235	1059 / 849	1538 / 1379	2073 / 1815	1589 / 1363		2108 / 1842	2687 / 2342
Louisville, KY	382 / 321	941 / 829	292 / 286	345 / 304	819 / 732	1120 / 1035	928 / 788	111 / 111	520 / 491	2108 / 1842		1037 / 911
Miami, FL	655 / 595	1504 / 1258	1329 / 1197	1264 / 1080	1300 / 1121	2037 / 1716	1190 / 964	1448 / 1021	1448 / 1252	2687 / 2342	1037 / 911	
Milwaukee, WI	761 / 669	1050 / 860	87 / 67	422 / 328	991 / 853	1029 / 908	1142 / 984	268 / 238	537 / 436	2087 / 1756	379 / 348	1416 / 1259
Minneapolis, MN	1068 / 906	1368 / 1124	405 / 334	740 / 622	936 / 852	841 / 693	1157 / 1034	586 / 503	447 / 394	1889 / 1536	697 / 603	1723 / 1501
Nashville, TN	242 / 214	1088 / 943	446 / 409	513 / 448	660 / 631	1156 / 1023	769 / 657	279 / 249	556 / 492	2025 / 1797	168 / 151	897 / 806
New Orleans, LA	479 / 425	1507 / 1367	912 / 837	1030 / 917	496 / 447	1273 / 1067	356 / 305	796 / 708	806 / 690	1883 / 1671	685 / 621	856 / 674
New York, NY	841 / 760	206 / 187	802 / 740	473 / 425	1552 / 1391	1771 / 1638	1608 / 1417	713 / 664	1198 / 1113	2786 / 2475	748 / 662	1308 / 1090
Philadelphia, PA	741 / 665	296 / 281	738 / 678	413 / 363	1452 / 1302	1691 / 1569	1508 / 1324	633 / 587	1118 / 1039	2706 / 2401	668 / 576	1208 / 1013
Phoenix, AZ	1793 / 1587	2604 / 2300	1713 / 1440	1992 / 1738	998 / 868	792 / 589	1149 / 1009	1698 / 1489	1214 / 1043	389 / 370	1733 / 1506	2298 / 1972
Portland, OR	2601 / 2172	3046 / 2537	2083 / 1739	2418 / 2046	2009 / 1616	1238 / 985	2205 / 1825	2227 / 1877	1809 / 1481	959 / 834	2320 / 1950	3256 / 2700
St. Louis, MO	541 / 484	1141 / 1046	289 / 258	529 / 487	630 / 550	857 / 781	779 / 667	235 / 229	257 / 238	1845 / 1592	263 / 254	1196 / 1068
San Francisco, CA	2496 / 2139	3095 / 2704	2142 / 1846	2467 / 2161	1753 / 1465	1235 / 956	1912 / 1635	2256 / 1944	1835 / 1498	379 / 337	2349 / 1989	3053 / 2585
Seattle, WA	2618 / 2181	2976 / 2496	2013 / 1720	2348 / 2021	2078 / 1660	1307 / 1019	2274 / 1874	2194 / 1866	1839 / 1489	1131 / 954	2305 / 1944	3273 / 2724
Washington, DC	608 / 533	429 / 413	671 / 589	345 / 288	1319 / 1171	1616 / 1464	1375 / 1190	558 / 476	1043 / 927	2631 / 2288	582 / 451	1075 / 921

Road Miles are on the top in roman; Air Miles are below in italic.

United States Road and Air Distances

Milwaukee	Minneapolis	Nashville	New Orleans	New York	Philadelphia	Phoenix	Portland	St. Louis	San Francisco	Seattle	Washington, DC	Major Cities
761 / 669	1068 / 906	242 / 214	479 / 425	841 / 760	741 / 665	1793 / 1587	2601 / 2172	541 / 484	2496 / 2139	2618 / 2181	608 / 533	Atlanta, GA
1050 / 860	1368 / 1124	1088 / 943	1507 / 1367	206 / 187	296 / 281	2604 / 2300	3046 / 2537	1141 / 1046	3095 / 2704	2976 / 2496	429 / 413	Boston, MA
87 / 67	405 / 334	446 / 409	912 / 837	802 / 740	738 / 678	1713 / 1440	2083 / 1739	289 / 258	2142 / 1846	2013 / 1720	672 / 589	Chicago, IL
422 / 328	740 / 622	513 / 448	1030 / 917	473 / 425	413 / 363	1992 / 1738	2418 / 2046	529 / 487	2467 / 2161	2348 / 2021	346 / 288	Cleveland, OH
991 / 853	936 / 852	660 / 631	496 / 447	1552 / 1391	1452 / 1302	998 / 868	2009 / 1616	630 / 550	1753 / 1465	2078 / 1660	1319 / 1171	Dallas, TX
1029 / 908	841 / 693	1156 / 1023	1273 / 1067	1771 / 1638	1691 / 1569	792 / 589	1238 / 985	857 / 781	1235 / 956	1307 / 1019	1616 / 1464	Denver, CO
353 / 237	671 / 528	528 / 457	1045 / 926	637 / 509	573 / 453	1957 / 1671	2349 / 1953	513 / 440	2399 / 2079	2279 / 1927	506 / 383	Detroit, MI
268 / 238	586 / 503	279 / 249	796 / 708	713 / 664	633 / 587	1698 / 1489	2227 / 1877	235 / 229	2256 / 1944	2194 / 1866	558 / 476	Indianapolis, IN
2087 / 1756	1889 / 1536	2025 / 1797	1883 / 1671	2786 / 2475	2706 / 2401	389 / 370	959 / 834	1845 / 1592	379 / 337	1131 / 954	2631 / 2288	Los Angeles, CA
379 / 348	697 / 603	168 / 151	685 / 621	748 / 662	668 / 576	1733 / 1506	2320 / 1950	263 / 254	2349 / 1989	2305 / 1944	582 / 451	Louisville, KY
1416 / 1259	1723 / 1501	897 / 806	856 / 674	1308 / 1090	1208 / 1013	2298 / 1972	3256 / 2700	1196 / 1068	3053 / 2585	3273 / 2724	1075 / 921	Miami, FL
	332 / 297	532 / 475	994 / 903	889 / 746	825 / 690	1751 / 1460	2010 / 1718	363 / 317	2175 / 1845	1940 / 1694	758 / 612	Milwaukee, WI
332 / 297		826 / 695	1214 / 1040	1207 / 980	1143 / 980	1616 / 1276	1678 / 1426	552 / 448	1940 / 1589	1608 / 1399	1076 / 908	Minneapolis, MN
532 / 475	826 / 695		517 / 471	892 / 675	792 / 675	1650 / 1448	2359 / 1972	299 / 271	2333 / 1968	2376 / 1977	659 / 542	Nashville, TN
994 / 903	1214 / 1040	517 / 471		1311 / 1182	1211 / 1088	1494 / 1301	2505 / 2051	673 / 604	2249 / 1911	2574 / 2086	1078 / 954	New Orleans, LA
889 / 746	1207 / 1028	892 / 766	1311 / 1182		100 / 94	2411 / 2153	2885 / 2454	948 / 892	2934 / 2586	2815 / 2421	233 / 228	New York, NY
825 / 690	1143 / 980	792 / 675	1211 / 1088	100 / 94		2331 / 2075	2821 / 2406	868 / 813	2866 / 2521	2751 / 2378	133 / 134	Philadelphia, PA
1751 / 1460	1616 / 1276	1650 / 1448	1494 / 1301	2411 / 2153	2331 / 2075		1266 / 1009	1470 / 1262	763 / 651	1437 / 1106	2256 / 1956	Phoenix, AZ
2010 / 1718	1678 / 1426	2359 / 1972	2505 / 2051	2885 / 2454	2821 / 2406	1266 / 1009		2060 / 1708	636 / 550	172 / 129	2754 / 2327	Portland, OR
363 / 317	552 / 448	299 / 271	673 / 604	948 / 892	868 / 813	1470 / 1262	2060 / 1708		2089 / 1735	2081 / 1709	793 / 696	St. Louis, MO
2175 / 1845	1940 / 1589	2333 / 1968	2249 / 1911	2934 / 2586	2866 / 2521	763 / 651	636 / 550	2089 / 1735		808 / 678	2799 / 2419	San Francisco, CA
1940 / 1694	1608 / 1399	2376 / 1977	2574 / 2086	2815 / 2421	2751 / 2378	1437 / 1106	172 / 129	2081 / 1709	808 / 678		2684 / 2306	Seattle, WA
758 / 612	1076 / 908	659 / 542	1078 / 954	233 / 228	133 / 134	2256 / 1956	2754 / 2327	793 / 696	2799 / 2419	2684 / 2306		Washington, DC

All distances in statute miles. To convert to kilometers, multiply by 1.6

Weight and Measure Equivalents

Linear Measure

	1 inch	2.54 cm.
12 inches	1 foot	0.3048 m.
3 feet	1 yard	0.9144 m.
5 1/2 yards	1 rod/pole/perch	5.029 m.
40 rods	1 furlong	201.168 m.
8 furlongs *or* 5,280 ft.	1 statute mile	1.609 km.
3 miles	1 land league	4.83 km.
6,076.115 feet	1 international nautical mile	1.852 km.

Area Measure

	1 sq. inch	6.452 sq. cm.
144 sq. inches	1 sq. foot	0.0929 m²
9 sq. feet	1 sq. yard	0.8361 m²
43,560 sq. feet	1 acre	0.4047 ha.
640 acres	1 sq. mile	259 ha.
1 sq. mile	1 section	259 ha.
36 sections	1 township	9,324 ha.

U.S. Liquid

8 drams	1 ounce *or* 1.8047 cu. in.	0.0295 l.
4 oz.	1 gill *or* 7.219 cu. in.	0.1183 l.
4 gills	1 pint *or* 28.875 cu. in.	0.4732 l.
2 pints	1 quart *or* 57.75 cu. in.	0.9464 l.
4 quarts	1 gallon *or* 231 cu. in.	3.7845 l.

U.S. Dry

2 pints	1 quart *or* 67.20 cu. in.	1.1012 l.
8 quarts	1 peck *or* 537.61 cu. in.	8.8098 l.
4 pecks	1 bushel *or* 2,150.42 cu. in.	35.2391 l.

Weight (Avoirdupois)

	1 grain	0.0648 g.
437.5 grains	1 ounce	28.3495 g.
7,000 grains	1 pound *or* 16 ounces	0.4536 kg.
100 pounds	1 hundredweight	45.36 kg.
2,000 pounds	1 short ton	0.9072 t.
2,240 pounds	1 long ton	1.016 t.

Customary U.S. Household

1 teaspoon	¹/₆ fluid ounce	4.9 ml.
3 teaspoons	1 tablespoon *or* ¹/₂ fluid ounce	14.8 ml.
16 tablespoons	1 cup *or* 8 fluid ounces	236.6 ml.
2 cups	1 pint *or* 16 fluid ounces	473.2 ml.
2 pints	1 quart *or* 32 fluid ounces	946.4 ml.
4 quarts	1 gallon *or* 128 fluid ounces	3.785 l.

Metric Linear

	1 millimeter	0.03937 in.
10 millimeters	1 centimeter	0.3937 in.
10 centimeters	1 decimeter	3.937 in.
10 decimeters	1 meter	3.2808 ft.
10 meters	1 dekameter	32.808 ft.
10 dekameters	1 hectometer	328.08 ft.
10 hectometers	1 kilometer	0.621 mi.

Metric Area

	1 sq. millimeter	0.00155 in.²
100 millimeters²	1 sq. centimeter	0.15499 in.²
100 centimeters²	1 sq. decimeter	15.499 in.²
100 decimeters²	1 sq. meter	1.196 yd.²
100 meters²	1 sq. dekameter	119.6 yd.²
100 dekameters²	1 sq. hectometer	2.471 acres
100 hectometers²	1 sq. kilometer	0.386 sq. mi. *or* 247.1 acres

Metric Capacity or Volume

10 milliliters	1 centiliter	0.338 fluid oz.
10 centiliters	1 deciliter	3.38 fluid oz. *or* 0.1057 liquid qt.
10 deciliters	1 liter	1.0567 liquid qt. *or* 0.9081 dry qt.
10 liters	1 dekaliter	2.642 gal. *or* 0.284 bu.
10 dekaliters	1 hectoliter	26.418 gal. *or* 2.838 bu.
10 hectoliters	1 kiloliter	264.18 gal. *or* 28.38 bu.

Metric Weight

10 milligrams	1 centigram	0.1543 gr.
10 centigrams	1 decigram	1.5432 gr.
10 decigrams	1 gram	15.432 gr.
10 grams	1 dekagram	0.35274 oz.
10 dekagrams	1 hectogram	3.5274 oz.
10 hectograms	1 kilogram	2.2046 lb.
1,000 kilograms	1 metric ton	2,204.6 lb.

Weight and Measure Conversions

When you know	Multiply by	To find*	When you know	Multiply by	To find*
Linear			**Linear**		
inches	25.4	millimeters	millimeters	0.039	inches
inches	2.54	centimeters	centimeters	0.39	inches
feet	30.0	centimeters	centimeters	0.033	feet
feet	0.3	meters	centimeters	0.01	yards
yards	90.0	centimeters	meters	3.3	feet
yards	0.9	meters	meters	1.1	yards
rods	5.0	meters	meters	0.2	rods
miles	1.6	kilometers	kilometers	0.62	miles
Capacity or Volume			**Capacity or Volume**		
teaspoons	5.0	milliliters	milliliters	0.2	teaspoons
tablespoons	15.0	milliliters	milliliters	0.07	tablespoons
fluid ounces	30.0	milliliters	milliliters	0.034	fluid ounces
fluid ounces	0.03	liters	milliliters	0.004	cups
cups	240.0	milliliters	liters	34.0	fluid ounces
cups	0.24	liters	liters	4.2	cups
pints	0.47	liters	liters	2.1	pints
quarts	0.95	liters	liters	1.06	quarts
gallons	3.8	liters	liters	0.26	gallons
bushels	35.0	liters	liters	0.03	bushels
Weight			**Weight**		
ounces	28.0	grams	grams	0.035	ounces
ounces	0.028	kilograms	grams	0.002	pounds
pounds	454.0	grams	kilograms	35.0	ounces
pounds	0.45	kilograms	kilograms	2.2	pounds
short ton	0.9	metric ton	metric ton	1.1	short ton

*Approximately

Temperature Conversions

FAHRENHEIT = 9 X CELSIUS ÷ 5 + 32

32°	50°	75°	100°	125°	150°	175°	200°	212°
0°	10°	23.9°	37.8°	51.7°	65.6°	79.4°	93.3°	100°

CELSIUS = FAHRENHEIT – 32 x 5 ÷ 9

Clothing Size Equivalents

Men's Suits and Overcoats

U. S.	36	38	40	42	44	46
U. K.	36	38	40	42	44	46
Europe	46	48	50	52	54	56

Men's Shoes

U.S.	7¹/₂	8	8¹/₂	9¹/₂	10¹/₂	11¹/₂
U. K.	7	7¹/₂	8	9	10	11
Europe	40¹/₂	41	42	43	44¹/₂	46

Men's Shirts

U.S.	14	14¹/₂	15	15¹/₂	16	17
U. K.	14	14¹/₂	15	15¹/₂	16	17
Europe	36	37	38	39	41	43

Women's Suits and Dresses

U. S.	6	8	10	12	14	16
U.K.	8	10	12	14	16	18
Europe	36	38	40	42	44	46

Women's Shoes

U.S.	6	6¹/₂	7	7¹/₂	8	8¹/₂
U. K.	4¹/₂	5	5¹/₂	6	6¹/₂	7
Europe	36¹/₂	37	37¹/₂	38	38¹/₂	39

Children's Clothes

U.S.	4	6	8	10	12	14
U.K. – Height(")	43	48	55	58	60	62
– Age	4-5	6-7	9-10	11	12	13
Europe – Height (cm)	125	135	150	155	160	165
– Age	7	9	12	13	14	15

Country Information

Country, *Capital*	Predominant Language(s)	Predominant Religion(s)	Currency
Argentina, *Buenos Aires*	Spanish	Roman Catholic	Peso
Australia, *Canberra*	English	Protestant	Dollar
Austria, *Vienna*	German	Roman Catholic	Euro
Belgium, *Brussels*	Flemish (Dutch)	Roman Catholic	Euro
Canada, *Ottawa*	English, French	Roman Catholic	Dollar
Chile, *Santiago*	Spanish	Roman Catholic	Peso
China, *Beijing*	Mandarin Chinese	Officially atheist	Yuan
Denmark, *Copenhagen*	Danish	Protestant	Krone
Egypt, *Cairo*	Arabic	Islamic	Pound
Finland, *Helsinki*	Finnish, Swedish	Protestant	Euro
France, *Paris*	French	Roman Catholic	Euro
Germany, *Berlin*	German	Protestant	Euro
Greece, *Athens*	Greek	Greek Orthodox	Euro
India, *Delhi*	Hindi, English	Hindu, Islamic	Rupee
Ireland, *Dublin*	Irish, English	Roman Catholic	Euro
Israel, *Jerusalem*	Hebrew, Arabic	Jewish	New Shekel
Italy, *Rome*	Italian	Roman Catholic	Euro
Japan, *Tokyo*	Japanese	Buddhist	Yen
Korea, South, *Seoul*	Korean	Buddhist	Won
Mexico, *Mexico City*	Spanish	Roman Catholic	Nuevo Peso
Netherlands, *Amsterdam*	Dutch	Roman Catholic	Euro
Norway, *Oslo*	Norwegian	Protestant	Krone
Peru, *Lima*	Spanish	Roman Catholic	Nuevo Sol
Philippines, *Manila*	Filipino, English	Roman Catholic	Peso
Poland, *Warsaw*	Polish	Roman Catholic	Zloty
Portugal, *Lisbon*	Portuguese	Roman Catholic	Euro
Romania, *Bucharest*	Romanian	Orthodox	Lev
Russia, *Moscow*	Slavic	Orthodox	Rouble
Saudi Arabia, *Riyadh*	Arabic	Islamic	Riyal
South Africa, *Cape Town*	English	Protestant	Rand
Spain, *Madrid*	Spanish	Roman Catholic	Euro
Sweden, *Stockholm*	Swedish	Protestant	Krona
Switzerland, *Bern*	German	Protestant	Franc
Syria, *Damascus*	Arabic	Islamic	Pound
Taiwan, *Taipei*	Chinese	Buddhist	Dollar
Thailand, *Bangkok*	Thai	Buddhist	Baht
Turkey, *Ankara*	Turkish	Islamic	Lira
United Kingdom, *London*	English	Protestant	Pound
Venezuela, *Caracas*	Spanish	Roman Catholic	Bolivar

Foreign Embassies in the United States

Albania
2100 S Street NW 20008
223-4942 (Tirana)

Algeria
2118 Kalorama Rd. NW 20008
265-2800 (Algiers)

Angola
2100-2108 16th St. NW 20009
785-1156 (Luanda)

Argentina
1600 New Hampshire
Avenue NW 20009
238-6400 (Buenos Aires)

Armenia
2225 R Street NW 20008
319-1976 (Yerevan)

Australia
1601 Massachusetts Avenue
NW 20036
797-3000 (Canberra)

Austria
3524 Intl. Court NW 20008
895-6700 (Vienna)

Azerbaijan
2741 34th St. NW 20008
337-3500 (Baku)

Bahrain
3502 Intl. Drive NW 20008
342-0741 (Manama)

Bangladesh
3510 Intl. Drive NW 20007
244-2745 (Baridhara)

Belarus
1619 New Hampshire
Avenue NW 20009
986-1606 (Minsk)

Belgium
3330 Garfield St. NW 20008
333-6900 (Brussels)

Belize
2535 Massachusetts Avenue
NW 20008
332-9636 (Belize City)

Benin
2124 Kalorama Road NW
20008
232-6656 (Cotonou)

Bolivia
3014 Massachusetts Avenue
NW 20008
483-4410 (La Paz)

Bosnia and Herzegovina
2109 E Street NW 20037
337-1500 (Sarajevo)

Botswana
1531-3 New Hampshire
Avenue NW 20036
244-4990 (Gaborone)

Brazil
3006 Massachusetts Avenue
NW 20008
238-2700 (Brasilia)

Bulgaria
1621 22nd Street NW 20008
387-0174 (Sofia)

Burkina Faso
2340 Massachusetts Avenue
NW 20008
332-5577 (Ouagadougou)

Burundi
2233 Wisc. Ave. NW 20007
342-2574 (Bujumbura)

Cambodia
4530 16th St. NW 20011
726-7742 (Phnom Penh)

Cameroon
2349 Massachusetts Avenue
NW 20008
265-8790 (Yaounde)

Canada
501 Penn. Ave. NW 20001
682-1740 (Ottawa)

Cape Verde
3415 Massachusetts Avenue
NW 20007
965-6820 (Praia)

Chad
2002 R Street NW 20009
462-4009 (N'Djamena)

Chile
1732 Massachusetts Avenue
NW 20036
785-1746 (Santiago)

China
2300 Conn. Ave. NW 20008
328-2500 (Beijing)

Colombia
2118 Leroy Place NW 20008
387-8338 (Bogota)

Congo, Dem. Republic of
1800 New Hampshire
Avenue NW 20009
234-7690 (Kinshasa)

Congo, Republic of
4891 Colorado Avenue NW
20011
726-5500 (Brazzaville)

Costa Rica
2114 S Street NW 20008
234-2945 or 46 (San Jose)

Cote d'Ivoire
2424 Massachusetts Avenue
NW 20008
797-0300 (Abidjan)

Croatia
2343 Massachusetts Avenue
NW 20008
588-5899 (Zagreb)

Czech Republic
3900 Spring of Freedom
Street NW 20008
274-9100 (Prague)

Denmark
3200 Whitehaven Street NW
20008
234-4300 (Copenhagen)

Dominican Republic
1715 22nd St. NW 20008
332-6280 (Santo Domingo)

Ecuador
2535 15th St. NW 20009
234-7200 (Quito)

Egypt
3521 Intl. Court NW 20008
895-5400 (Cairo)

All addresses are in Washington, D.C. All phone numbers are in area code 202. Location of the U.S. Embassy in the respective country is in parentheses after telephone number.

El Salvador
2308 California St. NW
20008
265-9671 (San Salvador)

Estonia
2131 Massachusetts Avenue
NW 20008
588-0101 (Tallinn)

Ethiopia
3506 Intl. Drive NW 20008
364-1200 (Addis Ababa)

Finland
3301 Massachusetts Avenue
NW 20008
298-5800 (Helsinki)

France
4101 Reservoir Rd. NW 20007
944-6000 (Paris)

Gambia
1156 15th St. NW #905 20005
785-1399 (Banjul)

Georgia
1615 New Hampshire
Avenue NW #300 20009
387-2390 (Tbilisi)

Germany
4645 Reservoir Rd. NW 20007
298-4000 (Berlin)

Ghana
3512 Intl. Drive NW 20008
686-4520 (Accra)

Greece
2221 Massachusetts Avenue
NW 20008
939-1300 (Athens)

Guatemala
2220 R Street NW 20008
745-4952 (Guatemala City)

Haiti
2311 Massachusetts Avenue
NW 20008
332-4090 (Port-au-Prince)

Honduras
3007 Tilden Street NW #4M
20008
966-7702 (Tegucigalpa)

Hungary
3910 Shoemaker Street NW
20008
362-6730 (Budapest)

Iceland
1156 15th Street NW 20005
265-6653 (Reykjavik)

India
2107 Massachusetts Avenue
NW 20008
939-7000 (New Delhi)

Indonesia
2020 Massachusetts Avenue
NW 20036
775-5200 (Jakarta)

Iran
2209 Wisc. Ave. NW 20007
965-4990 (Tehran)

Ireland
2234 Massachusetts Avenue
NW 20008
462-3939 (Dublin)

Israel
3514 Intl. Drive NW 20008
364-5500 (Tel Aviv)

Italy
3000 Whitehaven St. NW 20008
612-4400 (Rome)

Jamaica
1520 New Hampshire Ave.
NW 20036
452-0660 (Kingston)

Japan
2520 Massachusetts Avenue
NW 20008
238-6700 (Tokyo)

Jordan
3504 Intl. Court NW 20008
966-2664 (Amman)

Kazakhstan
1401 16th St. NW 20036
232-5488 (Almaty)

Kenya
2249 R St. NW 20008
387-6101 (Nairobi)

Korea
2450 Massachusetts Avenue
NW 20008
939-5600 (Seoul)

Kuwait
2940 Tilden St. NW 20008
966-0702 (Kuwait City)

Kyrgyzstan
1732 Wisc. Ave. NW 20007
338-5141 (Bishkek)

Laos
2222 S Street NW 20008
332-6416 (Vientiane)

Latvia
4325 17th Street NW 20011
726-8213 (Riga)

Lebanon
2560 28th Street NW 20008
939-6300 (Beirut)

Liberia
5201 16th Street NW 20011
723-0437 (Monrovia)

Lithuania
2622 16th Street NW 20009
234-5860 (Vilnius)

Luxembourg
2200 Massachusetts Avenue
NW 20008
265-4171 (Luxembourg)

Malaysia
3516 Intl. Court NW 20008
572-9700 (Kuala Lumpur)

Mali
2130 R Street NW 20008
332-2249 (Bamako)

Mexico
1911 Penn. Ave. NW 20006
728-1600 (Mexico City)

Moldova
2101 S Street NW 20008
667-1130 (Chisinau)

Mongolia
2833 M Street NW 20007
333-7117 (Ulaanbaatar)

Morocco
1601 21st Street NW 20009
462-7979 (Rabat)

Mozambique
1990 M St. NW #570 20036
293-7146 (Maputo)

Myanmar
2300 S Street NW 20008
332-9044 (Rangoon)

Netherlands
4200 Linnean Ave. NW 20008
244-5300 (The Hague)

New Zealand
37 Observatory Circle NW
20008
328-4800 (Wellington)

Nicaragua
1627 New Hampshire
Avenue NW 20009
939-6570 (Managua)

Niger
2204 R Street NW 20008
483-4224 (Niamey)

Nigeria
1333 16th Street NW 20036
986-8400 (Lagos and Abuja)

Norway
2720 34th Street NW 20008
333-6000 (Oslo)

Pakistan
3517 Intl. Court NW 20008
243-6500 (Islamabad)

Panama
2862 McGill Terr. NW 20008
483-1407 (Panama City)

Peru
1700 Massachusetts Avenue
NW 20036
833-9860 (Lima)

Philippines
1600 Massachusetts Avenue
NW 20036
467-9300 (Manila)

Poland
2640 16th Street NW 20009
234-3800 (Warsaw)

Portugal
2012 Massachusetts Avenue
NW 20036
328-8610 (Lisbon)

Romania
1607 23rd Street NW 20008
332-4848 (Bucharest)

Russia
2650 Wisc. Ave. NW 20007
298-5700 (Moscow)

Rwanda
1714 New Hampshire
Avenue NW 20009
232-2882 (Kigali)

Saudi Arabia
601 New Hampshire Avenue
NW 20037
337-4076 (Riyadh)

Senegal
2112 Wyoming Avenue NW
20008
234-0540 (Dakar)

Sierra Leone
1701 19th Street NW 20009
939-9261 (Freetown)

Singapore
3501 Intl. Place NW 20008
537-3100 (Singapore)

Slovakia
3523 Intl. Court NW 20008
237-1054 (Bratislava)

Slovenia
1525 New Hampshire
Avenue NW 20036
667-5363 (Ljubljana)

South Africa
3051 Massachusetts Avenue
NW 20008
232-4400 (Pretoria)

Spain
2375 Penn. Ave. NW 20037
452-0100 (Madrid)

Sri Lanka
2148 Wyoming Avenue NW
20008
483-4025 (Colombo)

Sudan
2210 Massachusetts Avenue
NW 20008
338-8565 (Khartoum)

Sweden
1501 M Street NW 20005
467-2600 (Stockholm)

Switzerland
2900 Cathedral Ave. NW 20008
745-7900 (Bern)

Syria
2215 Wyoming Ave. NW 20008
232-6313 (Damascus)

Tanzania
2139 R Street NW 20008
939-6125 (Dar Es Salaam)

Thailand
1024 Wisc. Ave. NW 20007
944-3600 (Bangkok)

Tunisia
1515 Massachusetts Avenue
NW 20005
862-1850 (Tunis)

Turkey
2525 Massachusetts Avenue
NW 20008
612-6700 (Ankara)

Turkmenistan
2207 Massachusetts Avenue
NW 20008
588-1500 (Ashgabat)

Uganda
5911 16th St. NW 20011
726-7100 (Kampala)

Ukraine
3350 M Street NW 20007
333-0606 (Kiev)

United Arab Emirates
3522 Intl. Court NW 20008
243-2400 (Abu Dhabi)

United Kingdom
3100 Massachusetts Avenue
NW 20008
588-6500 (London)

Uruguay
1913 Eye Street NW 20006
331-1313 (Montevideo)

Uzbekistan
1746 Massachusetts Avenue
NW 20036
887-5300 (Tashkent)

Venezuela
1099 30th Street NW 20007
342-2214 (Caracas)

Vietnam
1233 20th St. NW #400 20036
861-0737 (Hanoi)

Yemen
2319 Wyoming Ave. NW 20008
965-4760 (Sana'a)

Zambia
2419 Mass. Ave. NW 20008
265-9717 (Lusaka)

Zimbabwe
1608 New Hampshire
Avenue NW 20009
332-7100 (Harare)

All addresses are in Washington, D.C. All phone numbers are in area code 202. Location of the U.S. Embassy in the respective country is in parentheses after the telephone number.

Area Codes

UNITED STATES

Alabama
Birmingham	205
Huntsville	256
Mobile	251
Montgomery	334

Alaska
	907

Arizona
Flagstaff	928
Phoenix	480/602/623
Scottsdale	480/602
Tucson	520

Arkansas
Fayetteville	479
Jonesboro	870
Little Rock	501
Pine Bluff	870

California
Anaheim	714
Bakersfield	661
Barstow	760
Berkeley	510
Beverly Hills	310
Burbank	818
Claremont	909
Concord	925
Encinitas	760
Fresno	559
Hollywood	323
Irvine	949
Long Beach	562
Los Angeles	213
Monterey	831
Oakland	510
Palm Springs	760
Pasadena	626
Redding	530
Sacramento	916
San Bernardino	909
San Diego	619/858
San Francisco	415
San Jose	408
San Mateo	650
Santa Barbara	805
Santa Rosa	707
Stockton	209
Torrance	310/424

Colorado
Aspen	970
Boulder	303/720
Colorado Springs	719
Denver	303/720
Fort Collins	970

Connecticut
Hartford	860/959
New Haven	203/475
New London	860/959
Stamford	203/475
Waterbury	203/475

Delaware
	302

Florida
Clearwater	727
Daytona Beach	386
Fort Lauderdale	754/954
Fort Myers	239/941
Gainesville	352
Jacksonville	904
Lakeland	863
Miami	305/786
Orlando	321/407
Palm Beach	561
Pensacola	850
Port St. Lucie	772
St. Petersburg	727
Sanibel/Captiva	239
Sarasota	941
Tallahassee	850
Tampa	813

Georgia
Athens	706
Atlanta	404/470/678
Augusta	706
Columbus	706
Decatur	404/470/678
Macon	478
Marietta	470/678/770
Savannah	912
Valdosta	229

Hawaii
	808

Idaho
	208

Illinois
Addison	331/630
Aurora	331/630
Bloomington	309

Carbondale	618
Champaign	217
Chicago, INNER	312/872
Chicago, OUTER	773/872
Danville	217
Des Plaines	224/847
Joliet	815
Moline	309
Palos Heights	708
Peoria	309
Rockford	815
Springfield	217
Urbana	217
Waukegan	224/847

Indiana
Evansville	812
Fort Wayne	260
Gary	219
Indianapolis	317
Lafayette	765
Muncie	765
South Bend	574
Terre Haute	812

Iowa
Ames	515
Cedar Rapids	319
Council Bluffs	712
Davenport	563
Des Moines	515
Dubuque	563
Fort Dodge	515
Iowa City	319
Ottumwa	641
Sioux City	712

Kansas
Dodge City	620
Kansas City	913
Lawrence	785
Manhattan	785
Topeka	785
Wichita	316/620

Kentucky
Ashland	606
Bowling Green	270
Covington	859
Frankfort	502
Lexington	859
Louisville	502
Paducah	270

Multiple area codes are assigned in some areas. For long distance information, dial (area code) 555-1212. For the area code for a particular place, dial "0" (local operator).

Louisiana

Baton Rouge	225
Houma	985
Lafayette	337
New Orleans	504
Shreveport	318

Maine
207

Maryland

Annapolis	410/443/667
Baltimore	410/443/667
Cumberland	227/240/301
Frederick	227/240/301
Silver Spring	227/240/301

Massachusetts

Amherst	413
Boston	617/857
Cambridge	617/857
Cape Cod	508/774
Lowell	351/978
Lynn	339/781
New Bedford	508/774
Plymouth	508/774
Salem	351/978
Springfield	413
Worcester	508/774

Michigan

Ann Arbor	734
Bloomfield	248/947
Detroit	313
Grand Rapids	616
Kalamazoo	269
Lansing	517
Marquette, & ALL U.P.	906
Pontiac	248/947
Port Huron	810
Saginaw	989
Traverse City	231
Warren	586
Ypsilanti	734

Minnesota

Anoka	763
Bloomington	952
Duluth	218
Minneapolis	612
Rochester	507
St. Cloud	320
St. Paul	651

Mississippi

Biloxi	228
Gulfport	228
Hattiesburg	601
Jackson	601
Tupelo	662

Missouri

Aurora	417
Branson	417
Cape Girardeau	573
Columbia	573
Hannibal	573
Jefferson City	573
Kansas City	816/975
St. Charles	636
St. Joseph	816/975
St. Louis	314/557
Sedalia	660
Springfield	417

Montana
406

Nebraska

Grand Island	308
Lincoln	402
North Platte	308
Omaha	402

Nevada

Las Vegas	702
Reno	775

New Hampshire
603

New Jersey

Atlantic City	609
Caldwell	862/973
Camden	856
Cherry Hill	856
Elizabeth	908
Hackensack	201/551
Newark	862/973
New Brunswick	732/848
Princeton	609
Toms River	732/848
Trenton	609

New Mexico
505

New York

Albany	518
Binghamton	607
Buffalo	716
Long Island	
Nassau County	516
Suffolk County	631
New City	845
New York City	
Manhattan	212/646/917
Bronx	347/718
Brooklyn	347/718
Queens	347/718
Staten Island	347/718
All five boroughs	
(cellular, pagers)	917
Oswego	315
Plattsburgh	518
Port Chester	914
Poughkeepsie	845/914
Rochester	585
Syracuse	315
White Plains	914

North Carolina

Asheville	828
Cape Hatteras	252
Charlotte	704/980
Durham	919/984
Fayetteville	910
Greensboro	336
Raleigh	919/984
Wilmington	910
Winston-Salem	336

North Dakota
701

Ohio

Akron	234/330
Ashtabula	440
Canton	234/330
Cincinnati	283/513
Cleveland	216
Columbus	614
Dayton	937
Lima	419/567
Marion	740
Toledo	419/567
Youngstown	234/330

Oklahoma

Ardmore	580
Enid	580
Lawton	580
Oklahoma City	405
Stillwater	405
Tulsa	918

Oregon

Eugene	541
La Grande	541
Portland	503/971
Salem	503/971

Pennsylvania

Allentown	484/610/835
Altoona	814
Canonsburg	724/878
Erie	814

Harrisburg	717	**Vermont**	802	**Ontario**	
Lancaster	717			Belleville	613
New Castle	724/878	**Virginia**		Hamilton	289/905
Philadelphia	215/267/445	Arlington	571/703	London	519
Pittsburgh	412/878	Blacksburg	540	Niagara Falls	289/905
Reading	484/610/835	Bristol	276	Ottawa	613
Scranton	570	Charlottesville	434	Sault Ste. Marie	705
State College	814	Fairfax	571/703	Thunder Bay	807
West Chester	484/610/835	Fredericksburg	540	Toronto	416/647
Wilkes-Barre	570	Harrisonburg	540	Windsor	519
		Lynchburg	434	**Prince Edward Island**	902
Rhode Island	401	Newport News	757		
		Norfolk	757	**Québec**	
South Carolina		Petersburg	804	Hull	819
Charleston	843	Richmond	804	Laval	450
Columbia	803	Roanoke	540	Montréal	514
Greenville	864	Virginia Beach	757	Québec	418
Spartanburg	864			Sherbrooke	819
		Washington		**Saskatchewan**	306
South Dakota	605	Bellevue	425/564		
		Olympia	360/564	**Yukon**	867
Tennessee		Seattle	206/564		
Chattanooga	423	Spokane	509	ATLANTIC	
Clarksville	931	Tacoma	253/564	Anguilla	264
Jackson	731	Yakima	509	Antigua & Barbuda	268
Knoxville	865			Bahamas	242
Memphis	901	**Washington, D.C.**	202	Barbados	246
Nashville	615			Bequia	784
		West Virginia	304	Bermuda	441
Texas				British Virgin Islands	284
Abilene	325/915	**Wisconsin**		Cayman Islands	345
Amarillo	806	Eau Claire	715	Dominica	767
Austin	512/737	Green Bay	920	Dominican Republic	809
Bryan	979	La Crosse	608	Grenada	473
Corpus Christi	361	Madison	608	Grenadine Islands	784
Dallas	214/469/972	Milwaukee	414	Guadeloupe	590
Del Rio	830	Racine	262	Jamaica	876
El Paso	915	Sheboygan	920	Montserrat	664
Fort Worth	682/817	Wausau	715	Mustique	784
Galveston	409			Palm Island	784
Houston	281/713/832	**Wyoming**	307	Puerto Rico	787/939
Huntsville	936			St. Kitts & Nevis	869
Irving	214/469/972	CANADA		St. Lucia	758
Laredo	956	**Alberta**		St. Pierre & Miquelon	508
Lubbock	806	Calgary	403	St. Vincent	784
Odessa	432	Edmonton	780	Trinidad & Tobago	868
Plano	214/469/972			Turks & Caicos	649
Port Arthur	409	**British Columbia**		Union Island	784
San Antonio	210	Vancouver	604/778	U.S. Virgin Islands	340
Tyler	430/903	Victoria	250		
Waco	254	**Manitoba**	204	PACIFIC	
Wichita Falls	940	**New Brunswick**	506	Guam	671
		Newfoundland	709		
Utah		**Northwest Territories**	867		
Logan	435				
Moab	435	**Nova Scotia**	902		
Ogden	385	**Nunavut**	867		
Salt Lake City	801				

International Dialing Codes

The procedure for dialing **Station-to-Station Calls** from the United States is as follows: A – dial 011, the international access code; B – dial the country code number listed below; C – dial the city code number; D – dial the local number. If your central telephone office is not equipped for International Dialing, you must dial "0" (local operator) in order to place a call. **Operator-Assisted Calls:** For person-to-person, collect, credit card, or calls charged to another number, dial "0" (local operator).

Afghanistan	93	Cape Verde	238	France	33
Albania	355	Central African Rep.	236	Paris	1
Algeria	213	Chad	235	French Antilles	596
American Samoa	684	Chile	56	French Guiana	594
Andorra	376	China	86	French Polynesia	689
Angola	244	Beijing	10	Gabon	241
Antarctica	672	Hong Kong	(Sep. listing)	Gambia	220
Argentina	54	Colombia	57	Georgia	995
Buenos Aires	11	Comoros	269	Germany	49
Armenia	374	Congo, Dem. Rep.	243	Berlin	30
Aruba	297	Congo, Rep. of	242	Ghana	233
Ascension Island	247	Cook Islands	682	Gibraltar	350
Australia	61	Costa Rica	506	Greece	30
Sydney	2	Cote d'Ivoire	225	Athens	1
Austria	43	Croatia	385	Greenland	299
Vienna	1	Cuba	53	Guatemala	502
Azerbaijan	994	Cyprus	357	Guinea	224
Bahrain	973	Czech Republic	420	Guinea-Bissau	245
Bangladesh	880	Prague	2	Guyana	592
Belarus	375	Denmark	45	Haiti	509
Belgium	32	Diego Garcia	246	Honduras	504
Brussels	2	Djibouti	253	Hong Kong	852
Belize	501	Easter Island	56	Hungary	36
Benin	229	Ecuador	593	Budapest	1
Bhutan	975	Egypt	20	Iceland	354
Bolivia	591	Cairo	2	India	91
Bosnia-Herzegovina	387	El Salvador	503	New Delhi	11
Botswana	267	Equatorial Guinea	240	Indonesia	62
Brazil	55	Eritrea	291	Jakarta	21
Rio de Janeiro	21	Estonia	372	Iran	98
Brunei	673	Ethiopia	251	Iraq	964
Bulgaria	359	Falkland Islands	500	Ireland	353
Burkina Faso	226	Faroe Islands	298	Dublin	1
Burundi	257	Fiji Islands	679	Israel	972
Cambodia	855	Finland	358	Tel Aviv-Jaffa	3
Cameroon	237			Italy	39
Canada	1			Rome	6
				Japan	81
				Tokyo	3

Jordan	962	Netherlands Antilles	599	Barcelona	93
Kazakhstan	7	Curacao	9	Sri Lanka	94
Kenya	254	New Caledonia	687	Sudan	249
Kiribati	686	New Zealand	64	Suriname	597
Korea, North	850	Nicaragua	505	Swaziland	268
Korea, South	82	Leon	311	Sweden	46
Seoul	2	Niger	227	Stockholm	8
Kuwait	965	Nigeria	234	Switzerland	41
Kyrgyzstan	996	Niue	683	Geneva	22
Laos	856	Norway	47	Zurich	1
Latvia	371	Oman	968	Syria	963
Lebanon	961	Pakistan	92	Taiwan	886
Beirut	01	Palau	680	Taipei	2
Lesotho	266	Palestinian National Authority	970	Tajikistan	992
Liberia	231			Tanzania	255
Libya	218	Panama	507	Thailand	66
Liechtenstein	423	Papua New Guinea	675	Bangkok	2
Lithuania	370	Paraguay	595	Togo	228
Luxembourg	352	Peru	51	Tonga	676
Macao	853	Philippines	63	Tunisia	216
Macedonia	389	Manila	2	Turkey	90
Madagascar	261	Poland	48	Istanbul	216/212
Malawi	265	Warsaw	22	Turkmenistan	993
Malaysia	60	Portugal	351	Uganda	256
Maldives	960	Qatar	974	Ukraine	380
Mali	223	Reunion Island	262	Kiev	44
Malta	356	Romania	40	United Arab Emirates	971
Martinique	596	Russia	7	Abu Dhabi	2
Mauritania	222	Moscow	095	United Kingdom	44
Mexico	52	St. Petersburg	812	Belfast, N. Ire.	1232
Mexico City	55	Rwanda	250	Cardiff, Wales	2920
Micronesia	691	Saipan	670	Glasgow, Scot.	141
Moldova	373	San Marino	378	London, Eng.	207/208
Monaco	33	Saudi Arabia	966	United States	1
Mongolia	976	Senegal	221	Uruguay	598
Morocco	212	Serbia	381	Uzbekistan	998
Casablanca	2	Sierra Leone	232	Vatican City	39
Mozambique	258	Singapore	65	Venezuela	58
Myanmar	95	Slovak Republic	421	Caracas	212
Namibia	264	Slovenia	386	Vietnam	84
Nepal	977	Solomon Islands	677	Hanoi	4
Netherlands	31	Somalia	252	Ho Chi Minh City	8
Amsterdam	20	South Africa	27	Western Samoa	685
The Hague	70	Johannesburg	11	Yemen	967
		Spain	34	Zambia	260
				Zimbabwe	263

Toll-Free Numbers

Airlines
Aer Lingus	800-223-6537
Aeroflot	888-340-6400
Aero Mexico	800-237-6639
Air Canada	888-247-2262
Air France	800-237-2747
Air India	800-223-7776
Air New Zealand	800-262-1234
Alaska Airlines	800-426-0333
Alitalia Airlines	800-223-5730
Aloha Airlines	800-367-5250
American Airlines, American Eagle	800-433-7300
America West	800-235-9292
ANA: All Nippon Airways	800-235-9262
Asiana Airlines	800-227-4262
Austrian Airlines	800-843-0002
British Airways	800-247-9297
BWIA International	800-538-2942
Continental Airlines	800-525-0280
Delta Air Lines	800-221-1212
El Al Israel Airlines	800-223-6700
Finnair	800-950-5000
Iberia Airlines	800-772-4642
Icelandair	800-223-5500
Japan Airlines	800-525-3663
Jet Blue Airways	800-538-2583
KLM: Royal Dutch Airlines	800-225-2525
Korean Air	800-438-5000
Lufthansa	800-645-3880
Mexicana Airlines	800-531-7921
Northwest Airlines	800-225-2525
Olympic Airlines	800-223-1226
Qantas Airways	800-227-4500
SAS: Scandinavian Airlines	800-221-2350
Saudi Arabian Airlines	800-472-8342
Singapore Airlines	800-742-3333
Southwest Airlines	800-435-9792
Swiss International Airlines	877-359-7947
United Airlines	800-241-6522
USAirways	800-428-4322
Varig Brazilian Airlines	800-468-2744
Virgin Atlantic Airways	800-862-8621

Car Rental
Alamo Rent-A-Car	800-327-9633
Avis Rent-A-Car	800-331-1212
Budget Car & Truck Rental	800-527-0700
Dollar Rent-A-Car	800-800-4000
Enterprise Rent-A-Car	800-325-8007
Hertz Rent-A-Car	800-654-3131
National Car Rental	800-227-7368
Payless Car Rental	800-237-2804
Thrifty Car Rental	800-367-2277

Courier Services
Adcom Express	800-747-7424
BAX	800-882-3338
DHL Worldwide Express	800-225-5345
Federal Express	800-238-5355
UPS: United Parcel Service	800-742-5877
United States Postal Service	800-275-8777

Credit Cards (Lost or Stolen)
American Express	800-528-4800
Diners Club/Carte Blanche	800-234-6377
Discover Card	800-347-2683
MasterCard International	800-826-2181
Optima Card	800-635-5955
Visa Worldwide	800-336-8472

Hotels, Motels and Resorts
Best Western International	800-528-1234
Choice Hotels International	800-424-6423
Clarion Hotels & Resorts	800-252-7466
Comfort Inns & Suites	800-228-5150
Courtyard (by Marriott)	800-321-2211
Days Inns	800-325-2525
DoubleTree/Guest Quarters	800-424-2900
Econo Lodges	800-553-2666
Embassy Suites	800-362-2779
Fairmont Hotels	800-223-1818
Four Seasons Hotels	800-819-5053
Hampton Inns	800-426-7866
Helmsley Hotels	800-221-4982
Hilton Hotels	800-445-8667
Holiday Inn	800-465-4329
Howard Johnson Hotels	800-446-4656
Hyatt Hotels & Resorts	800-233-1234
Intercontinental Hotels	800-327-0200
Marriott Hotels & Resorts	800-228-9290
Motel 6	800-466-8356
Nikko Hotels International	800-645-5687
Novotel Hotels	800-668-6835
Omni International Hotels	800-843-6664
Quality Inns, Hotels & Suites	800-228-5151
Radisson Hotels	800-333-3333
Ramada Worldwide	800-228-2828
Red Roof Inns	800-843-7663
Renaissance Hotels	800-468-3571
Residence Inns (by Marriott)	800-331-3131
Ritz-Carlton Hotels	800-241-3333
Sheraton Worldwide	800-325-3535
Westin Hotels & Resorts	800-228-3000
Wyndham Hotels & Resorts	800-822-4200

Railways and Bus Lines
Amtrak	800-523-8720
Greyhound	800-231-2222
Trailways	800-858-8555

For additional toll-free listings, dial 1-800-555-1212 or check your local directory.

Abbreviations

Admin	Administration
AFB	Air Force Base
Afr	Africa
AK	Alaska
AL	Alabama
Amer	American
Ant	Antarctica
AR	Arkansas
Arg	Argentina
Arpt	Airport
Aust	Austria
Austral	Australia
AZ	Arizona
Bah	Bahamas
Bar	Barbados
Bel	Belgium
Bldg	Building
Bol	Bolivia
Bra	Brazil
Brdg	Bridge
C Arpt	County Airport
CA	California
Can	Canada
Cent Sta	Central Station
Chan	Channel
CO	Colorado
Col	Columbia
Conv Ctr	Convention Center
Corp	Corporation
CP	County Park
CR	Costa Rica
CRA	County Recreation Area
CT	Connecticut
Ctr	Center
Czech Rep	Czech Republic
DC	District of Coumbia
DE	Delaware
Dept	Department
Dom Rep	Dominican Republic
El *Sal*	El Salvador
Environ	Environment(al)
Exh	Exhibition
Falk Isl	Falkland Islands
FL	Florida
FP	Forest Preserve
Fr	France
GA	Georgia

Ger	Germany
Gdn(s)	Garden(s)
Govt	Government(al)
Gr	Greece
Hdqrs	Headquarters
HI	Hawaii
Hist	Historic(al)
HS	Historic Site
Hts	Heights
IA	Iowa
ID	Idaho
IL	Illinois
IN	Indiana
Indo	Indonesia
Info	Information
Inst	Institution(al)
Intl	International
IR	Indian Reservation
Ire	Ireland
Isl	Island
Jam	Jamaica
KS	Kansas
KY	Kentucky
LA	Louisiana
Lab	Laboratory
MA	Massachusetts
MD	Maryland
ME	Maine
Mem	Memorial
Mex	Mexico
MI	Michigan
Mil	Military
MN	Minnesota
MO	Missouri
Mon	Monument
Mong	Mongolia
MS	Mississippi
MT	Montana
Mt(s)	Mount / Mountain(s)
Mus	Museum
NAS	Naval Air Station
Natl	National
NC	North Carolina
ND	North Dakota
NE	Nebraska
Neth	Netherlands
NF	National Forest
NH	New Hampshire

NG	National Grasslands
NHS	National Historic Site
NHP	National Historical Park
Nic	Nicaragua
NJ	New Jersey
NL	National Lakeshore
NM	National Monument
NM	New Mexico
N Mem	National Memorial
NMP	National Military Park
Nor	Norway
N Pres	National Preserve
NP	National Park
NRA	National Recreation Area
NS	National Seashore
NV	Nevada
NWR	National Wildlife Refuge
NY	New York
Obs	Observatory
OH	Ohio
OK	Oklahoma
OR	Oregon
PA	Pennsylvania
Pen	Peninsula
Phil	Philippines
Pk	Peak
PNG	Papua New Guinea
Prov P	Provincial Park
Port	Portugal
PR	Puerto Rico
Pres	Preserve
Pt(e)	Point(e)
R	River
RA	Recreation Area
Res	Reservation
Rfg	Refuge
RI	Rhode Island
RR	Railroad
RP	Regional Park
R Pres	Regional Preserve
Rus	Russia

S Afr	South Africa	Sta	Station	*Uru*	Uruguay
SC	South Carolina	Stad	Stadium	UT	Utah
Sd	Sound	Str	Strait	VA	Virginia
SD	South Dakota	SU	State University	*Ven*	Venezuela
SF	State Forest	Svc	Service	Vol	Volcano
SHM	State Historical Monument	*Swe*	Sweden	VT	Vermont
		Switz	Switzerland	WA	Washington
SHP	State Historical Park	Syr	Syria	*WI*	West Indies
SHS	State Historic Site	Tech	Technology	WI	Wisconsin
SM	State Monument	Term	Terminal	WMA	Wildlife Management Area
SNA	State Natural Area	Terr	Territory		
SP	State Park	TN	Tennessee	WR	Wildlife Refuge
Sq	Square	TX	Texas	WV	West Virginia
SRA	State Recreation Area	U	University	WY	Wyoming
St(e)	Saint(e)	UK	United Kingdom	*Yug*	Yugoslavia

Index

A

Aachen, 23 **B3**
Aalen, 23 **D2**
Aalsmeer, 30 **C5**
Aalst, 31 **E3**
Aarberg, 37 **A3**
Aasiaat, 102 **C7**
Aba, 44 **D1**
Abadan, 49 **F4**
Abakan, 55 **A3**
Abassiya, 50 **C3**
Abbeville, SC 121 **E4**
ABC TV Ctr, CA 172 **D8**
Abcoude, 30 **D5**
Abdin, 50 **C2**
Abéché, 45 **E2**
Abelardo L Rodriguez Intl Arpt, 169 **H1**
Abeokuta, 44 **C1**
Aberdeen, *Austral* 75 **C1**
Aberdeen, ID 135 **F2**
Aberdeen, MS 129 **H5**
Aberdeen, SD 110 **F6**, 126 **D6**

Aberdeen, *UK* 14 **C2**, 18 **D6**
Aberdeen Country Park, 75 **C1**
Aberystwyth, 19 **C3**
Abha, 49 **E2**
Abiathar Pk, WY 180 **D5**
Abidjan, 44 **B1**
Abiko, 68 **E8**
Abilene, KS 127 **E2**
Abilene, TX 111 **F3**, 128 **D4**, 178 **D2**
Abingdon, VA 118 **C1**, 121 **E6**
Abington, PA 145 **E6**
Abitibi R, 124 **F8**
Ablis, 28 **A5**
Abramtsevo, 56 **D5**
Absaroka Beartooth Wilderness, MT 180 **C6**
Absaroka Range, MT 180 **C6**
Abu an-Numrus, 50 **B1**
Abu Dhabi, 49 **G3**
Abu Ghaush, 50 **C4**
Abu Kamal, 49 **E5**
Abud, 50 **C6**

Abuja, 44 **D1**
Academy Gdn, PA 145 **G5**
Acadia NP, ME 114 **F5**, 179 **H5**, 186 **C5**
Acadia Wild Gdn, ME 186 **D5**
Acapulco, 96 **C2**
Accomac, VA 119 **G2**
Accra, 44 **C1**
Achau, 42 **E6**
Achinsk, 55 **A3**
Acilia, 40 **B4**
Acklins Isl, 94 **D5**
Acoma IR, NM 131 **D3**
Acropolis, 43 **B2**
Ad Dahna, 49 **F4**
Ad Dammam, 49 **F4**
Ad Diwaniyah, 49 **F5**
Adachi-Ku, 68 **C7**
Adams, MA 115 **A3**, 117 **H3**
Adams NHS, MA 139 **E2**
Adams Park, GA 152 **A3**
Adamsville, FL 154 **D4**
Adana, 48 **D6**
Addis Ababa, 45 **G1**
Addison, IL 159 **B4**

Addison, TX 165 **F5**
Addyston, OH 151 **B2**
Adelaide, 76 **D3**, 80 **A3**
Adelphi, MD 148 **E8**
Aden, 49 **F1**
Adirondack Mts, 112 **E6**, 117 **G4**
Adirondack Park, NY 117 **G5**
Adjuntas, 122 **B2**
Adliswil, 37 **E1**
Admiralty Island NM, AK 136 **E5**, 178 **B1**
Admiralty Islands, 76 **C2**
Adobe Dam CRA, AZ 168 **B6**
Adriatic Sea, 17 **F4**, 24 **D4**
Aegean Sea, 17 **H3**, 25 **G3**, 48 **C6**
Aerial Tram, WY 181 **F2**
Aeroporto da Portela, 38 **B7**
Affori, 40 **B2**
Affton, MO 162 **B1**
Afghanistan, 49 **H6**, 58 **A7**
Africa, 44 – 48
Afton, WY 130 **C7**

Agacli, 43 **D4**

Agadez, 44 **D2**

Agadir, 44 **B4**

Agawam R, MA 184 **A6**

Agazzi NWR, MN 126 **E8**

Agerup, 36 **A6**

Agincourt, 104 **F7**

Agra, 58 **C6**

Agrate, 40 **D3**

Agricola Oriental, 98 **C3**

Agrigento, 24 **C1**

Agrinia, 25 **E3**

Agua Blanca, 99 **H4**

Agua Prieta, 131 **C1**

Aguadilla, 122 **A3**

Aguascalientes, 96 **C4**

Aguja Pt, 84 **B3**

Ahaggar, 44 **D3**

Ahames, 43 **B4**

Ahmadabad, 58 **B5**

Ahrensburg, 22 **D5**

Ahrensfelde, 32 **E7**

Ahumada, 131 **E1**

Ahvaz, 49 **F5**

Ahwar, 49 **F1**

Aiea, HI 177 **F3**

Aigáleo, 43 **B2**

Aiken, SC 121 **F4**

Aïr, 44 **D3**

Airport West, 79 **B4**

Aix-en-Provence, 21 **F4**

Ajaccio, 16 **D3**, 24 **A4**

Ajax, 116 **B4**

Ajdabiya, 48 **B5**

Ajijic, 99 **G1**

Ajuda, 38 **A6**

Ajusco, 98 **B2**

Akasaka, 69 **A3**

Akasaka Sta, 69 **A3**

Akashicho, 69 **F1**

Akersberga, 36 **F7**

Akharnaï, 43 **B4**

Akhisar, 25 **H3**

Akita, 66 **F6**

Akhmadkala, 53 **B3**

Akpinar, 43 **D4**

Akron, NY 116 **C3**

Akron, OH 112 **D5**, 118 **C5**

Akureyn, 14 **B5**

Al Amarah, 49 **F5**

Al Aqabah, 48 **D4**

Al Barajil, 50 **B2**

Al Basrah, 49 **F5**

Al Bayda, 45 **E4**, 48 **B5**

Al Buraymi, 49 **G3**

Al Fashir, 45 **F2**

Al Fayyum, 45 **F4**, 48 **C4**

Al Hasakah, 48 **E6**

Al Hillah, 49 **E5**

Al Hudaydah, 49 **E1**

Al Hufuf, 49 **F3**

Al Jawf, 45 **E3**, 48 **B3**

Al Jizah, 45 **F4**, 48 **C4**

Al Kasab, 49 **G4**

Al Kharijah, 45 **F3**

Al Kunayyisah, 50 **B1**

Al Mubarraz, 49 **F4**

Al Mukalla, 49 **F1**

Al Qadarif, 45 **G2**

Al Ubayyid, 45 **F2**, 48 **C1**

Alabama, 97 **F6**, 113 **C3**, 120 **C2**, 179 **F2**

Alabama R, 120 **C3**

Alachua, FL 123 **E5**

Alameda, CA 174 **C5**

Alameda Park, 98 **B3**

Alamo, CA 174 **D6**

Alamo, The, TX 163 **G2**

Alamo Band Navajo IR, NM 128 **A5**

Alamo Hts, TX 163 **G3**

Alamogordo, NM 128 **B4**, 131 **E2**

Alamosa, CO 127 **A3**, 131 **E4**

Alampur, 65 **D1**

Åland Isl, 15 **F3**, 22 **F8**

Alaska, 100 **A6**, 136, 178 **A3**

Alaska Falls SP, HI 137 **F2**

Alaska Peninsula, AK 136 **B5**

Alaska Peninsula NWR, AK 136 **B5**

Alaska Range, 100 **A6**, 136 **C6**

Albacete, 21 **C2**

Albán, 90 **A3**

Albania, 17 **G3**, 25 **E4**, 45 **E6**

Albany, Austral 76 **A3**

Albany, CA 174 **C6**

Albany, GA 113 **D3**, 120 **D3**

Albany, NY 112 **E6**, 117 **H2**, 179 **G5**

Albany, OR 134 **B3**

Albany, VT 114 **B3**

Albemarle Sd, NC 187 **E6**

Alberhill, CA 171 **G2**

Albert Lea, MN 124 **B4**

Alberta, 101 **D4**

Alberton, MT 135 **E5**

Alberton, S Afr 51 **G2**

Albertsland, 36 **B5**

Albertson, NY 143 **H4**

Albi, 21 **D4**

Albion, NY 116 **C4**

Alboranse, 21 **C1**

Ålborg, 15 **E2**, 22 **D6**

Albright Visitor Ctr, WY 180 **B5**

Albuquerque, NM 111 **D4**, 128 **B6**, 131 **E3**, 178 **C3**

Albury, 77 **E3**

Alcántara Reservoir, 21 **B3**

Alcorcon, 39 **A1**

Aldan, 55 **D4**

Aldan R, 55 **E4**

Aldershot, 26 **A5**

Aldine, TX 166 **B5**

Aleksandrovskaya, 57 **F1**

Alencon, 20 **D6**

Alenuihaha Chan, HI 137 **E2**

Aleppo, 48 **D6**

Alert, Can 82 **D6**, 102 **A8**

Alert, OH 151 **A4**

Alessandria, 24 **A5**

Ålesund, 14 **D3**

Alexander Archipelago, 101 **A4**, 136 **E5**

Alexander City, AL 120 **D3**

Alexander Isl, 83 **D4**

Alexandra, 51 **G3**

Alexandria, Egypt 45 **F4**, 48 **C5**

Alexandria, KY 118 **A3**

Alexandria, LA 113 **A3**, 129 **G4**

Alexandria, MN 124 **A6**, 126 **F6**

Alexandria, VA 112 **E5**, 119 **F3**, 148 **C5**

Alexandroupoli, 25 **G4**

Alfred, NY 116 **C2**

Algeria, 16 **C1**, 21 **E1**, 44 **C4**

Alghero, 24 **A3**

Algiers, 16 **C2**, 21 **E2**, 44 **C5**

Algona, WA 176 **C1**

Alhambra, CA 170 **C5**

Alibahadir, 43 **F4**

Alicante, 21 **D2**

Alice, TX 129 **E2**

Alice Springs, 76 **C4**

Alipur, 64 **D8**

Aliso Viejo, CA 171 **E1**

Aliso-Wood Canyons RP, CA 171 **E1**

Alkali Lake, OR 132 **C8**

Allahabad, 58 **C5**

Allegany SP, NY 116 **B2**, 119 **E6**

Allegheny C Arpt, PA 146 **C5**

Allegheny Mts, WV 119 **E3**

Allegheny NF, PA 116 **B1**, 119 **E6**

Allegheny NRA, PA 116 **B1**

Allegheny Obs, PA 146 **B7**

Allegheny Reservoir, PA 116 **B1**

Allegheny R, PA 119 D5

Allen Park, MI 156 C5

Allentown, PA 112 E6, 119 G5

Alley Isl, ME 186 A5

Alliance, NE 127 C4, 130 F6

Alligator Lake, NC 187 E4

Alligator River, NC 187 E4

Alligator River NWR, NC 187 F5

Allison Park, PA 146 C8

Allstate Arena, IL 158 B5

Alma, 103 D2

Alma-Ata, 59 C8

Almada, 38 B6

Almaden Quicksilver CP, CA 175 F1

Almagro, 89 A3

Almárgem do Bispo, 38 A8

Almería, 16 B2, 21 C2

Almirante Brown, 88 E5

Almkerk, 30 D1

Aloha, OR 177 E5

Alorton, IL 162 C1

Alpena, MI 112 C6, 124 F6

Alpharetta, GA 120 D4

Alphen aan den Rijn, 30 C4

Alpine, TX 128 C3, 131 F1

Alpine, WY 135 G2

Alps, 20 F5, 23 C1, 24 B6, 44 D6

Alsip, IL 159 D2

Alsónémedi, 42 B5

Alsopakony, 42 C5

Alta, 36 F6

Alta Plaza, CA 173 B2

Alta Vista, 105 B2

Altadena, CA 170 C6

Altamont, OR 132 B8

Altamonte Springs, FL 153 G5

Altamura, 24 D3

Altar of the Earth, 73 E3

Altay, 55 B2, 58 F8

Altay Mts, 55 A3, 58 E8

Altiplano, 84 D1

Altlandsberg, 32 F7

Altmannsdorf, 42 E7

Alto Da Moóca, 92 B4

Alton, NH 115 C4

Altona, 79 A3

Altona Bay, 79 A3

Altona East, 79 A3

Altona North, 79 A3

Altoona, PA 112 D5, 119 E5

Alturas, CA 132 C7, 134 C1

Altus, OK 128 D5

Alva, FL 123 E3

Alva, OK 127 E1, 129 E6

Álvaro Obregón, 98 A3

Ama, LA 163 E5

Amadora, 38 A7

Amagaski, 70 C5

Amarillo, TX 111 E4, 128 D5, 178 D3

Amaroúsion, 43 C3

Amazon Basin, 84 D4

Amazon R, 84 D3

Ambato, 84 B4

Ambler, PA 144 D6

Ambon, 61 F2, 80 A4

Amdanga, 65 F3

Amelia Earhart Pk, CA 182 D3

American Canyon, CA 174 C4

American Consulate, 74 C6

American Falls, ID 135 F2

American Highland, 83 D1

American Mem Library, 33 E1

American Mus of Natural History, NY 141 D4

American Samoa, 80 D3

American U, DC 148 C7

American West Arena, AZ 168 B3

Americus, GA 120 D3

Amersham, 26 A8

Amery Ice Shelf, 83 D1

Amherst, Can 103 E2

Amherst, MA 115 B2

Amiens, 20 D7

Amistad NRA, TX 128 D3

Amman, 48 D5

Ammassalik, 102 E7

Ammerstol, 30 C2

Ammon, ID 130 B7

Amora, 38 B5

Amritsar, 58 C6

Amstelveen, 30 D5

Amsterdam, Neth 16 D6, 20 E8, 23 B4, 30 D6

Amsterdam, NY 117 G3

Amsterdam Cent Sta, 30 D6

Amtrak Auto Train Term, FL 153 H6

Amtrak Sta, OH 150 D7

Amu Darya R, 53 C1

Amundsen Gulf, 100 D6, 136 F8

Amundsen Sea, 83 C4

Amuntai, 61 D2

Amur R, 55 E3, 66 A3

An Nafud, 49 E4

An Najaf, 49 E5

An Nasiriyah, 49 F5

Anaconda, MT 130 B8, 135 F4

Anadolufeneri, 43 F4

Anadoluhisari, 43 E3

Anadyr, 54 F7

Anaheim, CA 133 D2, 170 D3

Anaktuvuk Pass, AK 136 D8

Anápolis, 85 F1

Añasco, 122 A3

Anatakya, 48 D6

Anchorage, AK 82 A5, 100 A6, 136 C6, 178 B1

Ancient Tomb, 70 B5

Ancol Dreamland, 64 B8

Ancona, 17 E4, 24 C4

Anda, 66 C7

Andalusia, PA 145 G5

Andaman Islands, 59 E3

Andaman Sea, 59 F3

Andelfingen, 37 F3

Anderlecht, 31 F2

Anderson, CA 132 B7

Anderson, IN 118 A4, 125 E3

Anderson, SC 121 E5

Anderson Park, FL 154 B6

Andes, 84 B4, 84 D1, 86 A6

Andheri, 65 B3

Andijon, 53 E1

Andingmen, 73 E3

Andorra, 16 C3, 21 E4

Andover, ME 114 C5

Andover, MA 138 C7

Andrews, TX 128 C4, 131 F2

Andrews AFB, MD 148 F6

Andreyevskoye, 56 D2

Andria, 24 D3

Andros Isl, 94 C5

Androscoggin R, ME 114 D5

Andújar, 21 B2

Ang mo Kio, 63 F2

Angara R, 55 B3

Angarn, 36 E8

Angarsk, 55 B3

Angeles, 60 D5

Angers, 20 D6

Angleton, TX 129 F2

Angola, 47 E5

Angola, IN 118 A6, 125 E4

Angono, 62 D2

Angoulême, 20 D5

Anguilla, 95 G4

Ángyálföld, 42 B7

Anheuser-Busch Brewery, MO 162 C1

Aniakchak NM & Pres, AK 136 C5, 178 A1

Ankara, 45 F5, 48 D6

Ann Arbor, MI 112 C6, 118 B6, 125 F4

Anna Maria, FL 123 E3, 154 A1

Annaba, 16 D2, 24 A1, 44 D5

Annandale, VA 148 B5

Annandale-on-Hudson, NY 117 G2

Annapolis, MD 112 E5, 119 G3

Anne Frank House, 30 D6

Annecy, 23 B1

Annen, 34 F7

Annino, 57 F1

Anniston, AL 120 D4

Annobón, 46 C6

Ano Liosia, 43 B4

Anolaima, 90 A3

Anqing, 67 B3

Ansan, 72 B5

Ansel Adams Wilderness, CA 182 D2

Anshan, 55 E2, 60 C8, 66 C6

Antalya, 48 C6

Antananarivo, 47 H4

Antarctic Pen, 83 E4

Antarctica, 83

Antelope Flats, WY 181 G3

Anthony, NM 131 D1

Anticosti Isl, 103 E3

Antigo, WI 124 D6

Antigua & Barbuda, 95 H3

Antímono, 90 B4

Antioch, CA 174 F7

Antioch, IL 158 B8

Antipolo, 62 D2

Antler Pk, WY 180 A5

Antofagasta, 86 A6

Antsirabe, 47 H3

Antsiranana, 47 H4

Antwerp, 16 D6, 20 E7, 23 B3, 31 G6

Antwerp Intl Arpt, 31 G5

Anyang, 55 D1, 60 B7, 67 A4, 72 C5

Anza-Borrego Desert SP, CA 133 E2

Aomori, 66 F6

Aosta, 23 B1, 24 A5

Apalachee Bay, FL 122 D5

Apalachicola, FL 122 C5

Apalachicola NF, FL 120 D2, 122 C6

Apatity, 15 G5, 52 D6

Apennine, 24 C4

Apennines Mts, 17 E4

Apia, 80 D3

Apollo Beach, FL 154 D3

Apopka, FL 123 F4, 153 F5

Apoquindo, 87 H3

Apostle Islands NL, WI 124 C7, 179 E5

Appalachian Mts, 103 D1, 112 E5, 118 D2, 120 D5

Appio, 40 C5

Appleton, WI 112 B6, 124 D5

Appomattox, VA 119 E2

Appomattox Court House NHP, VA 179 G3

Aptucxet Trading Post Mus, MA 184 B5

Aqtau, 53 B2

Aqtobe, 53 C3

Aquarium, OH 150 D7

Aquarium, WA 176 B5

Ar Ram, 50 D5

Ar Ramadi, 49 E5

Ar Raqqah, 48 D6

Arab, AL 120 C4

Arabi, LA 163 G5

Arabian Pen, 49 F3

Arabian Sea, 49 H2, 59 A4

Aracaju, 85 H2

Arafura Sea, 76 A1, 76 C6, 80 A4

Araguaia R, 85 F2

Aral, 53 D2

Aral Sea, 53 C2

Arapaho NF, CO 127 A3

Aransas NWR, TX 129 F2

Aras R, 49 F6

Arashiyama, 70 E8

Aravaca, 39 A4

Arboga, 22 E8

Arboretum & Nature Ctr, TX 166 B4

Arbutus, MD 147 C2

Arc de Triomphe, 29 B3

Arc Dome, NV 132 E6

Arcadia, CA 170 D5

Arcadia, FL 123 E3

Arcata, CA 132 A7

Arch, 37 B4

Archbald, PA 117 F1

Archer, FL 123 E5

Arches NP, UT 130 C5, 178 C4

Arco, ID 135 F3

Arcola, TX 166 B1

Arctic Bay, 102 A6

Arctic Circle, 82, 100 A7, 102 D7, 136 A8

Arctic NWR, AK 136 D8

Arctic Ocean, 100 B8, 136 B8

Arctic Red River, 136 E8

Ardeatino, 40 C5

Ardebil, 49 F6

Arden Hills, MN 161 D4

Ardmore, OK 129 E5

Ardmore, PA 144 C3

Arecibo, 122 B2

Areeiro, 38 B6

Arendal, 22 C7

Arequipa, 84 C1

Arese, 40 B3

Arezzo, 24 B4

Arganzuela, 39 C2

Argenteuil, 28 C7

Argentina, 86 B4

Argonne Natl Lab, IL 159 B2

Århus, 15 E2, 22 D6

Arica, 84 C1

Arizona, 96 B6, 111 C4, 131 B2, 178 B3

Arizona Creek, WY 181 G6

Arizona SU, AZ 168 C3

Arkadelphia, AR 129 G5

Arkansas, 97 E6, 113 B4, 129 G5, 179 E3

Arkansas City, KS 127 F2

Arkansas R, 110 E5, 113 A4, 125 B1, 127 C2, 129 F6, 131 E4, 178 D3

Arkhangelsk, 15 H5, 52 D5, 82 E8

Arkhange I'skoye, 56 A4

Arlanda Arpt, 36 D8

Arlington, MA 139 C4

Arlington, TX 129 E4, 164 D2

Arlington, VT 115 A3

Arlington, VA 119 F3, 148 C6

Arlington Conv Ctr, TX 164 D3

Arlington Hts, IL 158 B5

Arlington Hts, OH 151 D3

Arlington Natl Cemetery, VA 148 C6

Armenia, 45 G5

Armenia, Col 84 C5

Armidale, 77 F3

Arncliffe, 78 E6

Arnhem, 20 E8, 23 B4

Arnhem Land, 76 C6

Arnold, IL 132 C5

Arnold, PA 146 F8

Arpádföld, 42 B7

Arpajon, 28 C5

Arqalyq, 53 E3

Arras, 23 A3

Arrecife, 90 A6

Arrentela, 38 C5

Arroyo, 122 C1

Arroyo Hondo, 99 G6

Arsenicker Keys, FL 188 D3

Art Gallery of Ontario, 104 D6

Art Museum, WA 176 B5

Artesia, NM 131 F2

Arthabaska, 114 B6

Arturo Merino Benítiz Intl Arpt, 87 E3

Aruba, 84 C6, 95 E2

Arujá, 92 **D6**

Arusha, 47 **G6**

Arvada, CO 167 **F4**

Arvada Ctr for the Arts & Humanities, CO 167 **F4**

Arviat, 101 **F4**

Arvika, 22 **D8**

Arvin, CA 133 **D3**

Aryiroupolis, 43 **B2**

As Sulayyil, 49 **F2**

Asahikawa, 66 **F7**

Asaka, 68 **B8**

Asansol, 58 **E5**

Asbestos, 114 **B6**

Ascensión, 128 **A3**

Ascension Isl, 46 **A5**

Ascoli Piceno, 24 **C4**

Asenovgrad, 25 **G5**

Ash Springs, NV 132 **F5**

Ashburton, 79 **D2**

Ashdod, 50 **A4**

Ashdown, AR 129 **F5**

Asheboro, NC 121 **G5**

Asheville, NC 113 **D4**, 121 **E5**

Ashfield, 78 **D6**

Ashford Hollow, NY 116 **B2**

Ashgabat, 49 **G6**, 53 **B1**

Ashiya, 70 **B6**

Ashkhabad, 58 **A8**

Ashland, CA 175 **D4**

Ashland, ME 114 **E7**

Ashland, OH 118 **C5**

Ashland, OR 132 **A8**

Ashland, WI 124 **C6**

Ashley NF, UT 135 **G1**

Ashmore & Cartier Islands, 76 **B4**

Asia, 58 – 61, 66

Asia Minor, 48 **C6**

Asmara, 45 **G2**, 49 **E1**

Aspen, CO127 **A3**, 130 **D5**

Aspen Park, CO 167 **E1**

Aspern, 42 **F7**

Aspropirgos, 43 **A3**

Assab, 45 **G2**

Assateague Island, MD 119 **H2**

Assateague Island NS, MD 179 **H4**

Asse, 31 **F3**

Assemblé Nationale, 29 **C2**

Assen, 20 **F8**, 23 **B4**

Assiniboia, 126 **A8**

Assiniboine Park & Zoo, 107 **F5**

Assinippi, MA 139 **F1**

Astana, 53 **E3**

Asti, 24 **A5**

Astor, FL 123 **F5**

Astoria, NY 143 **E4**

Astoria, OR 134 **B4**

Astrakhan, 53 **B3**

Astrodome, TX 166 **B3**

Astroworld, TX 166 **B3**

Asunción, 86 **B6**

Aswan, 45 **G3**, 48 **D3**

Aswan High Dam, 48 **D3**

Asyut, 45 **F4**, 48 **C4**

At Taif, 49 **E2**

At Talibiyah, 50 **B1**

At Tayyibah, 50 **D5**

Atacama Desert, 84 **D1**, 86 **A6**

Atar, 44 **A3**

Atarot Arpt, 50 **D5**

Atascadero, CA 133 **C4**

Ataturk Arpt, 43 **D2**

Atbarah, 45 **G3**

Atchison, KS 125 **A3**, 127 **F3**

Atequiaza, 99 **H2**

Athabasca R, 101 **D3**

Athens, AL 120 **C5**

Athens, GA 113 **D4**, 121 **E4**

Athens, Gr 17 **H2**, 25 **F3**, 43 **B3**, 45 **F5**, 48 **B6**

Athens, OH 118 **C4**

Athens, TN 120 **D5**, 125 **F1**

Athens U, 43 **B3**

Atherton, CA 175 **C3**

Athlone, 19 **B4**

Athol, MA 115 **B3**

Atikokan, 103 **A3**

Atizapán, 98 **A5**

Atlanta, GA 97 **F6**, 113 **D4**, 120 **D4**, 152 **A3**, 179 **G2**

Atlanta History Ctr, GA 152 **B5**

Atlanta Mem Park, GA 152 **B4**

Atlanta State Farmer's Market, GA 152 **B1**

Atlantic Beach, FL 123 **F6**

Atlantic Beach, NY 143 **G1**

Atlantic City, NJ 112 **F5**, 119 **H4**

Atlantic Coastal Plain, 113 **E4**

Atlantic Ocean, 16 **A5**, 20 **B6**, 85 **G6**, 86 **C5**, 95 **F6**, 97 **H6**, 103 **F1**

Atlas Mts, 16 **A1**, 21 **E1**, 44 **C5**

Atlavik, 136 **E8**

Atmore, AL 122 **B6**

Atomium, 31 **G2**

Atsugi, 68 **A6**

Atteridgeville, 51 **G6**

Attica, NY 116 **C3**

Atwater, CA 132 **C5**

Atyrau, 53 **C3**

Atzgersdorf, 42 **D7**

Auberry, CA 133 **C4**

Aubervilliers, 28 **D7**

Aubre Cliff, AZ 183 **A1**

Auburn, AL 120 **D3**

Auburn, CA 132 **C6**

Auburn, IN 118 **A6**

Auburn, ME 115 **D4**

Auburn, NE 127 **F3**

Auburn, NY 116 **D3**

Auburn, WA 176 **C2**

Auckland, 77 **H2**, 80 **C2**

Auckland Islands, 80 **C1**

Auderghem, 31 **G1**

Audubon, NJ 145 **F1**

Audubon, PA 144 **A6**

Audubon Park & Zoological Gdn, LA 163 **F5**

Augsburg 17 **E5**, 23 **D2**

Augusta, GA 113 **D4**

Augusta, ME 112 **F7**, 114 **F5**

Augusta, SC 121 **F4**

Aurelio, 40 **C5**, 41 **A3**

Aurillac, 20 **E5**

Aurora, CO 127 **A3**, 130 **E5**, 167 **H2**

Aurora, TX 164 **A6**

Austral Islands, 81 **E3**

Austin, MN 124 **B5**

Austin, NV 132 **E6**

Austin, TX 96 **D5**, 111 **F3**, 129 **E3**, 178 **D2**

Austral Islands, 81 **E3**

Australia, 76 **C4**, 80 **A3**

Australian Capital Terr, 77 **E3**

Austria, 17 **E5**, 23 **E2**, 24 **C6**, 44 **D6**

Autodrome, 40 **C3**

Auxerre, 23 **A3**

Avalanche Pk, WY 180 **D3**

Avalon, PA 146 **B7**

Avarua, 80 **D3**

Avellaneda, 86 **B5**, 88 **E6**

Avellino, 24 **C3**

Avenal, CA 133 **C4**

Aventine Hill, 41 **D1**

Aventura, FL 155 **G3**

Aviemore, 18 **D6**

Avignon, 16 **D4**, 20 **E5**

Ávila, 21 **B3**

Avon, NY 116 **C3**

Avon, NC 187 **H2**

Avon, OH 150 **A6**

Avon Lake, OH 150 **A7**

Avon Park, FL 123 **F3**

Avondale, LA 163 **E4**

Avondale, MO 162 **C6**

Avondale, TX 164 **A5**

Avondale Estates, GA 152 **D4**

Avtovo, 57 **F2**

Awsim, 50 **B3**

Axel Heiberg Isl, 100 **F8**

Ayacucho, 84 **C2**

Ayagoz, 53 **F2**

Ayanagar, 64 **D6**

Ayase, 68 **A6**

Aydin, 25 **H3**

Ayers Rock, 76 **C4**

Ayiá Paraskeví, 43 **C3**

Ayoun el Atrous, 44 **B2**

Ayr, 14 **C1**, 18 **C5**

Azcapotzalco, 98 **B4**

Azerbaijan, 45 **H5**, 49 **E6**

Azle, TX 164 **A4**

Azores, 44 **A6**

Aztec, NM 131 **D4**, 128 **A6**

Aztec Amphitheater, AZ 183 **C2**

Aztec Stad, 98 **B1**

Azul, 86 **B4**

Azusa, CA 170 **D5**

B

Baasrode, 31 **F4**

Bab el Mandab, 49 **E1**

Babelan, 64 **C8**

Babson College Map & Globe Mus, MA 139 **B3**

Babu Bheri, 65 **D3**

Babushkin, 56 **C5**

Babuyan Isl, 67 **C1**

Back Bay, MA 140 **A3**

Back R, 100 **E5**

Backbone Mt, MD 119 **E3**

Baclaran, 62 **C1**

Bacolod, 61 **E4**

Bacoor, 62 **B1**

Bad Hersfeld, 23 **C3**

Bad River IR, WI 124 **C6**

Bad Vilbel, 35 **C4**

Badajoz, 16 **A3**, 21 **B2**

Badalona, 38 **F6**

Badarpur, 64 **E6**

Baden, Aust 42 **D5**

Baden, Switz 37 **D2**

Badhoevedorp, 30 **C5**

Badlands NP, SD 126 **C5**, 130 **F7**, 178 **D3**

Badli, 64 **D8**

Badu, 91 **E2**

Baetic Mts, 21 **C2**

Baffin Bay, 82 **D5**, 102 **B7**

Baffin Isl, 82 **D5**, 102 **B6**

Bafoussam, 44 **D1**

Baggio, 40 **B1**

Baggs, WY 135 **H1**

Baghdad, 45 **H5**, 49 **E5**

Bagladesh, 58 **E5**

Baguio, 60 **D5**

Bahamas, 94 **D6**, 97 **H5**

Bahía Blanca, 86 **B4**

Bahía Grande, 86 **B3**

Bahla Honda SP, FL 188 **C2**

Bahrain, 45 **H4**, 49 **F4**

Bahtim, 50 **C3**

Baicheng, 55 **E2**, 66 **B2**

Baidyabati, 65 **E3**

Baie-Comeau, 103 **D3**

Baie-d'Urfe, 106 **A1**

Baileys Crossroads, VA 148 **C6**

Bailianjing, 74 **E5**

Bailianjingzhen, 74 **E5**

Bainbridge, GA 120 **D2**, 122 **D6**

Bainbridge Isl, WA 176 **A5**

Bainbridge SP, Fay, WA 176 **A6**

Baixa da Banheira, 38 **C6**

Bajianfang, 73 **F4**

Baj Baj, 65 **D1**

Baja California, 96 **A5**, 111 **B3**

Baker, NV 130 **A5**, 132 **F6**

Baker City, OR 134 **D3**

Baker Isl, 80 **D4**

Baker Isl, ME 186 **D2**

Baker Lake, 100 **F5**

Bakersfield, CA 111 **B4**, 133 **D3**, 178 **A3**

Bakhtaran, 49 **F5**

Bakhtawarpur, 64 **E8**

Bakirköy, 43 **D2**

Baku, 45 **H6**, 53 **B2**

Bal Harbour, FL 155 **G2**

Bala Cynwyd, PA 144 **D4**

Balashikha, 56 **D5**

Balboa Park, CA 169 **F3**

Balch Springs, TX 165 **H3**

Balcone Hts, TX 163 **F3**

Bald Eagle, MN 161 **F4**

Bald Eagle SF, PA 119 **F5**

Bald Eagle-Otter Lake RP, MN 161 **E4**

Baldwin, NY 143 **H2**

Baldwin, PA 146 **C5**

Baldwin Harbor, NY 143 **H2**

Baldwin Park, CA 170 **D5**

Baldwinsville, NY 117 **E3**

Balearic Islands, 16 **C2**, 21 **E3**, 44 **C5**

Balearic Sea, 21 **E3**

Balgowlah, 78 **F8**

Bali, 61 **D1**

Balikesir, 25 **H4**

Balikpapan, 61 **D2**

Balingen, 23 **C2**

Balizhuang, 73 **C2**

Balkan Mts, 25 **G5**

Balkan Pen, 17 **G4**, 25 **E5**

Balkash, 58 **E3**

Balkhash, 53 **E2**

Ballarat, 76 **D2**

Balleny Isl, 83 **A3**

Ballerup, 36 **A6**

Ballston Spa, NY 117 **G3**

Bally, 65 **E2**

Bally Bridge, 65 **E2**

Ballymena, 18 **C5**

Balqash, 53 **E2**

Balsas R, 96 **D3**

Baltic Sea, 15 **F2**, 22 **F6**, 52 **A6**, 82 **F7**

Baltimore, MD 112 **E5**, 119 **G3**, 147 **C2**, 179 **H4**

Baltimore Highlands, MD 147 **D2**

Baltimore Mus of Art, MD 147 **D3**

Baltimore-Washington Intl Arpt, MD 147 **C1**

Baltimore Zoo, MD 147 **C3**

Balvanera, 89 **B2**

Balwyn, 79 **D3**

Bamako, 44 **B2**

Bamangachi, 65 **F3**

Bambari, 45 **E1**

Bamberg, 23 **D3**

Bancalari, 88 **C8**

Banda Aceh, 59 **E2**

Banda Sea, 61 **F2**

Bandar Beheshti, 49 **H4**

Bandar Seri Begawan, 61 **D3**

Bandar-e Abbas, 49 **G4**

Bandar-e Bushehr, 49 **F4**

Bandel, 65 **E4**

Bandelier NM, NM 127 **A1**, 131 **D3**, 178 **C3**

Bandera, TX 128 **D3**

Bandirma, 25 **H4**

Bandra, 65 **A3**

Bandundu, 47 **E6**

Bandung, 61 **B1**

Banff, 101 **D3**

Banfield, 88 **E6**

Bang Kapi, 63 **H6**

Bang Khun Thian, 63 **F6**

Bang Kruai, 63 **F6**

Bang Na, 63 **H4**

Bang Phlat, 63 **F6**

Bang Su, 63 **F6**

Bangalore, 59 **C4**

Bangar, 64 **D8**

Banghazi, 45 **E4**, 48 **B5**

Bangkok, 61 **A4**, 63 **G5**

Bangkok Noi, 63 **F5**

Bangor, UK 19 **D3**

Bangor, ME 103 **D2**, 112 **F7**, 114 **E5**, 179 **H6**

Bangrak, 63 **F5**

Bángu, 91 **B2**

Bangui, 45 **E1**

Banja Luka, 17 **F4**, 24 **D5**

Banjarmasin, 61 **D2**

Banjul, 44 **A3**

Bank One Ballpark, 168 **C3**

Bankhead NF, William B, AL 120 **C4**

Banks Isl, 82 **C5**, 100 **D7**

Bankstown, 78 **C6**

Bansberia, 65 **E4**

Banska Bystrica, 17 **F5**

Banstead, 26 **C6**

Bantry, 19 **A3**

Baoding, 55 **D1**, 60 **B8**, 66 **A5**

Baoji, 60 **B7**

Baoshan County, 74 **D8**

Baotou, 55 **D1**, 60 **B8**

Baqubah, 49 **E5**

Bar Harbor, ME 112 **F7**, 114 **E5**, 186 **D5**

Bar Isl, ME 186 **D5**

Barabinsk, 53 **F3**

Barajas, 39 **E4**

Barajas Arpt, 39 **F4**

Barangar, 65 **F2**

Barasat, 65 **F3**

Barbados, 85 **E6**, 95 **H2**

Barberá del Vallès, 38 **E7**

Barberini Palace, 41 **D3**

Barbican, 27 **E3**

Barbourville, KY 118 **B1**

Barbuda, 95 **H3**

Barcarena, 38 **A7**

Barcelona, 16 **C3**, 21 **E3**, 38 **E6**, 44 **D6**

Barcelona Arpt, 38 **E5**

Barceloneta, 38 **F6**

Bardstown, KY 118 **A3**, 125 **E2**

Bareilly, 58 **C6**

Barendrecht, 30 **B1**

Barents Sea, 15 **G6**, 52 **E7**, 82 **E7**

Bargachia, 65 **D2**

Bari, 17 **F3**, 24 **D3**

Barking, 26 **D7**

Barletta, 24 **D3**

Barnacle State HS, FL 155 **F1**

Barnaul, 53 **F3**

Barnes Foundation, PA 144 **D3**

Barnes Sd, FL 188 **F4**

Barnet, 26 **C8**

Barnstable, MA 115 **D2**, 184 **D5**

Barnstable Harbor, MA 184 **D5**

Barnstaple, 19 **C2**

Barnwell, SC 121 **F4**

Barquisimeto, 84 **D5**, 95 **E1**

Barra da Tijuca, 91 **C1**

Barracas, 89 **D1**

Barrackpore, 65 **F3**

Barrancabermeja, 84 **C5**

Barranquilla, 84 **C6**, 94 **D1**

Barrarico, 87 **G5**

Barre, VT 115 **B4**

Barreiro, 38 **C6**

Barrie, 103 **C1**

Barrington, IL 158 **A6**

Barrington, NJ 145 **F1**

Barrow, AK 82 **B6**, 100 **B7**, 136 **C8**

Barstow, CA 111 **B4**, 133 **E3**

Bartlesville, OK 113 **A4**, 125 **A1**, 127 **F1**, 129 **F6**

Bartlett, IL 159 **A4**

Bartlett Isl, ME 186 **A4**

Barton, OR 177 **H4**

Barton NHS, Clara, MD 148 **C7**

Bartonville, TX 164 **C6**

Baruta, 90 **C4**

Barvikha, 56 **A4**

Basel, 16 **D5**, 20 **F6**, 23 **B1**, 24 **A6**

Baseline Flat, WY 181 **F3**

Bashtil, 50 **B3**

Basibuyük, 43 **F2**

Basildon, 26 **F7**

Basin, WY 135 **H3**

Bass Harbor, ME 186 **B2**

Bass Harbor Head, ME 186 **B1**

Bass Str, 77 **E2**, 80 **B2**

Bassersdorf, 37 **F1**

Basseterre, 95 **G3**

Bastia, 24 **B4**

Bastrop, LA 129 **G4**

Basus, 50 **B3**

Bat Yam, 50 **A6**

Batan Isl, 67 **C1**

Batavia, NY 116 **C3**

Batavia, OH 118 **B3**

Batdambang, 61 **A4**

Batesville, AR 120 **A6**, 129 **G6**

Bath, ME 115 **D4**

Bath, NY 116 **D2**, 119 **F6**

Bath, UK 19 **D2**

Baths of Caracalla, 41 **E1**

Bathurst, 103 **E3**

Batna, 21 **F1**, 44 **D5**

Baton Rouge, LA 113 **B3**, 120 **A3**, 129 **G3**, 179 **E2**

Batterkinden, 37 **C3**

Battery Park, NY 141 **E1**

Battle Creek RP, MN 161 **F2**

Battle Green, MA 138 **B5**

Battle Mt, NV 132 **E7**

Batumi, 53 **A3**

Baubau, 61 **F2**

Bauerstown, PA 146 **C7**

Baulkham Hills, 78 **C8**

Bauria, 65 **D1**

Bauru, 85 **F1**

Bay City, MI 124 **F5**

Bay City, TX 129 **F2**

Bay Harbor Islands, FL 155 **G2**

Bay Minette, AL 120 **B2**, 122 **A6**

Bay of Bengal, 59 **E4**

Bay of Biscay, 16 **B4**, 20 **C5**

Bay of Campeche, 97 **E3**

Bay of Fundy, 103 **E2**

Bay Pines, FL 154 **A4**

Bay Ridge, NY 142 **C2**

Bay Village, OH 150 **A7**

Bayamo, 94 **C4**

Bayamon, 122 **B2**

Bayanbayanan, 62 **D3**

Bayanhongor, 55 **C2**, 58 **F8**

Bayji, 49 **E5**

Bayonne, Fr 21 **C4**

Bayonne, NJ 142 **C2**

Bayou Segnette SP, LA 163 **F4**

Bayreuth, 23 **D3**

Bayshore Gdns, FL 154 **B1**

Bayside, NY 143 **F4**

Bayside, WI 157 **B4**

Bayswater, 79 **F2**

Beach Grove, IN 157 **F1**

Beach Park, IL 158 **C8**

Beachwood, OH 150 **F7**

Beacon, NY 117 **G1**

Beacon Hill, Austral 78 **F8**

Beacon Hill, MA 140 **B4**

Beaconsfield, Can 106 **A3**

Beaconsfield, UK 26 **A8**

Bear Isl, ME 186 **C3**

Bear Pk, WY 135 **H2**

Beatrice, NE 127 **E3**

Beatty, NV 133 **E4**

Beaufort, SC 121 **F3**

Beaufort Sea, 82 **B6**, 100 **C7**, 136 **D8**

Beaumont, TX 113 **A3**, 129 **F3**

Beaumont Place, TX 166 **D4**

Beauport, 105 **F3**, 114 **C7**

Beaux Arts Village, WA 176 **C5**

Beaver, PA 118 **D5**

Beaver, UT 130 **B5**

Beaver Creek, AK 136 D6
Beaver R, OK 128 D6
Beaverhead NF, MT 135 F3
Beaverton, OR 177 F5
Becancour, 114 B7
Béchar, 44 C4
Bechler R, 180 A3
Bechovice, 35 F3
Beckley, WV 118 C2
Beddington, ME 114 E5
Bedford, IN 125 E2
Bedford, OH 150 E6
Bedford, PA 119 E4
Bedford, TX 164 D4
Bedford, VA 119 E1
Bedford Hts, OH 150 F6
Bedford Res, OH 150 E5
Bedford-Stuyvesant, NY 142 D3
Bedfordview, 51 G3
Bedok, 63 H2
Bee Ridge, FL 123 E3
Beecroft, 78 D8
Beeville, TX 129 E2
Behala, 65 E1
Behing Auto Mus, CA 174 C6
Beian, 55 E3, 66 C7
Beijing, 55 E1, 60 C8, 66 A5, 73 D2
Beijing Amusement Park, 73 E1
Beijing Exh Ctr, 73 D3
Beijing Railway Station, 73 E2
Beijing Zoo, 73 C3
Beira, 47 G3
Beirut, 48 D5
Beit Sira, 50 C5
Beiwucun, 73 A4
Beixinjing, 74 A6
Beixuejiatang, 74 E8
Beja, 21 A3
Bejaïa, 16 D2
Bekasi, 64 C7
Békásmegyer, 42 A8
Bel Air, MD 119 G4

Belapurpada, 65 C2
Belarus, 15 G1, 52 A5
Belas, 38 A7
Belavista, 93 E1
Belcher Islands, 103 B3
Belém, Bra 85 F4
Belém, Port 38 B6
Beleutovo, 56 C1
Belfast, ME 114 E5
Belfast, UK 14 B1, 19 C4
Belford Roxo, 91 C3
Belgium, 16 D6, 20 E7, 23 A3
Belgrade, MT 135 G4
Belgrade, Yug 17 G4, 25 E6, 45 E6
Belgrano, 88 D7
Belgravia, 27 A1
Belize, 81 H5, 84 A6, 97 F3
Belize City, 97 F3
Bell, CA 170 C4
Bella Vista, 88 B4
Bellair Beach, FL 154 A5
Bellaire, TX 166 B3
Bellavista, 87 F5
Belle Chasse, LA 163 G4
Belle Fourche, SD 126 B6
Belle Harbor, NY 143 E1
Belle Isle, FL 153 G3
Belle Isle Park, MI 156 E6
Belle View, VA 148 D5
Belleair, FL 154 A5
Belleair, VA 148 A5
Belleair Shore, FL 154 A4
Bellefontaine, OH 118 B5
Bellefontaine Neighbors, MO 162 C3
Bellefonte, PA 119 E5
Belleville, Fr 29 F3
Belleville, IL 125 C2
Belleville, NJ 142 B5
Bellevue, KY 151 D2
Bellevue, NE 127 F4
Bellevue, PA 146 B7
Bellevue, WA 176 D5
Bellflower, CA 170 C3

Bellingham, WA 110 B8, 134 B6
Bellingshausen Sea, 83 C4
Bellmawr, NJ 145 F1
Bellows Falls, VT 115 B3
Bellwood, IL 159 C4
Belmont, CA 175 B3
Belmont, MA 139 C4
Belmont, NY 119 F6
Belmont Park, CA 169 E4
Belmont Park Racetrack, NY 143 G3
Belmopan, 84 A6, 97 F3
Belo Horizonte, 85 G1
Belomorsk, 15 G4, 52 C6
Belp, 37 C2
Belrose, 78 E8
Belsele, 31 E5
Beltrami Isl SF, MN 126 F8
Beltsville, MD 148 F8
Belvedere, CA 175 A6
Belvedere, GA 152 D3
Belyayevo Bogorodskoye, 56 B3
Bemidji, MN 112 A7, 124 B7, 126 F7
Bemis Hts, NY 117 H3
Ben Gurion Intl Arpt, 50 B6
Benbrook, TX 164 A3
Bend, OR 110 B7, 134 C3
Bendigo, 77 E2
Bene Re'en, 50 A4
Benevento, 24 C3
Benfica, 38 B7
Benfica Stad, 38 B7
Bengbu, 67 B4
Bengkulu, 61 A1
Benguela, 46 D4
Beni, 47 F6
Beni R, 84 D2
Benicia, CA 174 D7
Benin, 44 C2
Benito Juárez, 98 D2, D3
Benito Juárez Intl Arpt, 98 C3
Benjamin Constant, 84 D3

Bennettsville, SC 121 F5
Bennington, VT 115 A3, 117 H3
Benoni, 51 H3
Benrath, 34 B5
Bensalem, PA 145 H5
Bensenville, IL 159 B4
Bensonhurst, NY 142 D2
Bentleigh, 79 C1
Benue R, 44 D1
Benxi, 55 E2, 60 C8, 66 C6
Berazategui, 88 F5
Berbera, 45 H2
Berchem, 31 G5
Bercy, 29 F1
Berea, OH 150 B5
Berezniki, 53 D4
Bergama, 25 H3
Bergamo, 17 E4, 23 D1, 24 B5
Bergen, 14 D3, 22 B8
Bergen-Enkeim, 35 C3
Bergenfield, NJ 142 B4
Bering Land Bridge Natural Pres, AK 136 B7,178 A3
Bering Sea, 82 A6, 136 A6
Bering Str, 54 F8, 82 A6, 100 A7, 136 B8
Berkakit, 55 D4
Berkel, 30 B2
Berkeley, CA 174 C6
Berkeley, MO 162 B3
Berkeley, UC, 175 C6
Berkeley Springs, WV 119 E4
Berkersheim, 35 B4
Berkley, MI 156 C8
Berkner Isl, 83 D3
Berlaar, 31 H5
Berlare, 31 E4
Berlin, Ger 17 E6, 23 E4, 32 D7, 33
Berlin, NH 114 C5
Berlin Cathedral, 33 F3
Berlin Mus, 33 E2

Berlin-Schönefeld Arpt, 32 **E5**

Berlin-Tegel Arpt, 32 **C7**

Berlin-Tempelhof Arpt, 32 **D6**

Bermejillo, 128 **B1**

Bern, 16 **D5**, 20 **F6**, 23 **C1**, 24 **A6**, 37 **B2**

Bern Mus, 37 **B2**

Bern-Belp Arpt, 37 **C2**

Bernalillo, NM 128 **B6**, 131 **E3**

Bernard, ME 186 **B2**

Bernardsville, NJ 116 **A5**

Bernau, 32 **E8**

Bernebeu Stad, 39 **C3**

Bernière-St-Nicolas, 105 **D1**

Berregio, 40 **A1**

Berry Creek, WY 181 **F6**

Berrydale, WA 176 **D2**

Berryville, VA 119 **F3**

Bertem, 31 **H2**

Berwick-upon-Tweed, 18 **E5**

Berwyn, IL 159 **C3**

Berwyn, PA 144 **A4**

Berwyn Hts, MD 148 **E7**

Besançon, 20 **F6**, 23 **B1**

Beskudnikovo, 56 **B5**

Bessemer, AL 120 **C4**

Bet Nehemya, 50 **B5**

Bet Shemesh, 50 **B4**

Bethel, AK 136 **B6**

Bethel, VT 115 **A4**

Bethel Park, PA 146 **B5**

Bethesda, MD 148 **C8**

Bethlehem, PA 119 **G5**

Beulah, ND 126 **C7**

Beveren, 31 **F6**

Beverly, MA 138 **F6**

Beverly, NJ 145 **H5**

Beverly Hills, CA 170 **B4**,172 **A6**

Beverly Hills, FL 121 **E1**, 123 **E4**

Beverly Hills, MI 156 **C8**

Bevis, OH 151 **C3**

Bexley, 26 **E7**

Beykoz, 43 **F3**

Beyoglu, 43 **E2**

Béziers, 21 **E4**

Bhadreswar, 65 **E3**

Bhandup, 65 **C2**

Bhatpara, 65 **F3**

Bhayandar, 65 **B4**

Bhimpur, 65 **D3**

Bhiwandi, 65 **C4**

Bhopal, 58 **C5**

Bhutan, 58 **E5**

Bialystok, 15 **G1**

Biberist, 37 **C4**

Bibliotheque Nationale, 29 **E3**

Bicutan, 62 **C1**

Biddeford, ME 115 **C4**

Biedermannsdorf, 42 **E6**

Biel, 23 **B1**, 24 **A6**, 37 **A3**

Bielefeld, 16 **D6**, 23 **C4**

Biella, 23 **C1**

Bienville NF, MS 120 **B3**

Big Baldy Mt, MT 135 **G5**

Big Basin Redwoods SP, CA 175 **C1**

Big Bend NP, TX 128 **C2**, 178 **D2**

Big Bend SP, TX 128 **C3**

Big Coppitt Key, FL 188 **B1**

Big Creek Res, OH 150 **C6**

Big Cypress N Pres, FL 123 **F2**, 179 **G1**

Big Flats, NY 116 **D2**

Big Horn, WY 130 **D8**

Big Key, FL 188 **E4**

Big Lake, ME 114 **F6**

Big Pine, CA 132 **D5**

Big Pine Key, FL 123 **F1**,188 **C2**

Big Rapids, MI 124 **E5**

Big Rideau Lake, 117 **E6**

Big Sandy, MT 135 **G6**

Big South Fork NRA, TN 118 **A1**, 120 **D6**

Big Spring, TX 128 **D4**

Big Timber, MT 135 **G4**

Bighorn Canyon NRA, MT 130 **D8**, 135 **H4**, 178 **C5**

Bighorn NF, WY 126 **A6**, 130 **D7**

Bighorn R, 126 **A6**, 135 **H3**

Bijwasan, 64 **D6**

Bilbao, 16 **B4**, 21 **C4**

Bilk, 34 **B5**

Billerica, MA 138 **B6**

Billericay, 26 **F8**

Billings, MT 101 **F1**, 110 **D7**, 130 **D8**, 135 **H4**, 178 **C5**

Biloxi, MS 113 **B3**, 120 **B2**, 122 **A6**, 129 **H3**

Binangonan, 62 **D1**

Bingham, NY 112 **C8**

Binghamton, NY 112 **E6**, 117 **E2**, 119 **G6**

Bioko, 44 **D1**

Bi'r Zayt, 50 **D5**

Birch Cliff, 104 **D5**

Birchwood Village, MN 161 **F4**

Birds Hill, 107 **H6**

Birds Landing, CA 174 **F8**

Birjand, 49 **H5**

Birkenwerder, 32 **C8**

Birkerod, 36 **B7**

Birmensdorf, 37 **E1**

Birmingham, AL 113 **C3**, 97 **F6**, 120 **C4**, 179 **F2**

Birmingham, MO 162 **D6**

Birmingham, UK 14 **C1**, 19 **D3**, 20 **C8**

Birobidzhan, 55 **E3**

Birrong, 78 **C6**

Biryulevo, 56 **C2**

Bisbee, AZ 131 **C1**

Biscayne NP, FL 123 **G1**, 179 **G1**

Biscayne Park, FL 155 **G2**

Biscuit Basin, WY 180 **A3**

Bishan, 63 **F2**

Bishkek, 53 **E1**, 58 **C8**

Bishnupur, 65 **D1**

Bisho, 47 **F2**

Bishop, CA 132 **D5**

Bishop Mus, Bernice P, HI 177 **G2**

Biskra, 44 **C5**

Bismarck, ND 101 **F1**, 110 **F7**, 126 **C7**, 178 **D5**

Bismarck Archipelago, 76 **C2**

Bismarck Sea, 76 **C2**

Bissau, 44 **A3**

Bitola, 25 **E4**

Bitterroot NF, MT 135 **F4**

Bitterroot Range, ID 135 **E5**

Biysk, 53 **F3**

Bizerte, 24 **B1**

Björknäs, 36 **F6**

Black Betsy Keys, FL 188 **E4**

Black Canyon of the Gunnison NP, CO 130 **D5**, 178 **C3**

Black Diamond Mines R Pres, CA 174 **F6**

Black Forest, CO 130 **E5**

Black Gap WMA, TX 128 **C3**

Black Hills, 110 **E6**

Black Hills NF, SD 126 **B5**

Black Horse, PA 144 **B2**

Black Isl, ME 186 **A5**

Black Lake, ME 186 **B1**

Black Kettle NG, OK 127 **D1**, 128 **D6**

Black Lake, NY 117 **F6**

Black Pt, CA 174 **A8**

Black R, NY 117 **F4**

Black Sand Basin, WY 180 **A3**

Black Sea, 17 **H4**, 25 **H5**, 45 **F6**, 53 **A3**

Blackbeard Island NWR, GA 121 **F3**

Blackburn, 79 **D2**

Blackburn Hamlet, 105 **C3**

Blackfeet IR, MT 135 **F6**

Blackfoot, ID 130 **B7**, 135 **F2**

Blackmans Pt, MA 184 **A8**

Blackpool, 19 **D4**

Blacksburg, VA 118 **D1**, 121 **F6**

Blacktown, 78 **B8**

Blackwater NWR, MD 119 **G3**

Blackwell, OK 127 **E1**

Blad Porcupine Isl, ME 186 **D5**

Bladensburg, MD 148 **F7**

Blagoveshchensk, 55 **E3**, 66 **C8**

Blaine, WA 134 **B6**

Blainville, 106 **A4**

Blair, NE 125 **A4**

Blake Island SP, WA 176 **A4**

Blakehurst, 78 **D5**

Blakely, GA 120 **D2**

Blanding, UT 131 **C4**

Blankenfelde, 32 **D5**

Blantyre, 47 **G4**

Bleiswijk, 30 **B3**

Blida, 21 **E2**

Block Isl, RI 115 **C1**

Bloemfontein, 47 **F2**

Blois, 20 **D6**

Bloomfield, NJ 142 **B4**

Bloomingdale, IL 159 **A4**

Bloomington, CA 171 **G5**

Bloomington, IL 112 **B5**, 125 **D3**

Bloomington, IN 112 **C5**, 125 **E3**

Bloomington, MN 124 **B5**, 161 **C1**

Bloomsburg, PA 119 **F5**

Bloomsbury, 27 **C4**

Blossom Park, 105 **C1**

Blountstown, FL 122 **C6**

Blovstrod, 36 **B7**

Blue Ash, OH 151 **E3**

Blue Bell, PA 144, **D6**

Blue Hill Bay, ME 186 **A3**

Blue Hills State Reservoir, MA 139 **D2**

Blue Isl, IL 159 **D2**

Blue Jay, CA 171 **H6**

Blue Mosque, 43 **E2**

Blue Mound, TX 164 **B4**

Blue MT Lake, NY 117 **G5**

Blue Mts, OR 134 **D4**

Blue Nile R, 45 **G2**, 48 **D1**

Bluffton, IN 118 **A5**

Blumber, 32 **E8**

Blysk, 53 **F3**

Blythe, CA 131 **A3**, 133 **F2**

Blytheville, AR 120 **B6**

Bnei Brak Railway Sta, 50 **B6**

Bo Hai, 66 **B5**

Bo Hai Bay, 55 **E1**

Boa Vista, 85 **E4**

Boa Vista Park, 91 **D2**

Bobo-Dioulasso, 44 **B2**

Boca, 88 **E7**, 89 **E1**

Boca Raton, FL 123 **G2**, 155 **G6**

Boca Juniors Stad, 89 **E1**

Boccea, 40 **B6**

Bochum, 34 **D7**

Bockheim, 35 **B3**

Bodaybo, 55 **C4**

Bodegraven, 30 **C3**

Bodie Isl, NC 187 **G5**

Bodie Isl Lighthouse, NC 187 **C5**

Bodie Isl Visitor Ctr, NC 187 **H5**

Bodø, 15 **E5**

Bodrum, 25 **H2**

Boechout, 31 **H5**

Boedo, 89 **B1**

Boeing Field (Kings Co Intl), WA 176 **C4**

Boele, 34 **D7**

Bogalusa, LA 120 **A3**

Bogor, 61 **B1**, 64 **B5**

Bogotá, Col 84 **C5**, 90 **C2**

Bogota, NJ 142 **C6**

Bogotá Archeological Park, 90 **B3**

Bogotá Natl Mus, 90 **C2**

Bohnice, 35 **E3**

Bois de Boulogne, 28 **C7**, 29 **A3**

Bois de Vincennes, 28 **D7**

Bois des Filion, 106 **B4**

Boisbriand, 106 **A4**

Boise, ID 101 **C1**, 110 **C6**, 130 **A7**, 135 **E3**, 178 **B5**

Boise NF, ID 130 **A8**, 135 **E3**

Bojacá, 90 **A3**

Boksburg, 51 **H2**

Bolingbrook, IL 159 **A3**

Bolivar, MO 125 **B2**

Bolivia, 84 **D2**

Bollate, 40 **B2**

Bolligen, 37 **C2**

Bologna, 17 **E4**, 24 **B5**

Bolsa ChiCA Ecological Reserve, CA 170 **C2**

Bolshevo, 56 **D6**

Bol'shoy Theater, 57 **E6**

Bolton, Can 104 **A8**

Bolton, UK 19 **D4**

Bolzano, 23 **D1**, 24 **B6**

Bom Retiro, 92 **B5**, 93 **G6**

Boma, 46 **D5**

Bombay, 58 **B5**, 65 **A3**

Bombay Intl Arpt, 65 **B2**

Bombay, U of, 65 **A1**

Bommersheim, 35 **A4**

Bonaire, 84 **D6**, 95 **F1**

Bonames, 35 **B4**

Bondi, 78 **F6**

Bondy, 28 **D7**

Bonham, TX 129 **F5**

Bonita, CA 169 **G2**

Bonita Springs, FL 123 **F2**

Bonn, 16 **D6**, 20 **F7**, 23 **B3**

Bonners Ferry, ID 135 **E6**

Bonnyrigg, 78 **B6**

Bookertown, FL 153 **G6**

Boom, 31 **G4**

Boone, IA 125 **B4**

Boone, NC 121 **F6**

Boothbay Harbor, ME 115 **D4**

Boothia Pen, 100 **F6**

Bor, 25 **F6**

Borbeck, 34 **C7**

Bordeaux, 16 **C4**, 20 **D5**, 44 **C6**

Border Field SP, CA 169 **F1**

Borehamwood, 26 **C8**

Boring, OR 177 **H4**

Borivli, 65 **B3**

Borlange, 15 **F3**, 22 **E8**

Bornem, 31 **F4**

Borneo, 61 **D2**

Bornheim, 35 **C3**

Bornholm, 15 **F1**, 22 **E6**

Bornicke, 32 **A8**

Boron, CA 133 **D3**

Boronia, 79 **F2**

Borsbeek, 31 **H6**

Bos en Lommer, 30 **D6**

Bosa, 90 **B2**

Boskoop, 30 **C3**

Bosnia & Herzegovina, 17 **F4**, 24 **D5**, 25 **E6**, 45 **E6**

Boso Pen, 68 **E6**

Bosporus, 48 **D6**

Bosque del Apache NWR, NM 128 **A5**

Bosques, 88 **F5**

Boston, MA 103 **E1**, 112 **F6** 115 **C2**, 139 **E3**, 140, 179 **H5**

Boston, UK 19 **E3**

Boston Ctr for the Arts, MA 140 **B1**

Boston College, MA 139 **C3**

Boston Common, MA 140 **B3**

Boston Information Ctr, MA 40 **C3**

Boston Massacre Site, MA 140 **C4**

Boston NHP, MA 140 **D6**

Boston Tea Party Ship & Mus, MA 140 **D2**

Botafogo, 91 **D2**

Botanical Gdns, 89 **A4**

Botany, 78 **E6**

Botany Bay, 78 **E5**

Botany Bay NP, 78 **F5**

Botkyrka, 36 **D6**

Botswana, 47 **E3**

Bottineau, ND 126 **D8**

Bottrop, 34 **C8**

Bouaké, 44 **B1**

Bouar, 44 **D1**

Boucherville, 106 **D4**

Bougainville, 80 **B4**

Bouira, 21 **E2**

Boulder, CO 127 **A3**, 130 **E5**, 167 **E6**

Boulder, MT 135 **F4**

Boulder City, NV 131 **A3**, 133 **F4**

Boulder Mt Park, CO 167 **E5**

Boulder Pk, CA 134 **B1**

Boulogne, 88 **C8**

Boulogne-Billancourt, 28 **C7**

Boulogne-sur-Mer, 19 **F2**

Boundary Canal, NC 187 **F3**

Boundary Peak, NV 132 **D5**

Bountiful, UT 130 **B6**, 135 **G1**

Bourges, 20 **E6**

Bourke, 77 **E3**

Bourke Street Mall, 79 **B3**

Bourne, MA 184 **B5**

Bournedale, MA 184 **B6**

Bournemouth, 19 **E2**

Bovisa, 40 **B2**

Bow Mar, CO 167 **F2**

Bowen, 77 **E5**

Bowleys Quarters, MD 147 **F3**

Bowling Green, KY 113 **C4**, 120 **C6**, 125 **E2**

Bowling Green, OH 125 **F4**, 118 **B5**

Bowling Green, VA 119 **F2**

Bowman, ND 130 **F8**

Box Hill, *Austral* 79 **D2**

Box Hill, *UK* 26 **B5**

Box Springs Mt CP, CA 171 **H4**

Boxford, MA 138 **E7**

Boy Scouts Mus, 105 **A3**

Boyce Park, PA 146 **F7**

Boyd Hill Nature Ctr, FL 154 **B3**

Boydton, VA 119 **E1**

Boynton Beach, FL 123 **G2**

Bozeman, MT 110 **D7**, 130 **B8**, 135 **G4**

Brackenridge Park, TX 163 **G2**

Bracknell, 26 **A7**

Braddock, PA 146 **F7**

Bradenburg Gate, 33 **D3**

Bradenton, FL 123 **E3**, 154 **B1**

Bradenton Beach, FL 154 **B1**

Bradford, MA 138 **D8**

Bradford, PA 116 **B1**, 119 **E6**

Bradford, *UK* 19 **D4**

Bradley-Palmer SP, MA 138 **F7**

Bradley Woods Res, OH 150 **A6**

Brady, TX 128 **D3**

Braga, 16 **A4**, 21 **A4**

Bragança, 21 **B4**

Brahmapur, 59 **D4**

Brahmaputra R, 58 **E5**

Brainerd, MN 124 **B6**, 126 **F7**

Braintree, MA 139 **E2**

Braithwaite, LA 163 **H4**

Bramalea, 104 **B7**

Brampton, 104 **A6**

Brandenburg, 23 **D4**

Brandon, *Can* 101 **F2**

Brandon, FL 123 **E4**, 154 **D5**

Brandon, MS 120 **A3**

Brandon, VT 115 **A4**

Brant Rock, MA 184 **A8**

Brantford, 116 **A3**

Bras, 93 **H4**

Brasov, 17 **H5**

Brasília, 85 **F1**

Bratenahl, OH 150 **E8**

Bratislava, 17 **F5**, 23 **F2**, 24 **D6**

Bratsk, 55 **B3**

Brattleboro, VT 115 **B3**

Braunschweig, 23 **C4**

Brawley, CA 133 **F2**

Bray, 19 **C3**

Braybrook, 79 **A3**

Brazil, 85 **F3**, 86 **C6**

Brazilian Highlands, 85 **G2**

Brazos R, TX 128 **D4**

Brazzaville, 46 **D6**

Brea, CA 170 **D3**

Breakeyville, 105 **E1**, **F1**

Breckenridge Hills, MO 162 **A3**

Breckerfeld, 34 **F5**

Brecksville Res, OH 150 **E5**

Brecon, OH 151 **E4**

Breda, 20 **E8**, 23 **B4**

Breendonk, 31 **F4**

Breezy Pt, NY 143 **E1**

Breitenlee, 42 **F8**

Bremen, 15 **E1**, 20 **F8**, 23 **C4**

Bremerhaven, 22 **C5**

Bremgarten, 37 **D1**

Breña, 87 **F5**

Brent, 26 **C7**

Brentwood, MD 148 **E7**

Brentwood, MO 162 **B2**

Brentwood, NY 116 **B5**

Brentwood, PA 146 **C5**

Brentwood, *UK* 26 **E8**

Brescia, 24 **B5**

Bresso, 40 **C2**

Brest, 16 **B5**, 17 **G6**, 20 **B6**, 52 **A5**

Breton NWR, 120 **B1**, 122 **A5**

Breukelen, 30 **D4**

Brevard, NC 121 **E5**

Brevik, 36 **F5**

Brevnov, 35 **D3**

Brewer, ME 114 **D3**

Brewerton, NY 117 **E4**

Brewster, MA 184 **E5**

Brewster, WA 134 **C6**

Brewton, AL 120 **C2**, 122 **B6**

Bridal Trails SP, WA 176 **D5**

Bridalveil Falls, CA 182 **B3**

Bridesburg, PA 145 **F3**

Bridge City, LA 163 **F5**

Bridgeboro, NJ 145 **H4**

Bridgehampton, NY 116 **D6**

Bridgeport, CA 132 **D5**

Bridgeport, CT 112 **F6**, 115 **A1**

Bridgeport, WA 134 **C6**

Bridger-Teton NF, WY 130 **C7**, 135 **G2**, 180 **C1**, 181 **H2**

Bridgeton, MO 162 **A3**

Bridgetown, *Bar* 95 **H2**

Bridgetown, OH 151 **C2**

Bridgeville, PA 146 **B5**

Brie-Comte-Robert, 28 **E6**

Brieselang, 32 **B7**

Brigham City, UT 130 **B6**, 135 **G1**

Bright Angel Creek, AZ 183 **E2**

Brighton, *Austral* 79 **C1**

Brighton, CO 130 **E5**, 167 **H6**

Brighton, *UK* 19 **F2**

Brighton Beach, NY 142 **D1**

Brigittenau, 42 **E7**

Brindisi, 24 **D3**

Briones RP, CA 174 **D6**

Brisbane, *Austral* 77 **F4**, 80 **B2**

Brisbane, CA 175 **B4**

Bristol, FL 122 **C6**

Bristol, NH 115 **B4**

Bristol, RI 115 **C2**

Bristol, TN 118 **C1**, 121 **E6**

Bristol, *UK* 16 **C6**, 19 **D2**, 20 **C7**

Bristol, VT 115 **A4**

Bristol, VA 113 **D4**

Bristol Bay, AK 136 **B6**

Bristol Chan, 19 **D2**

British Columbia, 101 **C3**

British Columbia, U of, 107 **F2**

British Isles, 14 **C1**, 18

British Mus & Library, 27 **C3**

Brno, 17 **F5**, 23 **F2**

Broad Ripple Park, IN 157 **E3**

Broadmeadows, 79 **B4**

Broadmoor, CA 175 **A4**

Broadview, MT 135 **H4**

Broadview Hts, OH 150 **D5**

Broadview Park, TX 164 **A4**

Brochet, 101 **F4**

Brockport, NY 116 **C3**

Brockton, MA 115 **C2**

Brockville, 117 **E6**

Broederstroom, 51 **E5**

Broken Arrow, OK 125 **A1**, 127 **F1**, 129 **F6**

Broken Bow, NE 127 **D4**

Broken Hill, 76 **D3**

Bromley, KY 151 **D1**

Bromley, *UK* 26 **D6**

Bromma, 36 **D6**

Bromma Arpt, 36 **D6**

Bronson, FL 123 **E5**

Bronx, NY 116 **B5**, 143 **E5**

Bronx Zoo/Wildlife Conservation Park, NY 143 **E5**

Brook Park, OH 150 **C6**

Brookdale, NJ 142 **B5**

Brooker Creek Park, FL 154 **B6**

Brookfield, IL 159 **C3**

Brookfield Zoo, IL 159 **C3**

Brookhaven, GA 152 **C5**

Brookhaven, MS 120 **A3**

Brookhaven, PA 144 **B1**

Brookings, OR 132 **A8**, 134 **A3**

Brookings, SD 124 **A5**, 126 **E5**

Brooklandville, MD 147 **C4**

Brooklin, 92 **B4**

Brookline, MA 139 **C3**

Brooklyn, NY 116 **B5**, 141 **H2**, 142 **D2**

Brooklyn, OH 150 **C6**

Brooklyn Ctr, MN 161 **B4**

Brooklyn College, NY 142 **D2**

Brooklyn Hts, NY 142 **D3**

Brooklyn Hts, OH 150 **D6**

Brooklyn Mus & Botanical Gdn, NY 142 **D3**

Brooklyn Park, MD 147 **D1**

Brooklyn Park, MN 161 **B4**

Brooklyn Zoo, NY 142 **D2**

Brookmont, MD 148 **C7**

Brooks, 101 **D2**

Brooks AFB, TX 163 **G1**

Brooks Range, 100 **B7**, 82 **B6**, 136 **C8**

Brookside Park, OH 150 **C7**

Brookside Village, TX 166 **C2**

Brooksville, FL 123 **E4**

Brookvale, 78 **F8**

Brookville, PA 119 **E5**

Broomall, PA 144 **B3**

Broome, 76 **B5**

Broomfield, CO 167 **F5**

Brossard, 106 **D2**

Brottby, 36 **F8**

Brown Deer, WI 157 **B4**

Brown Deer Park, WI 157 **B4**

Brown Field, CA 169 **G1**

Brownfield, TX 128 **C4**

Brownsville, NY 143 **E2**

Brownsville, TN 120 **B5**

Brownsville, TX 96 **D5**, 111 **F1**, 129 **E1**

Brownwood, TX 128 **D4**

Broyhill Park, VA 148 **B6**

Brugg, 37 **A3**

Brugge, 23 **A3**

Brugherio, 40 **C2**

Brunei, 61 **D3**

Brunn, 42 **D6**

Brunna, 36 **D7**

Brunswick, *Austral* 79 **C3**

Brunswick, GA 113 **D3**, 121 **F2**, 123 **F6**

Brussels, 16 **D6**, 20 **E7**, 23 **A3**, 31 **G2**

Brussels Arpt, 31 **G2**

Bruzzano, 40 **B2**, 40 **C2**

Bryan, OH 118 **A6**

Bryan, TX 113 **A3**, 129 **F3**

Bryansk, 15 **H1**, 53 **B4**

Bryanston, 51 **F4**

Bryant Lake RP, MN 161 **A1**

Bryce Canyon NP, UT 131 **B4**, 178 **B4**

Bryn Athyn, PA 145 **F6**

Bryn Mawr, PA 144 **C4**

Bryn Mawr College, PA 144 **C4**

Brzeg, 23 **F3**

Bucaramanga, 84 **C5**

Bucharest, 17 **H4**, 25 **G6**, 45 **F4**

Buchholz, 34 **B6**

Buchs, 37 **E2**

Buchschlag, 35 **B2**

Buckhannon, WV 118 **D3**

Buckhead, GA 152 **C5**

Buckhead Ridge, FL 123 **F3**

Buckingham, TX 165 **G5**

Buckingham Palace, 27 **B1**

Bucyrus, OH 118 **B5**

Budafok, 42 **A6**

Budakalász, 42 **B8**

Budakeszi, 42 **A7**

Budaörs, 42 **A6**

Budapest, 17 **F5**, 24 **D6**, 42 **B7**

Budapest Egyptian Mus, 42 **B7**

Budatétény, 42 **A6**

Budge Budge, 65 **D1**

Buena Park, CA 170 **D3**

Buenaventura, 84 **B4**

Buenavista, 98 **B5**, 99 **E3**, 99 **H2**

Buenos Aires, 86 **B5**, 88 **E7**

Buer, 34 **C8**

Buffalo, NY 103 **C1**, 112 **D6**, 116 **B3**, 179 **G5**

Buffalo, WY 130 **D7**, 126 **A6**

Buffalo Bill's Mem Grave & Mus, CO 167 **E3**

Buffalo Grove, IL 158 **B6**

Buffalo Natl River, AR 125 **B2**

Buggenhout, 31 **F4**

Bugyi, 42 **B5**

Buhl, ID 132 **F8**, 135 **E2**

Buitenveldert, 30 **D5**

Bujumbura, 47 **F6**

Bukavu, 47 **F6**

Bukhara, 58 **B8**

Bukhoro, 53 **D1**

Bukit Batok, 63 **E3**

Bukit Panjang, 63 **E3**

Bukit Timah, 63 **E2**

Bukittinggi, 61 **A3**

Bülach, 37 **E3**

Bulaq ad-Dakrur, 50 **B2**

Bulawayo, 47 **F4**

Bulgaria, 17 **H4**, 25 **G6**, 45 **E6**

Bull Bay, NC 187 **E5**

Bullhead City, AZ 131 **A3**, 133 **F3**

Bullittsville, KY 151 **B1**

Bumba, 47 **E6**

Bunbury, 76 **A3**

Bund, The 74 **E7**

Bundaberg, 77 **F4**
Bundorra, 79 **C4**
Bung Kum, 63 **H6**
Bunker Hill Mon, MA 139 **D4**, 140 **C6**
Bunker Hill Village, TX 166 **A4**
Bunnell, FL 123 **F5**
Buona Vista, 63 **E1**
Buraydah, 49 **E4**
Burbank, CA 170 **B5**
Burbank, IL 159 **D3**
Burbank-Glendale-Pasadena Arpt, CA 170 **B6**
Bureau of Engraving & Printing, DC 149 **C2**
Buren, 37 **B3**
Burgas, 17 **H4**, 25 **H5**
Burgdorf, 37 **C3**
Burgos, 21 **C4**
Burholme, PA 145 **F5**
Burien, WA 176 **B3**
Burke Lake Park, VA 148 **A5**
Burke Lakefront Arpt, OH 150 **D7**
Burkesville, KY 118 **A1**
Burkina Faso, 44 **C2**
Burleson, TX 164 **B1**
Burley, ID 130 **A7**, 132 **F8**, 135 **F2**
Burlingame, CA 175 **B4**
Burlington, Can 116 **A4**
Burlington, CO 127 **C3**, 130 **F5**
Burlington, IA 125 **C3**
Burlington, KY 151 **B1**
Burlington, MA 138 **B5**
Burlington, OR 177 **E6**
Burlington, VT 103 **D2**, 114 **A5**, 117 **H6**
Burma, 58 **F5**
Burnaby, 107 **H2**
Burnet Woods, OH 151 **D2**
Burney, CA 132 **B7**, 134 **B1**
Burnhamthorpe, 104 **C5**

Burns, OR 134 **C3**
Burnt Porcupine Isl, ME 186 **D6**
Burr Ridge, IL 159 **C3**
Bursa, 25 **H4**
Burton, WA 176 **B3**
Burundi, 47 **F6**
Burwood, Austral 78 **D7**
Burwood, Austral 79 **D2**
Burzaco, 88 **E5**
Busch Gardens, FL 154 **D6**
Busch Mem Stad, MO 162 **C1**
Bushwick, NY 143 **E3**
Bustleton, PA 145 **E5**
Buta, 45 **F1**
Butano SP, CA 175 **C1**
Butantã, 92 **A4**
Butler, NJ 116 **A6**
Butler, PA 118 **D5**
Butler, WI 157 **A3**
Butler Pt, MA 184 **A5**
Butler U, IN 157 **E3**
Butovo, 56 **B2**
Butte, MT 110 **C7**, 130 **B8**, 135 **F4**, 178 **B5**
Buttonville, 104 **E8**
Butuan, 61 **F4**
Buxtehude, 22 **C5**
Buxton, NC 187 **H2**
Buxton Woods Coastal Reserve, NC 187 **H2**
Buyukada, 43 **F3**
Buyukdere, 43 **E3**
Buzzards Bay, MA 185 **A4**
Bydgoszcz, 22 **F5**
Byfield, MA 138 **E8**
Bylot Isl, 102 **A7**

C

C & O Canal NHP, MD 148 **B8**
Caballito, 89 **A1**
Cabangbungin, 64 **C8**
Cabimas, 84 **C6**
Cabin John, MD 148 **B8**
Cabin John RP, MD 148 **B8**

Cabinda, 46 **D5**
Cable Car Barn & Mus, CA 173 **D3**
Cabo Rojo, PR 122 **A1**
Caborca, 131 **B1**
Cabramatta, 78 **B6**
Cabrillo NM, CA 169 **E3**
Çabusbasi Çif, 43 **F3**
Cacém, 38 **A7**
Cáceres, 21 **B3**
Cachipay, 90 **A3**
Cadillac, MI 124 **E5**
Cadiz, OH 118 **D4**
Cádiz, Spain 16 **A3**, 21 **B1**
Caen, 21 **E1**, 20 **D7**
Caernarvon, 14 163 **H4**
Caetamo Campus, 93 **F4**
Cagayan de Oro, 61 **E4**
Cagliari, 17 **E2**, 24 **A3**
Caguas, 122 **C2**
Cahokia, IL 162 **C1**
Cahokia Mounds SHS, IL 162 **D2**
Caieiras, 92 **A6**
Cainta, 62 **D2**
Cairns, 77 **E5**
Cairo, Egypt 45 **F4**, 48 **C4**, 50 **C2**
Cairo, GA 122 **D6**
Cairo, IL 113 **B4**
Cairo Exh Grounds, 50 **C2**
Cairo Intl Arpt, 50 **D3**
Cairo Railway Sta, 50 **C2**
Cairo Stad, 50 **D2**
Cajamarca, 84 **B3**
Cajititlán, 99 **G3**
Caju, 91 **D2**
Caladest Island SP, CA 154 **A5**
Calais, Fr 19 **F2**, 20 **D7**
Calais, ME 112 **F7**, 114 **F6**
Calama, 86 **A6**
Calarasí, 25 **H6**
Calcutta, 58 **E5**, 65 **F1**

Calcutta Botanical Gdns, 65 **E2**
Calcutta, U of 65 **E2**
Calcutta Zoo, 65 **E1**
Caldes de Montbui, 38 **E8**
Caldwell, ID 134 **D3**
Caldwell, OH 118 **C4**
Calera de Tango, 87 **E1**
Calexico, CA 133 **F2**
Calgary, 101 **D2**, 110 **D8**
Calhoun, GA 120 **D5**
Cali, 84 **C4**
California, 101 **B1**, 110 **B5**, 132, 134 **B1**, 178 **A4**
California City, CA 134 **D3**
California Zoo, 65 **E1**
California-Irvine, U of, CA 171 **E1**
California-Riverside, U of, CA 171 **H4**
California-San Diego, U of, CA 169 **E5**
California State Polytechnic U, CA 171 **E4**
California SU Dominguez Hills, CA 170 **B3**
California SU Fullerton, CA 171 **E3**
California SU Hayward, CA 175 **D4**
California SU Long Beach, CA 170 **D2**
California SU Northridge, CA 170 **A6**
California SU San Bernardino, CA 171 **H5**
Calipatria, CA 133 **F2**
Callao, 84 **C2**, 87 **E3**
Callaway, FL 122 **C5**
Caloocan, 62 **C3**
Caltanissetta, 24 **C1**
Calumet City, IL 159 **E2**
Calusa Keys, FL 188 **E3**
Camaguey, 94 **C4**
Camas, WA 177 **H6**
Camberley, 26 **A6**
Camberwell, 79 **D2**
Cambodia, 61 **B4**

Cambrai, 23 **A3**

Cambria, CA 133 **B4**

Cambridge, MA 115 **C3**, 139 **C4**, 140 **A5**

Cambridge, MN 124 **B6**

Cambridge, NY 115 **A3**

Cambridge, OH 118 **C4**

Cambridge, UK 19 **F3**, 20 **D8**

Cambridge Bay, 100 **E6**

Camden, AR 129 **G5**

Camden, ME 114 **D5**

Camden, NJ 112 **E5**, 119 **H4**

Camden, NY 117 **E4**

Camden, SC 121 **F4**

Camden, UK 26 **C7**

Cameron, TX 129 **E3**

Cameron City, FL 153 **H6**

Cameroon, 44 **D1**, 46 **D6**

Camp Dennison, OH 151 **F3**

Camp Edwards Mil Res, MA 184 **B5**

Camp H R Smith, HI 177 **G3**

Camp Shelby Mil Res, MS 122 **A6**

Camp Springs, MD 148 **E5**

Camp Verde, AZ 131 **B3**

Campamento, 39 **A3**

Campbell, CA 175 **E4**

Campbell, FL 153 **F1**

Campbell River, 101 **B3**

Campbellsville, KY 118 **A3**, 120 **D6**, 125 **F2**

Campeche, 97 **E3**

Campestre, 98 **B2**

Campina Grande, 85 **H3**

Campinas, 86 **C6**

Campo Grande, 85 **E1**, 91 **A3**

Campobasso, 24 **C3**

Campos, 86 **C6**

Campos Elísios, 91 **C4**

Campton, KY 118 **B2**

Camurí Grande, 90 **D6**

Can Tho, 61 **B3**

Canaan, NH 115 **B4**

Canada, 100 – 103

Canada Place, 107 **G2**

Canadian R, TX 127 **C1**, 128 **D6**

Canadian Shield, 101 **E4**, 103 **C2**

Canadian Wonderland, 104 **C8**

Canakkale, 25 **G4**

Canandaigua, NY 116 **D3**

Canarsie, NY 143 **E2**

Canary Islands, 44 **A4**

Canary Wharf, 26 **D7**

Canaveral NS, FL 121 **F1**, 179 **G1**

Canberra, 77 **E3**, 80 **B2**

Cancún, 94 **A5**, 97 **F3**

Candiac, 106 **D1**

Caneças, 38 **A7**

Canillas, 39 **D4**

Canning, 88 **D5**

Cannonsville Reservoir, NY 117 **F2**

Canon City, CO 127 **A3**, 130 **E5**

Canso, 103 **F2**

Cantabrian Mts, 21 **B4**

Canterbury Woods, VA 148 **A5**

Canterbury, Austral 78 **D6**

Canterbury, Austral 79 **D2**

Canterbury, UK 19 **F2**

Canton, MA 139 **C1**

Canton, MS 120 **B3**

Canton, NY 117 **F6**

Canton, OH 112 **D5**, 118 **C5**

Canyon, CA 174 **D5**

Canyon, TX 128 **D5**

Canyon City, OR 134 **D3**

Canyon de Chelly NM, AZ 128 **A6**, 131 **C3**, 178 **C3**

Canyon Lake, CA 171 **H2**

Canyon Village, WY 180 **B4**

Canyonlands NP, UT 131 **C4**, 178 **C4**

Caojiazhai, 74 **D6**

Cap-Haitien, 95 **E4**

Cap Rouge, 105 **D2**

Cap San Antonio, 94 **A5**

Caparica, 38 **B2**

Cape Adare, 83 **B2**

Cape Agulhas, 47 **E2**

Cape Alava, WA 134 **A6**

Cape Ann, MA 115 **C3**

Cape Arnhem, 76 **D3**

Cape Bathurst, 136 **E8**

Cape Beale, 134 **A6**

Cape Beate, 95 **E3**

Cape Bon, 44 **D5**

Cape Canaveral, FL 113 **D2**, 123 **F4**

Cape Chelyuskin, 54 **A6**

Cape Clear, 19 **A3**

Cape Cod, MA 112 **F6**, 184 – 185

Cape Cod Bay, MA 115 **D2**, 184 **D7**

Cape Cod Canal, MA 184 **B6**

Cape Cod NS, MA 115 **D2**, 179 **H5**, 184 **F8**

Cape Comorin, 59 **B3**

Cape Coral, FL 123 **E2**

Cape Corrientes, 96 **B3**

Cape Disappointment, WA 134 **A5**

Cape Falcon, OR 134 **A4**

Cape Falso, 95 **E3**

Cape Farewell, 82 **F5**, 102 **F6**

Cape Fear R, 121 **G5**

Cape Ferreio, OR 134 **A3**

Cape Finisterre, 16 **A4**

Cape Flattery, WA 134 **A6**

Cape Girardeau, MO 113 **B4**, 125 **C2**

Cape Hatteras, NC 113 **F4**

Cape Hatteras Lighthouse, NC 187 **H2**

Cape Hatteras NS, NC 121 **H5**, 179 **H3**, 187 **G2**

Cape Hatteras Visitor Ctr, NC 187 **H2**

Cape Henlopen, DE 119 **H3**

Cape Horn, 86 **B2**

Cape Krusenstern NM, AK 136 **B8**, 178 **A3**

Cape Kumukahi, HI 137 **F2**

Cape Leeuwin, 76 **A3**

Cape Leveque, 76 **B5**

Cape Lisburne, AK 136 **B8**

Cape Lookout NS, NC 179 **H3**, 187 **F1**

Cape Lookout, OR 134 **A4**

Cape May Court House, NJ 119 **H3**

Cape May Pt, NJ 119 **H3**

Cape Mohican, AK 136 **A6**

Cape Morris Jesup, 82 **D6**

Cape Newewham, AK 136 **B6**

Cape Norvegia, 83 **E3**

Cape of Good Hope, 47 **E2**

Cape Palmas, 44 **B1**

Cape Poinsett, 83 **B1**

Cape Race, 103 **F3**

Cape Romain NWR, SC 121 **G4**

Cape Romano, FL 123 **E2**

Cape Royal, AZ 183 **E2**

Cape Sable, Can 103 **E2**

Cape Sable, FL 113 **D2**, 123 **F1**, 188 **D4**

Cape St. Vincent, 16 **A3**, 21 **A3**

Cape San Blas, FL 122 **C5**

Cape Town, 47 **E2**

Cape Tres Puntas, 86 **B3**

Cape York, 76 **D6**, 80 **B3**

Cape York Pen, 76 **B1**

Capela do Socorro, 92 **A3**

Capelle aan den Ijssel, 30 **B2**

Capital Children's Mus, DC 149 **F4**

Capitol, The, DC 149 **F2**

Capitol Hts, MD 148 **F6**

Capitol Reef NP, UT 131 **B4**, 178 **B4**

Capr Nao, 21 **D2**

Capulin, NM 131 **F4**

Caraballeda, 90 **C6**

Carabanchel, 39 **B1**

Caracal, 25 **G6**

Caracas, 84 **D6**, 90 **C5**, 95 **F1**

Caracas Botanical Gdns, 90 **C5**

Caracas Natl Mus of Art, 90 **C5**

Carayaca, 90 **A5**

Carbondale, IL 113 **B4**, 125 **D2**

Carbondale, PA 117 **E1**

Cardiff, 16 **C6**, 19 **D2**, 20 **C7**

Cardinal Stritch College, WI 157 **C4**

Caribbean Sea, 84 **C6**, 94 **D2**, 97 **G3**

Caribou, ME 114 **E8**

Carin RP, CA 175 **E4**

Caringbah, 78 **D5**

Carle Place, NY 143 **H4**

Carleton U, 105 **B2**

Carlin, NV 132 **E7**

Carlingford, 78 **C8**

Carlington, 105 **A3**

Carlisle, MA 138 **A6**

Carlisle, PA 178 **F4**

Carlisle, UK 18 **D5**

Carlsbad, NJ 142 **C5**

Carlsbad, NM 111 **E3**, 128 **B4**, 131 **F2**

Carlsbad Caverns NP, NM 128 **C4**, 131 **E2**, 178 **C2**

Carlstadt, NJ 142 **C5**

Carmacks, 100 **B5**

Carmacs, 136 **E6**

Carman, 126 **E8**

Carmel, IN 125 **E3**, 157 **E4**

Carmel, NY 117 **H1**, 119 **H6**

Carnarvon, 76 **A4**

Carnaxide, 38 **A6**

Carnegie, PA 146 **B6**

Carnegie Hall, NY 141 **G5**

Carney, MD 147 **E4**

Carol Beach, WI 158 **C8**

Carol City, FL 155 **F3**

Carol Stream, IL 159 **A4**

Carolina, 122 **C2**

Caroline Islands, 80 **B4**

Carondelet Park, MO 162 **B1**

Carpathian Mts, 17 **G5**

Carrabelle, FL 122 **C5**

Carrara, 24 **B5**

Carrizo Springs, TX 128 **D2**

Carroll, IA 125 **A4**

Carrollton, GA 120 **D4**

Carrollton, OH 118 **C5**

Carrollton, TX 165 **E6**

Carrollwood, FL 154 **C5**

Carry Falls Reservoir, NY 117 **F5**

Carson, CA 170 **C3**

Carson City, NV 110 **B5**, 132 **C6**

Carson NF, NM 127 **A1**

Cartagena, Col 84 **C5**, 94 **D1**

Cartagena, Spain 16 **B2**, 21 **D2**

Carter Presidential Ctr, GA 152 **C3**

Carteret, NJ 142 **A1**

Carthage, NY 117 **F5**

Carthage, TX 129 **F4**

Cartier-Brebeuf NHP, 105 **E3**

Cartierville Arpt, 106 **B3**

Cartwright, 103 **E4**

Carugate, 40 **D3**

Caruthersville, MO 120 **B6**, 129 **H6**

Casa de Campo, 39 **B3**

Casa Grande, AZ 111 **C3**, 131 **B2**

Casa Rosada, 89 **D3**

Casa Verde, 92 **B5**

Casablanca, 16 **A1**, 44 **B5**

Casalotti, 40 **B5**

Cascade, ID 135 **E3**

Cascade, MT 135 **G5**

Cascade Canyon, WY 181 **F3**

Cascade Corner, WY 180 **A3**

Cascade Creek, WY 181 **F3**

Cascade Head, OR 134 **A4**

Cascade Park, WA 177 **G6**

Cascade Range, 101 **B1**, 110 **B7**, 132 **B8**, 134 **B3**

Casco Bay, ME 115 **D4**

Caseros, 88 **C7**

Caserta, 24 **C3**

Caseyville, IL 162 **D2**

Cashion, AZ 168 **A3**

Casper, WY 110 **D7**, 126 **A5**, 130 **D7**, 178 **C4**

Caspers Wilderness Park, CA 171 **G1**

Caspian Sea, 45 **H6**, 49 **F6**, 53 **B2**

Cassiar, 101 **C4**, 136 **F6**

Cassiar Mts, 136 **F6**

Castel di Decima, 40 **C4**

Castel di Guido, 40 **A6**

Castel di Leva, 40 **C4**

Castel Porziano, 40 **B6**

Castel Sant'Angelo, 41 **B4**

Castelar, 88 **C6**

Castellar del Vallès, 38 **E8**

Castelldefels, 38 **D5**

Castellón de la Plana, 21 **D3**

Castle Amusement Park, CA 171 **G3**

Castle Hill, 78 **C8**

Castle Hills, TX 163 **F3**

Castle Park, CA 169 **G2**

Castle Rock, CO 130

Castle Rock SP, CA 175 **D1**

Castle Shannon, PA 146 **B5**

Castlebar, 19 **A4**

Castor Peak, WY 180 **D4**

Castries, 95 **H2**

Castro Valley, CA 175 **D4**

Castrop-Rauxel, 34 **E8**

Cat Isl, 94 **D5**

Catamarca, 86 **B6**

Catania, 17 **F2**, 24 **D1**

Cataño, PR 122 **C2**

Catanzaro, 24 **D2**

Cataumet, MA 184 **A5**

Catawba R, NC 121 **E5**

Caterham, 26 **D6**

Catford, 26 **D7**

Cathedral of the Annunciation, 57 **E4**

Cathedral of the Archangel Michael, 57 **F4**

Cathedral Peak, CA 182 **D4**

Cathedral Range, CA 182 **D3**

Catherine's Palace, 56 **C4**

Cathlamet, WA 134 **B4**

Catia la Mar, 90 **A6**

Catonsville, MD 147 **B2**

Catskill, NY 117 **G2**

Catskill Mts, NY 119 **H6**

Catskill Park, NY 117 **G1**, 119 **H6**

Caucagüita, 90 **D5**

Caucasus Mts, 45 **G6**, 53 **A3**

Caulfield, 79 **C2**

Causapscal, 103 **D3**

Causeway Bay, 75 **D2**

Cava, 91 **B4**

Cave Junction, OR 134 **A3**

Cavite, 62 **B1**

Caxias Belem Tower, 38 **A6**

Caxias do Sul, 86 **C6**

Cayagzi, 43 **F4**

Cayenne, 85 **F5**

Cayman Islands, 94 **B4**, 97 **G3**

Cayuga Lake, NY 116 **D3**

Cazenovia, NY 117 **E3**

CBS TV City, CA 172 **B7**

Ceballos, 128 **B1**

Cebu, 61 **E4**

Cecchignola, 40 **C4**

Cecil Park, 78 **A7**

Cedar City, UT
110 **C5**, 131 **B4**

Cedar Falls, IA 125 **B4**

Cedar Grove, GA 152 **C2**

Cedar Grove, NJ 142 **A6**

Cedar Hill, TX 165 **E1**

Cedar Hill SP, TX 165 **E1**

Cedar Hills, OR 177 **F5**

Cedar Isl, NC 187 **E1**

Cedar Key, FL 123 **E5**

Cedar Keys NWR, FL
121 **E1**

Cedar Mt, AZ 183 **F2**

Cedar Park, IL 162 **D3**

Cedar Rapids, IA 112 **B5**,
125 **C4**

Cedarbrook, PA 145 **E5**

Cedarhurst, NY 143 **G2**

Cedarpines Park, CA
171 **G6**

Cedartown, GA 120 **D4**

Cedarville, MA 184 **B6**

Cedros, 99 **H2**

Cedros Isl, 96 **A5**

Ceduna, 76 **C3**

Ceiba, 122 **D2**

Celebes, 61 **E2**

Celebes Sea, 61 **E3**

Celina, OH 118 **A5**

Celtic Sea, 19 **B2**, 20 **B7**

Cemke, 43 **F2**

Centennial Centre, 107 **G5**

Centennial Park, MD
147 **A3**

Center Hill Pt, MA 184 **B6**

Center Line, MI 156 **E8**

Center Square, PA 144 **C6**

Centerton, NJ 145 **H3**

Centerville, MA 184 **C5**

Centocelle, 40 **C5**

Central, AK 136 **D7**

Central African Republic,
45 **E1**

Central America, 97

Central Concert Hall,
57 **F5**

Central Exh Hall, 57 **E5**

Central Florida, U of, FL
153 **H4**

Central Florida Zoo, FL
153 **G6**

Central Lenin Mus, 57 **F5**

Central Park, NY 141 **G5**,
142 **D4**

Central Park Zoo, NY
141 **G5**

Central Plateau, WY 180 **B4**

Central Rail Sta, 65 **A1**

Central Range, 54 **B7**

Central Russian Upland,
53 **B4**

Central Siberian Plateau,
55 **B4**

Central Stad, 70 **A5**

Central Sta, 31 **G6**

Central Valley, CA 132 **B7**

Centre G. Pompidou,
29 **E2**

Centreville, IL 162 **C1**

Centro, 39 **C3**

Centro Simón Bolívar,
90 **B5**

Century, FL 122 **B6**

Cerdanyola del Vallès,
38 **E7**

Cerignola, 24 **C3**

Cernosice, 35 **D2**

Cernusco sul Naviglio,
40 **D2**

Cerrillos, 87 **F2**

Cerritos, CA 170 **D3**

Cerro Aconcague, 86 **A5**

Cerro de Pasco, 84 **C2**

Cesano Boscone, 40 **B1**

Cesena, 24 **B5**

Ceske Budejovice, 23 **E2**

Ceuta, 16 **A3**, 21 **B1**,
44 **C5**

Chabot RP, Anthony, CA
174 **D5**

Chacao, 90 **C5**

Chaco Culture NHP, NM
178 **C3**

Chaco Culture NHS, NM
128 **A6**

Chad, 45 **E2**, 48 **A3**

Chadron, NE 110 **E6**,
126 **B5**, 130 **F7**

Chadstone, 79 **D2**

Chagos Archipelago, 59 **B1**

Chai Wan, 75 **D3**

Chaillot, 29 **B3**

Chain O'Lakes SP, IL
158 **A8**

Chairmen Mao Mem Hall,
73 **D2**

Chalkida, 25 **F3**

Challis, ID 135 **F3**

Challis NF, ID 135 **E3**

Chalmette, LA 163 **G5**

Chalon-sur-Saône, 23 **B1**

Chalons-sur-Marne, 23 **B2**

Chamartín, 39 **C4**

Chambéri, 39 **C3**

Chamberlain, SD 126 **D5**

Chamberlain Lake, ME
114 **D7**

Chambersburg, PA 119 **F4**

Chambéry, 23 **B1**

Chamblee, GA 152 **C6**

Champ de Mars, 29 **B2**

Champaign, IL 112 **B5**,
125 **D3**

Chamberly, 20 **F5**

Chandannagar, 65 **E3**

Chandigarh, 58 **C6**

Chandler, AZ 168 **D2**

Chandrapur, 58 **C5**

Chang R, 60 **C6**

Changchun, 55 **E2**, 66 **C6**

Changde, 60 **B6**, 67 **A3**

Changi, 63 **H3**

Changi Intl Arpt, 63 **H2**

Changning District, 74 **B6**

Changsha, 60 **C6**, 67 **A3**

Changting, 67 **B2**

Changzhi, 67 **A4**

Changzhou, 67 **C4**

Chania, 17 **H2**, 25 **F1**

Channel Islands, CA
111 **A4**

Channel Islands, UK16 **B6**,
19 **D1**, 20 **C7**

Channel Islands NP, CA
178 **A3**

Channel-Port aux Basques,
103 **E3**

Channel Tunnel, 19 **F2**

Chantepec, 99 **F1**

Chanute, KS 127 **F2**

Chaoyang, 73 **F2**

Chaoyang District, 73 **F3**

Chaozhou, 67 **B2**

Chapala, 99 **H1**

Chapel Hill, NC 121 **E5**

Chapel of the Transfigur-
ation, WY 181 **F2**

Chapleau, 103 **B2**

Chappaquiddick Isl, MA
185 **C2**

Chapultepec Park, 98 **A3**

Chardzhou, 58 **A8**

Charing Cross Sta, 27 **C2**

Charjew, 53 **C1**

Charlemagne, 106 **D5**

Charleroi, 20 **E7**, 23 **B3**

Charles De Gaulle Arpt,
28 **E8**

Charles Town, WV 119 **F4**

Charlesbourg, 105 **E3**

Charleston, IL 125 **D3**

Charleston, MO 125 **C2**

Charleston, SC 113 **E3**,
121 **G3**, 179 **G2**

Charleston, WV 112 **D5**,
118 **C3**, 179 **G4**

Charlestown, MA 139 **D4**,
140 **C6**

Charleswood, 107 **F5**

Charleville, 77 **E4**

Charlotte, NC 113 **D4**,
121 **F5**, 179 **G3**

Charlotte Court House, VA
119 **E1**

Charlottesville, VA 112 E5, 119 E2

Charlottetown, 103 E2

Charneca, 38 B7

Charny, 105 E2

Charters Towers, 77 E5

Chartres, 20 D6

Chartwell, 26 D5

Chassahowitzka NWR, FL 121 E1

Chastain Mem Park, GA 152 B5

Chateaugay, NY 117 G6

Chateauguay, 106 B1

Chatfield SP, CO 167 F1

Chatham, MA 115 D2, 184 F5

Chatham, UK 26 F6

Chatham, VA 119 E1

Chatham Islands, 80 D1

Chatswood, 78 E3

Chattahoochee, FL 122 D6

Chattahoochee NF, GA 120 D5

Chattahoochee River NRA, GA 152 A6

Chattanooga, TN 113 C4, 120 D5, 125 F1

Chatuchak, 83 G6

Chaudière R, 114 C7

Chaumont, 23 B2

Cheb, 23 E3

Checkpoint Charlie, 33 C3

Cheektowaga, NY 116 B3

Chehalis, WA 134 B5

Cheju, 67 C4

Cheju Isl, 60 D7, 67 C4

Chelas, 38 B7

Chelles, 28 E7

Chelmsford, MA 138 A6

Chelmsford, UK 19 F3, 26 F8

Chelsea, MA 139 D4

Chelsea, PA 144 A1

Chelsea, UK 26 C7

Cheltenham, Austral 78 D8

Cheltenham, PA 145 F5

Chelyabinsk, 53 D3

Chembur, 65 B2

Chemnitz, 17 E6, 23 E3

Chenango R, NY 117 E2

Chene, 65 C4

Cheney, MA 134 D5

Cheng Sha Wan, 75 B3

Chengde, 66 B6

Chengdu, 60 A6

Chengjiaqiaozhen, 74 A5

Chenjiazha, 74 C8

Chequamegon NF, WI 124 C6

Cheraw, SC 121 F5

Cherbourg, 19 E1, 20 C7

Cheremushki, 56 B3

Cherepovets, 52 C5

Chernovtsy, 17 G5

Cherokee NF, NC 120 D5, 121 F6

Cherry Creek SRA, CO 167 H2

Cherry Grove, OH 151 F1

Cherry Hill, NJ 145 G2

Cherry Hills Village, CO 167 G2

Cherrydale, VA 148 C6

Cherskiy, 54 E7

Cherskiy Range, 54 E5

Chertanovo, 56 B3

Chertsey, 26 E6

Chesapeake, VA 119 G1

Chesapeake Bay, 112 E5, 119 G2

Chesham, 26 A8

Cheshunt, 26 D8

Chester, CA 132 B7

Chester, IL 125 C2

Chester, MT 135 G6

Chester, SC 121 F5

Chester, UK 19 D3

Chester, VT 115 D4

Chester Hts, PA 144 A1

Chesterbrook, PA 144 A5

Chesterbrook, VA 148 C7

Chesuncook, ME 114 D7

Chetenham, 79 C1

Chetumal, 97 F3

Cheverly, MD 148 F7

Cheviot, OH 151 C2

Chevreuse, 28 B6

Chevy Chase, MD 148 D8

Cheyenne, WY 110 E5, 127 B4, 130 E6, 178 D4

Cheyenne River, 126 C6

Cheyenne River IR, SD 126 C6, 130 F8

Chhalera Bangar, 64 F6

Chhaprauli, 64 F6

Chia, 90 C3

Chia Keng, 63 G2

Chiai, 67 C2

Chiang Kai-Shek Intl Arpt, 62 A5

Chiang Kai-Shek Mem Hall, 62 B5

Chiang Mai, 61 A4

Chiba, 68 E7

Chibougamau, 103 C2

Chicago, IL 103 B1, 112 B5, 125 D4, 159 E4, 160, 179 F4

Chicago, U of, IL 159 E3

Chicago Art Institute, IL 160 D6

Chicago Board of Trade, IL 160 C5

Chicago Botanic Gdn, IL 158 D6

Chicago Civic Opera House, IL 160 B6

Chicago Cultural Ctr, IL 160 D6

Chicago Hts, IL 159 D1

Chicago Mercantile Exchange, IL 160 C6

Chicago Midway Arpt, IL 159 D3

Chicago O'Hare Intl Arpt, IL 159 B4

Chicago Stock Exchange, IL 160 C5

Chicamacomico, NC 187 H4

Chickamauga & Chattanooga NMP, GA 179 F3

Chickasha, OK 129 E5

Chiclayo, 84 B3

Chico, CA 132 B6

Chicopee, MA 115 B2

Chicoutimi, 103 D2, 112 E8

Chido, 72 B7

Chieti, 24 C4

Chifeng, 66 B6

Chigasaki, 68 A5

Chigwell, 26 D8

Chihuahua, 96 C5, 111 D2, 128 B2

Chijiatang, 74 E8

Chikapanagi Pt, AZ 183 C3

Children's Mus, MA 140 D2

Childress, TX 128 D5

Chile, 84 C1, 86 A6

Chile, U of, 87 F2

Chillán, 86 A4

Chillicothe, MO 125 B3

Chillicothe, OH 118 B4, 125 F3

Chillum, MD 148 E7

Chilly-Mazarin, 28 D6

Chilmark, MA 185 A3

Chiloé Isl, 86 A4

Chilpancingo, 96 D3

Chilung, 62 D6, 67 C2

Chimayo, NM 131 E3

Chimbote, 84 B2

Chimoio, 47 G4

China, 55 E1, 58 E7, 60 A6, 67 A4

China Camp SP, CA 174 A7

China Grove, TX 163 H2

China Lake Naval Weapons Ctr, CA 133 D4

Chinatown, CA 174 A7

Chinatown, DC 149 D4

Chinatown, NY 141 F2

Chinatown, Phil 62 B2

Chincoteague, MD 119 H3

Chingola, 47 **F4**

Chinjop, 72 **E8**

Chinle, AZ 131 **C3**

Chino, CA 171 **F4**

Chino Hills, CA 171 **E4**

Chino Hills SP, CA 171 **E3**

Chinook, MT 135 **H6**

Chinquapin, CA 182 **A3**

Chinsnan, 62 **C6**

Chioggia, 24 **C5**

Chipaque, 90 **C1**

Chipata, 47 **G4**

Chipley, FL 122 **C6**

Chippewa Falls, WI 124 **C6**

Chippewa NF, MN 124 **B7**, 126 **F7**

Chipping Ongar, 26 **E8**

Chiputneticook Lakes, ME 114 **F6**

Chiricahua NM, AZ 131 **C1**

Chirner, 65 **C1**

Chisasibi, 103 **C3**

Chita, 55 **D3**, 66 **A8**

Chitral, 58 **B7**

Chitralada Palace, 63 **F6**

Chittagong, 58 **E5**

Chittenango, NY 117 **E3**

Chitu, 62 **D5**

Chiyoda-Ku, 69 **A4**

Chlef, 21 **E1**, 44 **C5**

Choachi, 90 **D1**

Chodov, 35 **F3**

Chofu, 68 **B7**

Choisy-le Roi, 28 **D6**

Choix, 128 **A1**

Chojnice, 22 **F5**

Chomedey, 106 **B3**

Chomutov, 23 **E3**

Chongjin, 55 **F2**, 66 **D6**

Chongju, 66 **C5**

Chongno, 62 **C7**

Chongqing, 60 **A6**

Chongwen District, 73 **E2**

Chonju, 66 **C5**

Chonos Archipelago, 86 **A3**

Chorrillos, 87 **G4**

Choteau, MT 135 **F5**

Chowchilla, CA 132 **C5**

Choybalsan, 55 **D2**, 66 **A7**

Christ the Redeemer Statue, 91 **D2**

Christchurch, 77 **H1**, 80 **C2**

Christiansborg Palace, 36 **C6**

Christiansburg, VA 118 **D1**, 121 **F6**

Chrysler Bldg, NY 141 **G4**

Chuansha County, 74 **F5**

Chubbuck, ID 130 **B7**

Chugach NF, AK 136 **D6**

Chukchi Pen, 136 **A8**

Chukchi Range, 54 **E8**, 82 **A6**

Chukchi Sea, 54 **E8**, 82 **B6**, 100 **A8**, 136 **A8**

Chula Vista, CA 133 **E2**, 169 **G2**

Chung, 72 **A6**

Chung Nang, 72 **D7**

Chungho, 62 **B4**

Chuo-Ku, 68 **C7**, 69 **E3**, 71 **B3**

Chur, 23 **C1**

Churchill, 101 **F4**

Churchill R, 101 **E3**

Churilkovo, 56 **D1**

Churubusco, 98 **B2**

Ciampino, 40 **D4**

Ciampino Arpt, 40 **D4**

Ciawi, 64 **B5**

Cibinong, 64 **B6**

Cibola NF, NM 128 **A5**, 131 **D2**, 131 **E3**

Cicero, IL 159 **D4**

Cienfuegos, 94 **A5**

Ciftalan, 43 **D4**

Cilandak, 64 **B7**

Cileungsir, 64 **C6**

Cilincing, 64 **C8**

Cimarron NG, KS 127 **C2**

Cincinnati, OH 112 **C5**, 118 **A3**, 125 **F3**, 151 **C2**, 179 **F4**

Cincinnati, U of, OH 151 **D2**

Cincinnati Gdns, OH 151 **E3**

Cincinnati Municipal Arpt, OH 151 **E2**

Cincinnati Zoo & Botanical Gdn, OH 151 **D2**

Cinecitta, 40 **C5**

Cinergy Field, OH 151 **D2**

Ciniselllo Balsamo, 40 **C3**

Cinkota, 42 **C7**

Cinnaminson, NJ 145 **G3**

Cipó, 92 **A3**

Circleville, OH 118 **B4**

Cisaura, 64 **C5**

Citadel, 50 **C2**

Citadelle, 105 **F3**

Citeureup, 64 **B6**

Citrus Bowl, FL 153 **G4**

Citrus Park, FL 154 **C6**

City, 27 **D3**

City Centre, 107 **G5**

City Mus Of Natural History, 70 **D5**

Ciudad Acuña, 128 **D2**

Ciudad Adolfo López Mateos Atizapán, 98 **A5**

Ciudad Azteca, 98 **C4**

Ciudad Bolívar, 84 **D5**

Ciudad Deportiva Boca Juniors, 89 **F2**

Ciudad de Valles, 96 **D4**

Ciudad del Carmen, 97 **E3**

Ciudad Granja, 99 **F5**

Ciudad Guayana, 85 **E5**

Ciudad Jiménez, 128 **B1**

Ciudad Juárez, 96 **B6**, 111 **D3**, 128 **A4**, 131 **D1**

Ciudad Lineal, 39 **D4**

Ciudad Mante, 96 **D4**

Ciudad Obregón, 96 **B5**

Ciudad Real, 21 **C2**

Ciudad Satelite, 98 **A4**

Ciudad Victoria, 96 **D4**

Civitavecchia, 24 **B4**

Clackamas, OR 177 **G4**

Clanton, AL 120 **C3**

Claremont, CA 171 **E5**

Claremont, NH 115 **B4**

Clarion, PA 119 **E5**

Clark Range, CA 182 **C2**

Clarks Summit, PA 117 **E1**

Clarksburg, WV 118 **D3**

Clarksdale, MS 120 **A5**, 129 **H5**

Clarkston, GA 152 **D4**

Clarksville, AR 125 **B1**

Clarksville, TN 113 **C4**, 120 **C6**, 125 **D1**

Claudius, 51 **G6**

Clawson, MI 156 **C8**

Clay, WV 118 **D3**

Claye-Souilly, 28 **E7**

Claypole, 88 **E5**

Clayton, Austral 79 **D1**

Clayton, CA 174 **E6**

Clayton, ID 135 **E3**

Clayton, MO 162 **B2**

Clayville, 51 **H5**

Clearfield, PA 119 **E5**

Clearlake, CA 132 **B6**

Clearwater, FL 123 **E4**, 154 **A5**

Clearwater Bay CP, 75 **F3**

Clearwater Marine Aquarium, FL 154 **A5**

Clearwater Mts, ID 135 **E4**

Clementi, 63 **E2**

Clemson, SC 121 **E5**

Clerkenwell, 27 **D4**

Clermont-Ferrand, 16 **C4**, 20 **E5**, 23 **A1**

Cleveland, MS 120 **A4**

Cleveland, OH 103 **C1**, 112 **D6**, 118 **C6**, 150 **C7**, 179 **G4**

Cleveland, TN 120 **D5**

Cleveland Hts, OH 150 **E7**

Cleveland Browns Stadium, OH 150 **D7**

Cleveland Hopkins Intl Arpt, OH 150 **B6**

Cleveland Metroparks Zoo, OH 150 **D6**

Cleveland Mus of Art, OH 150 **D7**

Cleveland Mus of Natural History, OH 150 **E7**

Cleveland NF, CA 171 **F2**

Cleves, OH 151 **A3**

Clichy, 28 **D7**

Cliffside Park, NJ 142 **D5**

Clifton, NJ 142 **B6**

Clifton Hts, PA 144 **C2**

Clifton Park, MD 147 **D3**

Clinton, CT 116 **D6**

Clinton, IL 125 **C4**

Clinton, MO 125 **A3**

Clinton, NC 121 **G5**

Clinton, SC 121 **E5**

Clinton Pt, 136 **F8**

Cliveden, PA 145 **E4**

Clock Tower, 37 **B2**

Cloisters, The, NY 143 **E5**

Cloncurry, 76 **D5**

Clonmel, 19 **B3**

Clontarf, 78 **F7**

Cloverdale, CA 132 **A6**

Cloverleaf, TX 166 **D3**

Clovis, CA 133 **C4**

Clovis, NM 111 **E4**, 128 **C5** 131 **F3**

Cluj-Napoca, 17 **G5**

Clyde, 78 **A7**

Clyde Hill, WA 176 **C5**

CN Tower, 104 **E5**

Coacalco, 98 **B6**

Coalinga, CA 133 **C4**

Coalville, UT 135 **G1**

Coamo, 122 **C1**

Coast Mts, 136 **F5**

Coast Ranges, 110 **A6**, 111 **A4**, 132 **A6**, 134 **A3**

Coaticook, 114 **B6**

Coats Isl, 102 **A5**

Coats Land, 83 **D3**

Coatzacoalcos, 97 **E3**

Cobb, CA 132 **A6**

Cobija, 84 **D2**

Cobleskill, NY 117 **G3**

Coburg, *Austral* 79 **C3**

Coburg, *Ger* 23 **D3**

Cochabamba, 84 **D1**

Cochin, 59 **B3**

Cochituate, MA 139 **A3**

Cockrell Hill, TX 165 **F3**

Coco R, 97 **G2**

Cocoa, FL 123 **F4**

Coconino Plateau, AZ 183 **B1**

Coconut Creek, FL 155 **G6**

Coconut Grove, FL 155 **F1**

Cocota, 91 **D3**

Cody, WY 110 **D6**, 130 **D7**, 135 **H3**

Coelho da Rocha, 91 **B3**

Coeur d'Alene, ID 135 **E5**, 110 **C7**

Coeur D'Alene IR, ID 134 **D5**

Coeur D'Alene NF, ID 135 **E5**

Coffeyville, KS 127 **F2**

Cohoes, NY 117 **H3**

Coiba Isl, 97 **G1**

Coimbatore, 59 **B3**

Coimbra, 16 **A3**, 21 **A3**

Coina, 38 **C5**

Coit Tower, CA 173 **E3**

Colby, KS 127 **C3**

Colby, WA 176 **A4**

Coldwater, MI 118 **A6**

Colebrook, NH 114 **B5**

Coleman, TX 128 **D4**

Coleraine, 18 **C5**

Colfax, WA 134 **D5**

College, AK 136 **D7**

College Park, GA 152 **A3**

College Park, MD 148 **E8**

College Pt, NY 143 **E4**

Colleyville, TX 164 **D4**

Collingdale, PA 144 **C2**

Collingswood, NJ 145 **F2**

Collington, NC 187 **G6**

Collinsville, IL 162 **D2**

Colma, CA 175 **A4**

Cologne, 16 **D6**, 20 **F7**, 23 **C3**

Cologno Monzese, 40 **C2**

Colombia, 84 **C4**, 94 **D1**

Colombo, 59 **C3**

Colón, 97 **H1**

Colón Theatre, 89 **D3**

Colonial NHP, VA 179 **G3**

Colonial Village, PA 144 **B5**

Colonie, NY 117 **G3**

Colony, The, TX 165 **F6**

Colorado, 110 **E5**, 127 **A3**, 130 **D5**, 178 **C4**

Colorado NM, CO 130 **D5**, 178 **C4**

Colorado Plateau, 110 **C5**

Colorado RR Mus, CO 167 **E4**

Colorado River, 110 **D5**, 111 **B4**, 128 **D4**, 130 **D5**, 131 **A3**, 133 **F2**, 178 **B3**, 183 **D2**

Colorado River IR, 131 **A3** 133 **F3**

Colorado Springs, CO 110 **E5**, 127 **A3**, 130 **D5**

Colosseum, 41 **E2**

Colquitt, GA 122 **D6**

Colstrip, MT 126 **A6**

Colter Bay, WY 181 **G4**

Colter Bay Visitor Ctr, WY 181 **G5**

Colter Pass, MT 180 **D6**

Colter Pk, WY 180 **C2**, 135 **G3**

Colton, CA 171 **H4**

Columbia, KY 118 **A1**

Columbia, MD 119 **H4**, 147 **H4**

Columbia, MS 120 **A3**, 129 **H4**

Columbia, MO 112 **B5**, 125 **B3**

Columbia, NC 187 **E5**

Columbia, SC 113 **D4**, 121 **F4**

Columbia, TN 125 **E1**, 120 **C5**

Columbia Hts, MN 161 **C4**

Columbia Park, MN 161 **C3**

Columbia Plateau, 110 **B6**

Columbia R, 101 **C2**, 110 **B7**, 134 **B4**, 178 **B5**

Columbia U, NY 142 **D5**

Columbine Valley, CO 167 **F2**

Columbus, GA 113 **D3**, 120 **D3**

Columbus, IN 125 **E3**

Columbus, MS 113 **B3**, 120 **B4**

Columbus, MT 135 **H4**

Columbus, NE 110 **F5**, 127 **E4**

Columbus, OH 112 **D5**, 118 **C4**, 125 **F3**, 179 **G4**

Columbus Mon, 38 **E6**

Colusa, CA 132 **B6**

Colville, WA 134 **D6**

Colville IR, WA 134 **D6**

Colville Lake, 136 **F8**

Colville NF, WA 134 **D6**

Colvin Run, VA 148 **A8**

Colwyn, PA 144 **D2**

Colyton, 78 **A8**

Coma, 24 **A5**

Comanche NG, CO 127 **B2**, 131 **F4**

Comas, 87 **F6**

Comerica Park, MI, 156 **C6**

Comiskey Park, IL 159 **D3**

Comitán, 97 **E2**

Commander Isl, 54 **B8**

Commerce City, CO 167 **H4**

Communism Peak, 53 **E1** 58 **C7**

Como Park, MN 161 **D3**

Comodoro Rivadavia, 86 **B3**

Comoros, 47 H5
Compiègne, 23 A3
Compton, CA 170 C3
Conakry, 44 A1
Concepción, 86 A4, 86 C6
Concepción del Oro, 96 C4
Conchalí, 87 F3
Conchos R, 96 C5
Concord, Austral 78 D7
Concord, CA 132 B5, 174 E7
Concord, KS 127 E3
Concord, MA 138 A5
Concord, NH 112 E6, 115 B3
Concord, NC 121 F5
Concord West, 78 D7
Concordia, Arg 86 B5
Concordia, KS 127 E3
Concorezzo, 40 D3
Condon, OR 134 C4
Conecuh NF, AL 120 C2, 122 B6
Coney Isl, NY 142 D1
Coney Isl, OH 151 E1
Conflans-Sainte-Honorine, 28 C8
Confucius Temple, 62 C5
Congaree R, SC 121 F5
Congaree Swamp NM, SC 121 F4
Congo, 46 D6
Congo Basin, 47 E6
Congo R, 47 E6
Congonhas Arpt, 92 B4
Conical Pk, MT 135 G4
Conley, GA 152 C2
Connaught Place, 64 E7
Connecticut, 103 D1, 112 E6, 115 B1, 179 H5
Connecticut R, NH 115 B3
Connell, WA 134 D5
Conrad, MT 135 F6
Conroe, TX 129 F3
Conshohocken, PA 144 C5
Constance, KY 151 C1
Constanta, 17 H4, 25 H6
Constantine, 21 E2, 44 D5

Constitución, 89 D2
Constitución Train Sta, 89 D1
Constitution, GA 152 C2
Constitution Gdns, DC 149 B2
Content Keys, FL 188 B2
Contreras, 98 A1
Convention Ctr, MN 161 C3
Converse, TX 163 H3
Conway, AR 125 B1, 129 G6
Conway, NH 115 C4
Coober Pedy, 76 C4
Cook Inlet, AK 136 C6
Cook Islands, 80 D3
Cook Str, 77 H1
Cooke City, MT 180 D6
Cookeville, TN 120 D6, 125 E1
Cooksville, 104 B5
Coolaroo, Austral 79 B4
Cooper City, FL 155 F4
Cooperstown, NY 117 F3
Coors Brewing Company, CO 167 E3
Coors Field, TX 167 G3
Coos Bay, OR 110 A7, 132 A8, 134 A3
Coot Bay, FL 188 D4
Copacabana, 91 D1
Copacabana Beach, 91 D1
Copenhagen, 15 E1, 22 D636 C6, 52 A6
Copenhagen Arpt, 36 C5
Copiapó, 86 A6
Copley Plaza, MA 140 A3
Coppell, TX 165 E5
Copper Butte, WA 134 D6
Coppermine, 100 D6
Coquille, OR 132 A8, 134 A3
Coral Gables, FL 155 F1, 123 G2
Coral Hills, MD 148 E6
Coral Sea, 76 C1, 77 F5, 80 B3

Coral Springs, FL 123 F2, 155 F6
Coraopolis, PA 146 A7
Corbeil-Essonnes, 28 D5
Corbin, KY 120 D6
Corcoran, CA 133 C4
Corcoran Gallery of Art, DC 149 B3
Cordele, GA 121 E3
Cordelia, CA 174 D8
Córdoba Arg 86 B5
Córdoba, Spain 16 B2, 21 B2
Cordova, AK 136 D6
Corfu, 17 G3, 25 E4
Corinth, Gr 17 G2, 25 F3
Corinth, MS 120 B5
Corinth, NY 117 G4
Cork, 14 B1, 19 A3, 20 A8
Corlu, 25 H5
Cormano, 40 B2
Cornaredo, 40 A3
Cornellá de Llobregat, 38 D6
Corner Brook, 103 E3
Corning, CA 132 B6
Corning, NY 116 D2
Cornish, ME 115 C4
Cornwall, 103 D2, 117 F6
Coro, Ven 84 C6
Corona, CA 171 F3
Corona, NY 143 E4
Coronado, CA 169 F3
Coronel Oviedo, 86 C6
Corpus Christi, TX 96 D5, 111 F2, 129 E2, 178 D1
Corrois, 38 B6
Corry, PA 116 A1
Corsica, 16 D3, 24 A4, 44 D6
Corsico, 40 B1
Corte Madera, CA 174 A6
Cortez, CO 131 C4
Cortez, FL 154 B1
Cortland, NY 117 E2
Corumbá, 85 E1

Corvallis, OR 110 A7, 134 B3
Corviale, 40 B5
Corwin Springs, MT 180 A6
Cosenza, 17 F3, 24 D2
Coshocton, OH 118 C4
Coslada, 39 F3
Costa Brava, 21 E4
Costa Da Caparica, 38 A6
Costa Mesa, CA 170 D2
Costa Rica, 81 H5, 84 A5 94 A1, 97 G1
Cota, 90 C3
Côte D'Ivoire, 44 B1
Côte-Saint-Luc, 106 B2
Coto De Caza, CA 171 F1
Cotopaxi, 84 B4
Cotsicana, TX 129 E4
Cottbus, 23 E4
Cotton Bowl, TX 165 G3
Cottonwood, AZ 131 B3
Cottonwood, CA 132 B7
Cottonwood Cove, NV 131 A3, 133 F4
Cotuit, MA 185 C4
Coubert, 28 E6
Coudersport, PA 116 C1, 119 F6
Council, ID 135 E3
Council Bluffs, IA 112 A5, 125 A4, 127 F4
Countryside, KS 162 B4
Coupeville, WA 134 B6
Cova da Piedade, 38 B6
Covedale, OH 151 C2
Covelo, CA 132 A6
Covent Garden, 27 C2
Covina, CA 171 E5
Covington, GA 121 E4
Covington, KY 118 A3, 125 F3, 151 D2
Covington, TN 120 B5, 129 H6
Covington, VA 118 D2
Cowan Hts, CA 171 E2

Cowansville, 114 **A5**

Coxsackie, NY 117 **G2**

Coyoacán, 98 **B2**

Coyote Creek, AZ 183 **B2**

Coyula, 99 **H5**

Cozumel Isl, 94 **A4**, 97 **F3**

Crabtree Fl, IL 158 **A6**

Crafton, PA 146 **B6**

Craig, CO 110 **D5**, 130 **D5**

Crailsheim, 23 **D2**

Craiova, 17 **G4**, 25 **F6**

Cranberry Isles, ME 186 **C2**

Cranberry Lake, NY 117 **F5**

Cranbrook, 101 **D2**

Crane, OR 132 **D8**

Crater Lake NP, OR
132 **B8**, 134 **B2**, 178 **A5**

Craters of the Moon NM,
ID 130 **B7**, 178 **B5**

Crawley, 26 **C5**

Cregy les Meaux, 28 **F7**

Cremona, 24 **B5**

Crescent City, CA 132 **A7**,
134 **A1**

Crescent City, FL 123 **F5**

Crescent Lake NWR, NE
127 **C4**

Crescenzago, 40 **C2**

Crest Hill, IL 159 **B1**

Crest Park, CA 171 **H6**

Crestline, CA 171 **H6**

Creston, CA 135 **A4**

Crestview, FL 120 **C2**,
122 **B6**

Crestview, HI 177 **E3**

Crestview, KY 151 **E1**

Crestwood, MO 162 **A1**

Crete, 17 **H2**, 25 **G1**,
45 **E5**, 48 **B5**

Creteil, 28 **D6**

Creve Coeur, MO 162 **A3**

Creve Coeur CP, MO
162 **A3**

Crewe, 19 **D3**

Crimea, 53 **A4**

Croatan NF, NC 121 **H5**

Croatan Sd, NC 187 **G5**

Croatia, 17 **F4**, 23 **F1**,
24 **D5**, 45 **E6**

Crockett, CA 174 **C7**

Crooked Isl, 94 **D5**

Crookston, MN 126 **E7**

Cross City, FL 122 **D5**

Cross Key, FL 188 **F4**

Crossville, TN 120 **D6**

Crotone, 24 **D2**

Crouch, ID 135 **E3**

Crow Ctr, MO 162 **C5**

Crow Creek IR, SD 126 **D5**

Crow IR, MT 130 **D8**,
135 **H4**

Crowley, TX 164 **B1**

Crown Pt, NY 117 **H5**

Crows Nest, IN 157 **E3**

Croyden, 26 **D6**

Croydon, *Austral* 79 **F3**

Croydon, PA 145 **H5**

Crum Creek, PA 144 **B3**

Cruzeiro do Sul, 84 **C3**

Crystal, MN 161 **B4**

Crystal, MS 120 **A3**

Crystal Beach, FL 154 **A6**

Crystal City, VA 148 **D6**

Crystal Cove SP, CA
171 **E1**

Crystal R, FL 123 **E4**

Csepel, 42 **B6**

Csillaghegy, 42 **B8**

Csomád, 42 **C8**

Csömör, 42 **B7**

Cuajimalpa, 98 **A3**

Cuauhtémoc, 98 **B3**,
128 **A3**

Cuautepec de Madero,
98 **C5**

Cuautitlán, 98 **B6**

Cuautitlán Izcalli, 98 **A6**

Cuba, 94 **C5**, 97 **H4**

Cubatão, 92 **D2**

Cucamonga Wilderness, CA
171 **H6**

Cucuta, 84 **C5**

Cudahy, WI 157 **C1**

Cuddy, PA 146 **A5**

Cudjoe Key, FL 188 **B2**

Cuenca, Ecuador 84 **B3**

Cuenca, Spain 16 **B3**

Cuence, 21 **C3**

Cuernavaca, 96 **D3**

Cuero, TX 129 **E2**

Cuescomatitlán, 99 **F2**

Cuiabá, 85 **E2**

Culhuacán, 98 **C2**

Culiacán, 111 **D1**

Culiacán, 96 **B4**

Cullman, AL 120 **C4**

Culpeper, VA 119 **F3**

Culver City, CA 170 **B4**,
172 **A5**

Cumaná, 84 **D5**

Cumberland, MD 112 **D5**,
119 **E4**

Cumberland Gap
NHP,118 **B1**, 179 **G3**

Cumberland Island, GA
123 **F6**

Cumberland Island NS, GA
121 **F2**, 179 **G2**

Cumberland R, 125 **E2**

Cummingsville, MA 138 **C5**

Cuneo, 24 **A5**

Cunningham Cabin HS,
WY 181 **G3**

Cupertino, CA 175 **D1**

Curacao, 84 **D6**, 95 **F1**

Curitiba, 86 **C6**

Curlew, FL 154 **B6**

Cusago, 40 **A1**

Cusano Milanino, 40 **B3**

Cushing, OK 127 **F1**

Custer NF, MT 126 **A6**,
180 **D6**

Custer SP, SD 126 **B5**

Cut Bank, MT 135 **F6**

Cut Off, LA 120 **A1**

Cutchogue, NY 116 **C6**

Cuthbert Lake, FL 188 **E4**

Cutler, ME 114 **F5**

Cuttact, 58 **D5**

Cuxhaven, 22 **C5**

Cuyahoga Hts, OH 150 **D6**

Cuyahoga Valley NP, OH
79 **G4**, 150 **E5**

Cuyamaca College, CA
169 **H3**

Cuzco, 84 **C2**

Cyclades, 17 **H2**, 25 **G2**

Cynthiana, KY 118 **B3**,
125 **F2**

Cypress, CA 170 **D3**

Cyprus, 45 **F5**, 48 **D5**

Cyrville, 105 **B3**

Czech Republic 17 **F6**,
23 **E3**

D

Da Hinggan Ling, 55 **D2**,
66 **B2**

Da Lat, 61 **B4**

Da Nang, 61 **B4**

Dabazi, 74 **E8**

Dachang, 74 **C8**

Dachnoye, 57 **F2**

Dadar, 65 **B2**

Dahl, 34 **F6**

Dahlhausen, 34 **D7**

Dahlonega, GA 120 **D5**

Dahlwitz, 32 **F7**

Daito, 70 **D5**

Dajing, 73 **B1**

Dakar, 44 **A3**

Dalaro, 36 **F5**

Dalhart, TX 127 **C1**,
128 **C6**, 131 **F3**

Dalhousie, 103 **E3**

Dalian, 55 **E1**, 60 **C8**,
66 **C5**

Dallas, OR 134 **B4**

Dallas, TX 81 **H6**, 96 **D6**,
111 **F3**, 129 **F4**, 165 **F3**,
179 **E2**

Dallas, U of, TX 165 **E4**

Dallas County Historical
Plaza, TX 165 **F3**

Dallas-Fort Worth
Intl Arpt, TX 164 **D5**

Dallas Mus of Art, TX
165 **G3**

Dallas Zoo, TX 165 F3
Dalles, The, OR 134 C4
Dallgow, 32 B7
Dalton, GA 120 D5
Dalton, MA 115 A3, 117 H2
Dalworthington Gdns, TX
164 D2
Daly City, CA 175 A4
Damascus, OR 177 H4
Damascus, Syr 45 G5
Dammartin-en-Goele,
28 E8
Dampier, 76 A5
Danbury, CT 115 A1
Dandenong North, 79 E1
Dandong, 55 E2, 60 C8,
66 C6
Dania, FL 155 G4
Daniel Boone NF, KY
118 B2, 121 E6, 125 F2
Dannemora, NY 117 G6
Dansville, NY 116 C2
Danube R 17 F5, 23 E2,
25 F6, 45 E6
Danvers, MA 138 E6
Danville, CA 174 E5
Danville, IL 125 D3
Danville, KY 118 A3
Danville, PA 119 G5
Danville, VA 113 D4,
119 E1, 121 G6
Daphni, 43 A3
Daphni Monastery, 43 A3
Dar es Salaam, 47 H5
Darby, MT 135 F4
Darby, PA 144 D2
Darby Creek, 144 B4
Dardanelles, 17 H3, 25 H4
Darhan, 55 C2
Darling Range, 76 A3
Darling R, 76 D3
Dartford, 26 E8
Dartmouth, 103 E2
Darwin, 76 C6
Dash Point SP, WA 176 B2
Dasht-e Kavir, 49 G6
Dasht-e Lut, 49 G5

Datong, 55 D1, 60 B8,
66 A5
Datun, 73 E4
Daugavpils, 15 G2
Dauphin, 101 F2
Davao, 61 F4
Davenport, IA 112 B5
Davenport, WA 134 D5
David, 97 G1
Davie, FL 155 F4
Davis Str, 102 C6
Davle, 35 E1
Dawkah, 49 G2
Dawson, Can 82 B5, 100 B6
Dawson, GA 120 D3
Dawson City, 136 E7
Dawson Creek, 101 C3
Dawson Range, 136 E6
Dayton, KY 151 D2
Dayton, OH 112 C5,
118 A4, 125 F3
Dayton, WA 134 D4
Daytona Beach, FL 113 E3,
121 F1, 123 F5, 179 G2
Dayville, OR 134 C3
De Funiak Springs, FL
120 C2, 122 C6
De Klinge, 31 E6
De Land, FL 123 F4
De Paul U, IL 159 D4
De Ridder, LA 129 G3
De Soto, TX 165 F1
De Soto NF, MS 120 B2,
122 A6, 129 H4
Deadwood, SD 130 F7
Dealey Plaza, TX 165 F3
Dearborn, MI 156 B6
Dearborn Hts, MI 156 B6
Dease Lake, 136 F6
Death Canyon, WY 181 E2
Death Valley, CA 110 B5
Death Valley NP, CA
133 E4, 178 B3
Debrecen, 17 G5
Decatur, AL 120 C5
Decatur, GA 120 D4, 152 C4
Decatur, IL 112 B5, 125 D3

Decatur, IN 118 A5
Deccan Plateau, 59 C4
Decin, 23 E3
Decorah, IA 124 C5
Dedham, MA 139 C2
Dee Why, 78 F8
Deep River, 103 C2
Deer Key, FL 188 F4
Deer Lodge, MT 135 F4
Deer Park, Austral 79 A3
Deer Park, OH 151 E3
Deerfield, IL 158 C6
Deerfield Beach, FL 155 G6
Defiance, OH 118 A5
Deggendorf, 23 E2
Del Este NP & Planetario
Humboldt, 90 C5
Del Mar, CA 169 E6
Del Rio, TX 111 F2, 128 D2
Del Valle, Mex 98 B2
Del Valle RP, CA 175 F4
Del Viso, 88 A8
Delanco, NJ 145 H4
Delano, CA 133 D4
Delaware, 112 E5, 119 G3,
179 H4
Delaware, OH 118 B4
Delaware Bay, 119 G3
Delaware R, 117 F1, 119 G6
Delaware SF, PA 119 G5
Delaware Water Gap NRA,
PA 119 G4
Delft, 30 A3
Delhi, India 58 C6, 64 E6
Delhi, NY 117 F2, 119 G6
Delhi Cantonment, 64 D7
Delhi Hills, OH 151 C2
Delhi U, 64 E8
Delicias, 128 B2, 96 C5
Dellwood, MO 162 B3
Delray Beach, FL 123 G2
Delson, 106 C1
Delta, UT 130 B5
Delta NF, MS 120 A3
Delta NWR, 120 B1,
122 A5, 129 H3
Deltona, FL 123 F4

Deming, NM 128 A4,
131 D2
Demopolis, AL 120 C3
Denakil, 45 G2
Denali NP & Pres, AK
136 C7, 178 A3
Denderleeuw, 31 E2
Dendermonde, 31 E4
Denison, IA 125 A4,
127 H4
Denizli, 25 H3
Denmark, 15 E1, 22 C6
Denmark Str, 14 A6,
82 E6, 102 E8
Dennis, MA 184 D5
Dennis Port, MA 184 E5
Denpasar, 61 D1
Dent, OH 151 B3
Denton, MD 119 G3
Denton, TX 129 E4
Denver, CO 110 E5,
127 A3, 130 E5,
167 G3, 178 C4
Denver, U of, CO 167 G2
Denver City, TX 131 F2
Denver Intl Arpt, CO
167 H4
Denver Zoo, CO 167 G3
Department of State, DC
149 A3
Depok, Indo 64 B6
Dera Mandi, 64 E5
Derby, 19 E3
Derendorf, 34 B5
Des Moines, IA 112 A5,
125 B4, 179 E4
Des Moines, WA 176 B3
Des Moines R, IA 124 A5
Des Peres, MO 162 A1
Des Plaines, IL 158 C5
Deschutes NF, OR 134 C3
Dese, 45 G2
Desert NWR, NV 133 F4
Desert Test Ctr, UT 130 A5
Desert View, AZ 183 F2
Desio, 40 C3
Desna, 56 A3

Desoto Mem Raceway, FL 154 D1

DeSoto N Mem, FL 154 B1

Dessau, 23 D4

Destin, FL 122 B6

Detroit, MI 103 B1, 112 C6, 118 B6, 125 F4, 156 C6, 179 F4

Detroit City Arpt, MI 156 F7

Detroit Civic Ctr, MI 156 D6

Detroit Lakes, MN 124 A7, 126 F7

Detroit Metro Wayne C Arpt, MI 156 B5

Detroit Zoo, MI 156 C8

Deurne, 31 G6

Deutch-Wagram, 42 F8

Deux Montagnes, 106 A3

Deva Temple, AZ 183 E2

Devils Lake, ND 126 D8

Devils Tower NM, WY 130 E8, 178 C5

Devon, PA 144 B4

Devon Isl, 100 F7, 102 A7

Devonport, 77 E2

Devoo Park, KY 151 D1

Devore, CA 171 G6

Devoto, 88 D7

Dexter, ME 114 D5

Dhaka, 58 E5

Dhauj, 64 E5

Dhrapetsona, 43 A3

Dhulagarh, 65 D2

Di Domitilla Catacombe, 40 C5

Diablo, CA 174 E5

Diadema, 92 B3

Diamond Bar, CA 171 E4

Diamond Creek, 79 D4

Diamond Head SM, HI 177 H1

Diamond Lake, OR 132 B8

Diamond Shoals, NC 187 H1

Diaspora Mus, 50 B6

Dibrugarh, 58 F6

Dickey, ME 114 D8

Dickinson, ND 110 E7, 126 C7

Diego Rivera Mus, 98 B2

Dielsdorf, 37 E2

Diemen, 30 D5

Diepkloof, 51 F2

Dieppe, 19 F1

Diepsloot Nature Reserve, 51 F4

Dietikon, 37 D2

Dietzenbach, 35 C1

Digby, 103 E2

Digul R, 76 B1

Dijon, 16 D5, 20 E6, 23 A1

Dikson, 82 D8

Dili, 61 F1

Dillon, MT 130 B8, 135 F4

Dillon, SC 121 G5

Dimitrovgrad, 25 G5

Dinamo Stad, 56 B4

Dinaric Alps, 24 D5

Dinosaur, CO 130 D5

Dinosaur NM, CO 130 D6, 178 C4

Dinslaken, 34 B8

Diósd, 42 A6

Dire Dawa, 45 H1

Discovery Park, WA 176 A6

Dismal Swamp NWR, VA 121 H6

Disney Animal Kingdom, FL 153 E2

Disney-MGM Studios Theme Park, FL 153 F2

Disneyland, CA 170 D3

Disney's Wide World of Sports Complex, FL 153 F2

District Hts, MD 148 F6

DC Convention Ctr, DC 149 D4

Ditch Creek, WY 181 G3

Diu, 58 B5

Dixie NF, UT 131 B4

Dixmont, ME 114 D5

Diyarbakir, 49 E6

Djibouti, 45 H2, 49 E1

Djursholm, 36 E7

Dnieper R, 52 A5

Dnipropetrovsk, 53 A4

Dobbins ARB, GA 152 A6

Dobbins Lookout, AZ 168 B2

Döbling, 42 D8

Dobrich, 25 H6

Dobson, NC 118 D1

Dobsonville, 51 E2

Dockton, WA 176 B2

Doctor Phillips, FL 153 F3

Dodecanese, 25 G2

Dodge City, KS 111 F4, 127 D2

Dodge Pt, ME 186 A3

Dodger Stad, CA 170 C5, 172 E7

Dodoma, 47 G5

Dogachia, 65 F4

Doha, 49 G4

Doigoye Ledovo, 56 D5

Dole, 23 B1

Dolgoprudnyy, 56 B6

Dollards-des-Ormeaux, 106 A3

Dolmabahce Palace, 43 E2

Dolni Brezary, 35 E2

Dolphin Research Ctr, FL 188 D2

Dom Pedro II Park, 93 H4

Dome, The, AZ 183 B3

Dominica, 85 E6, 95 H3

Dominican Republic, 95 E4

Dominjon Obs, 105 A3

Domjur, 65 D2

Domodedovo, 56 C1

Domodedovo Arpt, 56 D1

Domont, 28 D8

Don Bosco, 88 F6

Don Mills, 104 E7

Don R, 53 B4

Don Torcuato, 88 C8

Donaldsonville, LA 120 A3

Donalsonville, GA 122 D6

Donaustadt, 42 F8

Doncaster, Austral 79 D3

Doncaster, UK 19 E4

Doncaster & Templestowe, 79 D3

Donegal, 19 B4

Donetsk, 45 G6, 53 A4

Dongcaoheqing, 74 D5

Dongcheng District, 73 E3

Dongrancun, 73 B3

Dongtangqiaozhen, 74 F6

Dongting Hu, 67 A3

Dongzhimen, 73 E3

Donostia-San Sebastián, Spain 16 C4

Donvale, 79 E3

Doonside, 78 A8

Doordrecht, 30 C1

Doral, The, FL 155 F2

Doraville, GA 152 D6

Dorchester, MA 139 D4

Dorchester, UK 19 D2

Dordogne R, 20 D5

Dorer Mem SF, Richard J, MN 124 B5

Dorking, 26 C5

Dormont, PA 146 B5

Dornbach, 42 D7

Dornbirn, 23 D1

Dorris, CA 132 B7

Dorsey, MD 147 B1

Dorseyville, PA 146 D8

Dorstfeld, 34 F7

Dortmund, 23 C4, 34 F7

Dorval, 106 B2

Dorval Intl Arpt, 106 B2

Dothan, AL 113 C3, 120 D2, 122 C6

Douala, 44 D1

Double Bay, 78 F7

Double Oak, TX 164 D6

Douglas, AZ 131 C1

Douglas, GA 121 E3

Douglas, UK 19 C4

Douglas, WY 126 A5, 130 E7

Douglas FP, IL 158 A5

Douglass NHS, Frederick DC 148 E6

Dougting Hu Lake, 60 **B6**

Dourdan, 28 **B5**

Dover, DE 112 **E5**, 119 **G3**

Dover, MA 139 **B2**

Dover, NH 115 **C3**

Dover, NJ 116 **A5**

Dover, UK 16 **C6**, 19 **F2**, 20 **D7**

Dover-Foxcroft, ME 114 **D6**

Downers Grove, IL 159 **B3**

Downey, CA 170 **C4**

Downsview, 104 **D7**

Downsview Arpt, 104 **D7**

Doylestown, PA 119 **H5**

Dracut, MA 138 **A7**

Dragor, 36 **C5**

Drakensberg, 46 **F2**

Drama, 25 **G5**

Drammen, 15 **E2**, 22 **C8**

Dreieichenhain, 35 **B1**

Dreileich, 35 **B1**

Dresden, 17 **E6**, 23 **E3**

Dretzka Park, WI 157 **A4**

Drexel Hill, PA 144 **C2**

Driggs, ID 135 **G3**

Drobeta-Turnu Severin, 25 **F6**

Drogheda, 19 **C4**

Drottningholm, 36 **D6**

Drottningholm Palace, 36 **E6**

Druid Hill Park, MD 147 **C3**

Druid Hills, GA 152 **C4**

Drum Barracks Civil War Mus, CA 170 **C3**

Drummond, MT 135 **F5**

Drummondville, 114 **B6**

Drumoyne, 78 **E7**

Dry Creek Pioneer RP, CA 175 **F4**

Dry Tortugas NP, FL 179 **G1**

Dryden, 103 **A3**, 124 **B8**

Dubayy, 49 **E4**

Dubbo, 77 **E3**

Dubendorf, 37 **F2**

Dublin, CA 174 **E5**

Dublin, GA 121 **E3**

Dublin, Ire 14 **B1**, 19 **C4**, 20 **B8**

Dubois, ID 130 **B7**, 135 **F3**

Dubois, WY 135 **H3**

Dubravka, 57 **H2**

Dubrovnik, 17 **F4**, 24 **D4**

Dubuque, IA 112 **B6**, 125 **C4**

Duck, NC 187 **G6**

Duck Cove, ME 186 **A3**

Duck Key, FL 188 **D2**, 135 **E2**

Duck Valley IR, ID 132 **E8**, 135 **E2**

Dudingen, 37 **A1**

Duero, 21 **C3**

Duero R, 16 **B3**

Duffel, 31 **H4**

Dugway Proving Grounds, UT 130 **B5**

Duisburg, 23 **B4**, 34 **B7**

Dukou, 60 **A5**

Duluth, MN 103 **A1**, 112 **A7**, 124 **C7**, 179 **E5**

Dum-Dum, 65 **F2**

Dum-Dum Intl Arpt, 65 **F2**

Dumas, AR 120 **A4**

Dumas, TX 128 **D6**, 131 **F3**

Dumfries, 18 **D5**

Dun Laoghaire, 19 **C4**

Dunafoldvar, 24 **D6**

Dunaharaszti, 42 **B6**

Dunakeszi, 42 **B8**

Dunaujvaros, 24 **D6**

Duncan, OK 129 **E5**

Duncanville, TX 165 **E2**

Dund-Us, 55 **A3**

Dundalk, MD 147 **E2**

Dundalk, UK 19 **C4**

Dundee, 14 **C2**, **D6**

Dunderberg Pk, CA 182 **D5**

Dunedin, Austral 77 **G1**

Dunedin, FL 154 **A5**

Dunfermline, 18 **D5**

Dunkerque, 23 **A3**

Dunkirk, NY 116 **A3**

Dunlap, OH 151 **C4**

Dunn Loring, VA 148 **B6**

Dunnellon, FL 123 **E5**

Dunnville, 116 **A3**

Dunqian, 74 **A8**

Dunsmuir, CA 132 **B7**

Dunwoody, GA 152 **C6**

Duolun, 66 **A6**

Dupont, CO 167 **H4**

Duque de Caxias, 91 **C3**

Duquesne, PA 146 **D5**

Durango, CO 111 **D4**, 131 **D4**

Durango, Mex 96 **C4**

Durant, OK 113 **A3**

Durant Isl, NC 187 **F6**

Durants Neck, NC 187 **E6**

Durban, 47 **F2**

Durham, NC 113 **E4**, 121 **G6**

Durham, OR 177 **F4**

Durham, UK 19 **E4**

Durrës, 17 **G3**, 25 **E5**

Dushanbe, 53 **D1**, 58 **B7**

Dusit, 63 **F6**

Düsseldorf, 20 **F7**, 23 **B3**, 34 **B5**

Düsseldorf Arpt, 34 **B6**

Duvernay, 106 **B4**

Duxbury, MA 184 **A8**

Duxbury Bay, MA 184 **A8**

Dyer, IN 159 **E1**

Dyersburg, TN 125 **D1**, 129 **H6**

Dzerzhinskiy, 56 **D3**

Dzhugdzhur Range, 54 **E5**

Eakin Community Park, VA 148 **A6**

Ealing, 26 **C7**

Earlimart, CA 133 **C4**

East Aurora, NY 116 **B3**

East Boston, MA 139 **D4**

East Brewster,ma 184 **E6**

East Cape, FL 188 **C3**

East Carver, MA 184 **A7**

East Chicago, IN 159 **F2**

East China Sea, 60 **D7**, 67 **D3**

East Cleveland, OH 150 **E8**

East Dennis, MA 184 **E5**

East Entrance, WY 180 **D3**

East Falmouth, MA 185 **B4**

East Grand Forks, MN 126 **E7**

East Grinstead, 26 **D5**

East Hampton, NY 116 **D6**

East Harwich, MA 184 **F5**

East Hills, NY 143 **H5**

East Kew, 79 **C3**

East Kildonan, 107 **G6**

East Lake, NC 187 **F5**

East Lansdowne, PA 144 **D2**

East London, 47 **F2**

East Los Angeles, CA 170 **C4**

East Marion, MA 184 **A5**

East McKeesport, PA 146 **E5**

East Meadow, NY 143 **H3**

East Meredith, NY 117 **F2**

East New York, NY 143 **E3**

East Orange, NJ 142 **B4**

East Orleans, MA 184 **F6**

East Palo Alto, CA 175 **D3**

East Patchogue, NY 116 **C5**

East Point, CA 152 **A3**

East Potomac Park, DC 149 **C1**

East Rockaway, NY 143 **G2**

East Rutherford, NJ 142 **C5**

East St Louis, IL 125 **C2**, 162 **C1**

East San Diego, CA 169 **F3**

East Sandwich, MA 184 **C5**

E

Eagan, MN 161 **D1**

Eagle Creek, OR 177 **H4**

Eagle Lake, CA 132 **C7**

Eagle Lake, ME 114 **E8**, 186 **D5**

Eagle Pass, TX 128 **D2**

Eagle Pk, CA 182 **C6**

Eagle Pk, WY 180 **D2**

Eagle Village, IN 157 **D4**

Eagleville, PA 144 **B6**

East Siberian Sea, 54 **D7**, 82 **B7**

East Tampa, FL 154 **D4**

East Timor, 61 **F1**

East Wareham, MA 184 **A5**

East York, 104 **E6**

Eastern Bay, ME 186 **C6**

Eastern Desert, 48 **C4**

Eastern Ghats, 59 **C4**

Eastern Way, ME 186 **C3**

Eastgate, WA 176 **D5**

Eastham, MA 115 **D2**, 184 **F6**

Eastman, GA 121 **E3**

Easton, MD 119 **G3**

Easton, PA 119 **G5**

Eastpointe, MI 156 **E8**

Eastport, ME 114 **F5**

Eastport, NY 116 **C5**

Eastville, VA 119 **G2**

Eastwick, PA 144 **D1**

Eastwood, 78 **D8**

Eau Claire, WI 112 **B6**, 124 **C5**

Ebensburg, PA 119 **E5**

Ebergassing, 42 **F5**

Eberswalde-Finow, 23 **E4**

Ebina, 68 **A6**

Ebro R, 16 **C3**, 21 **C4**

Ebsjerg, 14 **D1**

Ecatepec, 98 **D5**

Echo Lake, ME 186 **B4**

Eckenheim, 35 **B4**

Eckerd College, FL 154 **B3**

Ecole Militaire, 29 **B1**

Ecorse, MI 156 **C5**

Ecuador, 84 **B4**

Eddystone, PA 144 **C1**

Edegem, 31 **G5**

Eden, ME 186 **B6**

Eden, NY 116 **B2**

Eden Park, OH 151 **D2**

Eden Prairie, MN 161 **A1**

Edenvale, 51 **G3**

Edgartown, MA 115 **C1**, 185 **B2**

Edgartown Harbor, MA 185 **B3**

Edgemere, MD 147 **F2**

Edgemont, PA 144 **A3**

Edgemont Key NWR, FL 154 **A3**

Edgewater, CO 167 **F3**

Edgewater, FL 121 **F1**

Edgewater Park, NJ 145 **H4**

Edgewater Park, OH 150 **C7**

Edgewood, KY 151 **D1**

Edina, MN 161 **B2**

Edinburg, TX 129 **E1**

Edinburgh, UK 14 **C2**, 18 **D5**

Edirne, 25 **G5**

Edison, NJ 116 **A5**

Edison International Field, CA 171 **E3**

Edison NHS, NJ 142 **A5**

Edisto Isl, SC 121 **F3**

Edmond, OK 127 **E1**, 129 **E6**

Edmonton, MD 148 **E7**

Edmonton, 101 **D3**

Edmundston, 103 **D2**, 114 **E8**

Edna, TX 129 **F2**

Edremit, 25 **H4**

Edwards Plateau, 111 **F3**

Edwardsville, KS 162 **A5**

Eel R, CA 132 **A6**

Effigy Mounds NM, IA 179 **E4**

Effinwild, PA 146 **C8**

Effretikon, 37 **F2**

Egelsbach, 35 **B1**

Egersund, 22 **B7**

Egham, 26 **A7**

Eglin AFB, FL 120 **C2**

Eglisau, 37 **E3**

Egypt, 45 **F4**, 48 **C4**

Egyptian Mus, 50 **C2**

Eichwalde, 32 **E5**

Eiffel Tower, 29 **B2**

Eindhoven, 20 **E8**, 23 **B4**

Eisenach, 23 **D3**

Eisenhower Mem Park, NY 143 **H4**

Eisenhüttenstadt, 23 **E4**

Ekáli, 43 **C4**

Ekeren, 31 **G6**

Ekero, 36 **D6**

El Aaiún, 44 **B4**

El Augustino, 87 **G5**

El Avila NP, 90 **C5**

El Batán, 39 **B2**

El Bire, 50 **D5**

El Bosque, 87 **F1**

El Cajon, CA 133 **E2**, 169 **H4**

El Capitan, CA 182 **B3**

El Carite, 90 **B4**

El Castillo, 99 **G3**

El Centro, CA 133 **F2**

El Cerrito, CA 171 **F3**, 174 **C6**

El Charquito, 90 **B1**

El Colegio, 90 **A1**

El Dorado, AR 113 **B3**, 129 **G4**

El Dorado, KS 127 **F2**

El Dorado Intl Arpt, 90 **C2**

El Fuerte, 128 **A1**

El Giza, 50 **B2**

El Granada, CA 175 **A3**

El Hatillo, 90 **D4**

El Junquito, 90 **A4**

El Maadi, 50 **C1**

El Malpais NM, NM 128 **A5**, 131 **D3**

El Matariya, 50 **D3**

El Molino, 99 **E2**

El Monte, CA 170 **D5**

El Noviciado, 87 **E3**

El Paso, TX 96 **C6**, 111 **D3**, 128 **B4**, 131 **E1**, 178 **C2**

El Portal, CA 182 **A3**

El Portal, FL 155 **G2**

El Prat de Llobregat, 38 **E5**

El Rodeo, 99 **E2**

El Rosal, 90 **B3**

El Rosario, 99 **G5**

El Salto, 99 **H3**

El Salvador, 81 **H5**, 84 **A6**, 97 **F2**

El Segundo, CA 170 **B3**

El Sobrante, CA 174 **C7**

El Sueco, 128 **A3**

El Tigre, 84 **D5**

El Vado, 99 **H4**

El Valle, 90 **B4**

El Verde, 99 **H4**

El Zamalik, 50 **C2**

El Zeitun, 50 **D3**

Elat, 48 **D4**

Elba Isl, 17 **E3**, 24 **B4**

Elbasan, 25 **E4**

Elbe R, 17 **E6**, 23 **D4**

Elbrus, 53 **A3**

Elburz Mts, 49 **F6**

Eldorado Springs, CO 167 **E5**

Eldoret, 47 **G6**

Electric Pk, MT 180 **A5**

Electric Science Mus, 71 **A3**

Elefsina, 43 **A3**

Elephant Butte Lake SP, NM 128 **B5**

Eleuthera, 94 **D6**

Elgin, IL 125 **D4**

Elgin, UK 18 **D6**

Elizabeth, NJ 116 **A5**, 119 **H5**, 142 **B2**

Elizabethton, TN 118 **C1**, 121 **E6**

Elizabethtown, NY 117 **G5**

Elizabethtown, OH 151 **A3**

Elk Grove Village, IL 158 **B5**

Elk Isl, WY 181 **G4**

Elk SF, PA 119 **E6**

Elkhovo, 25 **H5**

Elkins, WV 118 **D3**

Elkins Park, PA 145 **E5**

Elko, NV 110 **C6**, 130 **A6**, 132 **E7**, 135 **E1**

Elkridge, MD 147 **C1**

Elkton, MD 119 **G4**

Ellensburg, WA 134 **C5**

Ellenton, FL 154 **C1**

Ellenville, NY 117 **G1**

Ellenwood, GA 152 **D1**
Ellesmere Isl, 82 **D6**,
  100 **F8**, 102 **A8**
Ellicott City, MD 147 **B2**
Ellinghorst, 34 **C8**
Ellinikon, 43 **B2**
Elliniko Intl Arpt, 43 **B2**
Elliot Lake, 103 **B2**, 124 **F6**
Elliott Knob, VA 119 **E2**
Ellipse, The, DC 149 **C3**
Ellis Isl, NY 142 **C3**
Ellis Park Stad, 51 **G2**
Ellisport, WA 176 **B3**
Ellisville, MA 184 **B6**
Ellsworth, ME 114 **E5**
Ellsworth Land, 83 **D4**
Ellsworth Mts, 83 **D3**
Elm Grove, WI 157 **A3**
Elmali, 43 **F3**
Elmhurst, IL 159 **B4**
Elmira, NY 116 **D2**, 119 **F6**
Elmont, NY 143 **G3**
Elmstead, MI 156 **F6**
Elmwood, PA 144 **D2**
Elmwood Park, IL 159 **C4**
Elmwood Park, NJ 142 **B6**
Elmwood Place, OH 151 **D3**
Elstal, 32 **A7**
Eltham, 79 **E3**
Elwood, 79 **C2**
Ely, NV 110 **C5**, 130 **A5**,
  132 **F6**
Ely, UK 19 **F3**
Elyria, OH 118 **C5**
Elysian Park, CA 172 **E7**
Embarcadero Ctr, CA
  173 **E3**
Embrach, 37 **F2**
Embu Guaçu, 92 **A3**
Emden, 22 **B5**
Emerald, 77 **E4**
Emeryville, CA 174 **C6**
Emet, 25 **H3**
Emma Matilda Lake, WY
  181 **G4**
Emmett, ID 135 **E3**
Emory U Mus, GA 152 **C4**

Empire State Bldg, NY
  141 **E4**
Emporia, KS 112 **A5**,
  125 **A3**, 127 **F2**
Emporia, VA 119 **F1**,
  121 **G6**
Emporium, PA 119 **F6**
Emsworth, PA 146 **B7**
Encampment, WY 130 **D6**
Encarnación, 86 **C6**
Encinitas, CA 133 **D2**
Ende, 61 **E1**
Enderby Land, 83 **E1**
Endicott, NY 117 **E2**
Endwell, NY 117 **E2**
Enfield, 26 **D8**
Engativá, 90 **C2**
Engelhard, NC 187 **F3**
England, 14 **C1**, 16 **C6**,
  19 **E3**, 20 **D8**
Englewood, CO 167 **G2**
Englewood, FL 123 **B4**
Englewood, NJ 142 **D6**
Englewood Cliffs, NJ
  142 **D6**
English Chan, 16 **C6**,
  19 **E2**, 20 **C7**
English Turn, LA 163 **H4**
Enid, OK 111 **F4**, 127 **E1**,
  129 **E6**
Ennepetal, 34 **E6**
Ennerdale, 51 **E1**
Enschede, 20 **F8**, 23 **B4**
Ensenada, 133 **E1**, 96 **A6**
Enskede, 36 **E6**
Enterprise, OR 134 **D4**
Entrevías, 39 **C2**
Enugu, 44 **D1**
Epcot Ctr, FL 153 **F2**
Epernay, 23 **A3**
Ephraim, UT 130 **B5**
Ephrata, WA 134 **C5**
Epinal, 23 **B2**
Eppegem, 31 **G3**
Epping, Austral 78 **D8**
Epping, Austral 79 **C4**

Epping, NH 115 **C3**
Epsom, 26 **C6**
Epworth Hts, OH 151 **F3**
Equatorial Guinea, 46 **C6**
Erasmia, 51 **G6**
Érd, 42 **A6**
Erdőkertes, 42 **C8**
Erembodegem, 31 **E3**
Erenköy, 43 **E2**
Erfurt, 17 **E6**, 23 **D3**
Erie, CO 167 **F6**
Erie, PA 112 **D6**, 116 **A3**,
  118 **D6**
Erie Canal, NY 117 **F3**
Erie NWR, PA 116 **A1**,
  118 **D6**
Eritrea, 45 **G2**, 49 **E1**
Erkner, 32 **F6**
Erlangler, KY 151 **C1**
Ermelino Matarazzo, 92 **C5**
Ermington, 78 **D7**
Erqurum, 49 **E6**, 53 **A3**
Esbjerg, 22 **C6**
Escanaba, MI 112 **B6**,
  124 **E6**
Eschborn, 35 **A3**
Escondido, CA 133 **E2**
Escuintla, 97 **E2**
Esfahan, 49 **F5**
Eshta'ol, 50 **C4**
Eskişehir, 48 **C6**
Esla R, 21 **B4**
Esmeraldas, 84 **B4**
Esperance, 76 **B3**
Esplanade des Invalides,
  29 **C2**
Esquel, 86 **A4**
Essen, 16 **D6**, 23 **B4**, 34 **C7**
Essendon, 79 **B3**
Essex, MD 147 **E3**
Essex Junction, VT 117 **H5**
Essling, 42 **F7**
Estação Júlio Prestes, 93 **F6**
Esteban Echeverría, 88 **D5**
Estelle, LA 163 **F4**

Estes Park, CO 130 **E5**
Estevan, 101 **E2**, 126 **C8**
Estherville, IA 124 **A5**
Estonia, 15 **G3**, 52 **B6**
Ethiopia, 45 **G1**, 49 **E1**
Ethiopian Highlands,
  45 **G2**
Etna, CA 132 **A7**
Etna, Italy 24 **C2**
Etna, PA 146 **C7**
Etobicoke, 104 **C6**
Eton College, 26 **A7**
Etrechy, 28 **C5**
Etropole, 25 **F5**
Euclid, OH 150 **E8**
Euclid Creek Res, OH
  150 **E8**
Eufaula, AL 120 **D3**
Eugene, CA 174 **E5**
Eugene, OR 110 **A7**,
  134 **B3**, 178 **A5**
Eugenia Pt, 96 **A5**
Euless, TX 164 **D4**
Euphrates R, 45 **G5**, 49 **E5**
E.U.R., 40 **C5**
Eureka, CA 110 **A6**,
  132 **A7**, 134 **A1**
Eureka, MT 135 **E6**
Eureka, NV 132 **E6**
Disneyland Paris, 28 **F7**
Europa Ctr, 33 **B2**
Europe, 14 – 17, 22 – 25
European Economic Com-
  munity Hdqrs, 31 **G2**
Euston Sta, 27 **B4**
Evansburg SP, PA 144 **A4**
Evanston, IL 158 **D5**
Evanston, WY 130 **C6**,
  135 **G1**
Evansville, IN 112 **C5**,
  125 **E2**
Evendale, OH 151 **E3**
Evere, 31 **G2**
Everett, MA 139 **D4**
Everett, WA 110 **B8**,
  134 **B6**

Everglades NP, FL 123 F2, 179 G1, 188 E4
Everglades NP Visitor Ctr, FL 188 D4
Evergreen Park, IL 159 D3
Evergreen Park, MD 147 F2
Everman, TX 164 C2
Evesboro, NJ 145 H2
Eving, 34 F8
Évora, 21 A3
Evry, 28 D5
Ewa, HI 177 E2
Ewa Beach, HI 177 E2
Ewell, 26 C6
Exchange Square, 75 C2
Exeter, NH 115 C3
Exeter, UK 19 D2, 20 C7
Exhibition Park, Can 104 D6
Exhibition Park, Can 107 H2
Exhibition of Economic Achievements, 56 C5
Expo Mem Park, 70 D6
Exposition Park, CA 172 D5
Eyüp, 43 D3
Ezeiza Arpt, 88 C5
Ezine, 25 G4
Ezpeleta, 88 F6

F

Fabens, TX 131 E1
Fabreville, 106 A3
Facatativá, 90 A3
Faenza, 24 B5
Fahrland, 32 A6
Fairbanks, AK 82 B5, 100 B6, 136 D7, 178 A3
Fairchild Tropical Gdns, FL 155 F1
Fairfax, CA 174 A7
Fairfax, OH 151 E2
Fairfax, VA 119 F3, 148 A6
Fairfield, Austral 78 B7
Fairfield, CA 132 B5
Fairfield, ID 135 E2

Fairfield, NC 187 E3
Fairfield, OH 151 D4
Fairground Park, MO 162 C2
Fairmont, MN 124 B5, 126 F5
Fairmont, WV 118 D4
Fairmont City, IL 162 D2
Fairmont, NY 117 E3
Fairmount Hts, MD 148 F6
Fairmount Park, PA 144 D5
Fairview, GA 152 E1
Fairview, NJ 142 D5
Fairview, OR 177 H5
Fairview Hts, IL 162 D2
Fairview Park, OH 150 B6
Fairway, KS 162 C4
Faisalabad, 58 B6
Fajardo, 122 D2
Fakfak, 76 A3
Falcon Hts, MN 161 D3
Falfurrias, TX 129 E1
Falk Park, WI 157 B1
Falkensee, 32 B7
Falkland Islands, 86 B2
Fall River, MA 115 C2
Fallon, NV 132 D6
Fallon NWR, NV 132 D6
Fallon NAS, NV 132 D6
Falls Church, VA 148 B6
Falls City, NE 127 F3
Falls Creek, CA 182 B6
Falls of the Rhine, 37 F4
Falmouth, MA 185 A4
False Cape, 96 A4
Falun, 22 E8
Faneuil Hall, MA 140 C4
Fanhões, 38 B8
Fano, 24 C4
Far Rockaway, NY 143 F2
Farah, 49 H5, 58 A7
Farbach-Werner Nature Pres, OH 151 C3
Farghona, 53 E1
Fargo, ND 110 F7, 124 A7, 126 E7, 179 E5
Faridabad, 64 F5
Farmers Branch, TX 165 F5

Farmer's Market, CA 172 B7
Farmington, ME 114 D5
Farmington, MI 156 A8
Farmington, MO 125 C2
Farmington, NM 111 D4, 128 A6, 131 D4
Farmington, OR 177 E5
Farmington, UT 130 B6, 135 G1
Farmington Hills, MI 156 A8
Farmville, VA 119 E1
Farnborough, 26 A5
Farnham, 26 A5
Faro, Can 100 B5
Faro, Port 16 A3, 21 A3
Faroe Islands, 14 C3
Farrukhnagar, 64 F8
Farsta, 36 E5
Farum, 36 B7
Favoriten, 42 E7
Fawkner, 79 C4
Faya-Largeau, 45 E3
Fayetteville, AR 113 A4, 125 B1, 129 F6
Fayetteville, NC 113 D4, 121 G5
Fayetteville, TN 120 C5, 125 E1
Fayetteville, WV 118 C2
FBI Bldg, DC 149 D3
Feasterville, PA 145 G6
Fechenhein, 35 C3
Federal, PA 146 A5
Federal Hts, CO 167 G4
Federal Way, WA 176 B2
FedEx Field, MD 148 F6
Feira de Santana, 85 H2
Felix Neck Sanctuary, MA 185 B3
Fellowship, NJ 145 G2
Felsenthal NWR, AR 129 G4
Felsöpakony, 42 C5
Fengtai, 73 B1
Fengtai District, 73 C1
Fenino, 56 D4
Fentonville, PA 145 E4

Fenway Park, MA 139 D3
Ferbitz, 32 A7
Ferencváros, 42 B7
Fergus Falls, MN 126 E7
Ferguson, MO 162 B3
Ferihegy Arpt, 42 C6
Fermi Natl Accelerator Lab, IL 159 A3
Fernández Blanco Mus, 89 D4
Fernandina Beach, fl123 F6
Ferndale, FL 153 E5
Ferndale, MD 147 C1
Ferndale, MI 156 D8
Fernley, NV 132 C6
Fernsehtürm, 33 F4
Ferntree Gully, 79 F1
Ferrara, 24 B5
Ferraz de Vasconcelos, 92 D5
Ferris, TX 165 H1
Ferry Bldg, CA 173 F3
Fès, 16 A1, 44 B5
Fianarantsoa, 47 H3
Fidenae, 40 C6
Fiera Campionaria, 40 B2
Fife, WA 176 B1
Figino, 40 B2
Fiji, 80 C3
Filchner Ice Shelf, 83 D3
Fili, 43 B4
Filimonki, 56 A3
Fillmore, UT 130 B5
Fimbul Ice Shelf, 83 E3
Findlay, OH 125 F4, 118 B5
Fine Arts Palace, 98 F1
Finger Lakes NF, NY 116 D2
Finland, 15 G4, 52 G6, 82 F7
Finland Sta, 57 G2
Finneytown, OH 151 D3
Fiorito, 88 D6
Fircrest, WA 176 A1
Fire Island NS, NY 116 C5, 179 H4
First Union Center, 145 E1
Fish Camp, CA 182 B1

Fish Creek, WY 181 E1
Fish Lake NF, UT 130 B5
Fish Lake RP, MN 161 A4
Fisherman's Wharf, CA 173 D4
Fishermens Bend, 79 B2
Fishers, IN 157 F4
Fishguard, 19 C3
Fishing Bridge Visitor Ctr, WY 180 C3
Fitchburg, MA 115 B3
Fittja, 36 E6
Fitzgerald, GA 121 E3
Fitzwatertown, PA 145 E6
Fiumicino, 40 A4
Five Dock, 78 E7
Flagg Ranch, WY 181 F6
Flagler Beach, FL 123 F5
Flagstaff, AZ 111 C4, 131 B3, 178 B3
Flagstaff Lake, ME 114 C4
Flaming Geyser SP, WA 176 D1
Flaming Gorge NRA, WY 130 C6, 135 H1
Flamingo, FL 188 D4
Flat Creek, WY 181 G1
Flatbush, NY 142 D2
Flathead IR, MT 135 E5
Flathead NF, MT 135 F6
Fleischer Mus, AZ 168 D5
Flensburg, 22 C5
Flin Flon, 101 E3
Flingern, 34 B5
Flint, MI 112 C6, 124 F5
Flint R, GA 120 D2
Floral Park, NY 143 G3
Florala, AL 122 C6
Florence, AL 113 B4, 120 B5
Florence, AZ 131 B2
Florence, CA 170 C4
Florence, Italy 17 E4, 24 B4
Florence, KY 151 C1
Florence, SC 113 E4, 121 F4

Florencia, 84 C4
Florencio Varela, 88 F5
Flores, Arg 88 D6
Flores, Indo 61 E1
Floresville, TX 129 E2
Floriano, 85 G3
Florianópolis, 86 C6
Florida, 51 F3, 97 G5, 113 D2, 122, 179 G2
Florida Bay, FL 123 F1, 188 E3
Florida/Intl U, FL 155 E1
Florida Keys, 113 E1, 188
Florida State Fairgrounds, FL 154 D5
Floridsdorf, 42 E8
Florin, CA 132 B5
Florissant, MO 162 B3
Flourtown, PA 144, D5
Flower Mound, TX 164 D6
Floyd Bennett Field, NY 143 E1
Flushimi-Ku, 71 E1
Flushing, NY 143 F4
Flushing Meadows-Corona Park, NY 143 E4
Fly R, 76 B1
Foerster Peak, CA 182 D2
Foggia, 17 F3, 24 C3
Foggy Bottom, DC 149 A4
Folcroft, PA 144 C1
Foligno, 24 C4
Folkestone, 19 F2
Folkston, GA 123 E6
Fomeque, 90 D1
Fond du Lac, WI 124 D5
Fond du Lac IR, MN 124 B7
Fontana, CA 171 G5
Fontenay-Trésigny, 28 F6
Fontibón, 90 C2
Foot Hall IR, ID 130 B7
Footscray, 79 B3
Ford Estate, Henry, MI 156 C6

Ford Isl, HI 177 F3

Ford Mus & Greenfield Village, Henry, MI 156 C6
Fordham U, NY 143 E6
Ford's Theater, DC 149 D3
Forest, MS 120 B3
Forest City, FL 153 G5
Forest Grove, PA 146 A7
Forest Hts, MD 148 E5
Forest Hill, Austral 79 E2
Forest Hill, Can 104 D6
Forest Hill, TX 164 C2
Forest Hills, MA 139 C3
Forest Hills, NY 143 E3
Forest Park, GA 152 B2
Forest Park, MO 162 B2
Forest Park, NY 143 E4
Forest Park, OH 151 D4
Forestdale, MA 184 B5
Forestville, Austral 78 E8
Forestville, MD 148 F6
Forestville, OH 151 E1
Forêt D'Armainvilliers, 28 E6
Forêt de Marly, 28 B7
Forêt de Notre Dame, 28 E6
Forêt de Rambouillet, 28 A6
Forêt de Senart, 28 D6
Forêt de St Germain, 28 B7
Forks NHP, The, 107 G5
Forlì, 24 B5
Formentera, 21 E2
Former Imperial Palace, 71 E4
Formosa, 86 B6
Forrest City, AR 120 A5
Forsyth, MT 130 D8
Forsyth Pk, CA 182 B6
Forsythe NWR, Edwin B, NJ 119 H4
Fort & Portuguese Ruins, 65 A4
Fort Apache IR, AZ 131 C2
Fort Belknap IR, MT 135 H6
Fort Harrison, SP, IN 157 F3
Fort Benton, MT 135 G6
Fort Berthold IR, ND 126 C7

Fort Bliss Mil Res, NM 128 B4, 131 E2
Fort Bragg, CA 132 A6
Fort Bridger, WY 130 C6
Fort Chaffee Mil Res, AR 129 F5
Fort Collins, CO 110 D5, 127 A3, 136 F6
Fort-de-France, 95 H2
Fort Desoto, FL 154 B2
Fort Desoto Park, FL 154 B2
Fort Dodge, IA 112 A5, 125 B4, 126 F5
Fort DuPont Park, DC 148 E6
Fort Edward, NY 117 H4
Fort Erie, 116 B3
Fort Frances, 103 A3, 124 B7
Fort Franklin, 100 C5, 136 F7
Fort Garland, CO 131 E4
Fort Garry, 107 G4
Fort Good Hope, 136 F7
Fort Hall IR, ID 135 F2
Fort Hamilton, NY 142 C2
Fort Hood Mil Res, TX 129 E3
Fort Howard, MD 147 F1
Fort Irwin Mil Res, CA 133 E3
Fort Jones, CA 132 A7
Fort Kent, ME 114 E8
Fort Landing, NC 187 F5
Fort Laramie, WY 130 E6
Fort Lauderdale, FL 113 E2, 123 G2, 155 G4
Fort Lauderdale/Hollywood Intl Arpt, FL 155 G4
Fort Lauzon, 105 F3
Fort Lee, NJ 142 D5
Fort McDermitt IR, NV 132 D7
Fort McHenry NM & Historic Shrine, MD 147 D2, 179 H4
Fort McMurray, 101 E3

Fort McPherson, *Can*
100 **C6**, 136 **E7**

Fort McPherson, GA
152 **B3**

Fort Mitchell, KY 151 **D1**

Fort Morgan, CO 127 **B3**,
130 **F5**

Fort Myers, FL 94 **B6**,
113 **D2**, 123 **E2**

Fort Myers Beach, FL
123 **E2**

Fort Nelson, 101 **C4**

Fort Peck, MT 126 **A8**

Fort Peck IR, MT 126 **A8**

Fort Peck Lake, MT
126 **A7**, 135 **H6**

Fort Pickett Mil Res, VA
119 **F1**

Fort Pierce, FL 113 **E2**,
123 **F3**

Fort Raleigh NHS, NC
187 **D3**

Fort Robinson, NE 126 **B5**,
130 **F7**

Fort St John, 101 **C4**

Fort Sam Houston, TX
163 **G2**

Fort Scott, KS 125 **A3**,
127 **F2**

Fort Sheridan, IL 158 **C6**

Fort Sill Mil Res, OK 129 **E5**

Fort Simpson, 100 **C5**

Fort Smith, AR 113 **A4**,
125 **A1**, 129 **F6**

Fort Smith, *Can* 101 **E4**

Fort Snelling SP, MN
161 **D1**

Fort Stockton, TX 111 **E3**,
128 **C3**, 131 **F1**

Fort Sumter NM, SC 179 **G2**

Fort Thomas, KY 151 **E1**

Fort Totten, ND 126 **D7**

Fort Totten IR, ND 126 **D7**

Fort Vancouver NHS, OR
177 **F6**

Fort Walton Beach, FL
120 **C2**, 122 **B6**

Fort Ward SP, WA 176 **A5**

Fort Washakie, WY 135 **H2**

Fort Washington, PA 144 **D6**

Fort Washington SP, PA
144 **D6**

Fort Wayne, IN 112 **C5**,
118 **A5**, 125 **E4**

Fort William, 18 **C6**, 65 **E2**

Fort Worth, TX 96 **D6**,
111 **F3**, 129 **E4**, 164 **C3**,
178 **D2**

Fort Worth Alliance Arpt,
TX 164 **B6**

Fort Worth Cultural
District, TX 164 **B3**

Fort Worth Nature Ctr &
Refuge, TX 164 **A4**

Fort Wright, KY 151 **C1**

Fort Yukon, AK 100 **B6**,
136 **D7**

Fort Zachary Taylor SHS,
FL 188 **A1**

Fortaleza, 85 **H3**

Fortuna, CA 132 **A7**

Fossil, OR 134 **C4**

Fossil Butte NM, WY
130 **C6**, 178 **C4**

Foster, OH 151 **F4**

Foster City, CA 175 **C3**

Foster Village, HI 177 **F3**

Fót, 42 **B8**

Fountain, CO 130 **E5**

Fountain Valley, CA 170 **D2**

Fox Chapel, PA 146 **D7**

Fox Chase, PA 145 **F5**

Fox Creek, WY 181 **E2**

Fox Lake Hills, IL 158 **A8**

Fox Pt, WI 157 **C4**

Fox River Grove, IL 158 **A6**

Foxe Basin, 102 **B3**

France, 16 **C5**, 19 **F1**,
20 **D6**, 23 **A3**

Franceville, 46 **D6**

Francistown, 47 **F3**

Francisville, KY 151 **B2**

Franco da Rocha, 92 **A6**

Franconia, VA 148 **C5**

Frankford, PA 145 **F4**

Frankfort, IL 159 **C1**

Frankfort, KY 112 **C5**,
118 **A3**, 125 **F2**

Frankfurt, 16 **D6**, 20 **F7**,
23 **C3**, 23 **E4**, 35 **B3**

Frankfurt am Main Intl
Arpt, 35 **A3**

Franklin, MI 156 **B8**

Franklin, NH 115 **B4**

Franklin, PA 118 **D6**

Franklin, TN 120 **C6**,
125 **E1**

Franklin, VA 119 **F1**

Franklin Bay, 136 **E8**

Franklin Mts SP, NM
128 **A4**

Franklin Park, DC 149 **C4**

Franklin Park, IL 159 **C4**

Franklin Park, PA 146 **B8**

Franklin Square, NY 143 **G3**

Franz Josef Land, 52 **F7**,
82 **D7**

Frascati, 40 **D4**

Fraser, MI 156 **E8**

Fraser Plateau, 101 **B3**

Fraser R, 101 **C3**

Frattocchie, 40 **D4**

Frazier Park, CA 133 **D3**

Fredensborg, 36 **B8**

Frederick, MD 119 **F4**

Frederick, OK 128 **D5**

Frederick Law Olmsted
NHS, MA 139 **C3**

Fredericksburg, TX 129 **E3**

Fredericksburg, VA 119 **F2**

Fredericksburg & Spotsyl-
vania NMP, VA 179 **H4**

Fredericton, 103 **D2**

Frederiksberg, 36 **C6**

Fredonia, NY 116 **B2**

Fredrikstad, 22 **D8**

Freeport, *Bah* 94 **C6**

Freeport IA, 125 **C4**

Freeport, NY 116 **B5**,
143 **H2**

Freetown, 44 **A1**

Fregene, 40 **A5**

Freiburg, 20 **F6**, 23 **C2**,
24 **A6**

Fremantle, 76 **A3**

Fremont, CA 175 **E3**

Fremont, NE 127 **E4**

Fremont, OH 118 **B5**

Fremont NF, OR 132 **B8**,
134 **C2**

French Guiana, 85 **F5**

French Polynesia, 81 **E3**

French Quarter, LA 163 **G5**

French RP, MN 161 **A3**

Frenchman Bay, ME
186 **D6**

Fresnillo, 96 **C4**

Fresno, CA 110 **A5**,
133 **C4**, 178 **E4**

Fresno, TX 166 **B1**

Frestaby, 36 **E7**

Fribourg, 37 **A1**

Frick Park, PA 146 **D6**

Friday Harbor, WA 134 **B6**

Fridley, MN 161 **C4**

Friedersdorf, 32 **F5**

Friedrichshain, 32 **D7**

Friendswood, TX 166 **D1**

Frimley, 26 **A6**

Frisco, NC 187 **G2**

Frisco, UT 130 **B5**

Front Royal, VA 119 **E3**

Frostproof, FL 123 **F3**

Frosunda, 36 **F8**

Fruit Hill, OH 151 **E1**

Fruitvale, CO 130 **D5**

Fry Canyon, UT 131 **C4**

Frying Pan Landing, NC
187 **F5**

Fuchu, 68 **B7**

Fuencarral-el Pardo, 39 **B4**

Fuji, 66 **F5**

Fujim, 68 **B8**

Fujisawa, 68 **A5**

Fujita Art Mus, 71 **C3**

Fukui, 66 **E5**

Fukuoka, 67 **D4**

Fukushima-Ku, 71 **A4**

Fulda, 23 C3
Fullerton, CA 170 D3
Fulton, MO 125 C2
Fulton, NY 117 E4
Funabashi, 68 D7
Funafuti, 80 C4
Funchal, 44 A5
Funza, 90 B2
Fushimi-Ku, 70 F7, 71 E1
Fushun, 55 E2, 60 C8,
  66 C6
Futtsu, 68 C5
Fuxin, 66 B6
Fuyang, 67 A4
Fuzhou, 60 D6, 67 B2
Fyn, 22 D6

G

Gabbs, NV 132 D6
Gabon, 46 D6
Gaborone, 47 E3
Gadsden, AL 113 C4,
  120 C4
Gaffney, SC 121 F5
Gages Lake, IL 158 B7
Gaggiano, 40 A1
Gainesville, FL 113 D3,
  121 E1, 123 E5
Gainesville, GA 121 E4
Gainesville, TX 129 E5
Galapagos Islands, 81 H4, '
  84 A3
Galátsion, 43 B3
Galati, 17 H5
Galax, VA 121 F6
Galdhøpiggen, 15 E3
Gale Peak, CA 182 D1
Galena Park, TX 166 D3
Galesburg, IL 125 C4
Gallatin, TN 120 C6
Gallatin NF, MT 135 G4,
  180 B6
Gallatin Petrified Forest,
  MT 180 A6
Gallatin Range, 180 A5
Gallatin R, 180 A6
Galle, 59 C3

Gallipolis, OH 118 C3
Galloo Isl, NY 117 E5
Gallup, NM 111 D4,
  128 A6, 131 D3
Galveston, TX 113 A3,
  129 F2, 179 E1
Galway, 14 B1, 19 A4,
  20 A8
Gambia, 44 A3
Gamboa, 91 D2
Gander, 103 F3
Ganea, 53 B2
Ganges R, 58 D5
Ganlose, 36 A7
Ganshoren, 31 F2
Ganzhou, 60 C6, 67 A3
Gao, 44 C2
Garbagnate Milanese, 40 B3
Garbatella, 40 C5
Garden City, Egypt 50 C2
Garden City, KS 127 C2
Garden City, MI 156 B6
Garden City, NY 143 G3
Garden Grove, CA 170 D2
Garden Reach, 65 E2
Gardena, CA 170 B3
Gardenale, TX 163 H2
Gardenstadt, 34 F7
Gardiner, Austral 79 C2
Gardiner, ME 114 D5
Gardiner, MT 180 B5
Gare d'Austerlitz, 29 F1
Gare de l'Est, 29 F4
Gare du Nord, 29 F4
Gare St. Lazare, 29 D4
Garfield, NJ 142 C6
Garfield Hts, OH 150 E6
Garfield Park, IN 157 E2
Garfield Park Res, OH
  150 D6
Garges-Les-Gonesse, 28 D8
Gariya, 65 F1
Garland, TX 165 H5
Garment District, CA 172 E6
Garonne R, 16 C4, 20 D5
Garoua, 44 D1
Garrett Park, MD 148 C8

Garrison, MD 147 B4
Garryowen, MT 126 A6,
  130 D8
Garulia, 65 F3
Gary, IN 112 C5, 125 D4,
  159 F2
Gary Regional Arpt, IN
  159 F2
Gaspé, 103 E3
Gaspé Pen, 103 E3
Gastonia, NC 121 E5
Gates of the Arctic NP &
  Pres, AK 136 C8, 178 B2
Gatesville, NC 119 F1
Gatesville, TX 129 E3
Gateway of India, 65 B1
Gateway NRA, NY 116 B5,
  142 C1, 143 E2
Gatineau, 105 A1
Gatineau Prov P, 105 A3
Gatorland, FL 123 G2
Gatwick Arpt, 26 C5
Gauley River NRA, WV
  118 C2
Gava, 38 D5
Gävle, 15 F3, 22 F8
Gaza, 48 D5
Gaziosmanpasa, 43 D3
Gdansk, 15 F1, 22 F5,
  52 A6
Gdynia, 22 F5
Geddes, SD 126 E5
Gedera, 50 A4
Gedser, 22 D5
Geelong, 77 E2
Geilo, 22 C8
Gejiu, 60 A5
Gela, 24 C1
Gelsenkirchen, 34 D8
Gem Lake, MN 161 E4
General Mitchell Intl Arpt,
  WI 157 C1
General San Martín, 88 C7
General San Martín
  Cultural Centre, 89 C3
General Sarmiento, 88 B7
Genesee R, NY 116 C2

Geneseo, NY 116 C3
Geneva, NY 116 D3
Geneva, Switz 16 D4,
  20 F5, 23 B1
Genoa, 17 E4, 24 A5
Gentilly, 28 D6
Gentofte, 36 C6
George Bush Intl Arpt, TX
  166 C6
George Mason U, VA
  148 A6
George Town, 61 A3
George Washington Brdg,
  NY 142 D5
George Washington NF, OH
  119 E3
George Washington U, DC
  149 B3
Georges Hall, 78 C6
Georgetown, DE 119 G3
Georgetown, MA 138 E8
Georgetown, SC 121 G4
Georgetown, Guyana
  85 E5
Georgia, 97 F6, 113 D3,
  121 D2, 179 G2
Georgia, Rus 45 G6
Georgia Dome, GA 152 B3
Georgia Tech, GA 152 B4
Gera, 23 D3
Geraldton, 76 A3, 103 B2
Gerardsville, 51 F5
Gerasdorf, 42 F8
Gering, NE 130 F6
Gerlafingen, 37 C4
Gerli, 88 E6
Germann, TX 165 G3
Germantown, PA 145 E4
Germantown, TN 120 B5,
  129 H6
Germany, 17 E6, 20 F8,
  23 D4, 24 B6, 44 D6
Germiston, 51 H2
Gerona, 21 E4
Gerthe, 34 E8
Gettysburg, PA 119 F4

Getty Mus, J Paul, CA 170 **A5**

Gettysburg NMP, PA 179 **G4**

Gevelsberg, 34 **E6**

Ghadamis, 44 **D4**

Ghana, 44 **C1**

Ghardaïa, 44 **C4**

Ghatkopar, 65 **B2**

Ghaziabad, 64 **F7**

Ghent, 20 **E7**, 23 **A3**

Ghiradelli Square, CA 173 **C4**

Gianicolense, 40 **C5**, 41 **A1**

Gianicolo, 41 **B2**

Giardini del Quirinale, 41 **D3**

Gibraltar, 16 **A3**, 21 **B1**

Gibson Desert, 76 **B4**

Gibsonton, FL 154 **D4**

Giessen, 23 **C3**

Gifford, FL 123 **F3**

Gig Harbor, WA 176 **A3**

Gijón, 16 **B4**, 21 **B4**

Gila NF, NM 128 **A5**, 131 **D2**

Gila River IR, AZ 131 **B2**, 168 **B3**

Gillespie Field, CA 169 **H4**

Gillette, FL 154 **C2**

Gillette, WY 126 **A5**, 130 **E7**

Gilmore, GA 152 **A5**

Gilroy, CA 133 **B4**

Ginkakuji, 71 **F3**

Ginkakuji Temple, 70 **F8**

Ginnhein, 35 **B3**

Ginza, 69 **D2**

Gion, 71 **F3**

Gisborne, 77 **H2**

Giv'at Ze'ev, 50 **D5**

Gjirokastër, 25 **E4**

Gjøvik, 22 **D8**

Glacier NP, MT 135 **F6**, 178 **B6**

Glacier Bay NP & Pres, AK 136 **E6**, 178 **B1**

Glacier Pt, CA 182 **B3**

Gladbeck, 34 **C8**

Gladesville, 78 **D7**

Gladsakse, 36 **B6**

Gladstone, *Austral* 77 **F4**

Gladstone, OR 177 **G4**

Gladwyne, PA 144 **C4**

Glama R, 15 **E3**

Glasgow, KY 120 **D6**

Glasgow, MT 110 **E7**, 126 **A8**

Glasgow, UK 14 **C2**, 18 **C5**

Glasgow Village, MO 162 **C3**

Glattbrugg, 37 **D2**

Glattfelden, 37 **E3**

Glen, NH 115 **C4**

Glen Avon, CA 171 **G4**

Glen Burnie, MD 147 **D1**

Glen Canyon NRA, 131 **C4**, 178 **B3**

Glen Cove, NY 116 **B5**, 143 **H6**

Glen Echo, MD 148 **C7**

Glen Ellyn, IL 159 **A4**

Glen Mills, PA 144 **A3**

Glen Riddle, PA 144 **A1**

Glen Ridge, NJ 142 **B5**

Glen Waverly, 79 **E2**

Glenarden, MD 148 **F7**

Glencoe, IL 158 **D6**

Glendale, AZ 131 **B2**, 168 **A4**

Glendale, CA 133 **D3**, 170 **C5**, 172 **E8**

Glendale, CO 167 **G3**

Glendale, MO 162 **A1**

Glendale, OH 151 **D4**

Glendale, OR 134 **B2**

Glendale, VA 148 **A7**

Glendale, WI 157 **B4**

Glendale Hts, IL 159 **A4**

Glendive, MT 126 **B7**

Glendora, CA 171 **E5**

Glenfield, 78 **B5**

Glenolden, PA 144 **C1**

Glenroy, 79 **B4**

Glenshaw, PA 146 **C7**

Glenside, PA 145, **E5**

Glenview, CA 170 **A5**

Glenview, IL 158 **C5**

Glenvista, 51 **G2**

Glenwillow, OH 150 **F5**

Glenwood, IL 159 **D1**

Glenwood Springs, CO 130 **D5**

Glifada, Gr 43 **C1**

Glin, AZ 131 **C2**

Gloria, 91 **D2**

Glostrup, 36 **B6**

Gloucester, Can 105 **C2**

Gloucester, MA 115 **C4**

Gloucester, UK 19 **D3**

Gloucester, VA 119 **G2**

Gloucester City, NJ 145 **E1**

Gobancho, 69 **A4**

Gobi Desert, 55 **C1**, 58 **F8**, 60 **A3**, 66 **A6**

Godalming, 26 **B5**

Gödöllő, 42 **C8**

Goethals Brdg, 142 **B2**

Goiâna, 85 **F1**

Gokalpur, 64 **E8**

Gold Beach, OR 132 **A8**, 134 **A3**

Gold Horn, 43 **E2**

Gold Mus, 90 **C2**

Gold Reef City, 51 **F2**

Golden, CO 130 **E5**, 167 **E3**

Golden Beach, FL 155 **G3**

Golden Gate, FL 123 **F2**

Golden Gate Brdg, CA 174 **A5**

Golden Gate NRA, CA 173 **B4**, 174 **A5**, 175 **A4**, 178 **A4**

Golden Valley, MN 161 **B3**

Goldendale, WA 134 **C4**

Goldenrod, FL 153 **H4**

Goldfield, NV 132 **F6**

Goldsboro, NC 121 **G5**

Goldwater Air Force Range, Barry M, AZ 131 **A3**

Golf Manor, OH 151 **D3**

Golfo de Santa Clara, 133 **F1**

Golmud, 58 **F7**

Goma, 47 **F6**

Gomel, 15 **H1**

Gonaives, 94 **D4**

Gonder, 45 **G2**

Gonesse, 28 **D8**

Gonzales, CA 133 **B4**

Gonzalez, AL 122 **B6**

González Catán, 88 **C5**

Gooding, ID 132 **F8**, 135 **E2**

Goodland, KS 127 **C3**

Goodwell, OK 127 **C1**

Gooik, 31 **E1**

Goose Cove, ME 186 **A3**

Goose Lake, OR 132 **C8**

Gordon, *Austral* 78 **E8**

Gordon, Can 107 **F6**

Gorelovo, 57 **F1**

Gorgan, 49 **G6**

Gorgonzola, 40 **D2**

Gorham, ME 114 **C5**

Gorinchem, 30 **D1**

Gor'ky Park, 56 **B4**

Gorla, 40 **C2**

Görlitz, 23 **E3**

Gorlose, 36 **A8**

Gorna Oryakhovitsa, 25 **G6**

Gorontalo, 61 **E3**

Gorzow Wielkopolski, 23 **E4**

Goshen, NY 119 **H6**

Goshute IR, NV 132 **F6**

Göteborg, 15 **E2**, 22 **D7**

Gotland, 15 **F2**, 22 **F7**

Gotse Delchev, 25 **F5**

Göttingen, 23 **D4**

Gouda, 30 **C3**

Goupilieres, 28 **A7**

Goussainville, 28 **D8**

Gouverneur, NY 117 **F5**

Governador Valadares, 85 **G1**

253

Government Ctr, MA 140 C4

Government Pt, OR 134 A4

Governors Isl, NY 142 D3

Gowanda, NY 116 B2

Grace Cathedral, CA 173 D3

Graceville, FL 122 C6

Gracia, 38 E6

Gradyville, PA 144 A3

Grafton, Austral 77 F3

Grafton, ND 126 E8

Grafton, WV 118 D3

Graham, TX 129 E4

Graham Lake, ME 114 E5

Grajaú, 91 C2

Gran Chaco, 86 B6

Granada, Nic 90 A1, 97 F1

Granada, Spain 16 B2, 21 C2

Granby, 114 A6

Grand Bahama, 94 C6

Grand Canal, 60 C7, 67 B4

Grand Canyon, AZ 111 C4, 131 B3

Grand Canyon Arpt, AZ 183 E1

Grand Canyon Lodge, AZ 183 E2

Grand Canyon NP, AZ 131 B4, 133 F4, 178 B3, 183 D3

Grand Canyon of the Tuolumne R, CA 182 B4

Grand Canyon of the Yellowstone, WY 180 C4

Grand Canyon Village, AZ 183 E2

Grand Central Sta, NY 141 G4

Grand Falls, Can 103 D2

Grand Falls, Can 103 F3

Grand Falls/Grand Sault, 114 F8

Grand Forks, MN 124 A7

Grand Forks, ND 101 F2, 110 F7, 126 E7, 178 E5

Grand Hotel, 62 C5

Grand Isl, NE 110 F5, 127 D4

Grand Junction, CO 110 D5, 130 C5

Grand-Mère, 114 A7

Grand Palace, 63 F5

Grand Palais, 29 C3

Grand Place Market, 31 F2

Grand Prairie, TX 165 E3

Grand Rapids, Can 101 F3

Grand Rapids, MI 112 C6, 124 E5, 179 F5

Grand Rapids, MN 124 B7

Grand R, 116 A3

Grand River NG, SD 126 C6

Grand Terrace, CA 171 H4

Grand Teton, WY 130 C7

Grand Teton NP, WY 130 C7, 135 G3, 178 C5, 180 A1, 181 F5

Grand Trianon, 28 B7

Grand View, ID 135 E2

Grande Pointe, 107 H4

Grande Prairie, 101 D3

Grande R, 85 F1

Grandview Pt, AZ 183 E1

Grangeville, ID 130 A8, 135 E4

Granite City, IL 162 C3

Granite Falls, MN 126 F6

Granite Gorge, AZ 183 D2

Granite Narrows, AZ 183 C3

Granite Pk, MT 135 F4

Granollers, 38 F8

Grant Park, CA 152 C3

Grant Park, IL 160 D6

Grant Park, WI 157 C1

Grant Village Visitor Ctr, WY 180 C3

Grants, NM 128 A6, 131 D3

Grants Pass, OR 132 A8, 134 B2

Granville, NY 115 A4, 117 H4

Granville Isl, Can 107 G2

Grapevine, TX 164 D5

Grapevine RA, TX 164 C6

Grasfontein, 51 H6

Grasmere, 51 E1

Grass R, NY 117 F6

Grass Valley, CA 132 B6

Grasslands NP, 126 A8

Grassy Key, FL 188 D2

Gravenbruch, 35 C2

Gravesend, NY 142 D1

Gravesend, UK 26 F7

Grays, 26 E7

Grayslake, IL 158 B7

Grayson, KY 118 B3

Graz, 17 F5, 23 E1, 24 C6

Grazhdanka, 57 G3

Great Abaco, 94 C6

Great America, CA 175 E2

Great Artesian Basin, 76 D4

Great Australian Bight, 76 C3

Great Barrier Reef, 77 E5

Great Barrington, MA 115 A3, 117 H2

Great Basin, NV 132 E6

Great Basin NP, NV 130 A5, 132 F6, 178 B4

Great Bear Lake, 100 D5

Great Bend, KS 127 E2

Great Brook Farm SF, MA 138 A6

Great Buddha, 68 B5

Great Cranberry Isl, ME 186 C2

Great Dismal Swamp NWR, VA 119 G1

Great Dividing Range, 77 E3, 80 B3

Great Exuma, 94 C5

Great Falls, MT 101 D2, 110 D7, 135 G5, 178 C6

Great Falls, VA 148 A8

Great Falls Park, VA 148 A8

Great Fountain Geyser, WY 180 B3

Great Gott Isl, ME 186 B1

Great Hall of the People, The, 73 D2

Great Inagua, 94 D4

Great Indian Desert, 58 B6

Great Lakes Naval Training Ctr, IL 158 C7

Great Meadows NWR, MA 138 A5

Great Neck, NY 143 G5

Great Neck Plaza, NY 143 G4

Great Notch, NJ 142 B6

Great Plains, 101 D2, 110 E6

Great Pt, MA 185 F2

Great Sacandaga Lake, NY 117 G3

Great Salt Lake, UT 110 C5, 130 B6, 135 F1, 178 B4

Great Sand Dunes NP, CO 127 A3, 131 E4, 178 C3

Great Sandy Desert, 76 B5

Great Slave Lake, 101 D4

Great Smoky Mts NP, 121 E5, 125 F1, 179 F3

Great Thumb Mesa, AZ 183 C3

Great Thumb Pt, AZ 183 C3

Great Victoria Desert, 76 B3

Great White Heron NWR, FL 123 F1, 188 A3

Great Yarmouth, 19 F3

Greater Cincinnati Intl Arpt, KY 151 B1

Greco, 40 C2

Greece, 17 G2, 25 F3

Greece, NY 116 C3

Greeley, CO 110 E5, 127 B3, 130 E6

Green Bay, MI 103 A1

Green Bay, WI 112 **B6**, 124 **D5**, 179 **F5**

Green Harbor, MA 184 **A8**

Green Isl, ME 186 **A5**

Green Mountain NF, VT 115 **A3**, 117 **H5**

Green Oaks, IL 158 **C5**

Green Park, 27 **B2**

Green R, KY 125 **E2**

Green R, UT 130 **C5**

Green River, WY 135 **H1**

Green Valley, AZ 131 **B1**

Greenacres, CA 133 **C3**

Greenbelt, MD 148 **F8**

Greenbelt Park, MD 148 **F7**

Greenbrae, CA 174 **A6**

Greendale, WI 157 **B1**

Greenfield, MA 115 **A3**

Greenfield, WI 157 **B1**

Greenfield Park, Can 106 **D2**

Greenfield Park, WI 157 **A3**

Greening Isl, ME 186 **C3**

Greenland Sea, 82 **E6**

Greenock, 18 **C5**

Greenpoint, NY 141 **H2**

Greenport, NY 116 **D6**

Greensboro, AL 120 **C3**

Greensboro, NC 113 **D4**, 121 **F6**

Greensborough, 79 **D4**

Greensburg, IN 118 **A4**

Greensburg, PA 119 **E4**

Greenup, KY 118 **B3**

Greenville, AL 120 **C3**

Greenville, CA 132 **C6**

Greenville, ME 114 **D6**

Greenville, MS 113 **B3**, 120 **A4**, 129 **H5**

Greenville, NC 121 **H5**

Greenville, SC 113 **D4**, 121 **E5**

Greenwich, CT 115 **A1**, 116 **B6**

Greenwich, UK 26 **D7**

Greenwich Village, NY 141 **F3**

Greenwood, SC 121 **E4**

Greenwood Village, CO 167 **G2**

Gregg, PA 146 **A6**

Greifswald, 22 **E5**

Grembergen, 31 **E4**

Grenada, MS 120 **B4**, 129 **H5**

Grenada, WI 85 **E6**, 95 **H1**

Grenchen, 37 **B4**

Grenelle, 29 **A1**

Grenoble, 16 **D4**, 20 **F5**

Gresham, OR 177 **H5**

Gresham Park, GA 152 **C3**

Gretna, LA 163 **G5**

Greve, 36 **A5**

Greve Strand, 36 **B5**

Greymouth, 77 **G1**

Griffin, GA 120 **D4**

Griffith, *Austral* 77 **E3**

Griffith, IN 159 **F1**

Griffith Obs, CA 172 **D8**

Griffith Park, CA 170 **C5**, 172 **D8**

Grimbergen, 31 **G3**

Grimsby, 19 **E4**

Grimstad, 22 **C7**

Grinter Place SHS, KS 162 **A5**

Grise Fiord, 102 **A7**

Grobschmidt Park, WI 157 **B1**

Grodinge, 36 **D5**

Grodno, 15 **G1**

Groenendaal, 31 **G1**

Groesbeck, OH 151 **C3**

Groningen, 14 **D1**, 20 **E8**, 23 **B4**

Gros Ventre R, WY 181 **G2**

Gros Ventre Slide, WY 181 **G2**

Gros Ventre Wilderness Area, WY 181 **H1**

Grossenzersdorf, 42 **F7**

Gross Glienicke, 32 **B6**

Grossaffoltern, 37 **B3**

Grossbeeren, 32 **C5**

Grosse Pointe, MI 156 **F7**

Grosse Pointe Farms, MI 156 **F7**

Grosse Pointe Park, MI 156 **F7**

Grosse Pointe Shores, MI 156 **F7**

Grosse Pointe Woods, MI 156 **F7**

Grosser Muggelsee, 32 **E6**

Grosseto, 24 **B4**

Grossjedleresdorf, 42 **E8**

Grossmont College, CA 169 **G4**

Grotta-Ferrata, 40 **D4**

Groveland, MA 138 **D8**

Groveton, NH 114 **B5**

Grundy, VA 118 **C1**

Grune Municipal Park, 35 **B3**

Grunewald, 32 **B6**

Guadalajara, *Mex* 99 **F5**

Guadalajara, Spain 21 **C3**, 96 **C3**

Guadalquivir R, 21 **C2**

Guadalupe, AZ 168 **B3**

Guadalupe, CA 133 **C3**

Guadalupe Mountains NP, TX 128 **B4**, 131 **E1**, 178 **C2**

Guadalupe Pk, TX 131 **E2**

Guadalupe Victoria, 98 **C5**

Guadeloupe, 95 **H3**

Guadiana R, 21 **B3**

Guaianazes, 92 **D4**

Guajará-Mirim, 84 **D2**

Guam, 80 **A5**

Guang'anmen Railway Sta, 73 **C1**

Guangzhou, 60 **C5**, 67 **A3**

Guánica, 122 **A1**

Guantánamo, 94 **D4**

Guaporá R, 84 **D1**

Guaratiba, 91 **A1**

Guarda, 21 **A3**

Guarulhos, 92 **C5**

Guasca, 90 **D3**

Guatemala, 81 **H5**, 84 **A6**, 97 **E2**

Guatemala City, 84 **A6**, 97 **E2**

Guayama, 122 **C1**

Guayaquil, 84 **B3**

Guaymas, 96 **B5**

Guaynabo, 122 **C2**

Guelma, 24 **A1**

Guelph, 116 **A4**

Guernsey, *UK* 19 **D1**

Guernsey, WY 130 **E6**

Guggenheim Mus, NY 141 **H6**

Guia de Pacobaíba, 91 **D4**

Guiana Highlands, 84 **D5**

Guidonia, 40 **D6**

Guignes, 28 **F5**

Guildford, *Austral* 78 **C7**

Guildford, *UK* 19 **E2**, 26 **B5**

Guilford Courthouse NMP, NC 179 **G3**

Guilin, 60 **B6**

Guinea, 44 **A3**

Guinea-Bissau, 44 **A3**

Guiyang, 60 **B6**

Gujranwala, 58 **C6**

Gulf City, FL 154 **C3**

Gulf Coastal Plain, 113 **B3**

Gulf Island NS, FL 120 **C2**, 179 **F2**

Gulf of Aden, 45 **H2**, 49 **F1**

Gulf of Alaska, 82 **A5**, 100 **A5**, 136 **D5**

Gulf of Anadyr, 54 **F8**

Gulf of Aqaba, 48 **D4**

Gulf of Boothia, 15 **F4**, 52 **B6**, 102 **A6**,

Gulf of Cádiz, 21 **A3**

Gulf of California, 96 **A6**, 111 **C2**, 131 **A1**, 133 **F1**

Gulf of Carpentaria, 76 **D6**

Gulf of Finland, 15 **G3**

Gulf of Guinea, 44 **C1**

Gulf of Honduras, 97 **F2**

Gulf of Lion, 21 **E4**

Gulf of Mexico, 81 **H6**,
94 **A6**, 97 **E4**, 113 **C2**,
122 **C4**

Gulf of Oman, 49 **H4**

Gulf of Panama, 97 **H1**

Gulf of Papua, 76 **C1**

Gulf of Riga, 15 **G2**

Gulf of St Lawrence,
103 **E3**

Gulf of St Malo, 19 **E1**,
20 **C6**

Gulf of San Jorge, 86 **B3**

Gulf of Sidra, 45 **E4**, 48 **A5**

Gulf of Suez, 48 **D4**

Gulf of Thailand, 61 **A3**

Gulf of Tonkin, 60 **B5**

Gulf of Valencia, 21 **D3**

Gulf Shores, AL 122 **B6**

Gulfport, FL 154 **B3**

Gulfport, MS 120 **B2**,
122 **A6**, 129 **H3**

Gulfstream Park, FL 155 **G3**

Gulian, 66 **A3**

Gull Rock, NC 187 **F3**

GUM, 57 **F5**

Gum Neck, NC 187 **E4**

Gumet Pt, MA 184 **B8**

Gumpoldskirchen, 42 **D5**

Gümüşköy, 43 **E4**

Gunnison, CO 130 **D5**

Gunpowder Falls SP, MD
147 **E4**

Guntersville, AL 120 **C5**

Gunungsindur, 64 **A6**

Gurnee, IL 158 **C7**

Gurupi, 85 **F2**

Gustaf III's Pavilion, 36 **E6**

Gustava A Madero, 98 **B3**

Gustavsberg, 36 **F6**

Güstrow, 22 **D5**

Guterfelde, 32 **C5**

Guthrie, OK 127 **E1**,
129 **E6**

Guttenberg, NY 142 **D5**

Guyana, 85 **E5**

Guymon, OK 127 **C1**,
128 **D6**

Gweru, 47 **F4**

Gwynns Falls Park, MD
147 **C3**

Gyál, 42 **B6**

Gyda Pen, 50 **F5**

Gymea, 78 **D5**

Gympie, 77 **F4**

Gyor, 17 **F5**, 23 **F2**, 24 **D6**

H

Ha Kwai Chung, 75 **B4**

Haacht, 31 **H3**

Haan, 34 **C5**

Haang R, 55 **E1**

Haarlem, 30 **C6**

Habinghorst, 34 **E8**

Habiplet, 43 **D3**

Hachinohe, 66 **F6**

Hachioji, 68 **A7**

Hacienda Hts, CA 170 **D4**

Hackensack, NJ 142 **C6**

Hackensack, NY 119 **H5**

Hackettstown, NJ 116 **A5**

Hackney, 26 **D7**

Haddon Hts, NJ 145 **F1**

Haddonfield, NJ 145 **F1**

Hadfield, 79 **B4**

Hadian District, 73 **A4**

Hadley Pt, ME 186 **B6**

Hagen, 34 **F6**

Hagerstown, MD 112 **E5**,
119 **F4**

Hague, The, 16 **D6**, 20 **E8**,
23 **A4**, 30 **A3**

Hague Central Sta, The,
30 **A3**

Hahn SRA, Kenneth, CA
172 **B5**

Haidian, 73 **C4**

Haifa, 48 **D5**

Haikou, 60 **C5**

Hail, 49 **E4**

Hailar, 55 **D3**, 66 **B2**

Hailey, ID 135 **F2**

Hainan, 60 **B5**

Haines Junction, 136 **E6**

Hainesville, IL 158 **A7**

Haiphong, 60 **B5**

Haiti, 94 **D4**

Hakodate, 66 **F6**

Haldimand, 116 **A3**

Haleakala NP, HI 137 **E2**,
178 **C1**

Haleakala NP Visitor Ctr,
HI 137 **E3**

Hales Corners, WI 157 **A1**

Halethope, MD 147 **C2**

Half Dome, CA 182 **C3**

Half Moon Bay, CA 175 **B2**

Halfway, OR 134 **D3**

Halfway House, 51 **G4**

Halfax, Can 113 **E7**

Halifax, NC 119 **F1**

Halim Perdanakusuma
Arpt, 64 **C7**

Halisahar, 65 **F4**

Hall Quarry, ME 186 **B4**

Hallandale, FL 155 **G3**

Halle, *Bel* 31 **H1**, 16 **H6**

Halle, *Ger* 23 **D4**

Halmahera, 61 **F3**

Halmstad, 15 **E2**, 22 **D6**

Haltom City, TX 164 **C4**

Halver, 34 **F5**

Hamadan, 49 **F6**

Hamah, 48 **D5**

Hamamatsu, 66 **F5**

Hamborn, 34 **B7**

Hamburg, *Ger* 15 **E1**,
22 **D5**

Hamburg, NY 116 **B3**

Hamersley Range, 76 **A4**

Hami, 55 **B1**, 58 **E8**

Hamilton, AL 120 **B4**

Hamilton, *Austral* 77 **H2**

Hamilton, *Can* 103 **C1**,
112 **D6**, 116 **A4**

Hamilton, MT 135 **F4**

Hamilton, NY 117 **E3**

Hamilton, OH 118 **A4**

Hamilton Pond, ME 186 **C6**

Hamme, 31 **E4**

Hammerfest, 15 **F6**, 82 **E7**

Hammond, IN 159 **E2**

Hammond, LA 120 **A3**

Hammondsport, NY 116 **D2**

Hampstead, 106 **C2**

Hampstead Heath, 26 **C7**

Hampton, *Austral* 79 **C1**

Hampton, NH 115 **C3**

Hampton, VA 119 **G1**

Hampton Bays, NY 116 **D5**

Hampton Court Palace,
26 **B7**

Hampton NHS, PA 147 **D4**

Hamtramck, MI 156 **E7**

Hanam, 72 **C7**

Hancock, MA 117 **H2**

Hancock Tower, MA 140 **B2**

Handan, 55 **D1**, 60 **B7**,
66 **A5**

Handen, 36 **E5**

Haneda Arpt, 68 **C6**

Hanford, CA 133 **C4**

Hang Hau, 75 **F3**

Hanging Gardens, 65 **A1**

Hangkou District, 74 **E7**

Hangnam, 72 **D6**

Hangpu District, 74 **E6**

Hangzhou, 60 **D7**, 67 **B3**

Hanna, 101 **D2**

Hannibal, MO 112 **B5**

Hannover, 17 **E6**, 20 **F8**,
23 **C4**

Hanoi, 60 **B5**

Hanover, NH 115 **B4**

Hanover Park, IL 159 **A4**

Hansen Park, WI 157 **A3**

Haora, 65 **E2**

Haora Brdg, 65 **E2**

Hapeville, GA 152 **B2**

Happy Valley, 75 **D2**

Happy Valley, OR 177 **G5**

Happy Valley-Goose Bay,
103 **E4**

Harad, 49 **F3**

Harahan, LA 163 **E5**

Harare, 47 **F4**

Harbin, 55 **E2**, 66 **C7**

Harbinger, NC 187 **G6**

Harbord, 78 **F8**

Hardin, MT 135 **H4**

Harer, 45 **H1**

Hareskovby, 36 **B6**

Hargeysa, 45 **H1**

Harlan, IA 125 **A4**, 127 **F4**

Harlan, KY 118 **B1**

Harlem, NY 142 **D5**

Harlowton, MT 135 **G4**

Harmarville, PA 146 **D8**

Harmelen, 30 **D3**

Harney Lake, OR 132 **C8**

Harper Woods, MI 156 **E7**

Harpers Ferry NHP, WV 179 **G4**

Harrisburg, PA 112 **E5**, 119 **F4**

Harrison, AR 125 **B1**

Harrison, NJ 142 **B4**

Harrison, OH 151 **A3**

Harrisonburg, VA 119 **E3**

Harrods, 26 **C7**

Harrodsburg, KY 118 **A3**

Harrogate, 19 **E4**

Harrow, 26 **B8**

Harry S Truman NHS, MO 162 **D5**

Harry S Truman Sports Complex, MO 162 **D5**

Hart Mountain Natl Antelope Refuge, OR 132 **C8**, 134 **C2**

Hartbeespoort, 51 **E6**

Hartford, CT 112 **E6**, 115 **A3**

Hartford, PA 145 **H3**

Hartsfield Atlanta Intl Arpt, GA 152 **B2**

Hartwell, 79 **D2**

Hartwood Acres Park, PA 146 **D8**

Harvard U, MA 139 **C4**

Harvey, IL 159 **D2**

Harvey, LA 163 **F4**

Harvey Point Defense Testing Activity, NC 187 **E6**

Harwich, MA 184 **E5**

Harwich Port, MA 184 **E5**

Harwood Hts, IL 159 **D4**

Haryana, 64 **E6**

Hasbrouck Hts, NJ 142 **C6**

Haslet, TX 164 **B5**

Hässelby, 36 **D6**

Hässleholm, 22 **E6**

Hastings, NE 127 **E3**

Hat Yai, 61 **A3**

Hatboro, PA 145 **F6**

Hatchobori, 69 **E2**

Hatchobori Sta, 69 **F2**

Hatillo, 122 **B2**

Hatogaya, 68 **C8**

Hatteras, NC 187 **G2**

Hatteras Inlet, NC 187 **G1**

Hatteras Isl, NC 187 **H3**

Hattiesburg, MS 113 **B3**, 120 **B2**, 129 **H4**

Hattingen, 34 **D7**

Haugesund, 14 **D2**, 22 **B8**

Hausen, 35 **A3**

Havana, 94 **B5**, 97 **G4**, 113 **D1**

Havasu Canyon, AZ 183 **B3**

Havasu Creek, AZ 183 **B3**

Havasupai IR, AZ 183 **C2**

Havasupai Pt, AZ 183 **D2**

Haverford, PA 144 **C4**

Haverhill, MA 115 **C3**, 138 **D4**

Havering, 26 **E7**

Havertown, PA 144 **C3**

Havre, MT 101 **D2**, 110 **D7**, 135 **G6**

Havre-St Pierre, 103 **D3**

Hawaii, 137, 178 **C1**

Hawaii, HI 137 **F2**

Hawaii, U of, HI 177 **H2**

Hawaii Volcanoes NP, HI 137 **F1**, 178 **D1**

Hawaii Volcanoes NP Visitor Ctr, HI 137 **F1**

Hawaiian Islands, 80 **D6**

Hawawa Hts, HI 177 **F3**

Hawthorne, CA 170 **B3**

Hawthorne, FL 123 **E5**

Hawthorne, NV 110 **B5**, 132 **D5**

Hawthorne Army Depot, NV 132 **D5**

Hay R, 101 **D4**

Hayabusacho, 69 **B3**

Hayden Planetarium, MA 140 **B5**

Hayden Valley, WY 180 **B4**

Haydn Mus, 42 **E7**

Hayfork, CA 132 **A7**

Hays, KS 110 **F5**, 127 **D2**

Hays, MT 135 **H6**

Haystack Peak, CA 182 **B6**

Hayward, CA 132 **B5**, 175 **D4**

Hazard, KY 118 **B1**, 121 **E6**, 125 **F2**

Hazel Park, MI 156 **D8**

Hazelwood, MO 162 **B3**

Headingley, 107 **E5**

Heads, The, OR 134 **A3**

Healdsburg, CA 132 **A5**

Hearst, 103 **B2**

Heart Lake, WY 180 **C2**

Heathrow, FL 153 **G6**

Heathrow Arpt, UK 26 **B7**

Hebgen Lake, MT 180 **A4**

Hebrides, 14 **C2**

Hebron, Can 102 **D5**

Hebron, KY 151 **B1**

Hebron, TX 165 **F6**

Hedehusene, 36 **A5**

Hedingen, 37 **E1**

Hedwig Village, TX 166 **A4**

Heeresgeschichtliches, 42 **E7**

Hefei, 60 **C7**, 67 **B4**

Hegang, 66 **D7**

Heguri, 70 **E5**

Heidelberg, Austral 79 **D3**

Heidelberg, Ger 23 **C2**

Heidelberg West, 79 **C3**

Heilbronn, 23 **C2**

Heiligenhaus, 34 **C6**

Heimberg, 37 **C1**

Heineken Brewery, 30 **D5**

Heinersdorf, 32 **C5**

Heinz NWR, John, PA 144 **C1**

Heisingen, 34 **C7**

Hejaijiao, 74 **C5**

Hekelgem, 31 **E2**

Hekla, 14 **A5**

Helena, AR 120 **A5**

Helena, MT 110 **D7**, 135 **F5**

Helena NF, MT 135 **G5**

Heliopolis, 50 **D3**

Hellersdorf, 32 **F7**

Hellerup, 36 **C6**

Hells Canyon NRA, 130 **A8**, 134 **D4**

Helsingborg, 15 **E1**, 22 **D6**

Helsinki, 15 **G3**, 52 **B6**, 82 **F7**

Hemet, CA 133 **E2**

Hemiksem, 31 **F5**

Hempstead, NY 116 **B5**, 143 **H3**

Henderson, CO 167 **H5**

Henderson, KY 125 **D2**

Henderson, NV 111 **B4**, 133 **F4**

Henderson, NC 119 **F1**, 121 **G4**

Hendersonville, TN 125 **E1**

Hendon, 26 **C8**

Hengyang, 60 **C6**, 67 **A3**

Henningsdorf, 32 **C8**

Henson Creek Park, MD 148 **E5**

Henzada, 59 **F4**

Hepingli, 73 **E3**

Hepingli Railway Sta, 73 **E4**

Heppner, OR 134 **C4**

Heraklion, 17 **H2**, 25 **G1**, 48 **B6**

Herat, 49 **H6**, 58 **A7**

Hercules, CA 174 **C7**

257

Hereford, TX 128 **C5**, 131 **F3**

Hereford, UK 19 **D3**

Herkimer, NY 117 **F3**

Herlev, 36 **B6**

Hermitage, The, 57 **F2**

Hermit's Rest, AZ 183 **D2**

Hermosa Beach, CA 170 **B3**

Hermosillo, 96 **B5**, 111 **C3**

Hernals, 42 **D7**

Herne, 31 **E1**, 34 **D8**

Héroes de Padierna, 98 **A1**

Herring Cove Beach, MA 184 **D8**

Herring Run Park, MD 147 **D3**

Herrliberg, 37 **F1**

Herten, 34 **D8**

Hesperia, CA 133 **E3**

Hetch Hetchy Reservoir, CA 182 **A5**

Heusenstamm, 35 **C2**

Hewlett, NY 143 **G2**

HHH Metrodome, MN 161 **C3**

Hialeah, FL 155 **F2**

Hialeah Gdns, FL 155 **E2**

Hiawatha NF, MI 124 **E6**

Hibbing, MN 112 **A7**

Hibiya Park, 69 **C2**

Hibliya Public Hall, 69 **C2**

Hickory, NC 121 **F5**

Hickory Hills, IL 159 **C3**

Hicksville, NY 116 **B5**

Hidalgo del Parral, 96 **B5**, 128 **B1**

Hidden Falls, WY 181 **F3**

Hie Shrine, 69 **A3**

Hietzing, 42 **D7**

Higashi-Osaka, 70 **D5**

Higashikurume, 68 **B8**

Higashimurayama, 68 **A8**

Higashiyama-Ku, 71 **E3**

Higashiyamato, 68 **A7**

High Level, 101 **D4**

High Pt, FL 154 **B5**

High Pt, NC 121 **F6**

High Point SP, NJ 116 **A6**

High Springs, FL 123 **E5**

High Wycombe, 26 **A8**

Highgrove, CA 171 **H4**

Highland, CA 171 **H5**

Highland, IN 159 **F1**

Highland, NY 117 **G1**

Highland, PA 146 **B8**

Highland Hts, KY 151 **E5**

Highland Hts, OH 150 **F7**

Highland Lake Park Reserve, MN 161 **B1**

Highland Park, CA 172 **F7**

Highland Park, IL 158 **C6**

Highland Park, MI 156 **D7**

Highland Park, PA 146 **D7**

Highland Park, TX 165 **G4**

Highland Village, TX 164 **D6**

Highlands, NC 121 **E5**

Highlands Ranch, CO 167 **G1**

Highpoint, OH 151 **E4**

Highwood, IL 158 **C6**

Highwoods, IN 157 **D3**

Hilden, 34 **C5**

Hill Air Force Range, UT 130 **B6**, 132 **F7**, 135 **F1**

Hillandale, MD 148 **D8**

Hillcrest Hts, MD 148 **E5**

Hillegon, 30 **B5**

Hillerod, 36 **A8**

Hillingdon, 26 **B7**

Hillsboro, OH 118 **B3**

Hillsboro, OR 134 **B4**, 177 **E5**

Hillsboro, TN 120 **D5**

Hillsboro, TX 129 **E4**

Hillsboro Beach, FL 155 **H6**

Hillsborough, CA 175 **B3**

Hillsborough, NH 115 **B3**

Hillsdale, NY 115 **A3**

Hillside, NJ 142 **B3**

Hilltop, MN 161 **C4**

Hilo, HI 137 **F2**, 178 **D1**

Hilshire Village, TX 166 **A4**

Hilton, NY 116 **C4**

Hilton Head Isl, SC 121 **F3**

Himalayas, 58 **D6**

Himberg, 42 **E6**

Hims, 48 **D6**

Hinakawa, 68 **E5**

Hindar, 64 **F8**

Hindu Amphitheater, AZ 183 **D2**

Hindu Kush, 58 **B7**

Hinesville, GA 121 **F3**

Hingham, MA 139 **F2**

Hino, 68 **A7**

Hinsdale, IL 159 **C3**

Hinterbruhl, 42 **D6**

Hinton, WV 118 **D2**

Hipodromo de las Americas, 98 **A3**

Hippodrome, 88 **D8**

Hippodrome de la Zaezuela, 39 **B4**

Hirakata, 70 **E8**, 66 **E5**

Hiroshima, 60 **E8**, 66 **E5**

Hirshhorn Mus, DC 149 **D2**

Hisabpur, 65 **F3**

Hispaniola, 95 **E4**

Historic Richmond Town, NY 142 **B1**

Historical Library, 57 **G5**

Historical Mus, MI 156 **D6**

Ho Chi Minh, 61 **B3**

Ho Chung, 75 **E4**

Ho Man Tin, 75 **D3**

Hobart, Austral 77 **E1**

Hobart, IN 159 **F1**

Hobbs, NM 128 **C4**, 131 **F2**

Hobby Arpt, William P TX 166 **C2**

Hoboken, Bel 31 **G5**

Hoboken, NJ 141 **E4**, 142 **C4**

Hobsons Bay, 79 **B2**

Hochst, 35 **A3**

Hodgdon Pond, ME 186 **A4**

Hodogaya-Ku, 68 **B6**

Hoeilaart, 31 **G1**

Hof, 23 **D3**

Hofburg, 42 **E7**

Hoffman Estates, IL 158 **A5**

Hofgarten, 34 **B5**

Hofstade, 31 **G3**

Hohen Neuendor, 32 **C8**

Hohenlimburg, 34 **F6**

Hohhot, 55 **D1**, 60 **B8**, 66 **A5**

Hokkaido, 66 **F7**

Holbrook, AZ 131 **C3**

Holbrook, MA 139 **E2**

Holbrook, NY 116 **C5**

Holburn, 27 **D3**

Holcomb Botanical Gdns, IN 157 **E3**

Holdrege, NE 127 **D3**

Holesovice, 35 **E3**

Holguín, 94 **D4**

Holliday Park, IN 157 **E3**

Holliday Park, William P, MI 156 **A6**

Hollidaysburg, PA 119 **E4**

Hollister, CA 133 **E4**

Hollow Ground Swamp, NC 187 **E5**

Holly Springs NF, MS 120 **B5**

Hollywood, CA 172 **B8**

Hollywood, FL 123 **G2**, 155 **G3**

Hollywood Bowl, CA 172 **B8**

Holman, 100 **E6**

Holmes Beach, FL 154 **B1**

Holon, 50 **A6**

Holroyd, 78 **C7**

Holstebro, 22 **C6**

Holte, 36 **B7**

Holton Park, Frank, IL 162 **D1**

Holyhead, 19 **C3**

Holyoke, MA 115 **A3**

Homberg, 34 **A7**

Hombruch, 34 **F7**

Home Gdns, CA 171 **G3**

Home Place, IN 157 **E4**

Homecroft, IN 157 **F1**

Homer, NY 117 **E3**

Homerville, GA 123 **E6**

Homestead, FL 123 **F1**
Homestead, PA 146 **D6**
Homestead Canal, FL 188 **D4**
Homestead NM of America, NE 179 **E4**
Homewood, IL 159 **D1**
Homochitto NF, MS 120 **A3**
Homvel, 52 **A5**
Hondo, TX 128 **D2**
Honduras, 81 **H5**, 84 **A6**, 94 **A3**, 97 **G2**
Hønefoss, 22 **D8**
Honesdale, PA 117 **F1**, 119 **G6**
Honeymoon Island SRA, FL 154 **A6**
Hong Kong, 60 **C5**, 75
Hongkou Park and Stad, 74 **E8**
Hongmiao, 73 **F2**
Hongqiao Arpt, 74 **A5**
Honiara, 80 **B4**
Honolulu, HI 81 **E5**, 137 **C3**, 177 **G1**, 178 **C1**
Honolulu Intl Arpt, HI 177 **F2**
Honolulu Obs, HI 177 **E2**
Honolulu Stad, HI 177 **H1**
Honouliuli, HI 177 **E3**
Hönow, 32 **E7**
Honshu, 60 **F8**, 66 **F5**
Hood R, OR 134 **C4**
Hoofddorp, 30 **C5**
Hooghly-Chinsura, 65 **E4**
Hoogvliet, 30 **A3**
Hoomaluhia Botanical Gdns, HI 177 **E2**
Hoopa Valley IR, CA 134 **A1**
Hoosick Falls, NY 117 **H3**
Hoosier NF, IL 125 **E2**
Hooven, OH 151 **A3**
Hoover Wilderness, CA 182 **C6**
Hope, AR 129 **G5**

Hopewell, VA 119 **F2**
Hopi IR, AZ 131 **C3**
Hopkins, MN 161 **A3**
Hopkinsville, KY 125 **E1**
Horlivka, 53 **B4**
Hormigueros, 122 **B2**
Hornell, NY 116 **C2**
Horní Pocernice, 35 **F3**
Horomerice, 35 **E3**
Horse Ridge, CA 182 **B2**
Horseheads, NY 116 **D2**
Horseshoe Bend NMP, AL 179 **F2**
Horseshoe Lake SP, IL 162 **D2**
Horsholm, 36 **C8**
Horsley Park, 78 **A7**
Horta, 38 **E6**
Hortaleza, 39 **D4**
Hostivar, 35 **F3**
Hot Springs, AR 113 **B4**, 129 **F5**
Hot Springs, SD 126 **B5**, 130 **F7**
Hot Springs NP, AR 179 **E2**
Hotan, 58 **D7**
Hôtel de Ville, 29 **E2**
Hougang, 63 **G2**
Houghs Neck, MA 139 **E2**
Houghton, MI 112 **B7**, 124 **D7**
Houlton, ME 112 **F7**, 114 **E7**
Houma, LA 120 **A1**, 129 **H3**
Houmont Park, TX 166 **D5**
Hounslow, 26 **B7**
House of Seven Gables, MA 138 **F5**
House Rock Buffalo Ranch, AZ 183 **E3**
Houses of Parliament, 27 **C1**
Houston, TX 96 **D5**, 113 **A3**, 129 **F3**, 166 **A4**, 179 **E1**

Houston Lake, MO 162 **B6**
Hove, 31 **G5**
Howard Beach, NY 143 **E2**
Howell Park, Elisa, MI 156 **B7**
Howland Isl, 80 **D4**
Howrah, 65 **E2**
Howrah Bridge, 65 **E2**
Hoxton Park, 78 **A6**
Hoya, 68 **B7**
Hradec Králové, 23 **F3**
Hronda, 15 **G1**
Hsichih, 62 **D5**
Hsinchuang, 62 **B5**
Hsintien, 62 **C4**
Huai Khwang, 63 **G6**
Huainan, 67 **B4**
Hualapai Hilltop, AZ 183 **B2**
Hualapai IR, AZ 131 **B3**, 183 **A1**
Huambo, 47 **E4**
Huancayo, 84 **C2**
Huang R, 60 **A7**, 66 **B5**
Huanggenglang, 74 **B5**
Huangshi, 67 **B3**
Huánuco, 84 **C2**
Hubli, 59 **B4**
Huddinge, 36 **E6**
Hudson, NY 117 **H2**, 119 **H6**
Hudson Bay, 103 **A4**
Hudson Falls, NY 117 **H4**
Hudson R, 117 **G4**, 142 **D3**
Hudson Str, 102 **C5**
Huechuraba, 87 **G3**
Huejotitán, 99 **E2**
Huelva, 16 **A3**, 21 **A3**
Huentitán Alto, 99 **G5**
Huentitán Bajo, 99 **G6**
Huesca, 21 **D4**
Hugli-Chunchura, 65 **E4**
Hugo, OK 129 **F5**
Hujialou, 73 **F2**
Huldenberg, 31 **H1**
Hull, Can 103 **C2**

Hull, MA 139 **F3**
Hulls Cove, ME 186 **C6**
Hulls Cove Visitor Ctr, ME 186 **C6**
Hulst, 31 **E6**
Hulun Nur, 66 **B2**
Humacao, 122 **C2**
Humble, TX 166 **C6**
Humboldt- Toiyabe NF, CA/NV 132 **C5 E6 E7**, 134 **D1**, 182 **D6**
Humboldt R, 132 **D7**
Húmera, 39 **A3**
Humphreys Pk, AZ 131 **B3**
Hunewill Pk, CA 182 **C6**
Hung Hom, 75 **D3**
Hung Hom Railway Sta, 75 **D2**
Hungary, 17 **F5**, 23 **F1**, 24 **D6**, 45 **E6**
Hungnam, 60 **D8**
Hungnam, 55 **F2**, 66 **D5**
Hunjiang, 66 **C6**
Hunter, VA 148 **A7**
Hunters Creek Village, TX 166 **A4**
Hunters Hill, 78 **E7**
Hunters Valley, VA 148 **A7**
Huntingdon, PA 119 **F5**
Huntingdon Valley, PA 145 **F6**
Huntington, VA 148 **C5**
Huntington, WV 112 **D5**, 118 **C3**
Huntington Beach, CA 170 **D2**
Huntington Park, CA 170 **C4**
Huntington Res, OH 150 **B7**
Huntington Sta, NY 116 **B6**
Huntington Woods, MI 156 **C8**
Hunts Point, WA 176 **C5**
Huntsville, AL 113 **C4**, 120 **C5**
Huntsville, TN 118 **A1**

Huntsville, TX 129 **F3**
Hurley, NY 117 **G1**
Hurlingham, 88 **C7**
Huron, SD 126 **E5**
Huron NF, MI 124 **F5**
Hurst, TX 164 **C4**
Hurstville, 78 **D6**
Husinec, 35 **E4**
Hutchins, TX 165 **G2**
Hutchinson, MN 126 **F6**
Hutchinson, KS 111 **F4**,
127 **E2**
Hutchinson, 104 **A6**
Huttenheim, 34 **B6**
Huttonville, 104 **A6**
Huvosvoigy, 42 **A7**
Hvidovre, 36 **B5**
Hwajon, 72 **C7**
Hyannis, MA 115 **D2**,
184 **D5**
Hyannis Port, MA 185 **D4**
Hyattsville, MD 148 **E7**
Hyde Park, MA 139 **C3**
Hyde Park, NY 117 **G1**
Hyde Park, UK 27 **A3**
Hyderabad, 58 **B6**, 59 **C4**
Hysham, MT 135 **H4**

I

I-n-Amenas, 44 **D4**
I-n-Salah, 44 **D4**
Iahaina, HI 137 **D3**
Iao Valley SP, HI 137 **D3**
Iasi, 17 **H5**
Ibadan, 44 **C1**
Ibagué, 84 **C5**
Ibaraki, 70 **D6**
Iberian Mts, 21 **C4**
Iberian Pen, 16 **B3**
Ibiza, 16 **C3**, 21 **E2**
Ibri, 49 **H3**
Ica, 84 **C2**
Ice Stad, 37 **B2**
Iceland, 14 **A5**, 82 **F6**
Ichibancho, 69 **A4**
Ichigaya Sta, 69 **A4**
Ichihara, 68 **E6**
Ichikawa, 68 **C7**

Ichinomiya, 68 **F5**
Idabel, OK 129 **F5**
Idaho, 101 **C1**, 110 **C7**,
130 **A7**, 135 **F2**, 178 **B5**
Idaho City, ID 130 **A7**,
135 **E3**
Idaho Falls, ID 110 **C6**,
130 **B7**, 135 **F2**, 178 **B5**
Idaho Natl Engineering
Lab, ID 130 **B7**
Idar-Oberstein, 23 **C3**
Ide, 70 **F6**
Idemitsu Art Mus, 69 **D2**
Idledale, CO 167 **E2**
Idlewild, KY 151 **A1**
Igarka, 54 **A5**
Iglesias, 24 **A3**
Ignacio, CA 174 **A7**
Igreja Dos Enforcadas,
93 **G2**
Igreja NS Achiropita, 93 **E1**
Iguaçua, 91 **B4**
Iguala, 96 **C3**
Ihsaniye, 43 **D4**
Iiortaleza, 39 **D4**
Ijmuiden, 30 **B6**
Ikeda, 70 **C6**
Ikoma, 70 **E5**
Ilebo, 47 **E6**
Ile-Perrot, 106 **A1**
Ilerin, 44 **C1**
Îles-de-Boucherville
Prov P, 106 **D4**
Ilford, 26 **D7**
Ilha, 91 **A1**
Ilhéus, 85 **H2**
Iliamna Lake, AK 136 **C6**
Ililoueete Creek, CA
182 **C2**
I'linskoye, 56 **A4**
Ilion, NY 117 **F3**
Ilioúpolis, 43 **C2**
Illahee SP, WA 176 **A5**
Illinois, 112 **B5**, 125 **D4**,
179 **F4**
Illinois Beach SP, IL 158 **C8**
Illinois Ctr, IL 160 **D6**

Illinois Institute of
Technology, IL 159 **E3**
Illinois R, IL 125 **C3**
Iloilo, 61 **E4**
Ilsan, 72 **B8**
Imax, 30 **B2**
Imba, 68 **F8**
Imbabah, 50 **C2**
Imbariê, 91 **D4**
Imola, 24 **B5**
Imperatriz, 85 **G3**
Imperial Beach, CA 169 **F1**
Imperial Palace, 68 **C7**,
69 **B3**
Imperial Palace East Gdn,
69 **C3**
Imperial Palace Mus &
Forbidden City, 73 **E2**
Imperial Palace Outer Gdn,
69 **C3**
Imperial Theater, 69 **D2**
Imphal, 58 **F5**
Imuris, 131 **C1**
Imus, 62 **B1**
Inagawa, 70 **B7**
Inagi, 68 **A7**
Inárcs, 42 **C5**
Inari, 71 **E2**
Inchon, 55 **F1**, 72 **A6**
Incline Village, NV 132 **C6**
Independence, CA 133 **D4**
Independence, KS 125 **A3**
Independence, MO 125 **B3**,
162 **D5**
Independence, OH 150 **D5**
Independence, VA 118 **D1**
Independence NHP, PA
145 **E2**, 179 **H4**
Independencia, 87 **F6**
India, 58 **C5**
Indian Hills, CO 167 **E2**
Indian Key, FL 188 **E3**
Indian Lake, NY 117 **G4**
Indian Mounds Park, MN
161 **E2**
Indian Ocean, 59 **C2**
Indian Pt, ME 186 **A5**

Indian Rocks Beach, FL
154 **A4**
Indian Shores, FL 123 **E3**
Indiana, 112 **C5**, 125 **E2**,
179 **F4**
Indiana, PA 119 **E5**
Indiana Conv Ctr & RCA
Dome, IN 157 **E2**
Indiana Dunes NL, IN
159 **F2**, 179 **F4**
Indianapolis, IN 112 **C5**,
125 **E3**, 157 **D2**, 179 **F4**
Indianapolis, U of, IN
157 **E1**
Indianapolis Intl Arpt, IN
157 **D1**
Indianapolis Speedway, IN
157 **D2**
Indianola, PA 146 **D8**
Indianola, WA 176 **A6**
Indianópolis, 92 **B4**
Indiantown, FL 123 **F3**
Indigirka R, 54 **D6**
Indio, CA 133 **E2**
Indira Gandhi Intl. Arpt,
64 **D6**
Indonesia, 59 **F2**, 61 **D1**,
76 **A6**, 80 **A4**
Indonesia, U of, 64 **B7**
Indore, 58 **C5**
Indus R, 58 **B6**
Industrial Exh Hall, 74 **D6**
Ingleburn, 78 **A5**
Inglewood, CA 133 **D3**,
170 **B4**
Inglewood, WA 176 **D5**
Ingolstadt, 23 **D2**
Ingraham Pt, ME 186 **D8**
Inhambane, 47 **G3**
Inhaúma, 91 **C3**
Inkster, MI 156 **B6**
Inner Harbor, MD 147 **D2**
Innisbrook, FL 154 **B6**
Innoko NWR, AK 136 **C7**
Innsbruck, 17 **E5**, 23 **D1**,
24 **B6**
Inoã, 91 **F2**

Inspiration Pt, WY 181 **F3**
Inta, 52 **E5**
Intercession City, FL 153 **F1**
International Conference
    Ctr, 70 **A5**
International Court of
    Justice (World Court),
    30 **A3**
International Expo Ctr, OH
    150 **B6**
International Falls, MN
    112 **A7**, 124 **B7**
International Swimming
    Hall of Fame, FL 155 **G4**
International Trade Fair
    Exh Hall, 70 **C5**
Intracoastal Waterway, FL
    188 **D2**
Inukjuak, 103 **B4**
Inuvik, 82 **B5**, 100 **C6**,
    136 **E8**
Invalides, Hôtel des, 29 **C2**
Invercargill, 77 **G1**
Inverness, FL 121 **E1**,
    123 **E4**
Inverness, IL 158 **A5**
Inverness, UK 14 **C2**,
    18 **D6**
Inwood, NY 143 **G2**
Inyo NF, CA 132 **D5**,
    182 **D5**
Inzai, 68 **E8**
Ioannina, 17 **G3**, 25 **E4**
Ione, CA 132 **B5**
Ionian Islands, 25 **E3**
Ionian Sea, 17 **G2**, 25 **E2**
Iowa, 103 **A1**, 112 **A5**,
    124 **B4**, 179 **E4**
Iowa City, IA 125 **C4**
Ipanema, 91 **D1**
Ipiíba, 91 **F2**
Ipiranga, 92 **B4**
Ipiranga Mus, 92 **B4**
Ipoh, 61 **A3**
Ipswich, MA 138 **F7**
Ipswich, UK 19 **F3**, 20 **D8**
Iqaluit, 102 **C5**

Iquique, 84 **D1**
Iquitos, 84 **C3**
Iran, 45 **H5**, 49 **G5**, 58 **A7**
Iranshahr, 49 **H4**
Irapuato, 96 **C3**
Iraq, 45 **G4**, 49 **E5**
Irbil, 49 **E6**
Ireland, 14 **B1**, 19 **B4**,
    20 **A8**
Irifune, 69 **F2**
Iringa, 47 **G5**
Irish Sea, 19 **C4**, 20 **B8**
Irkutsk, 55 **B3**
Iron Mt, MI 124 **D6**
Irondequoit, NY 116 **D3**
Ironton, OH 118 **C3**
Iroquois Falls, 103 **B2**
Iroquois NWR, NY 116 **C3**
Iroquois Pt, HI 177 **F2**
Irrawaddy R, 58 **F5**
Iruma, 68 **A8**
Irvine, CA 171 **E1**
Irving, TX 129 **E4**, 165 **E4**
Irvington, NJ 142 **A3**
Isabela, 122 **B2**
Ísafjördhur, 14 **A5**
Ishim, 53 **E3**
Ishøj, 36 **B5**
Isidro Casanova, 88 **C6**
Isiro, 45 **F1**
Isis Temple, AZ 183 **E2**
Isla de Culebra, 122 **D2**
Isla de Pascua, 81 **G3**
Isla de Vieques, 122 **D1**
Islamabad, 58 **C7**
Islamorada, FL 123 **F1**,
    188 **E3**
Island Lake, IL 158 **A7**
Island Park, ID 135 **G3**
Island Pond, VT 114 **B5**
Islay, 18 **C5**
Isle au Haut, ME 115 **E4**
Isle of Wight, 20 **C7**
Isle of Youth, 94 **A5**
Isle Royale NP, MI 124 **D7**,
    179 **F6**
Islesford, ME 186 **C2**

Isleta IR, NM 128 **A5**
Islington, MA 139 **C2**
Islington, UK 27 **D4**
Israel, 48 **D5**
Issaquah, WA 176 **D4**
Istana, 63 **F1**
Istanbul, 17 **H4**, 25 **H5**,
    43 **D2**, 45 **E6**
Isthmus of Kra, 61 **A3**
Isthmus of Panama, 97 **H1**
Isthmus of Tehuantepec,
    97 **E3**
Itabuna, 85 **H2**
Itaipu, 91 **E1**
Ital Park, 89 **C4**
Italy, 17 **E3**, 20 **F5**, 23 **D1**,
    24 **C4**, 44 **D6**
Itambi, 91 **F4**
Itami, 70 **C6**
Itaquaquecetuba, 92 **D5**
Itaquera, 92 **C4**
Itasca, 159 **B4**
Ithaca, NY 112 **E6**, 117 **E2**
Ittingen, 37 **B2**
Iturup, 66 **F7**
Itzehoe, 22 **C5**
Iupeba, 92 **D3**
Ivalo, 15 **F5**
Ivanhoe, 79 **D3**
Ivanovo, 52 **C5**
Ivanteyevka, 56 **D6**
Ivry-sur-Seine, 28 **D7**
Iwaki, 66 **F5**
Ixtlahuacán de los
    Membrillos, 99 **H2**
Izembek NWR, AK 136 **A5**
Izhevsk, 53 **C4**
Izmaylovo, 56 **C4**
Izmir, 17 **H3**, 25 **G3**,
    45 **F5**, 48 **C6**
Iztacalco, 98 **C3**
Iztapalapa, 98 **C2**

J

Jabal Tuwayq, 49 **E3**
Jabalpur, 58 **C5**
Jabaquara, 92 **B4**

Jabavu, 51 **E2**
Jacarepaguá, 91 **C2**
Jacinto City, TX 166 **D3**
Jack Murphy Stad, CA
    169 **F4**
Jackman, ME 114 **C6**
Jackson, AL 120 **B3**
Jackson, CA 132 **C5**
Jackson, KY 118 **B2**
Jackson, MI 118 **A6**,
    125 **F4**
Jackson, MS 97 **E6**, 113 **B3**,
    120 **A3**, 129 **H4**, 179 **F2**
Jackson, OH 118 **C3**
Jackson, TN 113 **B4**,
    120 **B5**, 125 **D1**, 129 **H6**
Jackson, WY 110 **D6**,
    130 **C7**, 135 **G2**, 181 **F1**
Jackson Heights, NY 143 **E4**
Jackson Hole, WY 181 **F2**
Jackson Hole Arpt, WY
    181 **F2**
Jackson Lake, WY 180 **A1**,
    181 **G5**
Jackson Lake Lodge, WY
    181 **G4**
Jackson Natl Fish Hatchery,
    WY 181 **F1**
Jackson Park, IL 159 **E3**
Jackson Park, WI 157 **B3**
Jacksonville, AR 129 **G5**
Jacksonville, FL 113 **D3**,
    121 **F2**, 123 **E6**, 179 **G2**
Jacksonville, NC 121 **H5**
Jacksonville Beach, FL
    121 **F2**, 123 **F6**
Jacob Javits Conv Ctr, NY
    141 **F4**
Jacobs Field, OH 150 **D7**
Jadabpur, 65 **F1**
Jade Buddha Temple, 74 **C7**
Jaffna, 59 **C3**
Jagatpur, 64 **E8**
Jaipur, 58 **C6**
Jakarta, 61 **B1**, 64 **B7**
Jakobsberg, 36 **D7**
Jalan Kayu, 63 **G3**

Jalazun, 50 **D5**

Jamaica, NY 143 **F3**

Jamaica, WI 94 **C3**, 97 **H3**

Jamaica Bay WR, NY 143 **E2**

Jamaliya, 50 **C2**

Jambi, 61 **B2**

James Bay, 103 **B3**

James R, SD 126 **E6**

Jamestown, NY 112 **D6**, 116 **B2**, 119 **E6**

Jamestown, ND 110 **F7**, 126 **D7**

Jammu, 58 **C6**

Jampur, 65 **D4**

Jamshedpur, 58 **D5**

Jamul, CA 169 **H3**

Janai, 65 **E3**

Janalli, 78 **D5**

Janesville, WI 125 **C4**

Janos, 128 **A3**, 131 **D1**

Japan, 60 **E8**, 66 **E5**, 80 **A6**

Jaraguá, 92 **A5**

Jardim Da Luz, 93 **G6**

Jardim Paulista, 92 **B4**

Jardim Vera Cruz, 92 **C4**

Jardim Zoo, 38 **B7**

Jardin des Plantes, 29 **F1**

Jardin des Tuileries, 29 **D2**

Jardin du Carroussel, 29 **D2**

Jardin du Luxembourg, 29 **D1**

Jardine, MT 180 **B6**

Jardines de Morelos, 98 **D5**

Jarfalla, 36 **D7**

Jarvis Isl, 80 **D4**

Jask, 49 **H4**

Jasper, AL 120 **C4**

Jasper, TX 129 **G3**

Jataí, 85 **F1**

Java, 61 **C1**

Java Sea, 61 **C1**

Jayapura, 76 **B2**, 80 **A4**

Jayuya, 122 **B2**

Jean Lesage Intl Arpt, 105 **D3**

Jedediah, WY 181 **E5**

Jefferson, LA 163 **F5**

Jefferson, WI 124 **D5**

Jefferson City, MO 112 **B5**, 125 **B2**

Jefferson Mem, Thomas, DC 149 **C1**

Jefferson Natl Expansion Mem, MO 162 **C2**

Jefferson NF, VA 118 **B1**, 121 **E6**

Jefferson Square, CA 173 **C1**

Jeffersonville, VT 114 **A5**

Jegenstorf, 37 **C3**

Jejur, 65 **D4**

Jelenia Gora, 23 **F3**

Jena, 23 **D3**

Jenec, 35 **D3**

Jenkintown, PA 145 **E5**

Jennings, MO 162 **B3**

Jenny Lake, WY 181 **F3**

Jenny Lake Lodge, WY 181 **F3**

Jerada, 21 **C1**

Jeremy Pt, MA 184 **E6**

Jericho, 48 **D5**

Jerome, ID 130 **A7**, 132 **F8**, 135 **E2**

Jersey, 19 **D1**

Jersey City, NJ 119 **H5**, 142 **C3**

Jersey Village, TX 166 **A5**

Jerseyville, IL 125 **C3**

Jerusalem, 45 **G4**, 48 **D5**, 50 **D4**

Jesenice, 35 **F2**

Jestetten, 37 **E4**

Jesup, GA 121 **E3**

Jesus María, 87 **F5**

Jiading County, 74 **B7**

Jiamusi, 66 **C7**

Jian, 67 **A3**

Jiangjiaqiao, 74 **E7**

Jiaozuo, 67 **A4**

Jicarilla Apache IR, 128 **B6**, 131 **D4**

Jiddah, 45 **G3**, **E2**

Jihlava, 23 **E3**

Jiinsha R, 58 **F6**

Jijel, 21 **F2**

Jilin, 55 **F2**, 66 **C6**

Jílové u Prahy, 35 **F1**

Jílovîstiê, 35 **E1**

Jim Thompson's House, 63 **G5**

Jim Thorpe, PA 119 **G5**

Jima, 45 **G1**

Jinan, 55 **E1**, 60 **C7**, 66 **B5**

Jingan District, 74 **C6**

Jinganzhuang, 73 **E3**

Jingdezhen, 60 **C6**, 67 **B3**

Jingshan Park, 73 **E3**

Jining, 67 **B4**

Jinja, 47 **G6**

Jinocany, 35 **D2**

Jinzhou, 55 **E2**, 60 **C8**, 66 **B6**

Jixi, 55 **F3**, 66 **D7**

João Pessoa, 85 **H3**

Jocotepec, 99 **F1**

Jodhpur, 58 **B6**

Joensuu, 15 **G4**

Johannesburg, 47 **F3**, 51 **F3**

Johannesburg Arpt, 51 **H3**

Johannesburg Zoological Gdn, 51 **F3**

John Hancock Ctr, IL 160 **D8**

John Wayne Airport, CA 171 **E2**

Johns Hopkins U, MD 147 **D3**

Johnson, VT 114 **A5**

Johnson City, NY 117 **E3**

Johnson City, OR 177 **G4**

Johnson City, TN 113 **D4**, 121 **E6**

Johnson Mem, Lyndon B, DC 149 **A1**

Johnston Key, FL 188 **A3**

Johnstown, NY 117 **G3**

Johnstown, PA 119 **E4**

Joinvile, 86 **C6**

Joka, 65 **E1**, 125 **D4**

Joliet, IL 112 **B5**, 125 **D4**, 159 **A1**

Jones Beach SP, NY 143 **H1**

Jonesboro, AR 113 **B4**, 120 **A6**, 125 **C1**, 129 **H6**

Jönköping, 15 **E2**, 22 **E7**

Joplin, MO 113 **A4**, 125 **A3**, 129 **F6**

Jordan, 45 **G4**, 48 **D5**

Jordan Pond, ME 186 **C4**

Jordan Valley, OR 134 **D2**

Jordbro, 36 **E5**

Jorge Chávez Intl Arpt, 87 **F5**

Joshua Tree NP, CA 133 **F3**, 178 **B3**

José C Paz, 88 **B8**

Joyo, 70 **F7**

Joyous Pavilion Park, 73 **D1**

Juan Fernández Islands, 81 **H2**

Juana Díaz, 122 **B1**

Juanacatlán, 99 **H3**

Juázeiro do Norte, 85 **G3**

Juba, 45 **F1**

Júcar, 21 **C3**

Juhu Beach, 65 **A3**

Juiz de Fora, 85 **G1**

Juliaca, 84 **C2**

Jumpup Canyon, AZ 183 **C4**

Jumpup Pt, AZ 183 **C4**

Junction City, KS 127 **E3**

Junction City, OR 134 **B3**

Juneau, AK 82 **A5**, 101 **B4**, 136 **E6**, 178 **B1**

Juneau Park, WI 157 **C3**

Jungleland, FL 153 **F2**

Junín, 86 **B5**

Jupiter, FL 123 **G3**

Jurong East, 81 **E2**

Juruá R, 84 **D3**

Justice, IL 159 **C3**

Jutland, 15 **E2**, 22 **C6**

Jyväskylä, 15 **F4**

K

K Wilhelm Gedachtnis-
kirche, 33 B2
K2 Mt, 58 C7
Ka Lae, HI 137 E1
Kaarst, 34 A5
Kabinda, 47 F5
Kabukiza Theater, 69 E1
Kabul, 58 B7
Kabwe, 47 F4
Kadiköy, 43 E2
Kadoma, 70 D6
Kaena Pt, HI 137 B3
Kaesong, 66 E5
Kafr Hakim, 50 A3
Kagiso, 51 E3
Kagithane, 43 E3
Kagoshima, 60 E7, 67 D4
Kagran, 42 E8
Kahnawake, 106 B1
Kahoolawe, HI 137 D2
Kahuku Pt, HI 137 C4
Kahului, HI 137 D3
Kai Tak Arpt, 75 D3
Kaibab NF, AZ 183 D4
Kaibab Plateau, AZ 183 D4
Kaifeng, 67 A4
Kailu, HI 137 C3
Kailua-Kona, HI 137 E2
Kaisariani Monastery, 43 C2
Kaiser dom Cathedral,
35 B3
Kaiserebersdorf, 42 E7
Kaiserstuhl, 37 E3
Kaiwi Channel, HI 137 C3
Kaktovik, AK 136 D8
Kalahari Desert, 47 E3
Kalamakion, 43 B2
Kalamata, 17 G2, 25 E2
Kalamazoo, MI 112 C6,
118 A6, 125 E4
Kalaupapa NHP, HI
137 D3
Kalemie, 47 F5
Kalgoorlie, 76 B3

Kaliningrad, 15 F1, 52 A6,
56 D6
Kalispell, MT 110 C7,
135 F6
Kallhall, 36 D7
Kallithea, 43 B2
Kallnach, 37 A3
Kalmar, 15 F2, 22 E6
Kalundborg, 22 D6
Kalwa, 65 C3
Kam Shan CP, 75 B4
Kama R, 53 D4
Kamagaya, 68 D8
Kamakura, 68 B5
Kaman, 65 C3
Kamarhati, 65 F2
Kamat Gan, 50 B6
Kamaterón, 43 B3
Kamchatka Pen, 54 B7,
82 A8
Kamenice, 35 F1
Kameoka, 70 D8
Kamiak Mt, WA 135 D5
Kamigyo-Ku, 71 E3
Kamina, 47 F5
Kamloops, 101 C2
Kampala, 47 F6
Kampong Cham, 61 B4
Kampong Saom, 61 A3
Kanab Canyon, AZ 183 C3
Kanab Creek, AZ 183 C4
Kanab Creek Wilderness,
AZ 183 C4
Kanab Plateau, AZ 183 B4
Kananga, 47 E5
Kanazawa, 66 E5
Kanazawa-Ku, 68 B5
Kanchrapara, 65 F4
Kanda-Nishikicho, 69 D4
Kandy, 59 C3
Kaneohe, HI 137 C3,
177 H3
Kaneohe FP, HI 177 H3
Kangaroo Isl, 76 D2
Kangdong, 72 E7
Kangnam, 72 D6
Kangso, 72 C7

Kanheri Caves, 65 B3
Kankan, 44 B2
Kannapolis, NC 121 F5
Kano, 44 D2
Kanpur, 58 C5
Kansaripara, 65 D4
Kansas, 110 F5, 127 E2,
178 D3
Kansas City, KS 112 A5,
125 A3, 127 F3, 162 B6
Kansas City, MO 112 A5,
125 A3, 162 C5, 179 E3
Kansas City Downtown
Arpt, MO 162 B6
Kansas City Mus, MO
162 C5
Kansas City Zoo, MO
162 C4
Kansk, 55 B3
Kanuti NWR, AK 136 C7
Kaohsiung, 60 D6, 67 B2
Kaolack, 44 A3
Kapaa, HI 137 B4
Kapenhout, 31 H3
Kaposvar, 24 D6
Kapuskasing, 103 B2,
124 F3
Kara Kum, 53 C1
Kara Sea, 52 E6, 82 D8
Karachi, 58 A6
Karamay, 53 F2, 58 D8
Karawang Pt, 64 C8
Karbala, 49 E5
Karkuk, 49 E6, 53 A1
Karlebo, 36 B8
Karlovac, 23 F1, 24 D5
Karlshamn, 22 E6
Karlskrona, 22 F6
Karlslunde, 36 A5
Karlslunde Strand, 36 A5
Karlsruhe, 20 F7, 23 C2
Karlstad, 15 E2, 22 E8
Kartal, 43 F2
Kasai R, 47 E5
Kashan, 49 F5
Kashi, 53 E1, 58 C7
Kashiwa, 68 D8

Kasinathpur, 65 F2
Kassala, 45 G2, 48 D1
Kassel, 17 E6, 23 C3
Kastoria, 25 E4
Kastrup, 36 C5
Kasumigaseki, 69 E3
Katama, MA 185 B2
Katanga Plateau, 47 F5
Katano, 70 E6
Katerini, 25 F4
Katherine, 76 C6
Kathmandu, 58 D6
Katlehong, 51 G1
Katmai NP & Pres, AK
136 C6, 178 A1
Katowice, 17 F6
Katsina, 44 D2
Katsura, 71 D2
Kattegat, 15 E2, 22 D7
Katwijk aan Zee, 30 B4
Kauai, HI 137 B4
Kauai Chan, HI 137 B4
Kaulakahi Chan, HI 137 A4
Kauna Pt, HI 137 E1
Kaunas, 15 G1, 52 A5
Kavala, HI 13, 25 G4
Kawaguchi, 68 C8
Kawaiahao Church, HI
177 G2
Kawaihoa Pt, HI 137 A3
Kawanishi, 70 C6
Kawasaki, 66 F5, 68 C6
Kayenta, AZ 131 C4
Kayes, 44 B2
Kayseri, 48 D6
Kazakhstan, 45 H6, 58 C8
Kazan, 53 C4
Kazan Cathedral, 57 G2
Kazanluk, 25 G5
Kbely, 35 F3
Keahole Pt, HI 137 E2
Keaiwa Heiau SRA, HI
177 G3
Kearney, NE 110 F5, 127 D3
Kearny, NJ 142 B4
Kecskemet, 17 F5
Kedawung, 64 C8

Keene, NH 115 B3

Keerbergen, 31 H4

Keetmanshoop, 47 E3

Keflavík, 14 A5

Keilor, 79 A4

Keilor East, 79 A3

Kelafo, 45 H1

Kelang, 61 A3

Kelenfold, 42 A6

Keller, TX 164 C5

Kelleys Isl, OH 118 C6

Kelly, WV 181 G2

Kelly AFB, TX 163 F2

Kelly Park, Dr Howard A, FL 153 F6

Kelowna, 101 C2

Kelso, OR 177 H4

Kelso, WA 134 B4

Kelsterbach, 35 A3

Kemerburgaz, 43 D3

Kemi, 15 F5

Kemmerer, WY 130 C6, 135 G1

Kempten, 23 D2, 24 B6

Kempton Park, 51 H3

Ken Caryl Ranch, CO 167 F1

Kenai, AK 100 A6, 136 C6

Kenai Fjords NP, AK 136 C6, 178 B1

Kenburma, MA 139 F2

Kendal, 19 D4

Kendall, FL 155 F1

Kendari, 61 E2

Keng Hau, 75 C4

Kennebeck R, ME 114 D6

Kennebunk, ME 115 C4

Kennedy Ctr For the Performing Arts, DC 149 A3

Kennedy Intl Arpt, NY 143 F2

Kennedy Library & Mus, MA 139 D3

Kennedy NHS, MA 139 C3

Kennedy Space Ctr, FL 121 F1, 123 F4

Kennedy Stad, Robert F, DC 148 E6

Kenner, LA 163 E6

Kennesaw, GA 120 D4

Kenneth City, FL 154 B4

Kennett, MO 120 B6, 125 C1

Kennewick, WA 110 B7

Kenora, 103 A3, 124 B8, 126 F8

Kenosha, WI 125 D4

Kensington, GA 174 C6

Kensington, MD 148 D8

Kensington, PA 145 E3

Kensington, UK 26 C7

Kent, WA 176 C3

Kentfield, CA 174 A6

Kentland, MD 148 F7

Kenton, OH 118 B5

Kentucky, 113 C4, 118 B2, 179 F3

Kentucky R, KY 118 B2

Kenwood, MD 147 E3

Kenwood, OH 151 E3

Kenya, 45 G1, 47 G6

Keokuk, IA 125 C3

Keratsinion, 43 A3

Kerby, OR 132 A8

Kerepestarcsa, 42 C6

Kérkira, 25 E4

Kermadec Isl, 80 D2

Kerman, 49 G5

Kermit, TX 128 C4

Kern Park, WI 157 C3

Kernville, CA 133 D4

Kerr Reservoir, John H, VA 121 G6

Kerrville, TX 128 D3

Kerzers, 37 A3

Kessariani Monastery, 43 C2

Ketchikan, AK 101 B4, 136 E5

Ketchum, ID 130 A7, 135 F3

Kettwig, 34 C6

Keuka Lake, NY 116 D2

Kew, Austral 79 C2

Kew, S Afr 51 G3

Kew Gardens, NY 143 F3

Kew Gardens, UK 26 C7

Keweenaw Pen, MI 124 D7

Key Biscayne, FL 155 G1

Key Colony Beach, FL 188 D2

Key Deer NWR, FL 188 B2

Key Largo, FL 123 G1, 188 F3

Key Largo Natl Marine Sanctuary, FL 188 F3

Key West, FL 94 B6, 113 D1, 123 E1, 188 A1

Key West Intl Arpt, FL 188 A1

Key West NAS, FL 188 A1

Keybayoran Baru, 64 B7

Keyser, WV 119 E4

Khabarovsk, 55 F3, 66 E7

Khalándrion, 43 C3

Khanty-Mansiysk, 53 E4

Kharkiv, 53 A4

Khartoum, 45 F2, 48 C1

Khimki, 56 B5

Khíos, 25 G3

Khlong Toey, 63 G5

Kholargós, 43 C3

Khon Kaen, 61 A4

Khorramabad, 49 F5

Khovrino, 56 B5

Khulna, 58 E5

Khuralji Khas, 64 E7

Kicevo, 25 E5

Kidderville, NH 114 C5

Kiel, 15 E1, 22 D5

Kielce, 17 G6

Kieldrecht, 31 F6

Kiesen, 37 C1

Kiev, 17 H6, 53 A4

Kifisia, 43 C4

Kigali, 47 F6

Kihei, HI 137 D3

Kikwit, 47 E5

Kilchberg, 37 E1

Kildare, NC 187 E4

Kill Devil Hills, NC 187 G6

Killara, 78 E8

Killarney, Can 107 G1

Killarney, Ire 19 A3

Killeen, TX 111 F3, 129 E3

Killington Pk, VT 117 H4

Kilmarnock, 18 C5

Kilsyth, 79 F3

Kilyos, 43 E4

Kimball, NE 127 B4

Kimberley, 47 E2

Kimberley Plateau, 76 B5

Kimchaek, 66 D6

Kimitsu, 68 D5

Kimp'o, 72 A7

Kimp'o Intl Arpt, 72 B7

Kinali, 43 E1

Kinderhook, NY 117 H2

Kindu, 47 F6

King City, CA 133 B4

King City, OR 177 F4

King Contrivance, MD 147 A1

King of Prussia, PA 144 B5

Kingman, AZ 111 B4, 131 A3, 133 F3

Kings Canyon NP, CA 133 D4, 178 A4

King's Cross Sta, 27 C4

Kings Landing, 114 F7

King's Lynn, 19 F3

Kings Mountain NMP, SC 179 G3

Kings Park, MD 147 A4

Kings Park, VA 148 B5

Kings Point, NY 143 G5

Kingsbury Reservoir, 79 C4

Kingsford, 78 F6

Kingsgrove, 78 D6

Kingsport, TN 118 B1, 121 E6

Kingston, Can 103 D1, 117 E5

Kingston, Jam 94 C3, 97 H3

Kingston, MA 184 A7

Kingston, NY 117 G1, 119 H6

Kingston upon Hull, 14 C1, 19 E4, 20 D8

Kingston upon Thames, 26 C6

Kingstown, 95 H2

Kingsville, TX 129 E1

Kinshasa, 47 E6

Kinston, NC 121 H5

Kioicho, 69 A3

Kiowa NG, NM 128 C6

Kirby, TX 163 H2

Kirchberg, 37 C3

Kirdasah, 50 A3

Kirensk, 55 C3

Kiribati, 80 D4

Kiribati Isl, 80 C4

Kiritimati, 81 E4

Kirkland, Can 106 A3

Kirkland, WA 176 C6

Kirkland Lake, 103 B2

Kirklareli, 25 H5

Kirksville, MO 125 B3

Kirkwall, 18 D7

Kirkwood, MO 125 C2, 162 A1

Kirov, 53 D4

Kirov Stad, 57 F3

Kirsirmandira, 43 D4

Kiruna, 15 E4

Kisangani, 47 F6

Kisarazu, 68 D5

Kishinev, 17 H5

Kisirkaya, 43 E4

Kismaayo, 47 H6

Kispest, 42 B6

Kisshoin, 71 D2

Kissimmee, FL 123 F4, 153 F2

Kissimmee Park, FL 153 G1

Kisumu, 47 G6

Kita-Ku, 71 B4

Kita-mido Temple, 71 B3

Kitakyushu, 60 E8, 67 E4

Kitanomaru Park, 69 B4

Kitchener, 103 C1

Kitimat, 101 B3, 136 F5

Kitsilano, 107 F2

Kittanning, PA 119 E5

Kittery, ME 115 C3

Kitty Hawk, NC 187 G6

Kitwe, 47 F4

Kitzbühel, 23 D2

Kiyose, 68 B8

Kizu, 70 F6

Kladow, 32 B6

Klagenfurt, 17 F5, 23 E1, 24 C6

Klaipeda, 15 F1

Klamath, CA 132 A7, 134 A1

Klamath Falls, CA 134 B2

Klamath Falls, OR 110 B6, 132 B8

Klamath NF, CA 132 A7, 134 A3

Klamath R, CA 132 A7

Kleinburg, 104 C8

Kleinmachnow, 32 C6

Klerksdorp, 47 F3

Klettgau, 37 D4

Kliprivier, 51 G1

Klipriviersberg Nature Reserve, 51 F2

Klodzko, 23 F3

Klosterneuburg, 42 D8

Kloten, 37 F2

Kluane NP, 136 E6

Klyaz'ma, 56 D6

Knesset, 50 D4

Knin, 24 D5

Knole Park, 26 E5

Knollwood, MD 148 E8

Knotts Berry Farm, CA 170 D3

Knox, 79 F2

Knoxville, TN 113 C4, 121 E6, 125 F1

Kóbánya, 42 B7

Kobe, 60 E8, 66 E5, 70 A5

Kobe U, 70 A6

Koblenz, 23 C3

Kobuk R, AK 136 C7

Kobuk Valley NP, AK 136 C8, 178 A3

Kochi, 60 E8, 67 E4

Kodaira, 68 A7

Kodiak, AK 136 C5

Kodiak Isl, AK 82 A5, 136 C5

Kodiak NWR, AK 136 C5

Koganei, 68 B7

Kogarah, 78 E6

Køge, 22 D6

Kojimachi, 69 A3

Kokkola, 15 F4

Kokomo, IN 125 E3

Kokshetau, 53 E3

Kokubunji, 68 A7

Kola Pen, 15 G5, 52 D6, 82 E8

Kolding, 22 C6

Kolobrzeg, 22 E5

Kolpashevo, 53 F3

Kolpino, 57 H1

Kolsher, 65 C3

Koltushi, 57 H2

Kolwezi, 47 E5

Kolyma, 82 B7

Kolyma Mts, 82 A7

Kolyma Range, 54 F6

Kolyma R, 54 E6

Kolyuchin Bay, 136 A8

Komae, 68 B7

Komatke, AZ 168 B1

Komorany, 35 E2

Komotini, 25 F4

Komsomolsk na Amure, 55 F4, 66 D8

Konduz, 58 B7

Kongresshalle, 33 C3

Kongsvinger, 22 D8

Konigs-Wusterhausen, 32 E5

Königsallee, 34 B5

Koniz, 37 B2

Konnagar, 65 E3

Konolfingen, 37 C2

Konstantinovo, 56 D1

Konstantinovskiy, 56 C1

Konstanz, 23 C2, 24 A6

Kontich, 31 G5

Konya, 48 D6

Kootenai NF, MT 135 E6

Kopenick, 32 E6

Korce, 25 E4

Korea Bay, 66 C5

Korea Exhib Ctr, 72 D6

Korea Stock Exchange, 72 C6

Korea Str, 60 E8, 66 D5

Korhogo, 44 B1

Koridhallós, 43 B3

Korla, 53 F1, E8

Koropion, 43 C2

Koror, 80 A5

Korsøor, 22 D5

Koryak Range, 54 F7

Kosciusko, MS 129 H5

Koshien Baseball Stad, 70 B5

Kosice, 17 G5

Kosino, 56 D4

Kostelec, 35 F4

Koszalin, 22 F5

Kota, 58 C5

Kota Baharu, 61 A3

Kota Kinabalu, 61 D3

Kotel'niki, 56 D3

Kotka, 15 G3

Kotlas, 52 D6

Koto-Ku, 68 C7

Kotzebue, AK 100 A7, 136 B7

Kourou, 85 F5

Kovalevo, 57 G3

Kowloon, 67 A3, 75 D3

Kowloon Park, 75 C3

Kowloon Tong, 75 D4

Koyomizu Palace, 71 F3

Koyukuk NWR, AK 136 C7

Kozani, 25 E4

Kozu Shrine, 71 B1

Kozugu Shrine, 71 C2

Kragujevac, 25 E6

Krakow, 17 F6

Kralupy, 35 D4

Krasnodar, 53 A3

Krasnogorsk, 56 **A5**
Krasnoye Selo, 57 **F1**
Krefeld, 34 **A6**
Kremlin, 56 **C4**, 57 **F5**
Kreuzberg, 32 **D7**, 33 **D1**, 33 **E1**
Krimpen aan de Ijssel, 30 **B2**
Krionérion, 43 **B4**
Kristiansand, 14 **D2**, 22 **C7**
Kristianstad, 22 **E6**
Kristinehamn, 22 **E8**
Kroger Hills Park, OH 151 **F2**
Kronshtadt, 57 **E3**
Krotoszyn, 23 **F4**
Krugersdorp, 51 **E3**
Kruibeke, 31 **F5**
Krusevac, 25 **E6**
Kryvyy Rih, 53 **A4**
Kuala Lumpur, 61 **A3**
Kuching, 61 **C2**
Kudan-Minami, 69 **A4**
Kulturforum, 33 **D3**
Kumamoto, 60 **E7**, 67 **E4**
Kumanovo, 25 **F5**
Kumasi, 44 **C1**
Kumch'on, 72 **B8**
Kumiyama, 70 **E7**
Kumla, 36 **F5**
Kummelnäs, 36 **F6**
Kumo, 44 **D2**
Kuna Peak, CA 182 **D3**
Kunashir, 66 **F7**
Kungsangen, 36 **D7**
Kunlun Mts, 58 **D7**
Kunming, 60 **A5**
Kunp'o, 72 **C5**
Kunsthaus, 37 **E1**
Kunsthistorisches Mus, 42 **E7**
Kuopio, 15 **G4**
Kupang, 61 **F1**
Kupchino, 57 **G2**
Kuraymah, 45 **G3**
Kurdzhali, 25 **G5**
Kurgar, 53 **D3**

Kuri, 72 **D7**
Kurla, 65 **B2**
Kurnell, 78 **F5**
Kuro, 72 **C6**
Kursk, 53 **A4**
Kursk Sta, 57 **H5**
Kushiro, 66 **F7**
Kuskokwim Bay, AK 136 **B6**
Kuskokwim Mts, AK 136 **B6**
Kuskokwim R, 100 **A6**
Kusnacht, 37 **F1**
Kusti, 45 **F2**
Kuujjuaq, 103 **C4**
Kuwait, 45 **H4**, 49 **F4**
Kwach'on, 72 **D5**
Kwagunt Butte, AZ 183 **F2**
Kwai Chung, 75 **B4**
Kwanak, 72 **C6**
Kwangju, 66 **C5**, 72 **E5**
Kwangmyong, 72 **C6**
Kwun Tong, 75 **E3**
Kyobashi, 69 **E2**
Kyoto, 60 **E8**, 66 **E5**, 70 **E8**, 71 **F3**
Kyoto Intl Conference Ctr, 70 **F8**
Kyoto U, 71 **F4**
Kyrgyzstan, 58 **C8**
Kyushu, 60 **E7**, 67 **E5**
Kyustendil, 25 **F5**
Kyzyl, 55 **B2**
Kyzyl Kum, 53 **D2**
Kzyl-Orda, 58 **B8**

L

La Belle, FL 123 **F3**
La Boca Stad, 88 **E7**
La Brea Tar Pits, CA 172 **B6**
La Calera, 90 **D2**
La Cañada, 99 **G2**
La Ceiba, 97 **F2**
La Cisterna, 87 **F2**
La Colmena, 98 **A5**
La Concepcíon, 39 **D3**

La Coruña, 16 **A4**, 21 **A4**
La Crosse, KS 127 **D2**
La Crosse, WI 112 **B6**, 124 **C5**
La Defense, 28 **C7**
La Fayette, GA 120 **D5**
La Florida, 90 **A3**
La Giustiniana, 40 **B6**
La Grande, OR 134 **D4**
La Grange, GA 120 **D4**
La Grange, IL 159 **C3**
La Grange, KY 118 **A3**
La Granja, 87 **G2**
La Guaira, 90 **B6**
La Guardia Arpt, NY 143 **E4**
La-Guepiere, 28 **A5**
La Habra, CA 170 **D4**
La Honda, CA 175 **C1**
La Jolla, CA 169 **E5**
La Junta, CO 111 **E4**, 127 **B2**, 131 **F4**
La Llagosta, 38 **E7**
La Loche, 101 **D3**
La Matanza, 88 **C6**
La Mesa, CA 169 **G4**
La Mesa, Col 90 **A3**
La Mirada, CA 170 **D3**
La Molina, 87 **H5**
La Montaña, 84 **C3**
La Paz, 84 **D1**, 96 **B4**
La Perouse, 78 **F5**
La Perouse Str, 66 **F7**
La Pintana, 87 **F1**
La Plaine, 106 **B6**
La Plata, 86 **B5**
La Prairie, 106 **D1**
La Puente, CA 170 **D4**
La Punta, 99 **H4**
La Quebrada, 98 **A5**
La Reina, 87 **G3**
La Reja, 88 **A7**
La Rinconada, 90 **B4**
La Rioja, 86 **B5**
La Rochelle, 16 **C5**, 20 **D5**
La Ronge, 101 **E3**
La Salle, 106 **C2**, 156 **D5**

La Scala, 40 **C1**
La Serena, 86 **A5**
La Spezia, 24 **B5**
La Tuque, 114 **A8**
La Unión del Cuatro,99 **F4**
La Ventra del Astillero, 99 **E5**
La Verne, CA 171 **E5**
Laau Pt, HI 137 **C3**
Labé, 44 **A3**
Labrador, 103 **D4**
Labrador City, 103 **D3**
Labrador Sea, 102 **E5**
Lac Courte Oreilles IR, WI 124 **C6**
Lac Du Flambeau IR, WI 124 **C6**
Lac-Mégantic, 114 **C6**
Lac St Pierre, 114 **A7**
Lachenaie, 106 **C5**
Lachine, 106 **B2**
Lackland AFB, TX 163 **E1**
Laconia, NH 115 **B4**
Ladera, CA 174 **C2**
Ladue, MO 162 **A3**
Lae, 76 **C1**, 80 **B4**
Lafayette, CA 174 **D6**
Lafayette, CO 167 **F6**
Lafayette, IN 112 **C5**, 125 **E3**
Lafayette, LA 113 **B3**, 129 **G3**
Lafayette Hill, PA 144 **B5**
Lafayette Park, CA 173 **C2**
Lafayette Square, DC 149 **C4**
Laferrere, 88 **C6**
Lagny-sur-Marne, 28 **E7**
Lagos, 44 **C1**
Laguna Beach, CA 171 **E5**
Laguna Hills, CA 171 **F1**
Laguna IR, NM 131 **D3**
Laguna Niguel, CA 171 **F1**

Lahat, 61 **B1**

Lahore, 58 **C6**

Lahti, 15 **G3**

Lai Chi Kok, 75 **B3**

Lainate, 40 **A3**

Lainyungang,55 **E1**

Lairg, 18 **C7**

Lajpat Nagar, 64 **E6**

Lake Accotink Park, VA 148 **A5**

Lake Albert, 47 **F6**

Lake Athabasca, 101 **E4**

Lake Baikal, 55 **C3**

Lake Balkhash, 53 **E2**, 58 **C8**

Lake Barcroft, VA 148 **C6**

Lake Bluff, IL 158 **C7**

Lake Buena Vista, FL 123 **E4**, 153 **F3**

Lake Butler, FL 123 **E5**

Lake Chad, 44 **D2**

Lake Champlain, 114 **A5**, 117 **H5**

Lake Chapala, 96 **C3**

Lake Charles, LA 113 **B2**, 129 **G3**

Lake City, FL 121 **E2**

Lake City, GA 152 **C1**

Lake City, SC 121 **G4**

Lake Clark NP & Pres, AK 136 **C6**, 178 **A1**

Lake Eleanor Reservoir, CA 182 **A5**

Lake Elsinore, CA 171 **H2**

Lake Erie, 103 **C1**, 112 **D6**, 116 **A3**, 118 **C6**, 125 **F4**, 179 **G4**

Lake Eyre, 76 **D4**

Lake Fairfax Park, VA 148 **A7**

Lake Forest, CA 171 **F1**

Lake Forest, IL 158 **C7**

Lake George, NY 117 **G4**,

Lake Havasu City, AZ 131 **A3**, 133 **F3**

Lake Huron, 103 **B1**, 112 **C6**, 124 **F5**, 179 **F5**

Lake Isabella, CA 133 **D4**

Lake Jem, FL 153 **E6**

Lake Kariba, 47 **F4**

Lake Key, FL 188 **F4**

Lake Khanka, 66 **D7**

Lake Ladoga, 15 **G3**, 52 **C5**

Lake Landing, NC 187 **F3**

Lake Malawi, 47 **G4**

Lake Managua, 97 **F1**

Lake Manatee SRA, FL 154 **D1**

Lake Manitoba, 101 **F2**, 110 **F8**

Lake Maracaibo, 84 **C5**, 95 **H1**

Lake Mary, FL 153 **G6**

Lake Mattamuskeet, NC 187 **E3**

Lake Mead NRA, AZ 131 **A3**, 133 **F4**, 178 **B3**, 183 **A3**

Lake Meredith NRA, TX 128 **D6**

Lake Michigan, 103 **B1**, 112 **C6**, 124 **E5**, 179 **F5**

Lake Monroe, FL 153 **G6**

Lake Mweru, 47 **F5**

Lake Nasser, 45 **F3**, 48 **C3**

Lake Nicaragua, 97 **G1**

Lake Nipigon, 103 **A3**, 112 **B7**, 124 **C8**

Lake of the Woods, 101 **F2**, 112 **A7**, 124 **A8**, 126 **F8**, 179 **E6**, 181 **F6**

Lake Okeechobee, FL 113 **E2**, 123 **F3**, 179 **G1**

Lake Onega, 15 **H4**, 52 **C5**

Lake Ontario, 103 **C1**, 112 **D6**, 116 **C4**, 179 **G5**

Lake Oswego, OR 177 **F4**

Lake Park, FL 154 **C6**

Lake Park, WI 157 **C3**

Lake Peipus, 15 **G2**

Lake Placid, FL 123 **F3**

Lake Placid, NY 117 **G5**

Lake Pontchartrain, LA 120 **A3**

Lake Poopó, 84 **D1**

Lake Powell, AZ 131 **B4**

Lake Providence, LA 120 **A4**

Lake Quannapowitt, 138 **D5**

Lake Quivira, KS 162 **A5**

Lake Region, 15 **G3**

Lake St Clair, MI 118 **C6**

Lake St-Francois, 114 **C6**

Lake Sammamish SP, WA 176 **D5**

Lake Superior, 112 **B7**, 124 **D7**, 179 **F5**

Lake Superior Prov P, 124 **E7**

Lake Tahoe, CA 132 **C6**

Lake Tana, 45 **G2**

Lake Tanganyika, 47 **F5**

Lake Titicaca, 84 **D2**

Lake Turkana, 45 **G1**

Lake Urmia, 49 **F6**

Lake Van, 49 **E6**

Lake Victoria, 47 **G6**

Lake Volta, 44 **C1**

Lake Wales, FL 123 **E3**

Lake Winnipeg, 101 **F3**, 110 **F8**, 124 **A8**

Lake Winnipesaukee, NH 115 **C4**

Lake Worth, TX 164 **A3**

Lake Zurich, IL 158 **B6**

Lakefront Arpt LA, 163 **G6**

Lakeland, FL 123 **E4**

Lakeland Village, CA 171 **H1**

Lakemba, 78 **D6**

Lakeport, CA 132 **A6**

Lakeside, CA 133 **E2**, 169 **H5**

Lakeside, CO 167 **F4**

Lakeside, TX 164 **A4**

Lakeview, NY 143 **H3**

Lakeview, OR 132 **C8**, 134 **C2**

Lakeview, TX 164 **A5**

Lakewood, CA 170 **C3**

Lakewood, CO 167 **F2**

Lakewood, NY 116 **A3**

Lakewood, OH 150 **C7**

Lakewood FP, IL 158 **A6**

Lakewood Park, GA 152 **B3**

Lakshadweep, 59 **B3**

Lale, HI 137 **C3**

Lalor Park, 78 **B8**

Lamar, CO 131 **F4**

Lamar R, WY 180 **C5**

Lambaréné, 46 **D6**

Lambert-St. Louis Intl Arpt, MO 162 **B3**

Lambeth, 27 **D1**

Lambeth Bridge, 27 **C1**

Lambrate, 40 **C2**

Lamesa, TX 128 **C4**

Lamma Island, 75 **B1**

Lampagnano, 40 **B2**

Lampasas, TX 129 **E3**

Lanai, HI 137 **D3**

Lancaster, CA 133 **D3**

Lancaster, OH 118 **B4**

Lancaster, PA 119 **F4**

Lancaster, SC 121 **F5**

Lancaster, TX 165 **G1**

Lancaster, UK 19 **D4**

Lancaster Sound, 102 **A7**

L'Ancienne-Lorette, 105 **D3**

Land Between the Lakes, KY 120 **C6**

Lander, WY 110 **D6**, 130 **C7**, 135 **H2**

Landfall, MN 161 **F2**

Landmark Ctr, MN 161 **E2**

Landover, MD 148 **F7**

Land's End, 16 **B6**, 19 **C2**

Landsdowne, 78 **C6**

Landshut, 23 **D2**

Landskrona, 22 **E6**

Landsmeer, 30 **A9**

Landstrasse, 42 **E7**

Lane Cove, 78 **E7**

Langen, 35 **B1**

Langenberg, 34 **D6**

Langenzersdorf, 42 **E5**

Langley, VA 148 **B7**

Langley Park, MD 148 E8
Langnau, 37 E1
Langsa, 61 A3
Langstaff, 104 E8
Lank-Latum, 34 A6
Lansdowne, MD 147 C2
Lansdowne, PA 144 C2
L'anse IR, MI 124 D6
Lansing, IL 159 E1
Lansing, MI 112 C6, 125 E4
Lanús, 88 E6
Lanzhanchang, 73 B3
Lanzhou, 60 A7
Laoag, 60 D5, 67 C1
Laobaiduzhen, 74 E6
Laon, 20 E7, 23 A3
Laos, 61 A4
Lapa, 91 D2, 92 A5
Lapakahi SHP, HI 137 E2
Lapland, 15 F5, 82 E7
Laptev Sea, 54 B6, 82 C7
L'Aquila, 24 C4
Laramie, WY 110 D5,
  127 A4, 130 E6
Laredo, TX 96 D5, 111 F2,
  128 D1, 178 D1
Lares, 122 B2
Largo, FL 154 A4
Larisa, 17 G3, 25 F4
Larkspur, CA 174 A6
Larnia, 25 F3
Larsen Ice Shelf, 83 E4
Las Adjuntas, 90 B4
Las Condes, 87 H3
Las Cruces, NM 111 D3,
  128 B4, 131 E2
Las Fuentes, 99 F4
Las Juntas, 99 F4
Las Palmas, 44 A4
Las Piedras, 122 C2
Las Pinas, 62 B1
Las Pintas de Arriba, 99 G4
Las Trampas Regional
  Wilderness, CA 174 D5
Las Tunitas, 90 A6
Las Vegas, NV 111 B4,
  131 A4, 133 F4, 178 B3

Las Vegas, NM 111 E4,
  127 A1, 128 B6, 131 E3
Lasalle U, PA 145 E4
Lassen NF, CA 132 B7,
  134 B1
Lassen Pk, CA 132 B7
Lassen Volcanic NP, CA
  132 B7, 178 A4
L'Assomption, 106 D6
Lat Phrao, 63 G6
Latakia, 48 D6
Lathrup Village, MI 156 C8
Latin Quarter, 29 E1
Latina, Italy 24 B3
Latina, Spain 39 B2
Latino, 40 C5
Latvia, 15 G2, 52 B6
Lauderdale, MN 161 D3
Lauderdale-by-the-Sea, FL
  155 G5
Lauderdale Lakes, FL 155 G5
Lauderhill Sunrise, FL
  155 F5
Launceston, 77 E2
Laurel, MS 120 B3, 129 H4
Laurel, MT 130 C8
Laurel, OR 177 E4
Laurentides, 106 B6
Lausanne, 20 F6, 23 B1,
  24 A6
Lausannem, 16 D5
Lava Beds NM, CA 132 B7,
  178 A5
Lava Creek, WY 181 H4
Lava Hot Springs, ID
  130 B7
Laval, 106 B3
Laval-Ouest, 106 A3
Lavallol, 88 D5
Lavras, 92 D6
Lavriki, 57 G3
Lawndale, CA 170 B3
Lawndale, PA 145 F4
Lawnside, NJ 145 F5
Lawrence, IN 156 F3
Lawrence, KS 112 A5,
  127 F3

Lawrence, MA 115 C3,
  138 C8
Lawrence, NY 143 G1
Lawrenceburg, KY 118 A3
Lawrenceburg, TN 120 C5
Lawrenceville, VA 119 E3
Lawton, OK 111 F4,
  129 E5
Laxenburg, 42 E6
Layton, FL 188 D2
Layton, UT 135 G1
Laytonville, CA 132 A6
Lázaro Cárdenas, 96 C3
Le Bourget Arpt, 28 D8
Le Creusot, 20 E6
Le Gardeur, 106 D5
Le Havre, 16 C6, 19 E1,
  20 D7
Le Kremlin, 28 D6
Le Mans, 16 C5, 20 D6
Le Mars, IA 126 E5
Le Perray-en-Yvelines,
  28 A6
Le Plessis-Belleville, 28 F8
Le Puy, 20 E5
Le Roy, NY 116 C3
Le Val-Saint-Germain,
  28 B5
Lead, SD 126 B5
Leadore, ID 135 F3
Leadville, CO 127 A3,
  130 D5
Leaside, 104 E6
Leatherhead, 26 C6
Leavenworth, KS 125 A3,
  127 F3
Leavenworth, WA 134 C5
Lebanon, 45 G5, 48 D5
Lebanon, KY 118 A3
Lebanon, MO 125 B2
Lebanon, NH 115 B4
Lebanon, OH 118 B4
Lebanon, PA 119 G4
Lebanon, TN 120 C6
Lebanon, VA 118 C1
Lebanon SF, NJ 119 H4
Lebbeke, 31 E3

Leblon, 91 D1
Lecce, 24 D3
Leech Lake IR, MN 124 B7,
  126 F7
Leeds, 14 C1, 19 E4,
  20 C8
Leerbeek, 31 E1
Leesburg, VA 119 F3
Leesville, LA 129 G3
Leeward Islands, 95 G3
Leganés, 39 A4
Legazpi, 67 C4
Legler Barn Museum,
  Adam, KS 162 A4
Legok, 64 A7
Lehi, UT 130 B6
Leicester, 19 E3
Leichhardt, 78 E7
Leiden, 31 E4
Leidschendam, 30 B3
Leigh Lake, WY 181 F4
Leimuiden, 30 C4
Leipzig, 17 E6, 23 D4
Leitrim, 105 C1
Lemay, MO 162 B1
Leme, 91 D2
Lemmon, SD 126 C6
Lemon Grove, CA 169 G3
Lemont, IL 159 B2
Lemoore, CA 133 C4
Lena R, 54 C5, 82 B8
Lenasia, 51 E1
L'Enfant Plaza, DC 149 D2
Lengnau, 37 D3
Lenin Stad, 56 B4
Lenino, 56 C3
Leninsk, 53 D2
Lenox, MA 115 A3
Lens, 23 A3
Lensk, 55 C4
Leominster, MA 115 B3
León, Mex 96 C3, 97 F1
León, Spain 16 B4, 21 B4
Leon Valley, TX 163 E3
Leonardo Da Vinci
  Intl Arpt, 40 A4
Leonardtown, MD 119 G2

Leonia, NJ 142 D6

L'Epiphanie, 106 D6

Leppington, 78 A6

Lérida, 16 C3, 21 D4

Lerma, K, 96 C3

Lerwick, 18 E8

Lesbos, 25 G3

Les Eboulements, 114 C8

Les Halles, 29 E2

Les Mureaux, 28 B8

Les Ulis, 28 C6

Leskovac, 25 E6

Lesosibirsk, 55 A3

Lesotho, 47 F2

Lesser Antilles, 95 G2

Leszno, 23 F4

Letchworth SP, NY 116 C3

Lethbridge, 101 D2, 110 D8

Letmathe, 34 F6

Leuwiliang, 64 A5

Levallois-Perret, 28 C7

Level Green, PA 146 F6

Levelland, TX 128 C5,
131 F2

Levendas Park, 87 F5

Levin RP, Ed, CA 175 F3

Lévis, 105 F3, 114 C7

Levittown, NY 116 B5

Lewis, 18 C7

Lewis & Clark NF, MT
135 G5

Lewis & Clark NHP, OR-WA
134 A4, 178 A6

Lewis Lake, WY 180 B2

Lewis R, WY 180 B2

Lewis Smith Lake, AL
120 C4

Lewisburg, PA 119 F5

Lewisburg, TN 120 C5

Lewisburg, WV 118 D2

Lewisdale, MD 148 E7

Lewiston, ID 110 C7,
134 D4

Lewiston, ME 112 F7,
115 D4

Lewistown, MT 135 H5

Lewistown, PA 119 F5

Lewisville, TX 165 E6

Lexington, KY 112 C5,
118 A3, 125 F2, 179 F3

Lexington, MA 139 B4

Lexington, NE 127 D4

Lexington, VA 119 E2

Leyden, CO 167 E4

Leyte, 61 E4

Lhasa, 58 E6

L'Hospitalet de Llobregat,
38 E6

Lianxian, 67 A3

Lianyungang, 60 C7, 67 B4

Liaoyuan, 66 C3

Liard R, 102 C6

Libby, MT 135 E6

Libcice nad Vitavou, 35 E4

Liben, 35 E3

Liberal, KS 127 C1, 128 D6

Liberdade, 93 H2

Liberec, 17 F6, 23 E3

Liberia, 44 B1

Libertad, 88 B6

Liberty, NY 117 F1

Liberty Plain, MA 139 F1

Libertyville, IL 158 B7

Libeznice, 35 E4

Liboc, 35 D3

Library of Congress, DC
149 F2

Libreville, 46 D6

Libya, 17 G1, 45 E4, 48 A4

Libyan Desert, 45 F3, 48 B3

Lichtenberg, 32 E6

Lichtenrade, 32 D5

Lidingo, 36 E9

Lido Beach, NY 143 H1

Lido di Faro, 40 A4

Lido di Ostia, 40 A4

Liechtenstein, 17 E5,
23 C1, 24 B6

Liège, 16 D6, 20 E7, 23 B3

Liepaja, 15 F2

Lier, 31 H5

Liesing, 42 D6

Lighthouse Park, 107 F3

Lighthouse Pt, FL 155 G6

Lignumvitae Key, FL 188 E3

Lignumvitae Key St
Botanical Site, FL 188 E3

Ligurian Sea, 24 A4

Lihue, HI 137 B4

Likasi, 47 F5

Lille, 16 D6, 20 E7, 23 A3

Lillehammer, 15 E3, 22 D8

Lillerod, 36 A7

Lilongwe, 47 G4

Lilydale, Austral 79 F3

Lilydale, MN 161 D2

Lilymoor, IL 158 A7

Lima, OH 118 A5, 125 F3

Lima, PA 144 A3

Lima, Peru 84 C2, 87 G6

Lima, MT 135 F3

Limaburg, KY 151 B1

Limassol, 48 D5

Limbour, 28 B5

Limerick, 14 B1, 19 A3,
20 A8

Limito, 40 D2

Limoges, 16 C4, 20 D5

Limours, 105 A4

Limpopo R, 47 F3

Linate Arpt, 40 C1

Lince, 87 F5

Lincoln, CA 132 B6

Lincoln, ME 114 E6

Lincoln, MA 139 A4

Lincoln, NE 112 A5,
127 F4, 178 D4, 179 E4

Lincoln, NM 131 E2

Lincoln, UK 19 E4

Lincoln Ctr, NY 141 G5

Lincoln Hts, OH 151 D3

Lincoln Mem, DC 149 A3

Lincoln Mon, IL 160 D5

Lincoln NF, NM 128 B5

Lincoln Park, IL 159 D6

Lincoln Park, MI 156 C5

Lincoln Park, WI 157 C3

Lincolnia, VA 148 B5

Lincolnwood, IL 158 D5

Linden, NJ 142 A3

Lindenberg, 32 E8

Lindenhurst, IL 158 B8

Lindenhurst, NY 116 C5

Lindesberg, 22 E8

Lindfield, 78 E8

Lindholmen, 36 E8

Line Islands, 81 E4

Liniers, 88 D7

Linköping, 15 F2, 22 E7

Linkou, 62 B5

Linndale, OH 150 C6

Lint, 31 H5

Linthicum, MD 147 C1

Lintorf, 34 B6

Linz, 17 E5, 23 E2

Lion Park, 51 F4

Lion Rock CP, 75 D4

Lipetsk, 53 B4

Lisbon, OH 118 D5

Lisbon, Port 16 A3, 21 A3,
38 B7, 44 B5

Lisiy Nos, 57 F3

Lisle, IL 159 A3

L'Isle-Adam, 28 C7

Lismore, 77 F4

Lisse, 30 B5

Lissone, 40 C3

Litchfield, MN 126 F6

Lithuania, 15 G1, 52 B5

Little Bighorn Battlefield
NM, MT 178 C5

Little Canada, MN 161 E3

Little Colorado R, AZ 183 F2

Little Cranberry Isl, ME
186 D2

Little Falls, MN 124 B6,
126 F6

Little Falls, NJ 142 A6

Little Falls, NY 117 F3

Little Ferry, NJ 142 C5

Little Gott Isl, ME 186 B1

Little Italy, NY 141 F2

Little Kinnakeet US
Lifesaving Svc Sta, NC
187 H3

Little Manatee River SRA,
FL 154 D3

Little Mermaid, The, 36 C6

269

Little Missouri NG, ND 126 B7

Little Missouri R, MT 126 B6

Little Neck, NY 143 F4

Little Rock, AR 113 B4, 129 G5, 179 E2

Little Tokyo, CA 172 E6

Littlefield, TX 128 C5, 131 F2

Littleton, CO 167 G2

Littleton, NH 114 B5

Liulitun, 73 F3

Liupukeng, 73 E3

Liuzhou, 60 B5

Live Oak, FL 121 E2, 123 E5

Live Oak, TX 163 H3

Livermore, CA 175 F4

Livermore, ME 114 C5

Liverpool, Austral 78 B6

Liverpool, UK 14 C1, 19 D4, 20 C8

Liverpool Bay, 136 E8

Liverpool Street Sta, 27 F3

Livingston, MT 130 C8, 135 G4

Livingston, TX 129 F3

Livingstone, 47 F4

Livonia, MI 156A7

Livorno, 24 B4

Livry-Gargan, 28 E7

Ljubljana, 17 F4, 23 E1, 24 C6

Ljungby, 22 E6

Llanos, 84 C5

Llissá de Munt, 38 E8

Lloydminster, 101 E3

Lo Espejo, 87 F2

Lo Prado, 87 F3

Lobito, 46 D5

Loch Ness, 18 C6

Loch Raven, MD 147 D4

Lochearn, MD 147 C3

Lock Haven, PA 119 F5

Lockport, IL 159 B2

Lockport, NY 116 B3

Locust Valley, NY 143 H6

Lod, 50 B6

Lodge Grass, MT 135 H4

Lodi, CA 132 B5

Lodi, NJ 142 C6

Lodz, 17 F6

Logan, OH 118 C4

Logan, PA 145 E4

Logan, UT 110 C6, 130 B6, 135 G1

Logan, WV 118 C2

Logan Hts, CA 169 F3

Logan Intl Arpt, MA 139 E3, 140 D5

Logroño, 21 C4

Loia, 84 B3

Loire R, 16 C5, 20 D6

Lolo, MT 135 F5

Lolo Pk, MT 135 E5

Loma Linda, CA 171 H4

Loma Mar, CA 175 C1

Lomas de Zamora, 88 E6

Lomas Verdes, 98 A4

Lombard, IL 159 A4

Lomé, 44 C1

Lomita, CA 170 B3

Lomonosov, 57 E2

Lompoc, CA 133 C3

Londerzeel, 31 F3

London, Can. 103 C1, 112 D6

London, KY 118 B1, 120 D6

London, UK 16 C6, 19 E2, 20 D7, 26 D7, 27

London Arena, 26 C7

London Bridge Sta, 27 F2

London City Arpt, 26 D7

Londonderry, 14 B1, 18 B5

Londrina, 86 C6

Lone Star Geyser, WY 180 B3

Lonerock, OR 134 C4

Long Beach, CA 111 A4, 133 D2, 170 C3

Long Beach, NY 116 B5, 143 G1

Long Branch, Can 104 C5

Long Branch, NJ 119 H4

Long Island, 94 D5, 112 F6

Long Island City, NY 142 D4

Long Island Sd, 115 B1, 116 C6

Long Key SP, FL 188 E2

Long Lake, NY 117 G5

Long Lake RP, MN 161 D4

Long Pt, 78 B5

Long Pt, MA 184 E8

Long Pond, ME 186 B4

Long Pond, MA 184 B6

Long Porcupine Isl, ME 186 D6

Long Shoal R, NC 187 F4

Longboat Key, FL 123 E3

Longchamp Hippodrome, 28 C7

Longdaocun, 73 E4

Longhua Park, 74 C5

Longhuazui, 74 E5

Longlac, 124 E8

Longmont, CO 130 E5

Longreach, 77 E4

Longueuil, 106 D3, 114 A6

Longview, TX 113 A3, 129 F4

Longwood, FL 153 G5

Lonholt, 36 B8

Loni, 64 E8

Looe Key Nat Marine Sanctuary, FL 188 B2

Lookout Canyon, AZ 183 D4

Lookout Pt, ME 186 C6

Lookout Pts, WY 180 C4

Loop, The, IL 160 C6

Lopaus Pt, ME 186 B2

Lords Cricket Ground, 26 C7

Lordsburg, NM 131 D2

Loreto, 96 A5

Loretteville, 105 D3

Lorient, 20 C6

Lorraine, 106 B4

Los Alamos, NM 127 A1, 128 B6, 131 D3

Los Altos, CA 175 D2

Los Altos Hills, CA 175 D2

Los Angeles, CA 81 G6, 111 A4, 133 D3, 170 C5, 172, 178 A3

Los Angeles Civic Ctr, CA 172 E6

Los Angeles Conv Ctr, CA 172 C4

Los Angeles County Mus of Art, CA 172 B6

Los Angeles Intl Arpt, CA 170 B4

Los Angeles Mem Coliseum, CA 172 D5

Los Banos, CA 133 C4

Los Beleres, 99 F6

Los Gatos, CA 175 E1

Los Gavilares, 99 F4

Los Lunas, NM 128 B5, 131 E3

Los Mohis, 96 B5

Los Molinos, CA 132 B6

Los Padres NF, CA 133 B4, 133 C3

Los Penasquitos Canyon Pres, CA 169 F6

Los Pínamos P, 98 A1

Los Reyes, 98 D2

Lostwood NWR, ND 126 C8

Lot R, 20 D5

Louanghprabang, 60 A5

Loudixia, 74 E5

Loughman, FL 153 F1

Louisa, KY 118 B2

Louisa, VA 119 F2

Louiseville, 114 A7

Louisiana, 97 E6, 113 A3, 129 H3, 179 E2

Louisiana Superdome, LA 163 F5

Louisville, CO 167 F6

Louisville, KY 112 C5, 125 E2, 179 F3

Louisville, MS 120 B4

Loures, 38 B8

Lousa, 38 A8

Louvre, The, 29 E2
Louvres, 28 E8
Lovech, 25 G6
Loveland, OH 151 F4
Loveland Park, OH 151 F4
Lovelock, NV 132 D6
Lovington, NM 128 C4, 131 F2
Lowe Art Mus, FL 155 F1
Lowell, MA 138 A7
Lowell NHP, MA 138 A7
Lower Brule IR, SD 126 D5
Lower Geyser Basin, WY 180 A3
Lower Hadlock Pond, ME 186 C3
Lower Matecumbe Key, FL 188 E2
Lower Mills, 139 D2
Lower Red Lake, MN 124 A7
Lower Slide Lake, WY 181 G2
Lower Suwannee NWR, FL 121 E1
Lower Templestowne, 79 D3
Lower Tunguska R, 55 A4
Lowestoft, 19 F3
Lowry Park, FL 154 C5
Lowville, NY 117 F4
Loyalton, CA 132 C6
Loyola U, IL 158 D5
Luanda, 46 D5
Luanshya, 47 F4
Lubango, 46 D4
Lubbock, TX 96 C6, 111 E3, 128 D5, 178 D2
Lübeck, 15 E1, 22 D5
Lubin, 23 F4
Lublin, 17 G6
Lubumbashi, 47 F5
Lucena, 61 E4
Luchou, 62 B5
Luchu, 62 A5
Lucknow, 58 D5
Lüderitz, 46 D3
Ludiana, 58 C6

Ludlow, VT 115 A4
Ludvika, 22 E8
Ludwigsfelde, 32 C5
Luena, 47 E5
Lufkin, TX 113 A3, 129 F3
Lugano, 78 C5
Lugo, 21 A4
Lugouqiao, 73 A1
Lugu, 73 A3
Luhansk, 53 B4
Lujiazui, 74 E7
Luleå, 15 F4
Luleburgaz, 25 H5
Lumpkin, GA 120 D3
Lund, 22 E6
Lunda, 36 E8
Lunen, 34 F8
Lung Shan Temple, 62 B5
Lunghezza, 40 D6
Luoyang, 60 B7, 67 A4
Luray, VA 119 E3
Lusaka, 47 F4
Lutherville, MD 147 D4
Luton, 19 E3
Lutz, FL 154 C6
Luwan District, 74 D6
Luxembourg, 16 D6, 20 F7, 23 B3
Luxembourg City, 20 F7
Luxembourg Palace, 29 D1
Luxmanor, MD 148 C8
Luxor, 45 F4, 48 D3
Luzern, 23 C1, 24 A6
Luzon, 60 D5
Luzon Str, 60 D5, 67 C1
Lyell Canyon, CA 182 D3
Lynbrook, NY 143 G2
Lynchburg, VA 119 E2
Lyndhurst, NJ 142 B5
Lyndhurst, OH 150 F7
Lyngby, 36 C7
Lynge, 36 A7
Lynn, NH 155 C3, 138 E5
Lynn Canyon Park, 107 H3
Lynn Haven, FL 122 C6
Lynn Lake, 101 F3

Lynnfield, MA 138 D6
Lynnhurst, MA 138 E5
Lynwood, CA 170 C3
Lynwood, IL 159 E1
Lyon, 16 D4, 20 E5, 23 A1, 44 D6
Lyon Arboretum, HI 177 H2
Lyons, IL 159 C3
Lyons, NY 116 D3
Lyss, 37 A3
Lysterfield, 79 F1
Lytkarino, 56 D2
Lytle Creek, CA 171 G6
Lyttelton, 51 H6
Lyubertsy, 56 D3
Lyublino, 56 C3

M

MCI Center, DC 149 D3
Ma On Shan CP, 75 E4
Ma'ale Adummim, 50 D4
Maan, 48 D4
Maasdam, 30 B1
Maassluis, 30 A3
Maastricht, 23 B3
Mac Robertson Land, 83 D1
Macapá, 85 F4
Macarao NP, 90 A4
Macau, 60 C5, 67 A3
Maccarese, 40 A5
Macclenny, FL 123 E6
Macdona, TX 163 E1
Macdonnell Ranges, 76 C4
Macedonia, 17 G3, 25 F5, 45 E6
Macedonia, OH 150 F5
Maceió, 85 H2
Machakos, 47 G6
Machala, 84 B3
Machias, ME 114 F5
Machida, 68 A6
Mack, OH 151 B2
Mackay, 77 E5
Mackay Island NWR, NC 119 G1
Mackenzie, 101 C3

Mackenzie Mts, 100 C5, 136 F7
Mackenzie R, 82 B5, 100 C6
Mackeral Cove, ME 186 A1
Mâcon, Fr 20 E6, 23 A1
Macon, GA 113 D3, 121 E3
Macon, MO 125 B3
Macquarie Fields, 78 B5
Macquarie Isl, 83 A3
Macuto, 90 C6
Macwahoc, ME 114 E6
Macy's, NY 141 E4
Madagascar, 47 H3
Madaket, MA 185 H4
Madama Palace, 41 C3
Madang, 76 C2, 80 B4
Madeira, OH 151 E3
Madeira Beach, FL 154 A4
Madeira Islands, 44 B5
Madeira R, 84 D3
Madeleine, 29 D2
Madera, CA 133 C4
Madgeburg, 17 E6
Madiera Bickel Mound HS, FL 154 B2
Madison, FL 122 D6
Madison, IL 162 C2
Madison, IN 118 A3, 125 E2
Madison, SD 126 E5
Madison, WV 118 C2
Madison, WI 112 B6, 124 C5, 179 F4
Madison Hts, MI 156 D8
Madison IR, WA 176 A6
Madison Plateau, WY 180 A3
Madison R, WY 180 A4
Madison Square Gdn, NY 141 E4
Madison Valley, WY 180 A4
Madisonville, KY 125 E2
Madras, *India* 59 C4
Madras, OR 134 C3

Madrid, *Col* 90 **B2**
Madrid, *Spain* 16 **B3**,
 21 **C3**, 39 **D3**, 44 **C6**
Madrid City U, 39 **B3**
Madrid Geographical &
 Cadestral Inst, 39 **C4**
Madurai, 59 **C3**
Madureira, 91 **C2**
Magadan, 54 **A7**, 54 **F5**
Magaliesberg Natural Area,
 51 **E6**
Magdagachi, 55 **E3**
Magdalena Contreras,
 98 **A3**
Magdalena R, 84 **C5**
Magdeburg, 23 **D4**
Magdalena del Mar, 87 **F5**
Magic Kingdom Park, FL
 153 **F3**
Magic Land, 63 **G6**
Magnitogorsk, 53 **D3**
Magog, 118 **B6**
Magoúla, 43 **A4**
Mahajanga, 47 **H4**
Mahlow, 32 **D5**
Mahmutsevketpasa, 43 **F3**
Mahmutbey, 43 **D2**
Mahogany Hammock, FL
 188 **E4**
Mahrauli, 64 **E6**
Mahtomedi, MN 161 **F4**
Maidan, 73 **D4**
Maidenhead, 26 **A7**
Maidstone, *Can* 156 **F5**
Maidstone, *UK* 19 **F2**,
 26 **F6**
Maiduguri, 44 **D2**
Main RR Sta, 35 **B3**
Maine, 103 **D2**, 112 **F7**,
 114 **E5**, 179 **H6**
Mainz, 20 **F7**, 23 **C3**
Maipú, 87 **F2**
Maiquetía, 90 **B6**
Mairiporã, 92 **B6**
Maisons-Laffitte, 28 **C7**
Maitland, FL 123 **F4**,
 153 **G5**

Majé, 91 **F4**
Majorca, 16 **C3**, 21 **E3**
Majors House, Alexander,
 MO 162 **B4**
Majoshaza, 42 **A5**
Majuro, 80 **C5**
Makapuu Pt., HI 137 **D3**
Makassar Strait, 61 **E2**
Makati, 62 **C2**
Makhachkala, 53 **B2**
Makoti, ND 126 **C7**
Makurdi, 44 **D1**
Malabo, 44 **D1**
Malabon, 62 **B3**
Malacanang Palace, 62 **C2**
Malad, 65 **B3**
Malad City, ID 135 **F2**
Málaga, 16 **B2**, 21 **B2**
Malagrotta, 40 **B5**
Malakal, 45 **G1**
Malang, 61 **D1**
Malanje, 47 **E5**
Malawi, 47 **G5**
Malaysia, 61 **A3**, 61 **D2**
Malden, MA 139 **D4**
Maldives, 59 **B2**
Male, 59 **B2**
Malheur or, 134 **C2**
Malheur NF, OR 134 **D3**
Malheur NWR, OR 132 **D8**
Mali, 44 **B2**
Mall, The, DC 149 **D2**
Mall of America, MN
 161 **C1**
Malmo, 15 **E1**, 22 **E6**
Malone, NY 117 **G6**
Måløv, 36 **A6**
Malta, 17 **F1**, 24 **C1**,
 44 **D5**, 48 **A6**
Malta, MT 135 **H6**
Maltepe, 43 **F1**
Malton, 104 **B7**
Malvern, *Can* 104 **A5**
Malvern, AR 120 **D4**
Malvern, *Austral* 79 **C2**
Malverne, NY 143 **G3**
Mamelodi, 51 **H6**

Mamie, NC 187 **F6**
Mammoth Cave NP, KY
 120 **D6**, 125 **E2**, 179 **F3**
Mammoth Hot Springs, WY
 180 **B5**
Mammoth Lakes, CA
 132 **C5**
Mammoth Pk, CA 182 **D4**
Mamo, 90 **A6**
Mamontovka, 56 **D6**
Manado, 61 **F3**
Managua, 84 **A6**, 94 **A1**,
 97 **F1**
Manama, 49 **F4**
Manassas, VA 119 **F3**
Manati, 122 **B2**
Manaus, 85 **E4**
Manchester, CT 115 **B2**
Manchester, NH 112 **F6**,
 115 **B3**
Manchester, TN 120 **D5**
Manchester, *UK* 14 **C1**,
 19 **D4**, 20 **C8**
Manchester, VT 117 **H3**
Manchester, WA 176 **A4**
Manchester SF, SC 121 **F4**
Manchester SP, WA
 176 **A5**
Manchurian Plain, 66 **C3**
Mandal, 22 **C7**
Mandalay, 58 **F5**
Mandaluyong, 62 **C2**
Mandan, ND 126 **C7**
Mandaoli, 64 **F7**
Mandaula, 64 **E8**
Mandi, 64 **D5**
Mandra, 43 **A3**
Mandurah, 76 **A3**
Manfredonia, 24 **D3**
Mangalia, 25 **H6**
Mangalore, 59 **B4**
Mangus Corner, TX 163 **E1**
Manhasset, NY 143 **G5**
Manhattan, KS 110 **F5**,
 127 **E3**
Manhattan, NY 116 **B5**,
 141 **E4**, 142 **D4**

Manhattan Beach, CA
 170 **B3**
Manila, *Phil* 61 **D4**, 62 **C4**
Manila, UT 135 **H1**
Manila Intl Arpt, 62 **C1**
Manisa, 25 **H3**
Manistee NF, MI 124 **E5**
Manitoba, 101 **F3**
Manitoulin Isl, 124 **F6**
Manitowoc, WI 124 **D5**
Manitsoq, 102 **D6**
Manizales, 84 **C5**
Mankato, MN 112 **A6**,
 124 **A5**, 126 **F5**
Manlius, NY 117 **E3**
Manly, 78 **F8**
Mannheim, 16 **D6**, 20 **F7**,
 23 **C3**
Manns Harbor, NC 187 **G5**
Manoa Falls, HI 177 **H2**
Manokwari, 76 **A3**
Manomet Pt, MA 184 **B2**
Manorhaven, NY 143 **F5**
Mansel Isl, 103 **B4**
Manset, ME 186 **B2**
Mansfield, LA 129 **G4**
Mansfield, OH 112 **C5**,
 118 **C5**
Mansfield, TX 164 **D1**
Mansfield, WA 134 **C5**
Manteca, CA 132 **C5**
Manteo, NC 187 **G5**
Mantes-la-Jolie, 28 **A8**
Mantova, 24 **B5**
Mantua, VA 148 **A6**
Manuel F. Correllus SF, MA
 185 **G1**
Manvel, TX 166 **C1**
Manzanillo, 94 **C4**
Manzhouli, 66 **A7**
Maoming, 67 **A1**
Maple, 104 **C8**
Maple Grove, MN 124 **B6**
Maple Hts, OH 150 **E6**
Maple Leaf Gdns, 104 **C6**
Maple Shade, NJ 145 **G3**
Maple Valley, WA 176 **D4**

Maplewood, MN 161 E3

Maplewood, MO 162 B1

Map'o, 72 C7

Maputo, 47 G3

Mar del Plata, 86 B4

Maracaibo, 84 C6, 95 E1

Maracana Stad, 91 D2

Maracay, 84 D5, 95 F1

Maradi, 44 D2

Marais, 29 F2

Maraisburg, 51 F3

Marajó Isl, 85 F4

Marathon, Can 103 B2, 124 E7

Marathon, FL 123 F1, 188 C2

Marayong, 78 B8

Marble Arch, 27 A3

Marble Canyon, AZ 183 F4

Marblehead, MA 138 F5

Marbleton, WY 135 G2

Marco, FL 123 E2

Marcos Paz, 88 A6

Margarita Isl, 95 G1

Margate, FL 155 G5

Mari Girgis Sta, 50 C1

Maria Lanzendorf, 42 E6

Marianna, AR 120 A5

Marianna, FL 120 D2, 122 C6

Mariano Acosta, 88 A4

Marias Islands, 96 B4

Maribor, 23 F1, 24 C6

Maricopa, AZ 168 A3

Maricopa, CA 133 C3

Marie Byrd Land, 83 C3

Mariemont, OH 151 E2

Marienfelde, 32 D6

Mariestad, 22 E7

Marietta, GA 113 C4, 120 D4

Marietta, OH 118 C4

Marikina, 62 D3

Marin City, CA 174 A6

Marina, CA 133 B4

Marina District, CA 173 B3

Marina del Rey, CA 170 A4

Marinette, WI 124 D6

Marino, 40 D4

Mar'ino, 56 C3

Marinwood, CA 174 A7

Marion, IN 118 A5, 125 E3

Marion, OH 118 B5, 125 F3

Marion, SC 121 G4

Marion, VA 118 C1

Marion NF, Francis, SC 121 F4

Mariposa, CA 132 C5

Mariposa Grove, CA 182 B1

Maritime Mus & Planetarium, 107 G2

Mariupol, 53 A4

Mark Twain NF, MO 120 A6, 125 B2

Marka, 47 H6

Markham, Can 104 F8

Markham, IL 159 D2

Markleeville, CA 132 C5

Marksville, LA 129 G3

Marlboro, MA 138 F4

Marlborough, MA 115 C2

Marley, IL 159 B1

Marlin, TX 129 E3

Marlton, NJ 145 H1

Marmot Pk, MT 135 E5

Marne R, 20 E6

Marona, 44 D2

Maronouchi, 69 D3

Maroubra, 78 F6

Marquesas Islands, 81 F4

Marquette, MI 112 B7, 124 D6

Marra Mts, 45 E2

Marrakech, 44 B4

Marrero, LA 163 F4

Marrickville, 78 E6

Marrot Park, IN 157 E3

Mars Hill, ME 114 F7

Marsa al Burayqah, 48 B5

Marsa Matruh, 48 C5

Marsabit, 47 G6

Marsala, 24 C2

Marseille, 16 D4, 21 E4, 44 D6

Marsfield, 78 D8

Marshall, CO 167 E5

Marshall, MN 124 A5, 126 F6

Marshall Creek, TX 164 C6

Marshall Islands, 80 C5

Marshall Loxahatchee NWR, Arthur R, FL 155 F6

Marshalltown, IA 125 B4

Marshfield, MA 184 A8

Marsta, 36 D8

Marstons Mills, MA 184 C5

Martha's Vineyard, MA 115 D1, 185 G1

Marthalen, 37 F4

Martin Luther King Jr Mem Library, DC 149 D3

Martin Luther King Jr NHS, GA 152 C3

Martin Luther King Jr Park, TX 163 G2

Martínez, Arg 88 D8

Martinez, CA 174 D7

Martinez, TX 163 H2

Martinique, 95 H2

Martinsburg, WV 119 F4

Martinsville, VA 118 D1, 121 F6

Martorell, 122 C1

Mary, 53 C1

Maryborough, 77 F4

Maryland, 112 E5, 119 F3, 179 G4

Maryland, U of, MD 148 E7

Maryland Hts, MO 162 A3

Marystown, 103 F3

Marysville, CA 132 B6

Marysville, OH 118 B4

Maryville, MO 125 A3, 127 F3

Marzahn, 32 E7

Masan, 66 D5

Mascot, 78 E6

Mascouche, 106 C5

Mascuala, 99 H6

Maseru, 47 F2

Masha, 50 C6

Mashhad, 49 H6, 58 A3

Mashoes, NC 187 G5

Mashpee, MA 184 B5

Masirah, 49 H3

Mason City, IA 112 A6, 124 B5

Maspeth, NY 143 E3

Massa, 24 B5

Massachusetts, 103 D1, 112 E6, 115 B2, 179 H5

Massachusetts Inst of Technology, MA 139 D3

Massawa, 45 G2, 49 E1

Massena, NY 117 F6

Masset, AK 161 B3

Massif Central, 20 E5

Massimina, 40 B5

Massy, 28 C6

Mastic, NY 116 C5

Matadepera, 38 D8

Matadi, 46 D5

Matagami, 103 C2

Matamoros, 96 D4, 129 E1

Matane, 103 D3

Matanzas, 94 B5

Mataram, 61 D1

Matatlán, 99 H5

Matera, 24 D3

Mather, CA 182 A4

Mathias Church, 42 A7

Mato Grosso Plateau, 85 E2

Matsudo, 68 D8

Matsue, 66 E5

Matsuyama, 67 E4

Mattamuskeet NWR, NC 187 E3

Matterhorn, 16 D4, 23 C1, 24 A6

Matterhorn Canyon, CA 182 C5

Matterhorn Pk, CA 182 D6

Matteson, IL 159 D1

Mattituck, NY 116 C6

Matunga, 65 B2

Maturín, 84 **D5**, 95 **G1**
Mauá, 92 **C4**
Maubeuge, 23 **A3**
Maui, HI 137 **E3**
Mauna Kea, HI 137 **F2**
Mauna Loa, HI 137 **E1**
Maunawili, HI 177 **H3**
Maupin, OR 134 **C4**
Maurepas, 28 **B6**
Maurice NP, 114 **A7**
Mauritania, 44 **B3**
Mausoleum of Augustus, 41 **C4**
Mayaguana, 94 **D5**
Mayagüez, 95 **F3**, 122 **B2**
Mayfair, PA 145 **F4**
Mayfair, UK 27 **B2**
Mayfield, KY 120 **B6**
Mayfield, OH 150 **F8**
Mayfield Hts, OH 150 **F7**
Maymanah, 58 **A7**
Mayo, Can 100 **B5**
Mayo, FL 122 **D5**
Mays Landing, NJ 119 **H4**
Maysville, KY 118 **B3**
Maywood, OH 170 **C4**
Maywood, IL 159 **C4**
Maywood, NJ 142 **C6**
Maywood Park, OR 177 **G6**
Mazar-e Sharif, 58 **A7**
Mazatlán, 96 **B4**
Mbabane, 47 **F3**
Mbala, 47 **F5**
Mbandaka, 47 **E6**
Mbanza-Ngungu, 46 **D5**
Mbeya, 47 **G5**
M'boi Mirim, 92 **A3**
Mbuji-Mayi, 47 **F5**
McAlester, OK 113 **A4**, 129 **F5**
McAllen, TX 111 **F2**, 129 **E1**
McCall, ID 130 **A8**
McCandless, PA 146 **B8**
McClintock Chan, 100 **F6**
McCloud, CA 132 **B7**
McComb, MS 120 **A3**

McConnellsburg, PA 119 **E4**
McCook, NE 127 **D3**
McDermitt, NV 132 **D7**, 134 **D1**
McFarland, CA 133 **D4**
McKees Rocks, PA 146 **B7**
McKeesport, PA 146 **E5**
McKelvie NF, Samuel R, NE 126 **C5**
McKinleyville, CA 132 **A7**
McLean, VA 148 **B7**
McLoughlin House, OR 177 **G4**
McMichael Canadian Collection, 104 **B8**
McMinnville, OR 134 **B4**
McMurdo Sd, 83 **B2**
McPherson, KS 127 **E2**
Meadow Brook Park, MN 161 **B2**
Meadowlands, Can 105 **A1**
Meadowlands, S Afr 51 **F2**
Meadowlands Sports Complex, NJ 142 **C5**
Meadows, The, TX 166 **A3**
Meadowvale, 104 **A5**
Meadowvale Village, 104 **A5**
Meadville, PA 116 **A1**, 118 **D6**
Meazza Stad, 40 **B1**
Mecca, CA 133 **E2**
Mecca, Saudi Arabia 45 **G3**, 49 **E2**
Mechelen, 31 **G4**
Mechigmen, 136 **A7**
Medan, 61 **A3**
Medellín, 84 **C5**
Medfield, MA 139 **A1**
Medfield Junction, MA 139 **A1**
Medford, MA 139 **C4**
Medford, OR 110 **A6**, 132 **B8**, 134 **B2**
Media, PA 144 **B2**

Medicine Bow NF, WY 127 **A4**, 130 **E7**
Medicine Hat, 101 **D2**
Medicine Lake, MN 161 **A3**
Medicine Lodge, KS 127 **D2**
Medina, NY 116 **B3**
Medina, OH 118 **C5**
Medina, Saudi Arabia 49 **E3**
Medina, WA 176 **C5**
Mediodia, 39 **C2**
Mediterranean Sea, 16 **C**, 221 **F2**, 24 **A3**, 25 **E1**, 45 **E5**, 48 **B5**
Medley, FL 155 **F2**
Meerbusch, 34 **B5**
Meeteese, WY 135 **H3**
Meiderich, 34 **B7**
Meidling, 42 **D7**
Méier, 91 **C2**
Meikirch, 37 **B3**
Meilen, 37 **F1**
Meir, 31 **G6**
Mekele, 45 **G2**
Mekinac Lake, 114 **A8**
Mekong R, 60 **A5**, 61 **B4**
Melbourne, Austral 77 **E2**, 79 **C3**, 80 **B2**
Melbourne, FL 113 **E2**, 123 **F4**
Melbourne, KY 151 **E1**
Melbourne Cricket Grounds, 79 **C2**
Melbourne Royal Exh Bldg, 79 **C2**
Melilla, 16 **B1**, 21 **C1**, 44 **C5**
Melíssa, 43 **C3**
Mellon Arena, 146 **C6**
Melo, 86 **C5**
Melrose, MA 138, **D5**
Melrose Park, PA 145 **E5**
Melun, 28 **E5**
Melville Isl, Austral 76 **C6**, 80 **A3**
Melville Isl, Can 100 **E7**

Melville Pen, 102 **A5**
Melvindale, MI 156 **C6**
Melzo, 40 **D2**
Memorial Park, TX 166 **B4**
Memphis, FL 154 **C1**
Memphis, TN 113 **B4**, 120 **B5**, 125 **D1**, 129 **H6**, 179 **E3**
Menai, 78 **C5**
Mende, 20 **E5**
Mendota, CA 133 **C4**
Mendota, MN 161 **D1**
Mendota Hts, MN 161 **D1**
Mendoza, 86 **A5**
Mengede, 34 **E8**
Menguiafen, 73 **B2**
Menlo Park, CA 175 **D3**
Mennecy, 28 **D5**
Menominee, WI 124 **D6**
Menongue, 47 **E4**
Menor's Ferry, WY 181 **F2**
Menzel Bourguiba, 24 **A1**
Merano, 23 **D1**
Merauke, 76 **B1**, 80 **A4**
Meraux, LA 163 **H5**
Mercado, 93 **G4**
Merced, CA 132 **C5**
Merced Pk, CA 182 **C2**
Merced R, CA 182 **C3**
Merchandise Mart, IL 160 **B7**
Merchantville, NJ 145 **F2**
Merchtem, 31 **F3**
Mergui, 61 **A3**
Mérida, Mex 97 **F3**
Mérida, Spain 21 **B3**
Mérida, Ven 84 **C5**
Meridan, CT 115 **A1**
Meridian, MS 113 **B3**, 120 **B3**, 129 **H4**
Meridian Hills, IN 157 **E4**
Merion, PA 144 **D4**
Merksem, 31 **G6**
Merlo, 88 **B6**
Merredin, 76 **B3**
Merriam, KS 162 **B4**
Merrifield, VA 148 **B6**

Merrill, OR 132 **B8**

Merrillville, IN 159 **F1**

Merrimack R, NH 115 **C3**

Merritt Isl, FL 123 **F4**

Merriweather Post Pavilion, MD 147 **A1**

Merrylands, 78 **C7**

Mersin, 48 **D6**

Merthyr Tydfil, 19 **D3**

Merton, 26 **C6**

Meru, 47 **G6**

Mesa, AZ 131 **B2**, 168 **D3**

Mesa, WA 134 **D5**

Mesa College, CO 169 **F4**

Mesa Verde NP, CO 131 **D4**, 178 **C3**

Mescalero Apache IR, NM 128 **B4**, 131 **E2**

Mesolonga, 25 **E3**

Mesquita, 91 **B3**

Mesquite, NV 133 **F4**

Mesquite, TX 165 **H3**

Messina, 17 **F2** , 24 **C2**, 47 **F3**

Metairie, LA 129 **H3**, 163 **F5**

Methuen, MA 138 **C8**

Metropolitan Mus of Art, NY 141 **H6**

Metropolitan Oakland Intl Arpt, CA 174 **C5**

Metropolitan Park, 87 **G3**

Metropolitan Stad, MN 161 **C1**

Mettmann, 34 **C5**

Metz, 20 **F7**, 23 **B2**

Metzger, OR 177**F5**

Meudon, 28 **C6**

Meulan, 28 **A8**

Meuse R, 20 **E7**

Mexicali, 96 **A6**, 111 **B4**, 133 **F2**

Mexican Customs, 169 **G1**

Mexican Hat, UT 131 **C4**

Mexico, 81 **H5**, 94 **A4**, 96 **C4**

Mexico, MO 125 **C3**

Mexico Bay, NY 117 **E4**

Mexico City, 96 **D3**, 98 **C2**

Mezieres-sur-Siene 28 **A7**

Miami, FL 94 **C6**, 97 **G5**, 113 **E2**, 123 **F2**, 155 **G2**, 179 **G1**

Miami, OK 127 **F1**

Miami, U of, FL 155 **F1**

Miami Beach, FL 123 **G2**, 155 **G2**

Miami Hts, OH 151 **B2**

Miamitown, OH 151 **B3**

Miamiville, OH 151 **F3**

Michigan, 103 **B1**, 112 **C6**, 124 **D5**, 179 **F5**

Michigan City, IN 125 **E4**

Michipicoten Isl, 124 **E7**

Michurinets, 56 **A3**

Micronesia, Federated States of, 80 **B4**

Middleburg, 23 **A4**, 47 **E2**

Middle Cape, FL 188 **C4**

Middle Church, 107 **G6**

Middle East, 45, 49

Middle Fork Tuolumne R, CA 182 **A4**

Middle Granite Gorge, AZ 183 **C3**

Middle R, MD 147 **F3**

Middle Village, NY 143 **E3**

Middleburg, FL 123 **F5**

Middleburg Hts, OH 150 **C5**

Middlebury, VT 115 **A4**, 117 **H5**

Middlesboro, KY 120 **D6**

Middlesbrough, 19 **E4**

Middleton, MA 138 **D6**

Middletown, CT 115 **B2**

Middletown, NY 117 **G1**

Middletown, NC 187 **F3**

Midland, MI 124 **E5**

Midland, TX 111 **E3**, 128 **C4**, 178 **D2**

Midlothian, IL 159 **D2**

Midrand, 51 **G4**

Midway, FL 153 **H6**

Midway, OR 177 **E4**

Midway Geyser Basin, WY 180 **A3**

Midway Islands, 80 **C6**

Midwest City, OK 129 **E6**

Mifflintown, PA 119 **F5**

Miguel Hidalgo, 98 **A3**

Miguel Hidalgo Intl Arpt, 99 **G3**

Migum, 72 **E7**

Mijdrecht, 30 **D4**

Mikhaylovgrad, 25 **F6**

Milan, 17 **E4**, 23 **C1**, 24 **B5**, 40 **B2**

Milbank, SD 126 **E6**

Milbridge, ME 114 **F5**

Mildura, 76 **D3**

Mile High Stad, CO 167 **G3**

Miles City, MT 110 **E7**, 126 **A8**, 130 **E8**

Milford, CT 116 **C6**

Milford, NH 115 **B3**

Milford, NJ 116 **A6**

Milford, OH 151 **F3**

Milford, PA 119 **H5**

Military Academy of Colombia, 90 **C2**

Military Hospital, 93 **H6**

Military Mus, 35 **E3**

Military Reserve, 78 **B5**

Mill Grove, PA 144 **A6**

Mill Stream Run Res, OH 150 **C5**

Mill Valley, CA 174 **A6**

Millbrae, CA 175 **B4**

Mille Lacs Lake, MN 124 **B6**

Milledgeville, GA 121 **E4**

Milennium Dome, 26 **D7**

Miller Park, WI 157 **B2**

Millersburg, OH 118 **C5**

Milliken, 104 **F8**

Millinocket, ME 114 **E6**

Millis, MA 139 **A1**

Milltail Creek, NC 187 **F5**

Millvale, PA 146 **C7**

Milos, 25 **G2**

Milpitas, CA 132 **B5**, 175 **F2**

Milton, FL 120 **C2**, 122 **B6**

Milton, MA 139 **D2**

Milton, WA 176 **C1**

Milwaukee, WI 103 **A1**, 112 **B6**, 124 **D5**, 157 **C2**, 179 **F4**

Milwaukie, OR 177 **G5**

Mimico, 104 **C5**

Minami Mido Temple, 71 **A3**

Minami-Ku, Kyoto 71 **E2**

Minami-Ku, Osaka 71 **B2**

Minas, 86 **C5**

Minato, 69 **F2**

Minato Machi Sta, 71 **A1**

Minato-Ku, 68 **C7**, 69 **A1**

Mindanao, 61 **F4**

Minden, LA 129 **G4**

Minden, NE 127 **D3**

Minden, NV 132 **C6**

Mindoro, 61 **D4**

Mineola, NY 143 **H4**

Mingo NWR, MO 120 **B6**

Minna, 44 **C1**

Minneapolis, MN 103 **A1**, 112 **A6**, 124 **B6**, 161 **C2**, 179 **E5**

Minneapolis Chain of Lakes RP, MN 161 **C2**

Minneapolis Planetarium, MN 161 **C3**

Minneapolis-St. Paul Intl Arpt, MN 161 **C1**

Minnehaha, WA 177 **G6**

Minnehaha RP, MN 161 **D2**

Minnesota 103 **A3**, 112 **A8**, 124 **B6**, 179 **E5**

Minnesota R, 124 **A6**, 126 **F6**

Minnesota U, MN 161 C3

Minnetonka, MN 161 A3

Mino, 70 C6

Minorca, 16 D3,21 F3

Minot, ND 110 F7, 126 C8

Minshat al-Bakkari, 50 B2

Minsk, 15 G1, 52 A5

Minto, 78 A5

Minute Man NHP, MA
138 A5, 179 H5

Miquon, PA 144 D5

Mira Loma, CA 171 F4

Mirador, 99 G3

Miraflores, 87 F4

Miramar, FL 155 E3

Miramar College, CA
169 F5

Miramar NAS, CA 169 G5

Mirasierra, 39 B4

Miri, 61 D3

Mirnyy, 55 C4

Mirror Plateau, WY 180 C4

Misato, 68 D8

Miskolc, 17 F5

Misratah, 44 D4, 48 A5

Missinaibi R, 124 F8

Mission, KS 162 B4

Mission Bay Park, CA
169 E4

Mission Hills, KS 162 B4

Mission Pk R Pres, CA
175 E3

Mission Trails RP, CA
169 G5

Mission Viejo, CA 171 F1

Missisquoi NWR, VT
117 H6

Mississauga, 104 C5,
116 B4

Mississippi, 97 E6, 113 B3,
120 A3, 179 F2

Mississippi R, 97 E6,
112 A6, 113 B4, 120 A4,
124 B6, 125 C3, 129 H5,
179 E2

Missoula, MT 110 C7,
135 F5, 178 B6

Missouri, 113 A4, 125 C2,
179 E3

Missouri City, TX 129 F2,
166 A3

Missouri R, 101 D2,
110 E7, 112 A5, 125 B3,
126 C8, 127 F4, 135 H5,
178 C6, 179 E4

Mistassini, 103 C2

Misty Fiords NM, AK
136 F5, 178 B1

Mitaka, 68 B7

Mitchell, IL 162 D3

Mitchell, SD 126 E5

Mitchell Mem Forest, OH
151 B3

Mitilini, 25 G3

Mitry-Mory, 28 E8

Miyakojima-Ku, 71 C4

Miyazaki, 67 E4

Mmabatho, 47 E3

Mníšek pod Brdy, 35 D1

Mo-i-Rana, 15 E4

Moab, UT 110 D5, 130 C5

Moapa, NV 133 F4

Mobara, 68 F5

Mobile, AL 97 F6, 113 B3,
120 B2, 122 A6, 179 F2

Mobridge, SD 110 F6,
126 D6

Moca, 122 A3

Modderfontein, 51 G3

Modena, Italy 24 B5

Modena, UT 132 F5

Modesto, CA 132 C5

Modica, 24 C1

Mödling, 42 D6

Modoc NF, CA 132 C7,
134 C1

Modrany, 35 E2

Moers, 34 A7

Mofolo, 51 G3

Mogadishu, 47 H6

Mogilev, 15 H1

Mogocha, 55 D3

Mogyoród, 42 C8

Mohawk Canyon, AZ
183 A3

Mohawk R, NY 117 G3

Mojave Desert, CA 111 B4,
133 E3

Mojave NP, CA 133 F3,
178 A3

Mokena, IL 159 C1

Mokpo, 67 C4

Molde, 14 D4

Moldova, 17 H5, 45 F6

Molino, FL 122 B6

Molíns de Rey, 38 D6

Mollet del Valles, 38 F7

Molokai, HI 137 D3

Molokovo, 56 D2

Moluccas, 61 F2

Mombasa, 47 G6

Mona Passage, 95 F3,
122 A1

Monaco, 16 D4, 20 F5,
24 A4

Monahans, TX 128 C4

Monavoni, 51 G5

Mönchaltorf, 37 F1

Monclova-Aravaca, 39 B3

Monclova, 96 C5, 128 C1

Moncton, 103 E2

Moncucco, 40 B1

Monfort Hts, OH 151 C3

Mongolia, 58 F8, 60 A8,
66 A7

Mongolian Plateau, 55 C2,
60 A8

Monjolo, 91 F3

Monmorency, 79 D3

Mono Lake, CA 132 D5

Monomoy Isl, MA 115 D2,
185 E6

Monomoy NWR, MA
185 E6

Monomoy Pt, MA 185 E6

Monongahela NF, WV
118 D3

Monroe, LA 113 B3,
129 G4

Monroe, MI 118 B6

Monroe, NY 116 A6

Monroe, NC 121 F5

Monroeville, AL 120 C3

Monroeville, PA 146 E6

Monrovia, Afr 44 B1

Monrovia, CA 170 D5

Monserrat, 89 D2

Monster, 30 A3

Mont Blanc, 20 F5

Mont Clare, PA 144 A6

Mont-Laurier, 103 C2

Mont-Royal, 106 C2

Montana, 101 D2, 110 D7,
126 A7, 135 F6, 178 C5

Montara, CA 175 A3

Montauk, NY 115 B1,
116 D6

Montauk Pt, NY 115 B1

Montbéliard, 23 B2

Montcada i Reixac, 38 E7

Montclair, CA 171 F5

Montclair, NJ 142 A5

Monte Alto, 90 B5

Monte Grande, 88 D5

Monte Sacro, 40 C6

Monte Sereno, CA 175 E1

Monte Spacccato, 40 B5

Montebello, CA 170 D4

Montego Bay, 94 C4

Montenegro, 17 F4, 25 E6

Monterey, CA 110 A5,
133 B4

Monterey Park, CA 170 C5

Monteria, 84 C5

Monterrey, 96 D4, 111 F1,
128 D1

Montes Claros, 85 G1

Montesano, WA 134 B5

Montevideo, MN 124 B6

Montevideo, Uru 86 C5

Montezuma NWR, NY
116 D3

Montfoort, 30 D3

Montfort-l'Amaury, 28 A6

Montgat, 38 F7

Montge, 28 F8

Montgomery, AL 113 C3, 120 C3, 179 F2

Montgomery, OH 151 F3

Monticello, FL 122 D6

Monticello, KY 118 A1

Monticello, ME 114 E7

Monticello, NY 117 G1, 119 H6

Montjuïc Castle, 38 E6

Montmagny, 114 C7

Montmartre, 29 D4

Montmelo, 38 F7

Montparnasse, 29 C1

Montparnasse Cemetery, 29 C1

Montpelier, ID 135 G2

Montpelier, VT 112 F7, 114 A5

Montpellier, 16 D4, 21 E4

Montréal, 103 D2, 106 D3, 112 E7

Montréal Botanical Gdns, 106 C3

Montréal Conv Ctr, 106 C3

Montréal-Est, 106 D4

Montréal Forum, 106 C2

Montréal Nord, 106 C4

Montréal Olympic Stad, 106 D3

Montréal Zoological Gdns, 106 C2

Montreuil, 28 D7

Montrose, CO 110 D5, 130 D5

Montross, VA 119 F2

Montrouge, 28 D6

Montry, 28 F7

Montserrat, 95 H3

Montverde, FL 153 E4

Monumental Bullring, 99 G5

Monywa, 58 F5

Monza, 40 C3

Moon Run, PA 146 A6

Moonee Ponds, 79 B3

Moorabbin, 79 D1

Moorebank, 78 B6

Moorestown, NJ 145 H3

Moorhead, MN 124 A7, 126 E7

Moose, WY 181 F2

Moose Basin, WY 181 F5

Moose Creek, WY 181 F5

Moose Jaw, 101 E2

Moose MT Pres P, 126 C8

Moose Village Visitor Ctr, WY 181 F2

Moosehead Lake, ME 114 D6

Mooselookmeguntic Lake, ME 114 C5

Moosonee, 103 B3, 112 C8

Mopti, 44 B2

Moraga, CA 174 D6

Moran Creek, WY 181 F4

Moran Entrance Sta, WY 181 H4

Moran Junction, WY 181 H4

Moran Pt, AZ 183 F1

Moratalaz, 39 D2

Morden, 101 F2, 126 D8

Moreau R, SD 126 C6

Moree, 77 E4

Morehead, KY 118 B2

Morehead City, NC 121 H5

Moreland, Austral 79 B3

Moreland Hills, OH 150 F6

Morelia, 96 C3

Morena, 40 D4

Moreno, 88 A7

Moreno Valley, CA 171 H3

Mörfelden, 35 A1

Morgan City, LA 113 B2

Morgan Pierpont Library, NY 141 G4

Morgan Terr R Pres, CA 174 F6

Morgan, UT 135 G1

Morgantown, WV 112 D5, 118 D4

Moriguchi, 70 D6

Morioka, 66 F6

Morningside, MD 148 F5

Morocco, 16 A1, 21 B1, 44 B4

Morogoro, 47 G5

Morón, Arg 88 C7

Moron, Mong 55 B2

Moroni, 47 G5

Morris, MN 124 A6, 126 F6

Morris Isl, MA 184 F5

Morrison, CO 167 E2

Morristown, NJ 116 A5

Morrisville, NY 117 F3

Morro Bay, CA 133 B3

Morrow, GA 152 C1

Morton, PA 144 C2

Morton Grove, IL 158 D5

Mortsel, 31 G5

Morumbi, 92 A4

Morumbi Stad, 92 A4

Moscavide, 38 C7

Moscone Conv Ctr, CA 173 E1

Moscovskiy, 56 A3

Moscow, ID 134 D5

Moscow, Rus 15 H2, 52 B5, 56 C4, 57 F5, 82 F8

Moscow State U, 56 B3

Moselle R, 20 F6

Moshannon SF, PA 119 E5

Moskhaton, 43 B2

Mosman, 78 F7

Mosquera, 90 B2

Mosquito Coast, 97 G2

Moss, 22 D8

Moss Beach, CA 175 A3

Moss Park, FL 153 H2

Moss Park, Henry S, TX 165 G4

Mostar, 24 D4

Mosul, 49 E6, 53 A3

Motala, 22 E7

Motown Mus, MI 156 D6

Moulineaux, 28 C7

Moulins, 23 A1

Moulmein, 59 F4

Moultrie, GA 121 E2, 122 D6

Moundon, 45 E1

Mounds View, MN 161 C4

Moundsville, OH 118 D4

Mount Airy, NC 121 F6

Mount Airy Forest, OH 151 C2

Mount Angel, OR 134 B4

Mount Ararat, 49 F6

Mount Blanc, 16 D4, 24 A6

Mount Carmel, OH 151 F2

Mount Clark, CA 182 C2

Mount Conness, CA 182 D5

Mount Cook, 77 G1

Mount Dana, CA 182 D4

Mount Davis, PA 119 E4

Mount Demavend, 49 F6

Mount Desert, ME 186 B6

Mount Desert Isl, ME 114 F5, 186 B4

Mount Diablo SP, CA 174 E6

Mount Doane, WY 180 C3

Mount Dora, FL 153 E6

Mount Druitt, 78 A8

Mount Echo Park, OH 151 C2

Mount Elbert, CO 110 D5, 130 E5

Mount Etna, 17 F2

Mount Evans, CO 130 E5

Mount Everest, 58 E5

Mount Florence, CA 182 D3

Mount Gambier, 76 D2

Mount Greylock, MA 117 H2

Mount Hagen, 76 C1

Mount Hancock, WY 180 C2

Mount Hayden, AZ 183 E3

Mount Healthy, OH 151 D3

Mount Hebron, MD 147 A3

Mount Hoffman, CA 182 C4

Mount Holmes, WY 180 A5

Mount Hood, OR 134 B4, 178 A5

Mount Houston, TX 166 C5

Mount Isa, 76 D5

Mount Jefferson, NV 132 E6

Mount Jefferson, OR 134 B3

Mount Kenya, 47 G6

Mount Kirkpatrick, 83 C3

Mount Kisco, NY 116 B6

Mount Kosciusko, 77 E2

Mount Langford, WY
180 D3

Mount Laurel, PA 145 H2

Mount Lebanon, PA 146 C5

Mount Logan, 100 B5

Mount Mansfield, VT
117 H6

Mount Marcy, NY 117 G5

Mount McKinley, AK
82 A5, 100 A6

Mount McLoughlin, OR
134 B2

Mount Mitchell, NC
113 D4

Mount Moriah, NV 132 F6

Mount Morris, NY 116 C3

Mount Nebo, PA 146 B8

Mount of Olives, 50 D4

Mount Oliver, PA 146 C6

Mount Olympus, Greece
17 G3, 25 F4

Mount Olympus, WA
110 A8

Mount Pleasant, MI 112 C6

Mount Pleasant, TX 129 F4

Mount Plymouth, FL
153 F6

Mount Prospect, IL 158 C5

Mount Rainier, MD 148 E7

Mount Rainer, WA 110 B7,
134 B5

Mount Rainer NP, WA
134 B5

Mount Robson, 101 C3

Mount Rogers NRA, VA
118 C1

Mount Rushmore NM, SD
178 D5

Mount Schurz, WY 180 D2

Mount Shasta, CA 132 B7,
134 B1

Mount Sheridan, WY 180 B2

Mount Sterling, KY 118 B2

Mount Stimson, MT 135 F6

Mount Thielsen, OR 134 B2

Mount Trumbull, AZ 183 A3

Mount Vernon, IL 125 D2

Mount Vernon, NY 116 B6,
143 F6

Mount Vernon, OH 118 C5

Mount Vernon, WA 134 B6

Mount Vernon Square, DC
149 D4

Mount Vesuvius, 17 F3

Mount Waddington, 101 B3

Mount Warren, CA 182 D5

Mount Washburn, WY
180 C5

Mount Washington, NH
179 H5

Mount Washington
Inclines, PA 146 B6

Mount Waverley, 79 D2

Mount Whitney, CA
110 A5, 133 D4

Mount Wilhelm, 76 C2

Mount Wilson Obs, CA
170 C6

Mount Zimmer, MT 180 D6

Mount Zion, 50 D4

Mountain Creek Lake Park,
TX 165 E2

Mountain High, 142 A9

Mountain Home, AR
129 G6

Mountain Home, ID
130 A7, 132 E8, 135 E2

Mountain View, CA 175 D2

Mountain View, CO 167 F3

Mozambique, 47 G4

Mozambique Channel,
47 G3

Mratin, 35 F4

Mtwara, 47 G5

Muckleshoot IR, WA
176 D1

Mudaniiang, 55 E3

Mudanjiang, 66 C3

Mugla, 25 H2

Mühleberg, 37 A3

Muhlenbeck, 32 D8

Mühlhausen, 23 C3

Mülheim an der Ruhr,
34 C7

Muir Beach, CA 174 A6

Muir NHS, John, CA
174 D7

Muir Woods NM, CA
174 A6, 178 A4

Muko, 70 E7, 71 D1

Mulhouse, 20 F6, 23 B2,
24 A6

Mullingar, 19 B4

Multan, 58 B6

Mulund, 65 C3

Mumbra, 65 C3

Munchenbuchsee, 37 B3

Munchendorf, 42 E5

Muncie, IN 112 C5,
118 A4, 125 E3

Mundelein, IL 158 B7

Munhall, PA 146 D6

Munich, 17 E5, 23 D2,
24 B6, 44 D6

Municipal Ferry Bldg, NY
141 E1

Municipal Gallery of Art &
Culture & Modern Art
Center, 99 F5

Municipal Market, 93 H4

Municipal Park, MN 161 B1

Munsingen, 37 C1

Münster, Ger 23 C4

Munster, IN 159 E1

Münster Cathedral, 34 C7

Murcia 16 B2,21 C2

Murdo, SD 126 C5

Murfreesboro, TN 120 D5,
125 E1

Muri, 37 C2, 37 D1

Murino, 37 D4

Murmansk, 15 G6, 52 D6,
82 E7

Muroran, 66 F6

Murphy, ID 132 E8, 135 E2

Murphy, TX 165 H6

Murphy Candler Park, GA
152 C6

Murray R, 76 D3

Murrieta, CA 171 H1

Murrumbeena, 79 D1

Musashimurayama, 68 A8

Musashino, 68 A8

Muscat, 49 H3

Muscoy, CA 171 G5

Musè D'Orsay, 29 D2

Museo do Bellas Artes,
90 C5

Museu Memorias do Bixiga,
93 E1

Museum Folkwang, 34 C7

Museum of Art & Fort
Lauderdale Hist Mus, FL
155 G4

Museum of Chinese
History, 73 E2

Museum of Contemporary
Art, Chile 87 F3

Museum of Fine Arts, TX
166 B3

Museum of Flight, WA
176 D4

Museum of German
History, 33 E3

Museum of Modern Art,
Mex 98 B3

Museum of Modern Art, NY
141 G5

Museum of Oriental Art,
57 H5

Museum of Oriental
Ceramics, 71 B3

Museum of Sacred Art,
93 H6

Museum of Science, MA
140 B5

Museum of Science &
Industry, FL 154 D6

Museum of Science &
Industry, IL 159 D4

Museum of Stone Age
Antiquities, ME 186 D5

Museum of the Battle of Borodino, 56 **B4**

Museum of Transportation, 33 **D2**

Museuminsel, 33 **E4**

Musket Chan, MA 185 **G3**

Muskeget Isl, MA 185 **G4**

Muskegon, MI 112 **C6**, 124 **E5**

Muskogee, OK 113 **A4**, 125 **A1**, 127 **F1**, 129 **F6**

Musocco, 40 **B2**

Mustang Pt Park, TX 164 **A1**

Mutare, 47 **F4**

Mwanza, 47 **G6**

Mwene Ditu, 47 **F5**

Myingyan, 58 **F5**

Myitkyina, 58 **F5**

Mykonos, 25 **G2**

Myles Standish Mon, MA 184 **A8**

Myles Standish SF, MA 184 **A6**

Myrtle Beach, SC 113 **E4**, 121 **G4**

Myrtle Creek, OR 132 **A8**, 134 **B2**

Myrtle Pt, OR 132 **A8**, 134 **A3**

Mys Schmidta, 136 **A8**

Mysore, 59 **C4**

Mystery Castle, AZ 168 **B2**

Mytishchi, 56 **C6**

N

Naaldwijk, 30 **A3**

Naberezhnyye Chelny, 53 **D4**

Nacala, 47 **G4**

Nacka, 36 **F6**

Nacogdoches, TX 129 **F4**

Naestved, 22 **D5**

Naga, 61 **E4**

Nagano, 66 **F5**

Nagaokakyo, 70 **E7**, 71 **D1**

Nagareyama, 68 **D8**

Nagasaki, 60 **E7**, 67 **D3**

Nagatacho, 69 **B2**

Nagatino, 56 **C3**

Nagoya, 60 **F8**, 66 **E5**

Nagpur, 58 **C5**

Nags Head, NC 187 **G5**

Nags Head Wood Pres, NC 187 **G5**

Nagykanizsa, 23 **F1**, 24 **D6**

Nagytarcsa, 42 **C7**

Nagytétény, 42 **A6**

Naha, 60 **E6**, 67 **D3**

Nahanni NP, 136 **F7**

Nahant, MA 139 **F4**

Nahunta, GA 123 **E6**

Nahya, 50 **B2**

Naiguatá, 90 **D6**

Naihati, 65 **F4**

Nain, 103 **D4**

Nairobi, 47 **G6**

Naka-Ku, 68 **B5**

Nakagyo-Ku, 71 **E3**

Nakano-Ku, 68 **B8**

Nakanoshima Park, 71 **B3**

Nakhodka, 55 **F2**, 66 **C6**

Nakhon Ratchasima, 61 **A4**

Nakhon Sawan, 61 **A4**

Nakhon Si Thammarat, 61 **A3**

Nakurú, 47 **G6**

Naledi, 51 **E2**

Nalikul, 65 **D3**

Nam, 72 **A6**

Namangan, 53 **D1**, 58 **C8**

Namdong, 72 **A5**

Namhansan Prov P, 72 **E6**

Namib Desert, 46 **E3**

Namibe, 46 **D4**

Namibia, 47 **E3**

Nampo, 66 **C5**

Nampula, 47 **G4**

Namsos, 15 **E4**

Nanaimo, 101 **B2**, 134 **B6**

Nanakuli, HI 137 **C3**

Nanba Baseball Stad, 71 **B1**

Nanba Sta, 71 **B1**

Nanchang, 60 **C6**, 67 **B3**

Nancy, 16 **D5**, 20 **F6**, 23 **B2**

Nangi, 65 **E1**

Nangloi Jat, 64 **D7**

Naniwa-Ku, 71 **A1**

Nanjing, 60 **C7**, 67 **B4**

Nanning, 60 **B5**

Nanole, 65 **B2**

Nanpin, 67 **B3**

Nanshi District, 74 **E6**

Nantahala NF, NC 125 **F1**

Nantasket Beach, MA 139 **F2**

Nantes, 16 **C5**, 20 **C6**

Nanticoke, 116 **A3**

Nantong, 67 **C4**

Nantucket, MA 115 **D1**, 185 **H5**

Nantucket Harbor, MA 185 **G6**

Nantucket Isl, MA 115 **D1**, 185 **H5**

Nantucket NWR, MA 185 **G6**

Nantucket Sd, MA 115 **D2**, 185 **F4**

Nantucket SF, MA 185 **H5**

Nanyang, 60 **B7**, 67 **A4**

Napa, CA 132 **B5**

Naperville, IL 159 **A3**

Napier, 77 **H1**

Naples, FL 113 **D2**, 123 **E2**

Naples, Italy 17 **E3**, 24 **C3**, 44 **D5**

Naples Park, FL 123 **E2**

Napoleon, OH 118 **A6**

Napoleonic Mus, 41 **C3**

Nara, 66 **E5**, 70 **F5**

Nara Dreamland, 70 **F5**

Nara Park, 70 **F5**

Narashino, 68 **E7**

Narcoossee, FL 153 **H2**

Nari, 71 **C2**

Naricalps Mts, 17 **F4**

Narita, 68 **F8**

Narrogin, 76 **B3**

Narrows, The, ME 186 **B3**

Narvik, 15 **E5**

Naryan-Mar, 52 **E5**, 82 **D8**

Nashua, NH 115 **B3**

Nashville, GA 122 **D6**

Nashville, TN 113 **C4**, 120 **C6**, 125 **E1**, 179 **F3**

Nasik, 58 **B5**

Nasr City, 50 **D2**

Nassau, 94 **C6**, 97 **H5**, 113 **F2**

Natal, 85 **H3**

Natchez, MS 113 **B3**, 129 **H4**

Natchez Trace SP & Forest, TN 120 **B6**

Natchitoches, LA 129 **G4**

Natick, MA 139 **F3**

NASA Michoud Assembly Facility, LA 163 **H6**

National Agricultural Exh Ctr, 73 **F3**

National Air & Space Mus, DC 149 **E2**

National Aquarium, DC 149 **C3**

National Aquarium, MD 147 **D2**

National Arboretum, DC 148 **E6**

National Archives, DC 149 **D3**

National Art Mus, 98 **B3**

National Bunraku Theater, 71 **B1**

National Canyon, AZ 183 **B1**

National City, CA 169 **F2**

National City, IL 162 **C2**

National Congress, 100 **B7**

National Diet Bldg, 69 **B2**

National Elk Rfg, WY 181 **G1**

National Gallery Ger, 33 **D2**

National Gallery, UK 27 **C2**

National Gallery of Art, DC 149 **E3**

National Gallery of Art, East Wing, DC 149 **E2**
National Institutes of Health, MD 148 **C8**
National Library & Archives, 105 **A3**
National Maritime Mus, CA 17 **E3**
National Mem Cemetery of the Pacific, HI 177 **G2**
National Mus of American Art, DC 149 **D3**
National Mus of American History, DC 149 **C3**
National Mus of Anthropology, Mex 98 **B3**
National Mus of Fine Arts, Arg 89 **C4**
National Mus of Modern Art, Kyoto 71 **F3**
National Mus of Modern Art, Tokyo 69 **C4**
National Mus of Natural History, DC 149 **D2**
National Mus of Oriental Art, 41 **E3**
National Mus of Science & Technology, 105 **C2**
National Palace, 98 **B3**
National Palace Mus, 62 **C5**
National Park, NJ 145 **E1**
National Postal Mus, DC 149 **F3**
National Railways Mus, 89 **D4**
National Roman Mus, 41 **D4**
National Stad, India 64 **E7**
National Stad, Japan 68 **C7**
National Stad, Peru 87 **F5**
National Stad, Port 38 **A6**
National Tennis Ctr, NY 143 **F4**

National Theater, Japan 69 **B3**
National Theatre, UK 27 **D2**
National U of Colombia, 90 **C2**
Natuna Islands, 61 **B2**
Natural Bridge, WY 180 **B3**
Natural Bridges NM, UT 131 **C4**, 178 **C3**
Nature Reserve, 63 **E3**
Naucalpan de Juárez, 98 **A4**
Nauen, 32 **A8**
Nauru, 80 **C4**
Naushon Isl, MA 185 **F1**
Navajo IR, AZ 128 **A6**, 131 **C4**, 183 **F4**
Naval Air Sta, CA 169 **E3**
Naval Amphibious Base, CA 169 **F2**
Naval Avionics Ctr, IN 157 **F2**
Naval Comm Sta, Imperial Beach, CA 169 **F2**
Naval Landing Field, CA 169 **F1**
Naval Reserve, CA 169 **E3**
Naval Space Surv Sta, CA 169 **H1**
Naval Sta, CA 169 **F3**
Navojoa, 96 **B5**
Navotas, 62 **B3**
Navy Pier, IL 160 **F7**
Navy Pier Park, IL 160 **E7**
Naze, 67 **D3**
Nazilli, 25 **H3**
Nazlat as-Samman, 50 **B1**
Nazret, 45 **G1**
N'Djamena, 44 **D2**
Ndola, 47 **F4**
Nea Erithraia, 43 **C4**
Néa Ionía, 43 **C3**
Nea Liosia, 43 **B3**
Neah Bay, WA 134 **A6**
Nebitdag, 53 **B2**

Nebraska, 110 **F6**, 178 **D4**
Nebraska, NC 187 **F3**
Nebraska City, NE 125 **A3**, 127 **F3**
Nebraska NF, NE 127 **D4**
Necocea, 86 **B4**
Necropolis of the Port of Rome, 40 **A4**
Ned Brown FP, IL 158 **B5**
Nee Soon, 63 **F3**
Needham, MA 139 **B2**
Needles, CA 131 **A3**, 133 **F3**
Neffenbach, 37 **F3**
Negotin, 25 **F6**
Negro R, 84 **D4**
Negros, 61 **E4**
Neiderursel, 35 **B4**
Neihart, MT 135 **G5**
Neiva, 84 **C4**
Nellis Air Force Range, NV 131 **A4**, 132 **E5**
Nelson, AZ 131 **B3**
Nelson, New Zealand 77 **H1**
Nelson R, 101 **F3**
Nemchinovka, 56 **A4**
Neosho, MO 125 **A1**
Nepal, 58 **D6**
Nepean, 105 **A1**
Nepean City Hall, 105 **A1**
Neratovice, 35 **F4**
Nes Ziyyona, 50 **A5**
Neshaminy SP, PA 145 **H5**
Nespelem, WA 134 **D6**
Netherlands, 16 **D6**, 20 **E8**, 23 **B4**
Netherlands Antilles, 95 **F2**
Network Associates Coliseum, CA 174 **C5**
Neu Zittau, 32 **F5**
Neubrandenburg, 22 **E5**
Neuces R, TX 129 **E2**
Neuenegg, 37 **A3**

Neuenhagen, 32 **F7**
Neuhausen, 37 **F4**
Neu-Isenburg, 35 **B2**
Neukölln, 32 **D6**
Neunkirch, 37 **E4**
Neuquén, 86 **A4**
Neuss, 34 **A5**
Neustrelitz, 22 **E5**
Neusussenbrunn, 42 **F8**
Nevada, 110 **E5**, 132, 134 **D1**, 178 **B4**
Nevada, MO 125 **A3**
Nevada Great Basin, 110 **B5**
Nevada Test Site, NV 132 **E5**
Nevado de Colima, 96 **C3**
Nevers, 23 **A1**
Neves, 91 **E2**
New Albany, IN 125 **E2**
New Albany, MS 120 **B5**
New Amsterdam, 85 **E5**
New Baltimore, OH 151 **B4**
New Bedford, MA 112 **F6**, 115 **C2**
New Bern, NC 113 **E4**, 121 **H5**
New Braunfels, TX 129 **E2**
New Brighton, MN 161 **C4**
New Britain, CT 115 **A3**
New Britain, PNG 76 **D2**, 80 **B4**
New Brunswick, Can 114 **F7**
New Brunswick, NJ 119 **H5**
New Caledonia, 80 **B3**
New Carrollton, MD 148 **F7**
New Castle, PA 118 **D5**
New Chicago, 88 **D6**
New City, NY 116 **B6**, 119 **H6**
New Cumberland, OH 118 **D5**
New Delhi, 58 **C6**, 64 **E7**
New Dorp, NY 142 **C1**

New Eden, FL 153 H1

New England Aquarium, MA 140 D4

New Glasgow, 103 F2

New Guinea, 76 B2, 80 A4

New Hampshire, 103 D1, 112 E6, 115 C3, 179 H5

New Haven, CT 112 E6, 115 A1, 116 C6

New Haven, OH 151 B4

New Holland, NC 187 E3

New Hope, MN 161 B3

New Hyde Park, NY 143 G4

New Iberia, LA 129 G3

New Ireland, 76 D2, 80 B4

New Jersey, 103 D1, 112 E6, 116 A5, 119 H5, 179 H4

New Kensington, PA 146 F8

New Kowloon, 75 C4

New Lenox, IL 159 B1

New Lexington, OH 118 C4

New Liskeard, 103 C2

New London, CT 115 B1

New Martinsville, OH 118 C4

New Meadows, ID 135 E3

New Mexico, 111 D4, 128 B5, 131 E3, 178 C3

New Milford, CT 117 H1

New Orleans, LA 97 E5, 113 B2, 120 A1, 129 H3, 163 G5, 179 F1

New Orleans, U of, LA 163 G6

New Orleans Intl Arpt, LA 163 E6

New Palace, 37 C2

New Palace Bldg, 69 C3

New Paltz, NY 117 G1

New Philadelphia, OH 118 C5

New Plymouth, 77 H2

New Providence, 94 C6

New River Gorge Natl R, WV 118 D2

New Roads, LA 129 G3

New Sharon, ME 114 D5

New Siberian Isl, 54 C7, 82 C7

New Smyrna Beach, FL 123 F4

New South Wales, 77 E3

New Springville, NY 142 B1

New Ulm, MN 124 A5, 126 F6

New York, 103 D1, 112 E6, 116, 119 H6, 179 G5

New York, NY 103 D1, 112 F6, 116 B5, 119 H5, 141, 142 D4, 179 H4

New York Aquarium for Wildlife Conservation, NY 142 D1

New York Botanical Gdns, NY 143 E6

New York Public Library, NY 141 G4

New York Stock Exchange, NY 141 E1

New York U, NY 141 F3

New Zealand, 77 G2, 80 C2

Newark, CA 175 E3

Newark, DE 119 G4

Newark, NJ 112 F6, 116 A5, 119 H5, 142 B3

Newark, NY 116 D3

Newark, OH 118 C4

Newark, TX 164 A6

Newark Intl Arpt, NJ 142 B3

Newberry, SC 121 F4

Newberry Wildlife Sanctuary, OH 151 B3

Newburgh, NY 117 G1

Newburgh Hts, OH 150 D6

Newburyport, MA 115 C3

Newcastle, Afr 47 F2

Newcastle, Austral 77 E3

Newcastle, Can 103 E2

Newcastle, UK 14 C1, 18 E5

Newcastle, WY 126 B5, 130 E7

Newfane, NY 116 B4

Newfoundland, NC 187 E6

Newham, 26 D7

Newington, 27 E1

Newman, 76 B4

Newmarket, 79 B3

Newnan, GA 120 D4

Newport, AR 120 A5, 129 G6

Newport, Austral 79 B2

Newport, KY 151 D2

Newport, MN 161 F1

Newport, OR 134 A3

Newport, RI 115 C2

Newport, UK 19 D2

Newport, WA 134 D6

Newport Beach, CA 133 D2, 170 D1

Newport Hills, WA 176 C4

Newport News, VA 112 E5, 119 G1

Newry, 19 C4

Newton, IA 125 B4

Newton, KS 127 E2

Newton, MA 139 C3

Newton, NJ 116 A6, 119 H5

Newton Highlands, MA 139 B3

Newtown, Austral 78 E6

Newtown, OH 151 F2

Newtown Square, PA 144 B3

Neyagawa, 70 D6

Nez Perce, ID 135 E4

Nez Perce IR, ID 130 A8, 135 E4

Nez Perce NHP, ID 178 B6

Nezahualcóyotl, 98 D3

Ngau Chi Wan, 75 D4

Nha Trang, 61 C4

Niagara Falls, 116 B3

Niagara-on-the-Lake, 116 B4

Niamey, 44 C2

Nicaragua, 81 H5, 84 A6, 94 A3, 97 G2

Nice, CA 132 B6

Nice, Fr 16 D4, 20 F5, 24 A4

Niceville, FL 122 B6

Nicholasville, KY 118 A3

Nickerson SP, MA 184 F5

Nicobar Islands, 59 F3

Nicolás R Casillas, 99 E4

Nicolet, 114 A7

Nicolet NF, WI 124 D6

Nicosia, 48 D5

Nictau, 114 F8

Nied, 35 A3

Nieder-Neuendorf, 32 C8

Niederrad, 35 B2

Niel, 31 F5

Niemeyer, 91 D1

Nienburg, 23 C4

Nieuw Vennep, 30 C5

Nieuwerkerk aan de Ijssel, 30 C2

Nieuwkerken Waas, 31 F5

Niger, 44 D2

Niger R, 44 C2

Nigeria, 44 D1

Niguarda, 40 C2

Nihonbashi, 69 E3

Nihonbashi-Ningyocho, 69 F4

Niigata, 66 F6

Niihau, HI 137 A4

Niiza, 68 B8

Nijo Castle, 71 E3

Nikaia, 43 B2

Nikolayevsk-na-Amure, 55 F4

Niland, CA 133 F2

Nile R, 45 F4, 48 C4

Niles, IL 158 C5

Nilópolis, 91 B3

Nimes, 21 E4

Nine Mile Pond, FL 188 D4

Ningbo, 60 D7, 67 C3

Ninove, 31 E2

Ninoy Aquino Intl Arpt, 62 C1

Niobrara R, NE 127 C4

Nipigon, 103 A3, 124 D8

Nipomo, CA 133 C3

Nis, 17 G4, 25 F6

Nishi-Ku, 71 A3

Nishi-Kyogoku, 71 E2

Nishikyo-Ku, 71 D2

Nishijin Textile Ctr, 71 E4

Nishinomiya, 70 B6

Nishishinbashi, 69 C1

Niterói, 88 D6, 91 E2

Niue, 80 D3

Niva, 36 C8

Nizhnevartovsk, 53 F4

Nizhniy Novgorod, 53 B4

Nizhniy Tagil, 53 D4

No Man's Land, 50 C5

Noatak N Pres, AK 136 C8, 178 A3

Nob Hill, CA 173 D2

Nobska Pt, MA 185 F1

Nodebo, 36 A8

Nogales, AZ 111 C3, 131 B1

Nogales, Mex 96 B6, 131 B1

Nohili Pt, HI 137 A4

Noisy-le-Grand, 28 E7

Nokomis-Hiawatha RP, MN 161 C2

Nome, AK 82 A6, 136 B7

Nonantum, MA 139 B3

Noord, 30 D6

Noordwijk aan Zee, 30 B5

Noordwijkerhout, 30 B5

Norco, CA 171 F4

Norcross, GA 152 D6

Nordvik, 54 B6, 82 C8

Nordwest-stadt, 35 A3

Norfolk, NE 126 E4

Norfolk, VA 112 E5, 119 G1, 121 H6, 179 H3

Norfolk Isl, 77 G3, 80 C2

Norilsk, 54 A5, 82 C8

Normal, IL 125 D3

Norman, OK 129 E5

Norman Wells, 136 F7

Normandy Park, WA 176 B3

Nørre Herlev, 36 A8

Norridge, IL 159 C4

Norridgewock, ME 114 D5

Norris Geyser Basin, WY 180 B4

Norris Lake, TN 120 D6

Norristown, PA 119 G4, 144 C6

Norrköping, 15 F2, 22 F7

Norrsunda, 36 E8

North Absaroka Wilderness, WY 180 D4

North Adams, MA 115 A3, 117 H3

North Andover, MA 138 C8

North Arlington, NJ 142 C4

North Barrackpore, 65 F3

North Battleford, 101 E3

North Bay, Can 103 C2

North Bay Village, FL 155 G2

North Bend, OH 151 B2

North Bergen, NJ 142 C5

North Caldwell, NJ 142 A6

North Canadian R, OK 127 D1

North Cape, 15 F6, 82 E7

North Carolina, 113 E4, 121 F5, 179 G3

North Cascades NP, WA 134 C6, 178 B6

North Chagrin Res, OH 150 F8

North Channel, Can 124 F6

North Chan, UK 18 C5

North Chatham, MA 184 F5

North Chevy Chase, MD 148 D8

North Chicago, IL 158 C7

North China Plain, 66 A5

North College Hill, OH 151 D3

North Creek, NY 117 G4

North Crows Nest, IN 157 E3

North Dakota, 101 F2, 110 F7, 126 E7, 178 D6

North Decatur, GA 152 C4

North Druid Hills, GA 152 C4

North Dupo, IL 162 C1

North Eastham, MA 184 F6

North End, MA 140 B4

North Fair Oaks, CA 175 C3

North Harbor, 62 B2

North Houston, TX 166 B5

North Isl, 77 H2, 80 C2

North Kansas City, MO 162 C6

North Korea, 60 D8, 66 C3

North Lake Park, TX 165 E5

North Lauderdale, FL 155 G5

North Miami, FL 155 G3

North Miami Beach, FL 155 G3

North Mountain RA, AZ 168 B5

North Myrtle Beach, SC 121 G4

North New Hyde Park, NY 143 G4

North Oaks, MN 161 E4

North Olmsted, OH 150 B6

North Park, PA 146 C8

North Parramatta, 78 C8

North Plains, OR 177 E6

North Platte, NE 110 F5, 127C4

North Platte R, NE 127 B4, 130 F6

North Pt, Hong Kong 75 D2

North Pt, ME 186 A5

North Point SP, MD 147 F1

North Pole, 82 C7

North Port, FL 123 E3

North Powder, OR 134 D4

North Randall, OH 150 E6

North Randolph, MA 139 D1

North Reading, MA 138 D6

North Richland Hills, TX 164 C4

North Richmond, CA 174 B6

North Rim, AZ 183 E2

North Rocks, 78 D8

North Royalton, OH 150 C5

North Ryde, 78 D8

North St Paul, MN 161 F3

North Sea, 14 D1, 18 F5, 20 D8, 22 A6, 82 F7

North Siberian Lowland, 54 B6

North Springfield, VA 148 B5

North Sta & Fleet Ctr, MA 140 C4

North Stratford, NH 114 C7

North Sydney, 78 E7

North Tisbury, MA 185 G1

North Tonawanda, NY 116 B3

North Truro, MA 184 E8

North Valley Stream, NY 143 G3

North Vancouver, 107 G3

North Wellington, 77 H1

North West Cape, 76 A4

North Woburn, MA 138 C5

North York, 104 **D7**
Northbridge, 78 **E8**
Northbrook, IL 158 **C6**
Northbrook, OH 151 **C3**
Northcliff, 51 **F3**
Northcote, 79 **C3**
Northeast Creek, ME 186 **B6**
Northeast Entrance, MT 180 **D5**
Northeast Harbor, ME 186 **C3**
Northeast Philadelphia Arpt, PA 145 **G5**
Northern Cheyenne IR, MT 126 **A6**, 130 **D8**
Northern Dvina R, 52 **C5**
Northern European Plain, 15 **G1**, 52 **B5**
Northern Mariana Islands, 80 **B5**
Northern Terr, 76 **C5**
Northern Yukon NP, 136 **E8**
Northfield, IL 158 **C5**
Northfield, OH 150 **E5**
Northfield Ctr, OH 150 **E5**
Northglenn, CO 167 **G5**
Northlake, IL 159 **C4**
Northmead, 78 **C8**
Northport, WA 134 **D6**
Northwest Cape, FL 188 **C4**
Northwest Pk, MT 135 **E6**
Northwest Terr, Can 100 **E5**
Northwestern U, IL 158 **D5**
Northwestway Park, IN 157 **D3**
Northwoods, MO 162 **B2**
Norton Sd, AK 136 **B7**
Norwalk, CA 170 **D3**
Norwalk, CT 115 **A1**, 116 **B6**
Norway, 22 **C8**
Norway, ME 114 **C5**

Norwegian Sea, 14 **D4**, 52 **C7**, 82 **E7**
Norwich, CT 115 **B2**
Norwich, NY 117 **E2**
Norwich, UK 19 **F3**, 20 **D8**
Norwood, MA 139 **B1**
Norwood, OH 151 **E2**
Norwood, PA 144 **C1**
Nose, 70 **C8**
Notre Dame, 29 **E1**
Notre-Dame Basilica, 106 **C2**
Notting Hill, 79 **D1**
Nottingham, 14 **C1**, 19 **E3**, 20 **C8**
Nou Camp Stad, 38 **E6**
Nouadhibou, 44 **A3**
Nouakchott, 44 **A3**
Nouméa, 80 **C3**
Nova U, FL 155 **F4**
Novara, 20 **F5**, 24 **A5**
Novate Milanese, 40 **B2**
Novato, CA 174 **A7**
Novaya Zemlya, 52 **E6**, 82 **D7**
Novgorod, 15 **G3**, 52 **B5**
Novi Pazar, 25 **E6**
Novi Sad, 17 **G4**
Novo Iguaçu, 91 **B3**
Novonikol'skoye, 56 **C2**
Novokuznetsk, 55 **A3**
Novosaratovka, 57 **H2**
Novosel'tsevo, 56 **B6**
Novosibirsk, 53 **F3**
Nowitna NWR, AK 136 **C7**
Nowon, 72 **D8**
Noxubee NWR, MS 120 **B4**
Nuannuau, 62 **D6**
Nubian Desert, 45 **G3**, 48 **D2**
Nueva Casas Grandes, 96 **B6**, 131 **D1**
Nueva Gerona, 94 **B5**
Nueva Rosita, 128 **C2**

Nuevo España, 99 **F4**
Nuevo Laredo, 96 **D5**, 128 **D1**
Nuevo México, 99 **F6**
Nukualofa, 80 **D3**
Nukus, 53 **C2**, 58 **A8**
Nullarbor Plain, 76 **C3**
Nunavut, 100 **F6**
Nunawading, 79 **E2**
Nuñez, 88 **D7**
Nunivak Isl, AK 82 **A6**, 136 **A6**
Nuñoa, 87 **G2**
Nunyagmo, 136 **A7**
Nürnberg, 17 **E5**, 23 **D3**
Nutley, 81 **A2**
Nutter Pt, ME 186 **A3**
Nutting Lake, MA 138 **B5**
Nuuk, 82 **E5**, 102 **D6**
Nyack, NY 116 **B6**
Nyala, 45 **F2**
Nyssa, OR 134 **D3**

O

Oahu, HI 81 **E5**, 137 **C4**
Oak Bluff, 107 **F4**
Oak Bluffs, MA 115 **D2**, 185 **G2**
Oak Brook, IL 159 **B3**
Oak Forest, IL 159 **C2**
Oak Grove, OR 177 **G4**
Oak Hill, MA 139 **C2**
Oak Lane, PA 145 **E4**
Oak Lawn, IL 159 **C3**
Oak Park, *Austral* 79 **B4**
Oak Park, IL 159 **C4**
Oak Park, MI 156 **C8**
Oak Ridge, TN 120 **D6**, 125 **F1**
Oakdale, GA 152 **A4**
Oakdale, MN 161 **F3**
Oakhurst, CA 132 **C5**
Oakland, CA 110 **A5**, 132 **B5**, 174 **C5**
Oakland, FL 153 **E4**

Oakland, MD 119 **E4**
Oakland Mus, CA 174 **C5**
Oakland Park, FL 155 **G5**
Oakland Park, TX 165 **E6**
Oakleigh, 79 **D1**
Oakley, ID 135 **F2**
Oakley, KS 127 **C3**
Oaklyn, NJ 145 **F2**
Oakmont, PA 146 **E7**
Oakridge, *Can* 107 **G1**
Oakridge, OR 134 **B3**
Oaks, MO 162 **C6**
Oakton, VA 148 **A6**
Oakview, MD 148 **E8**
Oakville, CT 117 **H1**
Oakwood, OH 150 **F5**
Oamishirasato, 68 **F6**
Oaxaca, 96 **D2**
Ob R, 53 **E4**, 82 **D8**
Oban, 18 **C6**
Obatange PP, 124 **E7**
Obelisk, 89 **D3**
Oberbilk, 34 **B5**
Oberhausen, 34 **B7**
Oberlaa, 42 **E6**
Oberlin, KS 127 **D3**
Oberursel, 35 **A4**
Oboldino, 56 **D5**
Observatory Hill, 78 **E7**
Obsidian Cliff, WY 180 **B5**
Óbuda, 42 **A7**
Ocala, FL 113 **D2**, 121 **E1**, 123 **E5**
Ocala NF, FL 121 **F1**
Ocean Bluff, MA 184 **A8**
Ocean Falls, 101 **B3**
Ocean Park, Hong Kong 75 **C1**
Ocean Park, WA 134 **A5**
Oceanside, CA 111 **D2**
Oceanside, NY 143 **H2**
Ochakovo, 56 **B3**
Ochoco NF, OR 134 **C3**
Ocoee, FL 153 **F4**

Oconee NF, GA 121 E4

Ocracoke, NC 187 F1

Ocracoke Inlet, NC 187 F1

Ocracoke Isl, NC 187 F1

Ocracoke Isl Visitor Ctr, NC 187 F1

Ocracoke Lighthouse, NC 187 F1

Ócsa, 42 C5

October Stad, 56 B4

Odemis, 25 H3

Odense, 15 E1, 22 D6

Oder R, 17 F6, 23 E4

Odesa, 45 F6, 17 H5

Odessa, TX 111 E3, 128 C4, 131 F1

Odintsovo, 56 A3

Odivelas, 38 B7

Odolena Voda, 35 E4

Oeiras, 38 A6

Oeuzzane, 21 B1

O'Fallon Park, MO 162 C2

Offenbach, Ger 35 C3

Offenbach, Switz 37 D1

Offenburg, 23 C2

Offentahl, 35 C1

Ogallala, NE 127 C4, 130 F6

Ogbomosho, 44 C1

Ogden, UT 110 C6, 130 B6, 135 G1

Ogdensburg, NY 117 F6

Ogimachi Park, 71 B4

Ogo, 70 A6

Ogoki R, 124 D8

Ohatsu Tenjin Shrine, 71 A4

O'Higgins Park, 87 F2

Ohio, 103 C1, 112 C5, 118 A5, 179 G4

Ohio R, 112 C5, 118 B3, 125 E2, 179 F4

Ohiopyle SP, PA 119 E4

Ohrid, 25 E3

Oinville-sur-Montcient, 28 A8

Oita, 67 E4

Oji Park, 70 A5

Ojibway Prov P, 156 D5

Ojinaga, 128 B2

Okamedari, 71 F1

Okanogan, WA 134 C6

Okanogan NF, WA 134 C6

Okayama, 66 E5

Okeana, OH 151 A4

Okeechobee, FL 123 F3

Okefenokee NWR, GA 121 E2, 123 E6

Okha, 55 F4

Okhla, 64 E6

Okhotsk, 54 E5

Okinawa, 60 E6, 67 D3

Oklahoma, 96 D6, 111 F4, 129 E6, 178 D3

Oklahoma City, OK 111 F4, 127 E1, 129 E5, 178 D3

Okmulgee, OK 127 F1

Olalla, WA 176 A3

Öland, 15 F2, 22 F6

Olbia, 24 A3

Old Cairo, 50 C2

Old Crow, 136 D7

Old Faithful, WY 180 B3

Old Faithful Visitor Ctr, WY 180 B3

Old Man House SP, WA 176 A6

Old Mill Creek, IL 158 B8

Old North Church, MA 140 D5

Old Opera House, 35 B3

Old Orchard Beach, ME 115 D4

Old Saybrook, CT 116 D6

Old Shawnee Town, KS 162 A4

Old South Meeting House, MA 140 C3

Old Statehouse & Boston Massacre Site, MA 140 C3

Old Tampa Bay Park, FL 154 B5

Old Town, ME 114 E5

Old US Mint, CA 173 E1

Old Yafo, 50 A6

Oldcastle, 156 E5

Oldenburg, 23 C4

Oldsmar, FL 154 B5

Olean, NY 116 C2, 119 E6

Olenek R, 54 C5

Ol'gino, 57 F3

Olinda, 91 B3

Olivais, 38 C7

Olivar de los Padres, 98 A3

Olive Park, IL 160 E8

Oliver, 156 E5

Olivette, MO 162 B2

Olivon, 43 A4

Olivos, 88 D8

Olmos Park, TX 163 G3

Olmsted Falls, OH 150 B5

Olney, IL 125 D2

Olney, PA 145 E4

Olstykke, 36 A7

Olympia, WA 110 A7, 134 B5

Olympia Hts, FL 155 F1

Olympia Stad, 43 C3

Olympiastadion, 32 C7

Olympic NP, WA 134 B6, 178 A6

Olympic Sports Ctr, 73 D3

Olympic Stad, Indo 64 B7

Olympic Stad, Mex 98 B2

Olympic Stad, Spain 38 E4

Omagh, 19 B4

Omaha, NE 112 A5, 125 A4, 127 F4, 179 E4

Oman, 49 H3

Omdurman, 45 F2, 48 C1

Omiya Sento Palace, 71 E3

Oneco, FL 154 C1

Oneida, NY 117 F3

Oneida Lake, NY 117 E4

O'Neill, NE 127 E4

O'Neill NHS, CA 174 E5

O'Neill RP, CA 171 F1

Oneonta, NY 117 F2

Omsk, 53 E3

Once Train Sta, 89 B2

Onitsha, 44 D1

Onset, MA 184 A5

Ontario, CA 171 F4

Ontario Intl Arpt, CA 171 F4

Ontario Science Ctr, 104 E6

Oost, 30 D6

Oostende, 20 E7, 23 A4

Opa Locka, FL 155 F3

Opalikha, 56 A5

Opava, 23 F3

Opéra Bastille, 29 F1

Opera House, WA 176 A5

Opp, AL 120 C2

Opwijk, 31 F3

Oradea, 17 G5

Oral, 53 C3

Oran, 16 B1, 21 D1, 44 C5

Orange, Austral 77 E3

Orange, CA 171 E3

Orange, NJ 142 A4

Orange, OH 150 F6

Orange, VA 119 E2

Orange Bowl, FL 155 F2

Orange Co Conv Ctr, FL 153 F3

Orange Park, FL 123 F5

Orange R, 47 E2

Orangeburg, SC 121 F4

Oranienburg, 23 D4

Oranjestad, 95 E1

Orbottyán, 42 C8

Orcasitas, 39 B1

Orchard Beach, MD 147 E1

Orchards, WA 177 G6

Örebro, 15 F2, 22 E8

Oregon, 101 B1, 110 A7, 134 B4, 178 A5

Oregon City, OR 134 B4, 177 G4

Oregon Conv Ctr, OR 177 G5

Oregon Hist Ctr, OR 177 G5

Oregon Inlet, NC 187 H5

Oreland, PA 145 E6

Orem, UT 130 B6

Orenburg, 53 **C3**
Orense, 21 **A4**
Orford, NH 115 **B4**
Organ Pipe Cactus NM, AZ 131 **B2**, 178 **B2**
Orient, NY 116 **D6**
Orient, OR 177 **H5**
Orient Park, FL 154 **D5**
Oriental Plaza, 51 **F2**
Orinda, CA 174 **D6**
Orinoco R, 84 **D5**
Oriole Park at Camden Yards, MD 147 **D2**
Oriskany, NY 117 **F3**
Oristano, 24 **A3**
Orizaba, 96 **D3**
Orkney Islands, 14 **C2**
Orland, CA 132 **B6**
Orland Hills, IL 159 **C2**
Orland Park, IL 159 **C2**
Orlando, Afr 51 **F2**
Orlando, FL 113 **D2**, 121 **F1**, 123 **E4**, 153 **G4**, 179 **G1**
Orlando Arena, FL 153 **G4**
Orlando Intl Arpt, FL 153 **G3**
Orléans, Fr 16 **C5**, 20 **D6**
Orleans, MA 184 **F6**
Orlovista, FL 153 **F4**
Orly Arpt, 28 **D6**
Ormond Beach, FL 123 **F5**
Orofino, ID 135 **E4**
Orono, ME 114 **E5**
Oroville, CA 132 **B6**
Oroville, WA 134 **C6**
Orpington, 26 **D5**
Orsay, 28 **C6**
Orsk, 53 **D3**
Orszaghez, 42 **B7**
Orumiyeh, 49 **E6**
Oruro, 84 **D1**
Orwell, VT 115 **A4**
Osa, 40 **D5**
Osage IR, OK 127 **F1**, 129 **E6**
Osage R, MO 125 **B2**

Osaka, 60 **E8**, 66 **E5**, 70 **D5**, 71 **B2**
Osaka Castle, 70 **D5**, 71 **C3**
Osaka Chamber of Industry & Commerce, 71 **C3**
Osaka Festival Bldg, 71 **A3**
Osaka Intl Arpt, 70 **C6**
Osaka Mint & Mus, 70 **D5**, 71 **C3**
Osaka Scientific Tech Ctr, 71 **A3**
Osaka Sta, 71 **A4**
Osaka Stock Exchange, 71 **B3**
Osaka U, 70 **C5**, 71 **A3**
Osakajo Park, 71 **C3**
Osark NF, AR 129 **F6**
Osasco, 92 **A5**
Osceola NF, FL 121 **E2**
Oshawa, 103 **C1**, 116 **B5**
Oshkosh, WI 124 **D5**
Oshogbo, 44 **C1**
Osijek, 24 **D5**
Oskarshamn, 22 **F7**
Oskemen, 53 **F2**
Oslo, 15 **E3**, 22 **D8**, 82 **F7**
Osnabrück, 20 **F8**, 23 **C4**
Osorno, 86 **A4**
Osteen, FL 153 **H6**
Osteraker, 36 **F7**
Osterang, 36 **F5**
Osterath, 34 **A6**
Osterfeld, 34 **B7**
Osterhaninge, 36 **F5**
Osteria dell' Osa, 40 **D5**
Ostermundigen, 37 **C2**
Östersund, 15 **E4**
Osterville, MA 185 **E3**
Ostiense, 40 **C5**
Ostrava, 17 **F6**
Ostrov, 53 **D3**
Ostrup, 36 **A6**
Oswego, NY 117 **E4**
Otaki, 68 **F5**
Ota-Ku, 68 **C6**

Otaru, 66 **E7**
Otemachi, 69 **D4**
Othello, WA 134 **C5**
Otis, MA 115 **A3**
Otis ANG Base, MA 184 **B5**
Otradnoye, 57 **H1**
Otsu, 70 **F8**
Ottakring, 42 **D7**
Ottavia, 40 **B6**
Ottawa, Can 103 **C2**, 105 **B3**, 112 **E7**
Ottawa, KS 125 **A3**, 127 **F2**
Ottawa Civic Ctr, 105 **B2**
Ottawa Intl Arpt, 105 **B1**
Ottawa NF, MI 124 **D6**
Ottawa NWR, OH 118 **B6**
Otter Cove, ME 186 **D3**
Otter Creek, ME 186 **D4**
Otter Creek, VT 117 **H5**
Otter Pt, ME 186 **D3**
Ottumwa, IA 112 **A5**, 125 **B4**
Ouachita NF, AR 129 **F5**
Ouagadougou, 44 **C2**
Oud-Beijerland, 30 **B1**
Oud-Zuid, 30 **D5**
Oudewater, 30 **D3**
Oudja, 21 **C1**, 44 **C5**
Oulo, 15 **G4**
Oulu, 52 **C6**
Our Lady of Guadalupe Basilica, 98 **B4**
Our Lady of Lourdes Shrine, OH 150 **E8**
Outfall Canal, NC 187 **E3**
Outremont, 106 **C3**
Oveido, FL 153 **H5**
Overbrook, PA 144 **D3**
Overijse, 31 **H1**
Overland, MO 162 **B2**
Overland Park, MO 162 **B4**
Overlea, MD 147 **B3**
Overlook Mt, WY 180 **D2**
Overton, NV 133 **F4**
Overtoomse, 30 **D6**
Oviedo, 21 **B4**

Ovilla, TX 165 **F1**
Owasco Lake, NY 117 **E3**
Owatonna, MN 124 **B5**
Owego, NY 119 **F6**
Owen Sd, 103 **C1**
Owensboro, KY 113 **C4**, 125 **E2**
Owings Mills, MD 147 **B4**
Owyhee, NV 132 **E8**, 135 **E1**
Oxford, MS 120 **B4**
Oxford, NC 119 **E1**, 121 **G6**
Oxford, UK 19 **E3**
Oxnard, CA 133 **C3**
Oxon Hill, MD 148 **E5**
Oxon Hill Farm, MD 148 **D5**
Oyamazaki, 70 **E7**
Ozark, AL 120 **D3**
Ozark NF, AK 125 **B1**
Ozark Natl Scenic Riverways, MO 125 **C2**
Ozark Plateau, 113 **A4**
Ozoir-a-Ferriere, 28 **E6**
Ozona, FL 154 **A6**
Ozone Park, NY 143 **E3**

P

Pablo Iglesias, 39 **F1**
Pabst Brewery, WI 157 **C3**
Pacaembú Stad, 92 **B5**
Pace, FL 122 **B6**
Pace Railway Sta, 62 **C2**
Pacheco, CA 174 **D7**
Pachena Pt, 134 **A6**
Pachuca, 96 **D3**
Pacific, WA 176 **C1**
Pacific Beach, CA 169 **B4**
Pacific Bell Park, CA 173 **F1**
Pacific Coast Stock Exchange, CA 173 **E2**
Pacific Hts, CA 173 **B3**
Pacific Ocean, 80 – 81, 84 **A4**, 96 **C2**, 101 **A3**, 136 **D5**

Pacific Spirit RP, 107 F2
Pacifica, CA 175 A4
Padang, 61 A3
Paddington, 78 F7
Paderno Dugnano, 40 B3
Padova, 23 E1, 24 B5
Padre Hurlado, 87 E1
Padre Island NS, TX 178 D1
Padstow, 78 C6
Paducah, KY 113 B4,
120 B6, 125 D2
Page, AZ 131 B4
Pago Pago, 80 D3
Pahaska, WY 180 D3
Pahokee, FL 123 F3
Paianía, 43 C2
Painesville, OH 118 C6
Painted Desert, AZ 183 F3
Paintsville, KY 118 B2
Paio Pires, 38 C5
Paisley, OR 134 C2
Pakistan, 49 H5, 58 A6
Pakxe, 61 B4
Palace of Congresses, 57 E5
Palace of Chaillot, 29 A3
Palace of Fine Arts, CA
173 A3
Palace of Justice, 41 C4
Palace of Natl Assembly,
38 B6
Palace of the Arts, 40 B2
Palace of Versailles, 28 C6
Palaion Faliron, 43 B2
Palais de Chaillot, 29 A3
Palais du Justice, 29 E2
Palais Royal, 29 D2
Palais Unter den Linden,
33 E3
Palaiseau, 28 C6
Palam, 64 D7
Palana, 54 B8, 54 F6
Palapye, 47 F3
Palatine, IL 158 B6
Palatino Hill, 41 D2
Palatka, FL 121 F1, 123 F5
Palau, 80 A5
Palau-Solità, 38 E8
Palawan, 61 D4

Palazzo del Quirinale,
41 D3
Palazzo Venezia, 41 D3
Palembang, 61 B1
Palermo, Arg 88 D7,
89 A4
Palermo, CA 132 B6
Palermo, Italy 17 E2,
24 C2, 48 A6
Palhais, 38 C5
Pali, 62 B6, 64 E5
Palidoro, 40 A6
Palikir, 80 B4
Palisades Park, NJ 142 D5
Palm Bay, FL 123 F4
Palm Beach, FL 123 G3
Palm Coast, FL 123 F5
Palm Harbor, FL 154 A6
Palm Key, FL 188 E3
Palm R, FL 154 D5
Palm Springs, CA 133 E3
Palma de Mallorca, 16 C3,
21 E3
Palma Sola, FL 154 B1
Palmdale, CA 133 D3
Palmer Park, MD 148 F7
Palmerston, 77 H1
Palmetto, FL 154 B1
Palmira, 84 C4
Palmyra, NJ 145 G3
Palmyra, NY 116 D3
Palmyra Atoll, 80 D5
Palo Alto, CA 175 D2
Palomeras, 39 D2
Palopo, 61 E2
Palos FP, IL 159 C2
Palos Hts, IL 159 C2
Palos Hills, IL 159 C2
Palos Verdes Estates, CA
170 B3
Palu, 61 E2
Pamirs, 53 E1, 58 C7
Pamlico Sd, NC 121 H5,
187 F2
Pampa, TX 128 D6
Pampas, 86 B5
Pamplona, 16 B4, 21 C4

Panaca, NV 131 A4,
132 F5
Panaji, 59 B4
Panama, 81 H5, 84 B5,
97 H1
Panama Canal, 97 H1
Panama City, Pan 84 B5,
97 H1
Panama City, FL 113 C3,
120 C2, 122 C5
Panania, 78 C6
Panay, 61 E4
Panchiao, 62 B5
Pangkalpinang, 61 B2
Pangnirtung, 102 C6
Panhandle Key, FL 188 E3
Panihati, 65 F2
Pankow, 32 D7
Pantego, TX 164 C3
Pantelleria, 24 B1
Panthéon, Fr 29 E1
Pantheon, Italy 40 C5,
41 C3
Panthersville, GA 152 D3
Pantigliate, 40 D1
Pantitlán, 98 C3
Paoli, PA 144 A4
Paomachang, 73 C2
Papago Park, AZ 168 C3
Papeeté, 81 E3
Papendrecht, 30 C1
Papua New Guinea, 76 C1,
80 B4
Parabiago, 40 A3
Paradise, CA 132 B6
Paradise, NV 131 A4
Paradise Hills, CA 169 C3
Paradise Valley, AZ 168 C4
Paragould, AR 120 A6,
125 C1, 129 H6
Paraguay, 85 E1, 86 B6
Paraguay R, 85 E1, 86 B6
Paramaribo, 85 F5
Paramount Studios, CA
170 C3, 172 C7
Paraná, 86 B5
Paraná R, 86 B5, 86 C6

Paranapiacaba, 92 D3
Paranaque, 62 B1
Parasnath Jain Temple,
65 E2
Parc des Princes Stad, 28 C7
Parc Monceau, 29 C4
Parc Naturel Regional de la
Haute Vallee de
Chevreuse, 28 B5
Parco Traianeo, 41 E2
Parel, 65 B2
Parelheiros, 92 A3
Parent Naval Orange Tree,
CA 171 G4
Parepare, 61 E2
Parets del Vallès, 38 F8
Pargolovo, 57 F3
Parioli, 40 C6
Paris, Fr 16 C5, 20 E6,
23 A3, 28 D7, 29, 44 D6
Paris, ID 135 G2
Paris, IL 125 D3
Paris, KY 118 B2
Paris, TN 120 B6, 125 D1,
129 H6
Paris, TX 113 A3, 129 F5
Park City, IL 158 C7
Park City, UT 130 C6
Park Hills, KY 151 D1
Park Orchards, 79 E3
Park Ridge, IL 158 C5
Parker, TX 165 H6
Parker Ranch, HI 137 E2
Parker River NWR, MA
138 F8
Parker SF, Harold, MA
138 D7
Parkersburg, WV 112 D5,
118 C3
Parkland, FL 155 F6
Parkville, MD 147 E4
Parkville, MO 162 B6
Parliament, Aus 42 E7
Parliament, India 64 E7
Parliament Bldg, 64 B7
Parma, Italy 24 B5
Parma, OH 150 D6

Parma Hts, OH 150 C6

Parnaíba, 85 G3

Pärnu, 15 G2

Parque Almirante Guillermo Brown, 88 D6

Parque Ameghino, 89 C1

Parque Chacabuco, 89 A1

Parque Mus, 89 A3

Parque Colón, 89 E3

Parque del Centenario, 89 A3

Parque Do Estado, 92 B4

Parque Lezama, 89 E2

Parque Nacional da Tujica, 91 D2

Parque Natural Costanera Sur, 89 F3

Parque Paricios, 89 C1

Parque Rivadavia, 89 A3

Parramatta, 78 C7

Parrish, FL 154 D2

Parry Sound, 103 C1

Parsons, KS 127 F2

Parsons Pk, CA 182 D3

Parung, 64 A6

Pas, The, 101 F3

Pasadena, CA 133 D3, 170 C5

Pasadena, TX 129 F3, 166 D3

Pasarét, 42 A7

Pasaunda, 64 F7

Pasay, 62 C2

Pascagoula, MS 122 A6

Pasco, WA 134 D4

Pascoe Vale, 79 B3

Pasig, 62 C2

Pasir Panjang, 63 E1

Pasir Ris, 63 G3

Paso del Rey, 88 B6

Passage Key NWR, FL 154 B2

Passaic, NJ 116 B5, 142 B6

Passau, 21 D2

Passo Fundo, 86 C6

Passy, 29 A3

Pasteros, 62 C2

Pasto, 84 B4

Patagonia, 86 A3

Patapsco Valley SP, MD 147 B2

Pate, 62 A4

Paterson, NJ 112 E6, 116 A6, 119 H5

Paterson Mus, NJ 142 B6

Pathumwan, 63 G5

Patna, 58 D5, 65 E4

Patras, 17 G2, 25 E3

Patten, ME 114 F7

Patterson, NJ 142 B9

Patuxent River Park, MD 147 A1

Pau, 21 D4

Paul Revere House, MA 140 D4

Paulatuk, 136 F8

Paullo, 40 D1

Pauls Valley, OK 129 E5

Pavia, 24 A5

Pavillion, WY 135 H2

Pavlodar, 53 F3

Pawnee, OK 127 F1

Pawnee NG, CO 127 B4, 130 E6

Pawtucket, RI 115 C2

Paya Ledar, 63 G2

Paye, 65 C4

Payette, ID 134 D3

Payette NF, ID 130 A8, 135 E4

Paysandú, 86 B5

Payson, AZ 131 B3

Payson, UT 130 B5

Pazardzhik, 25 G5

Pea Island, NC 187 H4

Pea Island NWR, NC 187 H4

Pea Ridge NMP, AR 179 E3

Peabody, MA 138 E5

Peabody Institute, MD 147 B2

Peace R, Can 101 D3

Peace R, FL 123 E3

Peakhurst, 78 C6

Peania, 43 C2

Pearl City, HI 137 C3, 177 F3

Pearl Harbor, HI 137 C3

Pearl Harbor NWR, HI 177 E2

Pearl R, MS 129 H4

Pearland, TX 166 C2

Pearsall, TX 128 D2

Pearson Intl Arpt, 104 B6

Pec, 25 E5

Pecan Valley Park, TX 164 A3

Pecel, 42 C7

Peche Island Prov P, 156 F6

Pechora, 52 D5

Pechora R, 52 D5

Peco de Aneto, 21 D4

Pecos, TX 128 C3, 131 F1

Pecos R, NM 128 B4, 131 E3

Pecs, 17 F5, 24 D6

Pedley, CA 171 G4

Pedro García, 90 B5

Peekskill, NY 116 B6

Peel R, 136 E7

Pegu, 59 F4

Pekanbaru, 61 A3

Pelee Isl, 118 C6

Pelham, NH 138 A8

Pelham, NY 143 F6

Pelham Bay Park, NY 143 F6

Pelham Manor, NY 143 F6

Pell City, AL 120 C4

Pelly Crossing, 136 E7

Pelly R, 136 E6

Peloponnesus, 17 G2, 25 F3

Pelotas, 86 C5

Pematangsiantar, 61 A3

Pemba Isl, 47 G5

Pembina, ND 126 E8

Pembroke, Can 103 C2

Pembroke, UK 19 C2

Pembroke Park, FL 155 G3

Pembroke Pines, FL 155 E3

Peña Grande, 39 B4

Peñaflor, 87 E1

Peñalolén, 87 G1

Pendleton, OR 110 B7, 134 D4

Pengpu, 74 D8

Penha, 91 C3, 92 C4

Peniche, 21 A3

Penn Hills, PA 144 E7

Penn Square, PA 144 C6

Penn Wynne, PA 144 C3

Penn Yan, NY 116 D2

Penndel, PA 145 H6

Pennekamp Coral Reef SP, John, FL 188 F3

Pennsauken, NJ 145 F3

Pennsuco, FL 155 F2

Pennsylvania, 103 C1, 112 D5, 119 F5, 179 G4

Pennsylvania, U of, PA 144 D2

Pennsylvania Sta, NY 141 E4

Pennypack Park, PA 145 G5

Penobscot Bay, ME 114 D5

Penobscot R, ME 114 D5

Pensacola, FL 113 C3, 120 C2, 122 B6

Pensacola Mts, 83 D3

Pentagon, VA 148 D6

Penza, 53 C4

Penzance, 19 C2

Penzing, 42 D7

Peoria, AZ 168 A5

Peoria, IL 112 B5, 125 D3

Pepacton Reservoir, NY 117 F2

Pepper Pike, OH 150 F7

Pepsi Center, CO 167 G3

Perama, 43 A3

Perchtoldsdorf, 42 D6

Perdizes, 92 A5

Pereira, 84 C5

Périgueux, 20 D5

Peristerion, 43 B3

Perm, 53 D4

Pernik, 25 F5

Pero, 40 B2

Perovo, 56 C4

Perpignan, 16 C3, 21 E4

Perrine, FL 123 G2

Perry, FL 121 **E2**, 122 **D5**
Perry, GA 121 **D3**
Perry, NY 116 **C3**
Perry, OK 127 **E1**
Perry Hall, MD 147 **E4**
Perry Park, IN 157 **E1**
Perrysville, PA 146 **B8**
Perryton, TX 127 **D1**, 128 **D6**
Perryville, MO 125 **C2**
Persian Gulf, 45 **H4**, 49 **F4**
Perth, Can 117 **E6**
Perth, Austral 76 **A3**
Perth, UK 18 **D6**
Perth Road, 117 **E5**
Peru, 84 **C3**
Perugia, 24 **B4**
Perus, 92 **A6**
Pesaro, 24 **C4**
Pescadero, CA 175 **B1**
Pescadero Creek CP, CA 175 **C1**
Pescara, 24 **C4**
Peshawar, 58 **B7**
Pesthidegkút, 42 **A7**
Pestimre, 42 **B6**
Pestszenterzsébet, 42 **B6**
Pestszentimre, 42 **B6**
Petah Tiqwa, 50 **B6**
Petaluma, CA 132 **A5**
Petare, 90 **D4**
Peter & Paul Fortress, 57 **F2**
Peterborough, Can 103 **C1**
Peterborough, UK 19 **F3**
Peter's Palace, 56 **B4**
Petersburg, AK 101 **B4**
Petersburg, VA 112 **E5**, 119 **F1**, 121 **G6**
Petershagen, 32 **F7**
Petersham, 78 **E6**
Petinesca Castle, 37 **A3**
Petit Palais, 29 **C3**
Petoskey, MI 124 **E6**
Petrified Forest NP, AZ 131 **C3**, 178 **C3**
Petrified Tree, WY 180 **B5**

Petro-Slavyanka, 57 **H1**
Petrodvorets, 57 **E2**
Petrolina, 85 **G2**
Petropavl, 53 **E3**
Petropavlovsk-Kamchatskiy, 54 **C7**
Petroúpolis, 43 **B3**
Petrozavodsk, 15 **H4**, 52 **C5**
Pettit Pk, CA 182 **C5**
Pevek, 54 **E7**
Pfeiffers Corners, MD 147 **B1**
Pferderennbahn, 34 **F8**
Phalen Park, MN 161 **E3**
Phantom Ranch, AZ 183 **E2**
Phasi Charoen, 63 **E5**
Phelps Lake, WY 181 **F2**
Philadelphia, MS 120 **B3**
Philadelphia, PA 103 **D1**, 112 **E5**, 119 **H4**, 145 **E4**, 179 **H4**
Philadelphia College of Textile & Science, PA 144 **D4**
Philadelphia Intl Arpt, PA 144 **D1**
Philadelphia Mus of Art, PA 145 **E3**
Philharmonic Hall, 33 **D3**
Philippi, WV 118 **D3**
Philippine Sea, 60 **F5**
Philippines, 60 **E5**, 67 **C1**
Philippines, U of, 62 **C3**
Philips Arena, GA 152 **B4**
Philipsburg, MT 135 **F4**
Phillipsburg, KS 127 **D3**
Phipps Conservatory, PA 146 **C6**
Phitsanulok, 61 **A4**
Phnom Penh, 61 **B3**
Phoenix, AZ 96 **B6**, 111 **C4**, 131 **B2**, 168 **B4**, 178 **B3**
Phoenix Isl, 80 **D4**
Phongsali, 60 **A5**
Phra Khanong, 63 **H5**
Phra Nakhon, 63 **F5**

Phra Pradeng, 63 **F4**
Phuket, 61 **A3**
Piacenza, 24 **B5**
Piana del Sole, 40 **B5**
Picasso Mus, Fr 29 **F2**
Picasso Mus, Spain 38 **E6**
Picayune, MS 120 **B2**
Piccadilly Circus, 27 **B2**
Pickering, 116 **B4**
Pico de Aneto, 16 **C4**
Pico de Bandeira, 85 **G1**
Pico de Orizaba, 96 **D3**
Pico Duarte, 95 **E4**
Pico Rivera, CA 170 **D4**
Piedmont, CA 174 **C5**
Piedmont Park, GA 152 **C4**
Piedras Negras, 128 **D2**
Pierre, SD 110 **F6**, 126 **D5**, 178 **D5**
Pierrefonds, 106 **A3**
Pietermaritzburg, 47 **F2**
Pietralata, 40 **C6**
Piety Corner, MA 139 **B4**
Pijnacker, 30 **B3**
Pike NF, CO 127 **A3**
Pikes Pk, CO 110 **E5**, 127 **A3**, 130 **E5**
Pikesville, MD 147 **C4**
Pikeville, KY 118 **B2**
Pila, 22 **C7**
Pilcomayo R, 84 **D1**, 86 **B6**
Pilgram Creek, WY 181 **G5**
Pilgrim Mem SP, MA 184 **A7**
Pilisvörösvár, 42 **A8**
Pilot Pk, NV 135 **F1**
Pilot Rock, OR 134 **D4**
Pima Pt, AZ 183 **D2**
Pimlico Race Course, MD 147 **C3**
Pimmit Hills, VA 148 **B7**
Pinar del Rio, 94 **A5**
Pinchot NF, Gifford, WA 177 **H6**

Pindus Mts, 25 **E4**
Pine Bluff, AR 113 **A4**, 129 **G5**
Pine Grove, FL 153 **H1**
Pine Hills, FL 153 **F4**
Pine Island SF, MN 126 **F8**
Pine Lake, GA 152 **D4**
Pine Lawn, MO 162 **B2**
Pine Orchard, MD 147 **A3**
Pine Ridge, SD 126 **C5**
Pine Ridge IR, SD 126 **C5**, 130 **F7**
Pine Springs, MN 161 **F3**
Pine Springs, TX 131 **E1**
Pinedale, WY 135 **G2**
Pinehurst, MA 138 **B6**
Pinellas NWR, FL 154 **B3**
Pinellas Park, FL 154 **B4**
Pinerolo, 24 **A5**
Pineville, KY 118 **B1**
Piney Pt, FL 122 **D5**
Piney Pt Village, TX 166 **A4**
Pingdingshan, 67 **A4**
Pinghsi, 62 **D5**
Pinglin, 62 **D4**
Pingxiang, 67 **A3**
Pinnacles NM, CA 178 **A4**
Pinole, CA 174 **C7**
Pintendre, 105 **F2**
Pioche, NV 131 **A4**, 132 **F5**
Pioneer Village, 104 **D7**
Piraeus, 25 **F3**
Piratininga, 91 **E2**
Pireas, 43 **B2**
Pirgos, 25 **E3**
Piriniccikoy, 43 **D3**
Pirituba, 92 **A5**
Pirogovo, 56 **C6**
Pirque, 87 **G1**
Pisa, 17 **E4**, 24 **B4**
Pisgah, OH 151 **E4**
Pisgah NF, NC 121 **E5**
Pismo Beach, CA 133 **B3**
Pistakee Highlands, IL 158 **A8**
Pitcairn, 81 **F3**

Pitchstone Plateau, WY 180 **B2**

Pitlochry, 18 **D6**

Pittsburg, CA 174 **E7**

Pittsburgh, PA 112 **D5**, 118 **D5**, 146 **D7**, 179 **G4**

Pittsburgh, U of, PA 146 **C6**

Pittsburgh Civic Area, PA 146 **C6**

Pittsburgh Zoo, PA 146 **D7**

Pittsfield, ME 114 **D5**

Pittsfield, MA 115 **A3**, 117 **H2**

Pittsfield, NH 115 **C3**

Piura, 84 **B3**

Piute Mt, CA 182 **B5**

Place Charles de Gaulle, 29 **B3**

Place de la Bastille, 29 **F2**

Place de la Concorde, 29 **D3**

Place de la République, 29 **F3**

Place des Ternes, 29 **B4**

Place Royale, 105 **F3**

Placentia, CA 171 **E3**

Placentia Isl, ME 186 **B1**

Plainfield, IL 159 **A3**

Plainfield, NJ 116 **A5**

Plains of Abraham, 105 **E3**

Plainview, TX 111 **E4**, 128 **D5**

Planetarium & Jan Smut House, 51 **G3**

Plano, TX 129 **F4**, 165 **G6**

Plantation, FL 155 **F4**, 188 **F3**

Plantation Key, FL 188 **E3**

Plaster Rock, 114 **F8**

Plateau of Tibet, 58 **E6**

Platte R, 110 **F5**, 127 **D4**, 178 **D4**

Plattsburgh, NY 114 **A5**, 117 **H6**

Plattsmouth, NE 125 **A4**

Plaza de Armeria, 39 **B3**

Plaza de la Constitución, 89 **D1**

Plaza de Mayo, 88 **E7**, 89 **D3**

Plaza de Miserere, 89 **B2**

Plaza de Toros, 39 **C3**

Plaza de Toros Mon, 38 **E6**

Plaza del Congreso, 89 **C2**

Plaza Dorrego, 89 **D2**

Plaza General Lavalle, 89 **C3**

Plaza Libertad San Martin, 89 **D3**

Plaza Mexico, 98 **B3**

Plaza San Martín, 88 **E7**

Plaza V López, 89 **C4**

Pleasant Bay, MA 184 **F5**

Pleasant Hill, CA 174 **D6**

Pleasant Hills, PA 146 **C5**

Pleasant Lake, MA 184 **E5**

Pleasant Run, OH 151 **C4**

Pleasant View, CO 167 **F3**

Pleasanton, CA 175 **F4**

Pleasanton Ridge RP, CA 175 **E4**

Plessisville, 114 **B7**

Pleven, 17 **H4**, 25 **G6**

Pljevlja, 25 **E6**

Ploiesti, 17 **H4**

Plovdiv, 17 **H4**, 25 **G5**

Plum, PA 146 **F7**

Plumas NF, CA 132 **C6**

Plumpton, 78 **A8**

Plymouth, CA 132 **C5**

Plymouth, IL 153 **F5**

Plymouth, MA 115 **C2**, 184 **A7**

Plymouth, MN 161 **A3**

Plymouth, NH 115 **B4**

Plymouth, UK 16 **B6**, 19 **D2**, 20 **C7**

Plymouth Bay, MA 184 **A7**

Plymouth Meeting, PA 144 **C5**

Plymouth Plantation, MA 184 **A7**

Plzen, 17 **E6**, 23 **E3**

Po R, 16 **D4**, 24 **B5**

Poá, 92 **D5**

Pocahontas, AR 120 **A6**, 125 **C1**, 129 **H6**

Pocasset, MA 184 **A5**

Pocatello, ID 110 **C6**, 130 **B7**, 135 **F2**

Pocosin Lakes NWR, NC 187 **E4**

Podgorica, 17 **G3**, 25 **E5**

Podol'sk, 56 **B1**

Poeldijk, 30 **A3**

Pogliano, 40 **A3**

Pohang, 66 **D5**

Point Arena, CA 132 **A6**

Point Barrow, AK 82 **B6**, 100 **B7**, 136 **C8**

Point Brown, WA 134 **A5**

Point Defiance Park, WA 176 **A3**

Point Gammon, MA 185 **E4**

Point Harbor, NC 187 **G6**

Point Hope, AK 100 **A8**, 136 **B8**

Point Imperial, AZ 183 **E3**

Point Judith, RI 115 **C1**

Point Loma, CA 169 **E4**

Point Lookout, NY 143 **H1**

Point Pelee, 118 **C6**

Point Petre, 116 **D4**

Point Pleasant, OH 118 **C3**

Point Reyes NS, CA 178 **A4**

Point SP, PA 146 **B6**

Point Sublime, AZ 183 **D2**

Pointe-à-Pitre, 95 **H3**

Pointe aux Pins, 118 **C6**

Pointe aux Trembles, 106 **D4**

Pointe-Claire, 106 **B2**

Pointe Gatineau, 105 **B4**

Pointe-Noire, 46 **D6**

Poissy, 28 **B7**

Poitiers, 20 **D5**

Pok Fu Lam, 75 **B2**

Pok Fu Lam CP, 75 **B2**

Pokhara, 58 **D6**

Poland, 15 **E1**, 17 **F6**, 23 **F4**

Polar Plateau, 83 **D3**

Polba, 65 **E4**

Police, 22 **E5**

Pollux Pk, WY 180 **D4**

Polonezköy, 43 **F3**

Polpis, MA 185 **G6**

Polynesian Cultural Ctr, HI 137 **D3**

Polytechnical Mus, *Russia* 57 **F6**

Pom Prap Sattru Phai, 63 **F5**

Pomáz, 42 **A8**

Pomeroy, OH 118 **C3**

Pomona, CA 171 **E4**

Pompano Beach, FL 123 **G2**, 155 **G5**

Pompeys Pillar, MT 130 **D8**

Ponca City, OK 127 **E1**, 129 **E6**

Ponce, 95 **F3**, 122 **B1**

Ponce de Leon Bay, FL 123 **F1**, 188 **C4**

Pond Inlet, 102 **A7**

Pondicherry, 59 **C3**

Ponferrada, 21 **B4**

Ponkapoag, MA 139 **C1**

Ponta Grossa, 86 **C6**

Pontchartrain, 28 **A6**

Ponte Galeria, 40 **B4**

Pontiac, IL 125 **D4**

Pontiac, MI 125 **F4**

Pontianak, 61 **C2**

Pontoise, 28 **B8**

Pontonnyy, 57 **H1**

Pontoon Beach, IL 162 **D3**

Pont-Viau, 106 **B3**

Poopenaut Valley, CA 182 **A4**

Popayan, 84 **B4**

Poplar Bluff, MO 113 **B4**, 120 **A6**, 125 **C1**, 129 **H6**

Poplar Creek FP, IL 158 **A5**

Popponesset Beach, MA 185 **E3**

Porcupine R, AK 136 **D7**

Pordenone, 23 **D1**, 24 **C5**

Pori, 15 **F3**

Port Angeles, WA 134 **B6**

Port Arthur, TX 129 **G3**

Port-au-Prince, 94 **D3**

Port Augusta, 76 **D3**

Port Charlotte, FL 123 **E3**

Port Clinton, OH 118 **B6**

Port Colborne, 116 **B3**

Port Costa, CA 174 **C7**

Port Credit, 104 **C5**

Port Elizabeth, 47 **F2**

Port-Gentil, 46 **D6**

Port Harcourt, 44 **C1**

Port Hardy, 101 **B3**

Port Hedland, 76 **A5**

Port Huron, MI 124 **F5**

Port Jackson, 78 **F7**

Port Jefferson, NY 116 **C6**

Port Johnson, NY 115 **A1**

Port Lavaca, TX 129 **F2**

Port Lincoln, 76 **C3**

Port Macquarie, 77 **F3**

Port Madison, WA 176 **A5**

Port Madison IR, WA 176 **A6**

Port Melbourne, 79 **B2**

Port Moresby, 76 **C1**, 80 **B4**

Port-of-Spain, 95 **H1**

Port Orange, FL 123 **F5**

Port Orchard, WA 134 **B5**

Port Orford, OR 132 **A8**, 134 **A3**

Port Phillip Bay, 79 **B1**

Port Pirie, 76 **D3**

Port Richmond, NY 142 **B2**

Port Said, 45 **F4**, 48 **C5**

Port St Joe, FL 122 **C5**

Port St Lucie, FL 123 **F3**

Port Salerno, FL 123 **F3**

Port Sudan, 45 **G3**, 48 **D2**

Port Townsend, WA 134 **B6**

Port Union, OH 151 **D4**

Port-Villa, 80 **C3**

Port Washington, NY 143 **G5**

Portadown, 19 **B4**

Portage, IL 125 **E4**

Portage, ME 114 **E7**

Portage, WA 176 **B3**

Portage la Prairie, 101 **F2**

Portales, NM 131 **F3**

Porterville, CA 133 **D4**

Portland, IN 118 **A5**

Portland, ME 103 **E1**, 112 **F7**, 115 **D4**, 179 **H5**

Portland, OR 101 **B1**, 110 **A7**, 134 **B4**, 177 **G5**, 178 **A6**

Portland Intl Arpt, OR 177 **G6**

Portland SU, OR 177 **G5**

Porto, 16 **A3**, 21 **A3**, 44 **B6**

Pôrto Alegre, 86 **C5**

Porto-Novo, 44 **C1**

Porto Salvo, 38 **A6**

Pôrto Velho, 84 **D3**

Portola, CA 132 **C6**

Portola SP, CA 175 **C1**

Portola Valley, CA 175 **C2**

Portoviejo, 84 **B4**

Portree, 18 **C6**

Portsmouth, NH 112 **F6**, 115 **C3**

Portsmouth, OH 118 **B3**, 125 **F3**

Portsmouth, UK 16 **C6**, 19 **E2**, 20 **D7**

Portsmouth, VA 112 **E5**, 119 **G1**

Portsmouth Isl, NC 187 **E1**

Portsmouth Village, NC 187 **F1**

Portuense, 40 **B5**

Portugal, 16 **A3**, 21 **A3**, 44 **B5**

Posadas, 86 **C6**

Postholes, The, WY 181 **G4**

Poteau, OK 129 **F5**

Potenza, 24 **D3**

Potomac, MD 148 **B8**

Potomac R, MD 148 **D5**

Potosí, 84 **D1**

Potsdam, Ger 23 **E4**, 32 **B6**

Potsdam, NY 117 **F6**

Potsdamerplatz, 33 **D3**

Potters Bar, 26 **C8**

Pottstown, PA 119 **G4**

Pottsville, PA 119 **G5**

Poughkeepsie, NY 117 **H1**, 119 **H6**

Poultney, VT 115 **A4**

Povoa de Santa Iria, 38 **C8**

Povungnituk, 103 **B4**

Poway, CA 133 **E2**, 169 **H6**

Powder Horn Park, MN 161 **C2**

Powell, WY 130 **D8**

Powellhurst, OR 177 **G5**

Powells Pt, NC 187 **F6**

Poyang Hu, 67 **B3**

Poyang Hu Lake, 60 **C6**

Poydras, LA 163 **H4**

Poza Rica, 96 **D3**

Poznan, 17 **F6**, 23 **F4**

Pozuelo de Alarcon, 39 **A3**

Praça da Liberdade, 93 **G2**

Praça Da Republica, 93 **F4**

Prado Mus, 39 **C2**

Prados de Ecatepec, 98 **C6**

Prague, 17 **E6**, 23 **E3**, 35 **E3**

Praia Grande, 92 **C1**

Prairie Village, KS 162 **B4**

Prairie du Chien, WI 124 **C5**

Prater Mus, 42 **E7**

Prato, 24 **B4**

Pratt, KS 127 **E2**

Prawet, 63 **F3**

Precolumbian Mus, 87 **G3**

Pregnana, 40 **A3**

Prenestino, 40 **C5**

Prenzlauer Berg, 32 **D7**

Prescott, AZ 111 **C4**, 131 **B3**

Presidente Prudente, 85 **F1**

Presidential Palace, 87 **G5**

Presidential Palace & Natl Mon, 64 **B7**

Presidio,The CA 173 **A3**

Presque Isle, ME 112 **F7**, 114 **E7**

Presque Isle, PA 118 **D6**

Preston, Austral 79 **C3**

Preston, ID 135 **G1**

Preston, UK 19 **D4**

Prestonburg, KY 118 **B2**

Pretoria / Tshwane, 47 **F3**, 51 **H6**

Pretoria Church Square, 51 **G6**

Pretoria Natl Zoological Gdn, 51 **G6**

Pretty Marsh, ME 186 **A4**

Pretty Marsh Harbor, ME 186 **A4**

Preveza, 25 **E3**

Pribilof Islands, AK 136 **A6**

Price, UT 130 **C5**

Price Pk, CA 182 **C5**

Prilep, 25 **F5**

Primavalle, 40 **B6**

Prince Albert, 101 **E3**

Prince Charles Isl, 102 **B6**

Prince Edward Pt, 116 **D4**

Prince Frederick, MD 119 **G3**

Prince George, 101 **C3**

Prince of Wales Isl, 100 **F6**

Prince of Wales Mus, 65 **B1**

Princeton, IL 125 **D4**

Princeton, IN 125 **D2**

Princeton, NJ 119 **H5**

Princeton, KY 120 **C6**

Princeton, WV 118 **D2**

Principe, 46 **C6**

Prineville, OR 134 **C3**

Prins Hendrick Maritime Mus, 30 **B2**

Pristina, 25 **E5**
Progress Village, FL 154 **D4**
Prome, 59 **F4**
Promontory, UT 130 **B6**
Promontory, WY 180 **C2**
Pro Player Stad, FL 155 **G3**
Prospect Creek, AZ 183 **A3**
Prospect Hts, IL 158 **B5**
Prospect Park, PA 144 **C1**
Prosser, WA 134 **C4**
Prostejov, 23 **F3**
Providence, RI 112 **F6**, 115 **C2**
Providencia, 87 **G3**
Providenya, 54 **F8**
Providenya, 136 **A7**
Province Lands Visitor Ctr, MA 184 **D8**
Provincetown, MA 115 **D2**, 184 **D8**
Provincetown Harbor, MA 184 **D8**
Provo, UT 110 **C5**, 130 **B5**
Prudential Ctr, MA 140 **A3**
Prudhoe Bay, AK 136 **D8**
Pruhonice, 35 **F2**
Prut R, 17 **H5**
Pskov, 15 **G2**, 52 **B5**
Pucallpa, 84 **C3**
Puch'on, 72 **B6**
Pudahuel, 87 **E3**
Puebla, 96 **D3**
Pueblo, CO 110 **E5**, 127 **B2**, 131 **F4**
Pueblo Libre, 87 **F5**
Puente Alto, 87 **G1**
Puente de Vallecas, 39 **D2**
Puente Grande, 99 **H4**
Puerto Ayacueho, 84 **D5**
Puerto Barrios, 97 **F2**
Puerto Escondido, 96 **D2**
Puerto Limon, 97 **G1**
Puerto Maldonado, 84 **D2**
Puerto Montt, 86 **A4**
Puerto Peñasco, 96 **A6**, 131 **A1**

Puerto Princesa, 61 **D4**
Puerto Rico, 95 **F4**
Puget Sound Naval Shipyard, WA 176 **A5**
Puisieux-Pontoise, 28 **B8**
Puk, 72 **A6**
Pukalani, HI 137 **E3**
Puk'ansan NP, 72 **C8**
Pukaskwa NP, 124 **E7**
Pula, 24 **C5**
Pulaski, NY 117 **E4**
Pulaski, VA 118 **D1**
Pulau Ubin, 63 **H3**
Pulkovo, 57 **G1**
Pulkovo Arpt, 57 **F1**
Pune, 59 **B4**
Punggol, 63 **G3**
Punjabi Bagh, 64 **D7**
Puno, 84 **D1**
Punta Alta, 86 **B4**
Punta Arenas, 86 **A3**
Punta Brea, 122 **B1**
Punta Gorda, FL 123 **E3**
Punta Santíago, 122 **C2**
Punta Yeguas, 122 **C1**
Puntarenas, 97 **G1**
Puras, 84 **D3**
Pusan, 55 **F1**, 60 **D8**, 66 **D5**
Pushkin Mus of Fine Arts, 57 **E4**
Pushkino, 56 **D6**
Puskin, 57 **G1**
Putnam, CT 115 **B2**
Putte, 31 **H4**
Puttgarden, 22 **D5**
Putumayo R, 84 **C4**
Putuo District, 74 **B7**
Puuhonuao Honaunau NHP, HI 137 **E1**
Puurs, 31 **F4**
Puyallup, WA 176 **B1**
Pymble, 78 **D8**
Pyokche, 72 **C8**
Pyongyang, 55 **F2**, 60 **D8**, 66 **C5**
Pyramid Lake, NV 132 **C6**

Pyramid Lake IR, NV 132 **C7**
Pyramid Pk, WY 180 **D4**
Pyramids of Giza, 50 **B1**
Pyrenees Mts, 16 **C4**, 21 **D4**

Q

Qaanaaq, 82 **D6**, 102 **A8**
Qandahar, 58 **A7**
Qaqortok, 102 **E6**
Qaraghandy, 53 **E2**
Qarshi, 53 **D1**
Qatar, 45 **H4**, 49 **G3**
Qattara Depression, 45 **F4**, 48 **C4**
Qazvin, 49 **F6**
Qeqertarsuaq, 102 **C7**
Qibya, 50 **C5**
Qingdao, 55 **E1**, 60 **C7**, 66 **C5**
Qinghai Hu Lake, 58 **F7**
Qinghuayuan, 73 **D4**
Qinhuangdao, 66 **B5**
Qiqian, 60 **B8**
Qiqihar, 55 **E3**, 66 **C7**
Qom, 49 **F6**
Quail Valley, CA 171 **H2**
Quantico US Marine Corps Reserve, VA 119 **F3**
Quanzhou, 67 **B2**
Quartzsite, AZ 133 **F3**
Québec, 103 **D2**, 105 **E3**, 112 **E7**, 114 **B8**
Québec Aquarium, 105 **E2**
Québec City, 114 **B7**
Queen Charlotte Isl, 101 **A3**, 136 **F5**
Queen Elizabeth Isl, 82 **C5**
Queen Emma Summer Palace, HI 177 **H2**
Queen Mary, CA 170 **C2**
Queen Maud Land, 83 **E2**
Queen Maud Mts, 83 **D4**
Queens, NY 116 **B5**, 141 **H4**, 143 **E3**
Queensland, 77 **E4**

Queenstown, 63 **F1**, 77 **E2**
Queimados, 91 **A4**
Quelimane, 47 **G4**
Queluz, 38 **A7**
Querétaro, 96 **D3**
Quetico PP, 124 **C7**
Quetta, 58 **B6**
Quezaltenango, 97 **E2**
Quezon City, 62 **C3**
Qui Nhon, 61 **C4**
Quiapo Church, 62 **C2**
Quidnet, MA 185 **G6**
Quilicura, 87 **F3**
Quilmes, 88 **F6**
Quincy, CA 132 **B6**
Quincy, FL 122 **D6**
Quincy, IL 112 **B5**, 125 **C3**
Quincy, MA 115 **C2**, 139 **E2**
Quincy Market, MA 140 **D4**
Quinta Normal, 87 **F3**
Quinto Romano, 40 **B1**
Quiryat Mal'akhi, 50 **A5**
Quiryat 'Eqron, 50 **B5**
Quitman, GA 121 **E2**, 122 **D6**
Quito, 84 **B4**
Qujialang, 74 **C6**
Qustanay, 53 **D3**
Qyzylorda, 53 **D2**, 58 **B8**

R

Raasdorf, 42 **F8**
Raba, 61 **E1**
Rabat, 16 **A1**, 44 **B5**
Rabaul, 76 **D2**, 80 **B4**
Raccoon Key, FL 188 **B2**
Race Pt, MA 184 **D8**
Racine, WI 112 **B6**, 125 **D4**
Radevormwald, 34 **E5**
Radisson, 103 **C3**
Radnor, PA 144 **B4**
Radom, 17 **G6**
Radotín, 35 **D2**
Rafferty Pk, CA 182 **D3**

Rafael Castillo, 88 **C6**
Raffles Park, 63 **E2**
Raft, 37 **E3**
Ragged Pk, CA 182 **D4**
Raging Waters Theme
  Park, CA 171 **E5**
Ragusa, 24 **C1**
Rahkot, 58 **B5**
Rahway, NJ 142 **A3**
Railway Sta, 63 **F5**
Rainy Lake, 124 **B8**
Raipur, 58 **D5**
Raj Ghat, 64 **E7**
Rajpur, 65 **E1**
Rajshahi, 58 **E5**
Rákoscsaba, 42 **C7**
Rákoshegy, 42 **C7**
Rákoskert, 42 **C7**
Rákospalota, 42 **B8**
Raleigh, NC 113 **E4**, 121 **C6**
Ramallah, 50 **D5**
Ramanhati, 65 **D3**
Ramblewood, NJ 145 **H2**
Rambouillet, 28 **A5**
Ramla, 50 **B6**
Ramos, 91 **D2**
Ramrod Key, FL 188 **B2**
Rancagua, 86 **A5**
Ranchi, 58 **D5**
Rancho Cucamonga, CA
  171 **F5**
Rancho Grande, 92 **C3**
Rancho Palos Verdes CA,
  170 **B2**
Rancho Rinconada, CA
  175 **E1**
Rancho Santa Margarita,
  CA 171 **G1**
Rand Arpt, 51 **G2**
Randallstown, MD 147 **B4**
Randburg, 51 **F3**
Randolph, MA 139 **D1**
Randolph, MO 162 **D6**
Randolph, UT 135 **G1**
Randolph AFB, TX 163 **H3**
Randwick, 78 **F6**
Rangeley, ME 114 **C5**

Rangoon, 59 **F4**
Rangsdorf, 32 **D5**
Rankin Inlet, 100 **F5**
Ranst, 31 **H6**
Rapid City, SD 110 **E6**,
  126 **B5**, 130 **F7**, 178 **D5**
Raquette Lake, NY 117 **F4**
Rasht, 49 **F6**
Rat Burana, 63 **F4**
Ratak Chain, 80 **C5**
Ratcha Thewi, 63 **G6**
Rath, 34 **B5**
Ratingen, 34 **B6**
Raton, NM 127 **B1**,
  128 **C6**, 131 **E4**
Ravena, NY 117 **G2**
Ravenna, 24 **C5**
Ravenswood, IN 157 **E3**
Rawalpindi, 58 **B7**
Rawhide, AZ 168 **C6**
Rawlins, WY 130 **D6**
Rawson, 86 **B4**
Raymond James Stad, FL
  154 **C5**
Raytown, MO 162 **D4**
Razmetelevo, 57 **H2**
Reach RA, AZ 168 **C5**
Reading, MA 138 **D5**
Reading, OH 151 **E3**
Reading, PA 112 **E6**,
  119 **G5**
Reading, UK 19 **E2**
Real del Castillo, 133 **E1**
Real Felipe Castle & Mus,
  87 **E5**
Recife, 85 **H2**
Recklinghausen, 34 **D8**
Recoleta, Arg 89 **B4**
Recoleta, Chile 87 **G3**
Recoleta Cemetery, 89 **C4**
Reconquista, 86 **B6**
Red Bluff CA, 132 **B6**
Red Deer, 101 **D3**
Red Fort, 64 **E7**
Red Lake, MN 126 **F7**
Red Lake IR, MN 124 **A7**
Red Lodge, MT 135 **H4**

Red Mts, WY 180 **B2**
Red Oak, GA 152 **A1**
Red Oak, IA 127 **F4**
Red R, 101 **F1**
Red R, 111 **F4**, 113 **A3**,
  129 **G4**, 179 **E2**
Red River, NM 127 **A1**,
  131 **E4**
Red River of the North, MN
  124 **A7**
Red Rocks Park, CO
  167 **E2**
Red Sea, 45 **G3**, 48 **D3**
Red Square, 57 **F5**
Red Wing, MN 124 **B5**
Redbridge, 26 **D7**
Redding, CA 110 **A6**,
  132 **B7**, 134 **B1**
Redfield, SD 126 **D6**
Redhill, 26 **C5**
Redington Beach, FL 154 **A4**
Redington Shores, FL
  154 **A4**
Redlands, CA 171 **H4**
Redlands Bowl, CA 171 **H5**
Redmond, WA 176 **D6**
Redondo Beach, CA 170 **B3**
Redway, CA 132 **A6**
Redwood City, CA 132 **B5**,
  175 **C3**
Redwood NP, CA 132 **A7**,
  134 **A1**, 178 **A5** ●
Redwood RP, CA 174 **D5**
Reedley, CA 133 **C4**
Reedsport, OR 134 **A3**
Reerslev, 36 **A5**
Reese R, NV 132 **D6**
Refuge Hdqrs, WY 181 **F1**
Regattastrecke, 32 **E6**
Regensburg, 17 **E5**, 23 **D2**
Regensdorf, 37 **E2**
Regent's Park, 27 **A4**
Reggio di Calabria, 17 **F2**,
  24 **D2**
Regina, 101 **E2**, 110 **E8**
Rehovot, 50 **A5**
Reichstag, 33 **D3**

Reigate, 26 **C5**
Reims, 20 **E7**, 23 **A3**
Reinckendorf, 32 **C7**
Reindeer Lake, 101 **E3**
Reisenberg, 42 **F5**
Rembrandt House, 30 **D6**
Remington, OH 151 **F3**
Remscheid, 34 **D5**
Renaissance Ctr, MI
  156 **D6**
Renca, 87 **F3**
Rendezvous Mts, WY 181 **E2**
Rendon, TX 164 **C1**
Renfrew, 107 **G2**
Renmin Park, 74 **D6**
Rennes, 16 **C5**, 20 **C6**
Reno, NV 110 **B5**, 132 **C6**,
  178 **A4**
Rensselaer, IN 125 **E4**
Renton, WA 176 **D4**
Repentigny, 106 **D5**
Republic, WA 134 **D6**
Repulse Bay, Can 102 **A5**
Repulse Bay, Hong Kong
  75 **D1**
Resarö, 36 **F7**
Reservation Pk, WY 180 **D3**
Reservoir, 79 **C3**
Resistencia, 86 **B6**
Resolute, 82 **C5**, 100 **F7**
Retiro, Arg 89 **D4**
Retiro, Spain 39 **C3**
Retiro Sta, 88 **E7**, 89 **D4**
Retta, TX 164 **C1**
Reutov, 56 **D4**
Revelstoke, 101 **C2**
Revere, MA 139 **E4**
Revesby, 78 **C6**
Revnice, 35 **D1**
Rexburg, ID 130 **B7**, 135 **G3**
Rexdale, 104 **C7**
Rexhame, MA 184 **A8**
Reykjavik, 14 **A5**, 82 **F6**
Reynosa, 96 **D4**, 128 **D1**
Rhawnhurst, PA 145 **F5**
Rheinberg, 34 **A8**
Rheinhaussen, 34 **A7**

Rheinkamp, 34 **A7**

Rhine, 16 **D5**

Rhine R, 20 **F6**, 23 **B2**

Rhinebeck, NY 117 **G1**

Rhinelander, WI 124 **D6**

Rho, 40 **A3**

Rhode Island, 103 **D1**,
112 **E6**, 115 **C2**, 179 **H5**

Rhodes, 17 **H2**, 25 **H2**,
48 **C5**

Rhodope Mts, 25 **F5**

Rhome, TX 164 **A6**

Rhône R, 16 **D4**, 20 **E5**

Rialto, CA 171 **G5**

Rialto, OH 151 **D4**

Ribas de Jarama, 39 **F2**

Ribbon Falls, CA 182 **B3**

Ribeirão Pires, 92 **C3**

Ribeirão Prêto, 85 **F1**

Riberalta, 84 **D2**

Riccar Art Mus, 69 **D2**

Rice U, TX 166 **B3**

Richardson, TX 165 **G5**

Richardson FP, OH 151 **C4**

Richardson Mts, 136 **E8**

Richelieu R, 114 **A6**

Richfield, ID 135 **F2**

Richfield, MN 161 **C1**

Richfield, UT 110 **C5**,
130 **B5**

Richland Ctr, WI 124 **C5**

Richland Hills, TX 164 **C4**

Richmond, CA 174 **B6**

Richmond, Can 107 **G1**

Richmond, IN 118 **A4**,
125 **E3**

Richmond, KY 118 **A3**,
125 **F2**

Richmond, VA 112 **E5**,
119 **F2**

Richmond Hts, OH 150 **F8**

Richmond Hts, MO 162 **B2**

Richmond Hill, Can,
104 **D8**

Richmond Hill, NY 143 **F3**

Richmond upon Thames,
26 **C7**

Richton Park, IL 159 **C1**

Rickmansworth, 26 **B8**

Ridderkerk, 30 **C2**

Rideau Hall, 105 **B3**

Rideau R, 117 **E6**

Ridgecrest, CA 133 **E4**

Ridgefield, NJ 142 **D5**

Ridgefield Park, NJ 142 **C6**

Ridgewood, NY 143 **E3**

Ridley Creek SP, PA 144 **A3**

Ridley Park, PA 144 **C1**

Rietvlei Nature Reserve,
51 **H5**

Rift Valley, 45 **G1**, 47 **F5**

Riga, 15 **G2**, 52 **B5**

Rigby, ID 135 **G3**

Riggins, ID 135 **E4**

Riggisberg, 37 **B1**

Riiser-Larsen Ice Shelf,
83 **E3**

Riiser-Larsen Pen, 83 **E2**

Rijeka, 17 **F4**, 24 **C5**

Rijnsburg, 30 **B4**

Rijokri, 64 **D6**

Rijswijk, 30 **A3**

Riksten, 36 **E5**

Rímac, 87 **F5**

Rimforest, CA 171 **H6**

Rimini, 24 **C5**

Rimouski, 103 **D2**

Ringwood, Austral 79 **F2**

Ringwood, NJ 116 **A6**

Rio Branco, 84 **D2**

Rio Comprido, 91 **D2**

Rio Conchos R, 128 **B2**

Río Cuarto, 86 **B5**

Rio de Janeiro, 86 **D6**,
91 **C2**

Rio de Janeiro Intl Arpt,
91 **D3**

Río de la Plata, 86 **B5**, 89 **F4**

Rio Dell, CA 132 **A7**,
134 **A1**

Río Gallegos, 86 **A3**

Rio Grande, 96 **D5**, 111 **E2**

Rio Grande City, TX 129 **E1**

Rio Grande da Serra, 92 **C3**

Rio Grande NF, CO 131 **D4**

Rio Grande R, 128 **B6**,
131 **E1**, 178 **C2**

Rio Rancho, NM 128 **B6**,
131 **D3**

Rio Salado R, 128 **D1**

Rio Vista, MA 138 **A5**

Ripley, MS 129 **H5**

Ripley, WV 118 **C3**

Ri'ppollet, 38 **E7**

Rishon Leziyyon, 50 **A5**

Rishra, 65 **E3**

Risør, 22 **C7**

Rita Blanca NG, TX 127 **C1**

Ritchie, MD 148 **F6**

Ritzville, WA 134 **D5**

Rivaköy, 43 **F4**

River Hills, WI 157 **B4**

River Neck, NC 187 **E6**

River Oaks, TX 164 **B3**

River Pines, MA 138 **B6**

River Ridge, LA 163 **H5**

River Rouge, MI 156 **D5**

River Rouge Park, MI 156 **B6**

Rivera, 86 **C5**

Riverbend Nature Ctr, VA
148 **A8**

Riverdale, IL 159 **D2**

Riverdale, MD 148 **E7**

Rivergrove, OR 177 **F4**

Riverhead, NY 115 **B1**,
116 **C6**

Riverside, CA 111 **B4**,
133 **E3**, 171 **H4**

Riverside, MO 162 **C6**

Riverside, NJ 145 **G4**

Riverside Church, NY
142 **D5**

Riverside Park, IN 157 **E3**

Riverside Park, NY 141 **F6**

Riverton, NJ 145 **G4**

Riverton, WY 130 **D7**

Riverview, MI 156 **D5**

Riverview Park, PA 146 **B7**

Riverwoods, IL 158 **B6**

Riviera Beach, FL 123 **G3**

Rivière-à-Pierre, 114 **B8**

Rivière-aux-Rats, 114 **A8**

Riviere-du-Loup, 103 **D2**

Rivière-Matawin, 114 **A7**

Riyadh, 45 **H4**, 49 **F3**

Rizal Mem Coliseum, 62 **C2**

Roanoke, TX 164 **C6**

Roanoke, VA 112 **D5**,
118 **D1**, 121 **G6**

Roanoke Isl, NC 187 **G5**

Roanoke Rapids, NC 121 **H6**

Roanoke Sd, NC 187 **G5**

Robbinsdale, MN 161 **B3**

Robertsdale, AL 122 **A6**

Robinson Mt, MT 135 **K6**

Rochelle Park, NJ 142 **C6**

Rochester, MN 112 **A6**,
124 **B5**

Rochester, NH 115 **C4**

Rochester, NY 112 **E6**,
116 **D3**

Rochester Park, TX 165 **G3**

Rock Creek Park, DC
148 **D7**

Rock Hill, MO 162 **B1**

Rock Hill, SC 121 **F5**

Rock Isl, IL 112 **B5**, 125 **C4**

Rock Springs, WY 110 **D6**,
130 **C6**

Rockaway Beach, NY 143 **E1**

Rockburn Branch Park, MD
147 **B1**

Rockcliffe Park, 105 **B3**

Rockdale, Austral 78 **E6**

Rockdale, MD 147 **B3**

Rockefeller Ctr, NY 141 **G5**

Rockefeller Mem Parkway,
John D Jr, WY 180 **B3**

Rockefeller Park, OH 150 **E7**

Rockford, IL 112 **B6**, 125 **D4**

Rockhampton, 77 **F4**

Rockingham, NC 121 **G5**

Rockland, ME 114 **E5**

Rockledge, PA 145 **F5**

Rockville, MD 119 **F3**

Rockville Ctr, NY 143 **H2**

Rockwood, ME 114 **D6**

Rocky Mount, NC 121 **G6**

Rocky Mount, VA 118 D1

Rocky Mountain NP, CO 127 A3, 130 E6, 178 C4

Rocky Mts, 81 G6, 101 C4, 110 D6, 130 C7, 135 E6

Rocky Pt, MA 184 B2

Rocky Pt, NY 116 C6

Rocky Pt Park, MD 147 F2

Rocky Ripple, IN 157 E3

Rocky River, OH 150 B7

Rocky River Res, OH 150 B6

Rodanthe, NC 187 H4

Rodbyhavn, 22 D5

Rodeleheim, 35 A3

Rodeo, CA 174 C7

Rodermark, 35 C1

Rodin Mus, 29 C2

Rodovre, 36 B6

Roeland Park, KS 162 B5

Rogersville, TN 118 B1

Rogue R, 132 A8

Rokko Mts, 70 A6

Rokubancho, 69 A4

Rolla, MO 113 A4, 125 B2

Rolling Meadows, IL 158 B5

Rollins Savanna FP, IL 158 B8

Roma, 77 E4

Rómaifürdő, 42 B8

Roman Forum, 41 D2

Romania, 17 G5, 25 G6, 45 E6

Romashkovo, 56 A4

Rome, GA 120 D4

Rome, Italy 17 E3, 24 C4, 40 C5, 41, 44 D6

Rome, NY 117 F3

Romeoville, IL 159 B2

Romney, WV 119 E3

Romohr Acres, OH 151 F2

Romoland, CA 171 H2

Romulus, MI 156 A5

Ronald Reagan Washington Natl Arpt, VA 148 D6

Rønne, 22 E5

Ronne Ice Shelf, 83 D3

Rönninge, 36 D5

Roodepoort, 51 E3

Roosevelt Isl, 83 B3

Roosevelt Mem, Franklin D, DC 149 B2

Rooty Hill, 78 A8

Rosamond, CA 133 D3

Rosario, 86 B5

Rosarito, 96 A6, 133 E2

Roscommon, 19 B4

Rose Ball, CA 170 C5

Rose Center for Earth & Space, NY 141 G6

Rose Garden, The, OR 177 G5

Rose Valley, PA 144 B1

Roseau, 95 H2

Rosebank, NY 142 C2

Rosebud IR, SD 126 D5

Roseburg, OR 132 A8, 134 B2

Rosedale, MD 147 E3

Rosedale, NY 143 G2

Roselle, IL 159 A4

Roselle, NJ 142 A3

Roselle Park, NJ 142 A3

Rosemead, CA 170 C5

Rosemére, 106 B4

Rosenheim, 23 D2, 24 B6

Rosersberg, 36 D8

Rosetown, 101 E2

Roseville, CA 132 C6

Roseville, MI 156 F8

Roseville, MN 161 D4

Rosh Ha'Ayin, 50 B6

Rosicrucian Egyptian Mus & Planetarium, CA 175 E2

Roskilde, 22 D6

Roslags-Näsby, 36 E7

Roslyn, PA 145 E6

Roslyn Hts, NY 143 H5

Ross, OH 151 B4

Ross Ice Shelf, 83 C3

Ross Isl, 83 B3

Ross Sea, 83 B3

Rossmore, 78 A6

Rossville, MD 147 E3

Rostock, 15 E1, 22 D5

Rostorguyevo, 56 C2

Rostov, 53 A3

Roswell, NM 111 E3, 128 B5, 131 F2

Rotebro, 36 D7

Rotorua, 77 H2

Rotterdam, 16 D6, 20 E8, 23 A4, 30 B2

Rotterdam Arpt, 30 B2

Rouen, 16 C6, 19 F1, 20 D7

Round Lake Beach, IL 158 B7

Round Rock, TX 129 E3

Roundup, MT 135 H5

Rouyn-Noranda, 103 C2, 112 D7

Rovaniemi, 15 G5

Rovereto, 23 D1

Rovigo, 24 B5

Rowland Hts, CA 171 E4

Rowlett, TX 165 H5

Rowley, MA 138 F8

Rowville, 79 E1

Roxboro, NC 119 E1

Roxborough, PA 144 D4

Roxbury, MA 139 D3

Royal Botanic Gdns, 79 C2

Royal Canadian Mint, 107 H5

Royal Festival Hall, 27 C2

Royal Oak, MI 156 C8

Royal Observatory, 26 D7

Royal Palace, Bel 31 G2

Royal Palace, Swe 36 E6

Royal Park, 79 C3

Roztoky, 35 E3

Rub al Khali, 45 H3, 49 G2

Rubí, 38 D7

Rubidoux, CA 171 G4

Rubonia, FL 154 C2

Rubtsovsk, 53 F2

Ruby Lake Natl Wildlife Rfg, NV 132 F6

Rudersdorf, 32 F6

Rudná, 35 D2

Rudow, 32 E6

Rugby, ND 126 D8

Ruidoso, NM 131 E2

Ruins of Naniwa Palace, 71 C2

Ruins of Yuanmingyuan, 73 C4

Ruisbroek, 31 F1

Rum Cove, ME 186 B1

Rumbek, 45 F1

Rumeli Hisari, 43 E3

Rumelifeneri, 43 F4

Rumford, ME 114 C5

Rumlang, 37 E2

Rumpin, 64 A6

Rungsted, 36 C8

Rupelmonde, 31 F5

Rupert, ID 130 B7, 132 F8, 135 F2

Rural Ridge, PA 146 E8

Ruse, 17 H4, 25 G6

Rushville, IN 118 A4

Ruskin, FL 154 C3

Russell, IL 158 B8

Russell Key, FL 188 E3

Russell NWR, Charles M, MT 135 H5

Russellville, AL 120 B5

Russellville, KY 120 C6

Russia, 45 G6, 52 B5, 55 B3, 66 C8

Russian Hill, CA 173 D3

Russian Mus, 57 G2

Rustenfeld, 42 E6

Ruston, WA 176 A3

Rutherford, NJ 142 C5

Rutland, VT 112 E6, 115 A4, 117 H4

Ruttenscheid, 34 C7

Ruzyne Arpt, 35 D3

Rwanda, 47 F6

Ryazan, 53 B4

Rybatskoye, 57 G1

Rydbo, 36 E7

Ryde, 78 D7

Rye, FL 154 D1

Ryegate, MT 135 H4

Ryukyu Isl, 60 **E6**, 67 **D3**

Rzhevka, 57 **G2**

S

Saarbrücken, 16 **D5**,
20 **F7**, 23 **C2**

Saarmund, 32 **C5**

Sabac, 25 **E6**

Sabadell, 38 **E7**

Sabha, 48 **A4**

Sabinas, 128 **D2**

Sabinas Hidalgo, 128 **D1**

Sabine NWR, LA 129 **G3**

Sacajawea Pk, OR 134 **D4**

Sacavém, 38 **B7**

Sachs Harbour, 100 **D7**

Sachse, TX 165 **H5**

Saco, ME 115 **C4**

Saco, MT 135 **H6**

Sacramento, CA 110 **A5**,
132 **C5**, 178 **A4**

Sacré Coeur, 29 **D4**

Saddle Brook, NJ 142 **C6**

Saddle Mountain, WY
130 **C8**, 135 **G3**, 180 **D4**

Saddle Mountain Wilderness, AZ 183 **E3**

Saddlebag Lake, CA 182 **D5**

Sadler Pk, CA 182 **D2**

Sado, 66 **E6**

Safeco Field, WA 176 **B5**

Safety Harbor, FL 154 **B5**

Säffle, 22 **D7**

Safford, AZ 131 **C2**

Safi, 44 **B5**

Sag Harbor, NY 115 **B1**,
116 **D6**

Sagamihara, 68 **A6**

Sagamore, MA 184 **B6**

Sagamore Beach, MA 184 **B6**

Sagamore Hills, OH 150 **E5**

Saginaw, MI 112 **C6**, 124 **F5**

Saginaw, TX 164 **B4**

Saguaro NM, AZ 131 **B2**,
178 **B2**

Sahara, 44 **C3**

Sahel, 44 **C2**

Sai Ying Pun, 75 **B2**

Saida, 21 **D1**

Saidpur, 58 **E5**

St Adriá de Besós, 38 **F6**

St Albans, *Austral* 79 **A3**

St Albans, NY 143 **F3**

St Albans, VT 114 **A5**,
117 **H6**

St Andrews, *Can* 114 **F6**

St Andrews, *UK* 18 **D5**

St Ann, MO 162 **A3**

St Anthony, *Can* 101 **F4**

St Anthony, ID 135 **G3**

St Anthony, MN 161 **C3**

St Apolinaris Church, 35 **E3**

St-Arnoult-en-Yvelines,
28 **B5**

St-Athanase, 114 **D8**

St Augustine, FL 113 **E4**,
121 **F1**, 123 **F5**

St Austell, 19 **C2**

St Barthelemy, 95 **G3**

St Basil's Cathedral, 57 **F5**

St Bernard, OH 151 **D2**

St Bernard SP, LA 163 **H4**

St Boniface, 107 **H5**

St Catharines, 103 **C1**

St Catherines, 116 **B3**

St Charles, MD 119 **F3**

St Clair Beach, 156 **F6**

St Clair Shores, MI 156 **F8**

St Clairsville, OH 118 **D4**

St Cloud, FL 153 **H1**

St Cloud, MN 112 **A6**,
124 **A6**, 126 **F6**

St-Constant, 106 **C1**

St Croix, 95 **G3**

St Croix R, 114 **F6**

St Cyr l'Ecole, 28 **B6**

St David's, PA 144 **B4**

St-Denis, 28 **D7**

St-Dizier, 20 **E6**, 23 **B2**

St Edward SP, WA 176 **C6**

St-Emile, 105 **D4**

St-Etienne, 20 **E5**

St-Eustache, 106 **A3**

St Francis, SD 126 **C5**

St Francis, WI 157 **C2**

St François, 106 **C4**

St-Francois R, 114

St George, NY 142 **C2**

St George, UT 110 **C5**,
131 **A4**

St George Isl, AK 136 **A5**

St Georges, *Can* 103 **D2**,
114 **C7**

St George's, *Grenada* 95 **H1**

St George's Castle, 38 **B6**

St George's Chan, 19 **C3**

St Germain, 29 **C2**

St-Germain-en-Laye, 28 **B7**

St-Germain-Laxis, 28 **F5**

St Helena, *UK* 46 **B4**

St Helens, OR 134 **B4**

St-Hubert, 106 **D3**

St-Hyacinthe, 114 **A6**

St Ignatius, MT 135 **F5**

St James' Park, 27 **C1**

St-Janvier, 106 **A5**

St Jean-Chrysostome,
105 **F2**

St-Jean-de-Boischatel,
105 **F4**

St-Jean-sur-Richelieu,
114 **A6**

St Joe NF, ID 135 **E5**

St John, *Can* 103 **E2**,
112 **F7**

St John, MO 162 **B3**

St Johns, *WI* 95 **H3**

St Johns Park, 78 **B7**

St Johns R, 114 **F7**

St John's, *Can* 103 **F3**

St John's U, NY 143 **F4**

St Johnsbury, VT 114 **B5**

St Joseph, MO 112 **A5**,
125 **A3**, 127 **F3**

St Joseph Sd, FL 154 **A5**

St Katelijne Waver, 31 **H4**

St Kilda, 79 **C2**

St Kitts & Nevis, 95 **G3**

St-Lambert, 106 **D2**

St Laurent, 106 **B3**

St Lawrence Isl, AK 54 **F8**,
82 **A6**, 136 **A7**

St Lawrence R, 103 **D2**,
112 **F7**, 114 **C8**, 179 **H6**

St Léonard, 106 **C4**

St-Léonard, 114 **E8**

St-Louis, *Afr* 44 **A3**

St Louis, MO 112 **B5**,
125 **C2**, 162 **B2**, 179 **E3**

St Louis Park, MN 161 **B2**

St Louis Zoo, MO 162 **B2**

St Lucia, 85 **E6**, 95 **H2**

St Malo, 20 **C6**

St-Marcel, 114 **D8**

St Maries, ID 135 **E5**

St Marks NWR, FL 120 **D1**

St Martin, 95 **G3**

St Marylebone, 27 **A3**

St Marys, GA 121 **F2**, 123 **F6**

St Marys, PA 119 **E5**

St Mary's Cathedral, *Austral*
78 **F7**

St Mary's Cathedral, CA
173 **C2**

St Mary's U, TX 163 **F2**

St-Maur-des-Fosses, 28 **D6**

St-Nazaire, 20 **C6**

St-Ouen-l'Aumone, 28 **C8**

St-Pacôme, 114 **D8**

St Pancras Sta, 27 **C4**

St Patrick's Cathedral, NY
141 **G4**

St Paul, MN 112 **A6**,
124 **B6**, 161 **D2**, 179 **E5**

St Paul, TX 165 **H6**

St Paul Downtown Arpt,
MN 161 **E2**

St Paul Isl, AK 136 **A6**

St Paul's Cathedral, 27 **E2**

St Pete Beach, FL 154 **A3**

St Peter, MN 124 **B5**

St Peter's Basilica, 41 **A3**

St Petersburg, FL 97 **G5**,
113 **D2**, 123 **E3**, 154 **C4**

St Petersburg, *Rus* 15 **H3**,
52 **B5**, 57 **F2**, 82 **B7**

St Petersburg/Clearwater Intl Arpt, FL 154 B5

St Petersburg Mus of Fine Arts, FL 154 B3

St-Philippe, 106 D1

St Pierre & Miquelon, 103 F3

St Redempteur, 105 E2

St Roch-de-l'Achigan, 106 C6

St-Romuald, 105 E2

St-Soupplets, 28 F8

St Stephen, 114 F6

St Stephens, WY 130 C7

St Stephen's Cathedral, 42 E7

St-Tite, 114 A7

St-Tite-des-Caps, 114 C8

St Vincent & the Grenadines, 85 E6, 95 H2

St Vincent NWR, FL 120 D1

St Vital, 107 G4

Ste Anne-des-Plaines, 106 B5

Ste Catherine, 106 C1

Ste Etienne, 16 D4

Ste-Geneviéve, 106 A3

Ste-Genevieve des-Bois, 28 D5

Ste Maria at Aracoeli, 41 D2

Ste Maria at Cosmedin, 41 D2

Ste Maria Maggiore Basilica, 41 E3

Ste-Perpérue, 114 D8

Ste-Petronille, 105 F3

Ste-Rose, 106 B4

Ste-Therése, 106 A4

Sakae, 68 F8

Sakhalin, 55 F4, 66 F8

Sakura, 68 F7

Sakuranomiya Park, 71 C4

Sakyo-Ku, 71 F3

Sala Y Gomez, 81 G3

Salalah, 49 G2

Salamanca, NY 116 B2

Salamanca, Spain 16 B3, 21 B3, 39 C3

Salario, 41 E4

Salekhard, 52 F5

Salem, India 59 C3

Salem, MA 115 C3, 138 F5

Salem, NJ 119 G4

Salem, NY 115 A3

Salem, OR 110 A7, 134 B4, 178 A6

Salem, Swe 36 D5

Salem, VA 118 D1

Salem Maritime NHS, MA 138 F6

Salerno, 17 F3, 24 C3

Salina, KS 110 F5, 127 E2

Salina Cruz, 96 D2

Salinas, CA 133 B4

Salinas, PR 122 C1

Salisbury, MD 112 E5, 119 G3

Salisbury, UK 19 E2

Salisbury Cove, ME 186 C6

Salmon, ID 110 C7, 130 A8, 135 F4

Salmon NF, ID 135 E4

Salmon River, ID 135 E3

Salmon River Reservoir, NY 117 E4

Salt Lake, HI 177 F2

Salt Lake City, India 65 F2

Salt Lake City, UT 110 C5, 130 B6, 135 G1, 178 B4

Salt Plains NWR, OK 127 E1

Salt Pond Visitor Ctr, MA 184 F6

Salt River IR, AZ 168 D4

Salta, 86 A6

Saltillo, 96 C4

Salto, 86 B5

Salton Sea, CA 133 F2

Saltsjobaden, 36 F6

Saltwater SP, WA 176 B2

Salvador, 85 H2

Salvador Dali Mus, FL 154 B3

Salvo, NC 187 H3

Salyer NWR, J Clark, ND 126 C8

Salzburg, 17 E5, 23 E2, 24 C6

Sam Houston NF, TX 129 F3

Sam Rayburn Reservoir, TX 129 F3

Samalga Pass, AK 136 A5

Samandia, 43 F2

Samar, 61 E4

Samara, 53 C4

Samarinda, 61 D2

Samarkand, 58 B8

Samarqand, 53 D1

Samoset, FL 154 C1

Sampeng Market, 63 F5

Sampit, 61 C2

Samukawa, 68 A5

San Andres Atenco, 98 A5

San Andrés Totoltepec, 98 B1

San Angelo, TX 111 E3, 128 D3

San Anselmo, CA 174 A7

San Antonio, TX 96 D5, 111 F2, 129 E2, 163 F1, 178 D1

San Antonio Coliseum, TX 163 G2

San Antonio Conv Ctr, TX 163 G2

San Antonio Intl Arpt, LA 163 G3

San Antonio Missions NHP, TX 178 D1

San Antonio de Tequendama, 90 A3

San Antonio Tlayacapan, 99 H1

San Augustín, 99 E4

San Basilio, 40 D6

San Bernabe Ocotepec, 98 A3

San Bernardino, CA 111 B4, 133 E3, 171 H5

San Bernardino NF, CA 171 F6

San Bernardo, 86 A5, 87 F1

San Blás, 39 D3

San Boi de Llobregat, 38 D6

San Borja, 87 G5

San Bovio, 40 D1

San Bruno, CA 175 B4

San Bruno Mountain State & CP, CA 175 B4

San Carlos, CA 169 G4, 175 C3

San Carlos de Bariloche, 86 A4

San Carlos IR, AZ 131 C2

San Clemente, CA 133 D2

San Clemente de Llobregat, Spain 38 D5

San Cristobal, 84 C5, 89 C2

San Cristóbal Ecatepec, 98 C5

San Diego, CA 111 A4, 133 D2, 169 F4, 178 A3

San Diego, U of, CA 169 F4

San Diego Intl Arpt, CA 169 E3

San Diego SU, CA 169 G4

San Diego Zoo, CA 169 F3

San Dimas, CA 171 E5

San Donato Milanese, 40 C1

San Felípe, 131 A1, 133 F1

San Felipe de Jesús, 98 C4

San Fernando, Arg 88 A3

San Fernando, CA 170 B6

San Fernando de Apure, 84 D5

San Fernando de Henares, 39 F3

San Francisco, CA 81 F6, 110 A5, 132 A5, 173, 174 B5, 178 A4

San Francisco, U of, CA 173 A1

San Francisco Bay, CA
173 **F3**, 175 **C4**

San Francisco Bay NWR,
CA 175 **D3**

San Francisco Intl Aprt, CA
175 **B4**

San Francisco Mus of
Modern Art, CA 173 **E2**

San Francisco Tesistán,
99 **E6**

San Francisco Visitor Info
Ctr, CA 173 **D2**

San Francisco Watershed,
CA 175 **B3**

San Gabriel, CA 170 **D5**

San Gabriel Wilderness, CA
170 **D6**

San Gaspar de las Flores,
99 **G5**

San German, 122 **B1**

San Giovanni in Laterano
Basilica, 41 **F2**

San Gregorio, CA 175 **B2**

San Gregorio Atlapulco,
98 **D1**

San Ignacio de Loyola,
39 **A3**

San Isabel NF, CO 127 **A3**

San Isidro, 87 **F5**, 88 **D8**

San Jose, CA 94 **A1**, 97 **G1**,
110 **A5**, 132 **B5**, 175 **F1**

San José, CR 84 **A5**

San Jose Arena, CA 175 **F2**

San Jose Intl Aprt, CA
175 **E2**

San Jose SU, CA 175 **F2**

San Juan, *Arg* 86 **A5**

San Juan, *Mex* 99 **G2**

San Juan, *Phil* 62 **C2**

San Juan, PR 95 **F3**, 122 **C2**

San Juan Capistrano, CA
133 **D2**

San Juan Cosalá, 99 **G1**

San Juan de Lurigancho,
87 **G6**

San Juan de Miraflores,
87 **G4**

San Juan de Ocotán, 99 **F5**

San Juan NF, CO 131 **D4**

San Justo, 88 **C6**

San Leandro, CA 174 **D5**

San Lorenzo, CA 175 **D4**

San Lorenzo, PR 122 **C2**

San Lorenzo Tezonco, 98 **C2**

San Lucas, 96 **B4**

San Luis, 87 **G5**

San Luis Obispo, CA 133 **C3**

San Luis Potosi, 96 **C4**

San Luis Río Colorado,
131 **A3**, 133 **F2**

San Marcos, *Mex* 99 **E1**

San Marcos, TX 129 **E3**

San Marino, 17 **E4**, 24 **B4**

San Martín de las Flores,
99 **G4**

San Martín de Porras, 87 **F5**

San Martín Sq, 87 **F5**

San Mateo, CA 132 **B5**,
175 **C3**

San Mateo, *Phil* 62 **D3**

San Mateo Canyon
Wilderness, CA 171 **G1**

Sãn Mateus, 91 **C3**

San Matías Gulf, 86 **B4**

San Miguel, *Arg* 88 **B7**

San Miguel, CA 133 **C4**

San Miguel, *Chile* 87 **F2**

San Miguel, *El Sal* 97 **F2**

San Miguel, *Peru* 87 **F5**

San Miguel Cuyutlán, 99 **F2**

San Miguel de Tucumán,
86 **B6**

San Miguel Tatepozco,
99 **F6**

San Nicolas, 89 **D3**

San Nicolás de Ibarra,
99 **H1**

San Nicolas Isl, CA 133 **C2**

San Pablo, CA 174 **B7**

San Pablo Bay NWR, CA
174 **B8**

San Pedrito, 99 **F4**

San Pedro, CA 170 **B2**

San Pedro de Macorís,
95 **F4**

San Pedro Sula, 97 **F2**

San Pedro Xalostoc, 98 **C4**

San Po Kong, 75 **D3**

San Quentin, CA 174 **A6**

San Rafael, *Arg* 86 **A5**

San Rafael, CA 132 **A5**,
174 **A7**

San Ramon, CA 174 **E5**

San Remo, 24 **A5**

San Sebastián, 21 **C4**

San Sebastián, PR 122 **A3**

San Sebastián el Grande,
99 **F4**

San Severo, 24 **C3**

San Telmo, 89 **E2**

San Ysidro, CA 169 **G1**

Sanaa, 45 **H2**, 49 **F1**

Sanbancho, 69 **A4**

Sanborn Skyline CP, CA
175 **D1**

Sanchez Adobe HS, CA
175 **A4**

Sanchung, 62 **B5**

Sand Beach, ME 186 **D4**

Sand Point, ME 186 **C6**

Sanda, 70 **A7**

Sandakan, 61 **D3**

Sandberg, CA 133 **D3**

Sandpoint, ID 135 **E6**

Sandringham, 79 **C1**

Sands Point, NY 143 **G6**

Sandton, 51 **F3**

Sandusky, OH 118 **C6**

Sandwich, MA 184 **B5**

Sandy Lake, 103 **A3**

Sandy Neck, MA 184 **D5**

Sandy Springs, GA 152 **B6**

Sanford, FL 123 **F4**, 153 **H6**

Sanford, ME 115 **C4**

Sanga, 36 **D6**

Sangazi, 43 **F2**

Sangerhausen, 23 **D3**

Sanhsia, 62 **B4**

Sanibel, FL 123 **E2**

Sankaty Head, MA 185 **H6**

Sankt-Gallen, 23 **C1**, 24 **A6**

Sanlihe, 73 **C2**

Sanliurfa, 48 **D6**

Sans Souci, 78 **E5**

Sansom Park, TX 164 **B4**

Sant Andreu del la Barca,
38 **D7**

Sant Cugat del-Valles, 38 **E7**

Sant Feliu de Llobregat,
38 **D6**

Santa Ana, CA 171 **E2**

Santa Ana, *El Sal* 97 **F2**

Santa Ana, *Mex* 131 **C1**

Santa Ana River RP, CA
171 **G4**

Santa Ana Tepetitlán, 99 **F4**

Santa Anita, 99 **F4**

Santa Barbara, CA 111 **A4**,
133 **C3**

Santa Cecília, 93 **E5**

Santa Clara, CA 175 **E2**

Santa Clara, *Cuba* 94 **C5**

Santa Clara, *Mex* 98 **C5**

Santa Clarita, CA 133 **D3**

Santa Coloma de Gramanet,
38 **F6**

Santa Cruz, AZ 168 **B1**

Santa Cruz, *Bol* 84 **D1**

Santa Cruz, CA 133 **B4**

Santa Cruz, *India* 65 **B2**

Santa Cruz, *Spain* 44 **A4**

Santa Cruz de las Flores,
99 **E3**

Santa Cruz de la Soledad,
99 **H1**

Santa Cruz del Valle, 99 **G4**

Santa Cruz Isl, CA 133 **C2**

Santa Cruz Meyehualco,
98 **C2**

Santa Fe, *Arg* 86 **B5**

Santa Fe, NM 111 **D4**,
127 **A1**, 128 **B6**, 131 **E3**,
178 **C3**

Santa Fe NF, NM 127 **A1**, 128 **B6**, 131 **D4**

Santa Ifigênia, 93 **F5**

Santa Isabel, 122 **B1**

Santa Maria, *Arg* 86 **C5**

Santa Maria, AZ 168 **A3**

Santa Maria, CA 133 **C3**

Santa María Chiconautla, 98 **D6**

Santa María Chimalhuacán, 98 **D3**

Santa Maria in Trastevere, 41 **C2**

Santa Maria Tequepexpan, 99 **F4**

Santa Marta, 84 **C6**, 94 **D1**

Santa Monica, CA 170 **A4**

Santa Monica Mountains NRA, CA 170 **A5**, 172 **A8**, 178 **A3**

Santa Paula, CA 133 **D3**

Santa Rosa, *Arg* 86 **B4**

Santa Rosa, CA 110 **A5**, 132 **B5**

Santa Rosa, *Mex* 99 **H2**

Santa Rosa, NM 131 **E3**

Santa Rosa Isl, CA 133 **C2**

Santa Venetia, CA 174 **A7**

Santana, 92 **B5**

Santander, 16 **B4**, 21 **C4**

Santandercito, 90 **B1**

Santarém, 85 **F4**

Santee, CA 169 **H5**

Santee R, SC 121 **G4**

Santiago, *Chile* 86 **A5**, 87 **G2**

Santiago, *Dom Rep* 95 **E4**

Santiago de Compostela, *Spain* 21 **A4**

Santiago de Cuba, 94 **D4**, 97 **H4**

Santiago del Estero, 86 **B6**

Santo Amaro, 92 **A4**

Santo André, 92 **C4**

Santo Domingo, 95 **E3**

Santo Domingo's Church, 89 **D2**

Santo Tomé, 86 **C6**

Santos, 86 **C6**, 92 **D1**

Santos Dumont Arpt, 91 **D2**

Santpoort, 30 **C6**

Santuit, MA 185 **E3**

São Bernardo do Campo, 92 **C3**

São Caetano do Sul, 92 **C4**

São Francisco, 85 **G2**

São Gonçalo, 91 **F3**

São João de Meriti, 91 **C3**

São José do Rio Prêto, 85 **F1**

São Julião do Tojal, 38 **B8**

São Luís, 85 **G4**

São Mateus, 91 **B3**

São Miguel Paulista, 92 **C5**

São Paulo, 86 **C6**, 92 **B5**

São Paulo/Guarulhos Intl Arpt, 92 **C6**

São Tome and Principe, 46 **C6**

São Vicente, 92 **D1**

Saône R, 20 **E6**

Sappington, MO 162 **A1**

Sapporo, 66 **F7**

Sarajevo, 17 **F4**, 24 **D4**

Saranac Lake, NY 117 **G5**

Saransk, 53 **C4**

Sarasota, FL 113 **D2**, 123 **E3**

Saratoga, CA 175 **D1**

Saratoga Lake, NY 117 **H3**

Saratoga Springs, NY 117 **G3**

Saratov, 53 **C4**

Sarcelles, 28 **D8**

Sardinia, 17 **E3**, 24 **A3**, 44 **D5**

Sarh, 45 **E1**

Sari, 49 **G6**

Sariyer, 43 **E3**

Sarmiento Frigate & Naval Mus, 89 **E3**

Sarnia, 103 **B1**

Saronno, 40 **A3**

Sarriá, 38 **E6**

Sasad, 42 **A7**

Saskatchewan, 101 **E3**

Saskatoon, 101 **E2**, 110 **E8**

Sassari, 16 **D3**, 24 **A3**

Sassenheim, 30 **B4**

Sassnitz, 22 **E5**

Sassuolo, 24 **B5**

Sathorn, 63 **G5**

Satilla R, GA 123 **E6**

Sattahip, 61 **A3**

Sattra, 36 **F8**

Saúde, 92 **B4**

Saudi Arabia, 45 **H3**, 49 **E3**

Saugerties, NY 117 **G2**

Sauget, IL 162 **C1**

Saugus, MA 138 **E5**

Saugus Iron Works NHS, MA 138, **E5**

Sauk Ctr, MN 126 **F6**

Sauk Village, IL 159 **E1**

Sault Ste Marie, *Canada* 103 **B1**, 112 **C7**, 124 **F6**

Sault Ste Marie, MI 112 **C7**, 124 **E6**

Sausalito, CA 174 **A6**

Sava R, 24 **D5**

Savannah, GA 113 **D3**, 121 **F3**, 179 **G2**

Savannah, TN 120 **C5**, 125 **D1**

Savannah R, GA 121 **E4**

Savannakhet, 61 **A4**

Savigny-sur-Orpe, 28 **D6**

Savona, 24 **A5**

Sawtooth NF, ID 132 **F8**, 135 **F1**

Sawtooth NRA, ID 130 **A7**, 135 **E3**

Sayama, 68 **A8**

Sayan Mts, 55 **B3**

Sayhut, 49 **G1**

Sayre, PA 117 **E1**

Sayville, NY 116 **C5**

Saywun, 49 **F1**

SB Canyon, AZ 183 **B3**

SB Point, AZ 183 **B3**

Scarborough, 104 **F7**

Scarface Pk, MT 135 **F5**

Scarsdale, LA 163 **H4**

Sceaux, 28 **C6**

Schaerbeek, 31 **G2**

Schaffhausen, 23 **C2**, 37 **F4**

Schalksmühle, 34 **F5**

Scharnhorst, 34 **F8**

Schaumburg, IL 158 **A5**

Schauspielhaus, 33 **E3**

Schefferville, 103 **D4**

Schenectady, NY 117 **G3**

Schenley Park, PA 146 **D6**

Schererville, IN 159 **F1**

Schiedam, 30 **B2**

Schilde, 31 **H6**

Schildow, 32 **D8**

Schiller Park, IL 159 **C4**

Schipol Arpt, 30 **C5**

Schleswig, 22 **C5**

Schlieren, 37 **E2**

Schlitz Audubon Ctr, WI 157 **C4**

Schloss Bellevue, 33 **C3**

Schloss Charlottenburg, 32 **C7**

Schoemansville, 51 **E6**

Schoenfeld, 32 **E5**

Scholls, OR 177 **E4**

Schonebeck, 34 **C7**

Schoneberg, 32 **C6**, 33 **B1**

Schonwalde, 32 **D8**

School of Engineering, 89 **E2**

Schoonbrunn Palace, 42 **D7**

Schoonhoven, 30 **D2**

Schoten, 31 **G6**

Schroon Lake, NY 117 **H4**

Schupfen, 37 **B3**

Schurz, NV 132 **D6**

Schwanebeck, 32 **E8**

Schwanhein, 35 **A3**

Schwarzenburg, 37 **B1**

Schwechat, 42 **F6**

Schwedt, 23 **E4**

Schwelm, 34 **E6**

Schwerin, 22 **D5**

Schwerte, 34 **F7**

Scioto R, OH 118 **B5**

Scoresby, 79 **E2**
Scotia, NY 117 **G3**
Scotia Sea, 83 **F4**
Scotland, 14 **B2**, 18 **D6**
Scott City, KS 127 **C2**
Scott Isl, 83 **A3**
Scott Pk, ID 135 **F3**
Scottdale, GA 152 **D4**
Scotts Bluff NM, NE 178 **D4**
Scotts Run Nature Pres, VA 148 **B7**
Scottsbluff, NE 110 **E5**, 127 **B4**, 130 **F6**
Scottsboro, AL 120 **D5**
Scottsdale, AZ 131 **B2**, 168 **D6**
Scottsdale Ctr for the Arts & Dwtn Shopping District, AZ 168 **C4**
Scottsdale Municipal Arpt, AZ 168 **C5**
Scranton, PA 112 **E6**, 119 **G6**
Scripps Inst, CA 169 **E5**
Scunthorpe, 19 **E4**
Scuppernong, NC 187 **E6**
Scusset Beach SR, MA 184 **B6**
Sé, 93 **G3**
Sea Cliff, NY 143 **H5**
Sea of Azov, 53 **A3**
Sea of Crete, 17 **H2**, 25 **G2**
Sea of Japan, 55 **F2**, 60 **E8**, 66 **E6**
Sea of Marmara, 25 **H4**
Sea of Okhotsk, 54 **B7**, 82 **A8**
Sea Ranch Lakes, FL 155 **G5**
Sea Tac, WA 176 **C3**
Sea World, CA 169 **E4**
Sea World of Texas, TX 163 **C4**
Seabrook, MD 148 **F7**
Seagoville, TX 165 **H2**
Seal Beach, CA 170 **C2**
Seal Beach NWR, CA 170 **D2**

Seal Cove, ME 186 **A3**
Seal Cove Pond, ME 186 **A3**
Seal Harbor, ME 186 **C3**
Searingtown, NY 143 **G4**
Sears Tower, IL 160 **C6**
Seat Pleasant, MD 148 **F6**
Seattle, WA 101 **C2**, 110 **B8**, 134 **B5**, 176 **A5**, 178 **A6**
Seattle Ctr & Space Needle, WA 176 **B5**
Seattle-Tacoma Intl Arpt, WA 176 **C3**
Seawall, ME 186 **C2**
Seaworld, FL 153 **F3**
Sebago Lake, ME 115 **C4**
Sebastian, FL 123 **F3**
Sebastopol, CA 132 **A5**
Sebring, FL 123 **F3**
Secaucus, NJ 142 **C4**
Sedalia, MO 125 **B2**
Sedco Hills, CA 171 **H1**
Sedona, AZ 131 **B3**
Seeberg, 32 **F7**
Seefeld, 32 **E8**
Seeley, CA 133 **E2**
Ségou, 44 **B2**
Segura R, 21 **C2**
Seika, 70 **F6**
Seine R, 16 **C5**, 20 **E6**, 23 **A3**
Seixal, 38 **C6**
Selawik NWR, AK 136 **C7**
Selinia, 43 **A3**
Selkirk, 124 **A8**
Selma, AL 113 **C3**, 120 **C3**
Selma, CA 133 **C4**
Selvas, 84 **D3**
Selwyn Mts, 136 **F6**
Semarang, 61 **C1**
Semey, 53 **F2**
Seminole, FL 154 **A4**
Seminole, TX 128 **C4**
Seminole Indian Village, FL 155 **G4**
Seminole Park, FL 154 **A4**
Senago, 40 **B3**

Senaoane, 51 **E2**
Sendai, 66 **F6**
Seneca Falls, NY 116 **D3**
Seneca Lake, NY 116 **D3**
Sènègal, 44 **A3**
Sènègal R, 44 **A3**
Sengelose, 36 **A6**
Sentosa, 63 **F1**
Seoul, 55 **F1**, 60 **D8**, 66 **D4**, 72 **D7**
Seoul Grand Park, 72 **D6**
Seoul Natl Assembly Bldg, 72 **D6**
Seoul Olympic Stad, 72 **D6**
Seoul Sta, 72 **C7**
Seoul Tower, 72 **D7**
Sepik R, 76 **B2**
Sept-Iles, 103 **D3**
Serampore, 65 **E3**
Serangoon, 63 **F3**
Serbia, 17 **G4**, 25 **E6**
Serengeti Plain, 47 **G6**
Serov, 53 **E4**
Serowe, 47 **F3**
Serpong, 64 **A6**
Serra Da Cantareira, 92 **B6**
Serra Mesa, CA 169 **F3**
Serres, 25 **F4**
Sesto S. Giovanni, 40 **C2**
Sestroresk, 57 **E3**
Setagaya-Ku, 68 **B7**
Sete Pontes, 91 **E3**
Sétif, 21 **F1**
Seton Hall U, NJ 142 **A4**
Settala, 40 **D1**
Settecamini, 40 **D6**
Settimo Milanese, 40 **A1**
Settler's Cabin Park, PA 146 **A6**
Settsu, 70 **D6**
Setúbal, 16 **A3**, 21 **A3**
Seuzach, 37 **F3**
Seven Corners, VA 148 **B6**
Seven Hills, OH 150 **D5**, 151 **D4**

Seven Mile Brdg, FL 188 **C2**
Sevenoaks, 26 **E6**
Severn R, 19 **E3**
Severnaya Zemlya, 54 **A6**, 82 **C7**
Sevilla, 16 **A3**, 21 **B2**, 44 **C5**
Sevilleta NWR, NM 128 **B5**
Sevran, 28 **E7**
Seward, AK 100 **A5**
Seward, NE 127 **E4**
Seward Park, IL 160 **B8**
Seward Pen, AK 100 **A7**, 136 **B7**
Sewickley, PA 146 **A8**
Sewickley Hts, PA 146 **A8**
Sewri, 65 **B2**
Seydhisfjördhur, 14 **B5**
Sfax, 17 **E1**, 44 **D5**
Sforza Castle, 40 **B2**
Shabramant, 50 **B1**
Shache, 58 **C7**
Shackleton Ice Shelf, 83 **C1**
Shady Cove, OR 134 **B2**
Shahdara, 64 **E7**
Shaker Hts, OH 150 **E7**
Shaker Historic Mus, OH 150 **E7**
Sham Shui Po, 75 **C3**
Shandon, 151 **B4**
Shandong Pen, 66 **B5**
Shanghai, 60 **D7**, 67 **C4**, 74 **D7**
Shanghai County, 74 **B5**
Shanghai Exh Ctr, 74 **D6**
Shanghai Indoor Stad, 74 **C5**
Shanghai Mansions, 74 **E7**
Shanghai Sta, 74 **D7**
Shannon R, 19 **B3**
Shantou, 60 **C5**, 67 **B2**
Shaoguan, 67 **A3**
Shaoyang, 60 **B6**, 67 **A3**
Sharon, PA 118 **D5**
Sharon Hill, PA 144 **D2**
Sharon Woods, OH 151 **E4**

Sharonville, OH 151 E4

Shashi, 67 A3

Shasta NF, CA 134 B1

Shawano, WI 124 D5

Shawinigan, 103 D2, 114 A7

Shawnee, KS 162 A4

Shawnee, OK 129 E5

Shawnee Crowell SF, MA 184 B6

Shawnee Lookout Park, OH 151 A3

Shawnee NF, IL 125 D2

Shawnee NF, KY 120 B6

Shawseen Village, MA 138 C7

Shchelkovo, 56 D6

Shcherbinka, 56 B1

Shea Stad, NY 143 F4

Sheboygan, WI 112 B6, 124 D5

Sheep Mts, WY 181 G1

Sheep Mountain Wilderness, CA 171 E6

Sheep Porcupine Isl, ME 186 D5

Sheepshead Bay, NY 142 D1

Sheffield, 14 C1, 19 E4, 20 C8

Shek Kip Mei, 75 C3

Shek O, 75 F1

Shek O Country Park, 75 E1

Shelburne, 103 E2

Shelby, MT 135 G6

Shelbyville, KY 118 A3

Sheldon NWR, NV 132 C7, 134 C1

Shelikhov Gulf, 54 A8, 54 F6

Shell Key, FL 188 F4

Shelton, CT 116 C6

Shelton, WA 134 B5

Shenandoah Mts, 119 E3

Shenandoah NP, VA 119 E2, 179 G4

Sheng-Li Feng, 53 F1, 58 D8

Shenguasi, 73 F2

Shenkeng, 62 C5

Shenyang, 55 E2, 60 C8, 66 B6

Sherborn, MA 139 A3

Sherbrooke, 103 D2, 114 B6

Sheremet'yevo Arpt, 56 A6

Sheridan, CO 167 F2

Sheridan, WY 110 E6, 126 A6, 130 D8

Sheridan Park, WI 157 C2

Sherman, TX 129 F5

Sherwood, OR 177 F4

Shetland Isl, 14 C3

Sheung Wan, 75 C2

Sheva Nhava, 65 C1

Shibuya-Ku, 68 B7

Shihting, 62 D4

Shihung, 72 B6

Shijiazhuang, 55 E1, 60 B7, 66 A8

Shijingshan District, 73 B2

Shijo-omiya, 71 D3

Shijonawate, 70 E6

Shiki, 68 B8

Shikoku, 60 E8, 67 E4

Shikote Alin Range, 66 E7

Shiloh NMP, TN 179 F3

Shilong, 58 E5

Shimamoto, 70 E7

Shimogamo, 71 E4

Shimogyo, 71 E3

Shin-Kabuki-za Theater, 71 B1

Shinagawa-Ku, 68 C7

Shinbashi, 69 C1

Shinbashi Sta, 69 C1

Shindo, 72 C7

Shinkawa, 69 F2

Shintomi, 69 E2

Ship Harbor, ME 186 B2

Shiprock, NM 131 D4

Shipwreck Beach, HI 137 D3

Shiraz, 49 G4

Shiroi, 68 E8

Shisui, 68 F7

Shiziguan, 73 E1

Shizuoka, 66 F5

Shkodër, 17 G3, 25 E5

Sholapur, 59 C4

Shonan, 68 D8

Shore Acres, CA 174 E7

Shore Acres, IN 157 E3

Shoreview, MN 161 D4

Shorewood, IL 159 A1

Shorewood, WI 157 C3

Shorts Corner, TX 163 G3

Shoshone, ID 135 E2

Shoshone Lake, WY 180 B3

Shoshone NF, WY 135 H3, 180 D5

Shoshoni, WY 135 H2

Show Low, AZ 131 C3

Shreveport, LA 97 E6, 113 A3, 129 G4, 179 E2

Shrewsbury, MO 162 B1

Shrewsbury, UK 19 D3, 20 C8

Shrirampore, 65 E3

Shuangyashan, 55 F3, 66 B4

Shuangyushu, 73 C3

Shubra, 50 C3

Shubra El-Kheim, 50 C3

Shulin, 62 B4

Shumen, 25 H6

Shushary, 57 G1

Shymkent, 53 D1

Siasconset, MA 185 H6

Sibaté, 90 B1

Sibenik, 24 D4

Siberia, 82 B8

Sibolga, 61 A3

Sibu, 61 C2

Sicily, 17 F2, 24 C1, 44 D5, 48 A6

Sid Key, FL 188 E3

Sidi Bel Abbas, 21 D1

Sidney, Can 134 B6

Sidney, MT 126 B8

Sidney, NE 127 C4, 130 F6

Sidney, NY 117 F2

Sidney, OH 118 A4

Siegen, 23 C3

Siegessaule, 33 B3

Siegfried Pyre, AZ 183 F2

Siena, 24 B4

Sierra Blanca, TX 131 E1

Sierra Leone, 44 A1

Sierra Madre Del Sur, 96 C3

Sierra Madre Occidental, 96 B5, 111 D2

Sierra Madre Oriental, 96 C5, 111 E2

Sierra Morena, 21 B2

Sierra NF, CA 182 A1, 182 D2

Sierra Nevada, CA 110 A5, 132 C5

Sierra Vista, AZ 131 C1

Signal Hill, IL 162 D1

Signal Mt Lodge, WY 181 C4

Sigtuna, 36 D8

Sikasso, 44 B2

Sikeston, MO 120 B6

Sikhote Alin Range, 55 F3

Silistra, 25 H6

Sillery, 105 E2

Silver Beach, MA 185 H6

Silver City, ID 132 E8

Silver City, NM 111 D3, 128 A4, 131 D2

Silver Creek, NY 116 B2

Silver Gate, MT 180 D5

Silver Hill, MD 148 E5

Silver Hill, MN 139 A4

Silver Lake, MA 138 C6

Silver Spring, MD 148 D8

Silver Springs, FL 121 F1, 123 E5

Silver Springs, NV 132 D6

Silverton, OH 151 E3

Simmering, 42 E7

Simmons Park, E G, FL 154 C3

Simón Bolívar Intl Arpt, 90 B6

Simón Bolívar Plaza, 90 B5, 90 C1

Simón Bolívar Villa, 90 D2

Simpson Desert, 76 **D4**
Sinai, 48 **D4**
Sincelejo, 84 **C5**
Sing Pk, CA 182 **D1**
Singapore, 61 **A3**, 63 **G1**
Singapore Botanic Gdns, 63 **F1**
Singapore City, 61 **B2**
Singapore Natl Mus, 63 **F1**
Singapore Natl Stad, 63 **G1**
Singapore Railway Sta, 63 **F1**
Singapore, U of, 63 **F2**
Singapore War Mem, 63 **E3**
Singapore Zoological Gdns, 63 **F3**
Singawang, 61 **C2**
Singur, 65 **D3**
Sinjil, 50 **D6**
Sint Amands, 31 **F4**
Sint-Gensius-Rode, 31 **G1**
Sint-Gillis-Waas, 31 **E6**
Sint-Niklaas, 31 **E5**
Sinton, TX 129 **E2**
Sinuiju, 66 **C5**
Sioux Center, IA 126 **F5**
Sioux City, IA 125 **A4**, 126 **F5**
Sioux Falls, SD 110 **F6**, 124 **A5**, 126 **E5**, 179 **E4**
Sipe Island, 83 **B4**
Siping, 66 **C3**
Sippewisset, MA 185 **E1**
Siracusa, 24 **D1**
Sisimiut, 102 **C6**
Siskiyou NF, OR 134 **A3**
Sisseton Wahpeton IR, SD 126 **E6**
Sisters, OR 134 **B3**
Sitka, AK 101 **B4**, 136 **E5**
Sittwe, 58 **E5**
Siuslaw NF, OR 134 **A3**
Siwah, 45 **F4**, 48 **B4**
Six Flags Over Texas, TX 164 **D3**
Sixteen Mile Stand, OH 151 **F4**

Skaevinge, 36 **A8**
Skagerrak, 15 **E2**, 22 **C7**
Skagway, AK 100 **B5**
Skaneateles, NY 117 **E3**
Skaneateles Lake, NY 117 **E3**
Skånela, 36 **E8**
Skellefteå, 15 **F4**
Skhodnya, 56 **A6**
Skien, 15 **E2**, 22 **C8**
Skikda, 44 **D5**
Skodsborg, 36 **C7**
Skokie, IL 158 **D5**
Skopje, 17 **G3**, 25 **E5**
Skövde, 22 **E7**
Skovorodino, 55 **D3**
Skowhegan, ME 114 **D5**
Sky Harbor Intl Arpt, AZ 168 **C3**
Sky Lake, FL 153 **G3**
Skydome, 104 **D6**
Skye, 18 **C6**
Skyland, GA 152 **C5**
Skyway, WA 176 **C4**
Slangerup, 36 **A7**
Slavonski Brod, 24 **D5**
Sleeping Bear Dunes NL, MI 124 **E6**, 179 **F5**
Sleigh Ride Visitors Ctr, WY 181 **F1**
Slide Mt, NY 117 **G1**, 119 **H6**
Slidell, LA 120 **A3**
Sliedrecht, 30 **C1**
Sligo, 19 **B4**
Sliven, 25 **G5**
Slobozia, 25 **G6**
Slocomb, AL 122 **C6**
Slough, 26 **A7**
Slovakia, 17 **F5**, 45 **E6**
Slove, 45 **E6**
Slovenia, 17 **F4**, 23 **E1**, 24 **C6**
Smallwood Reservoir, 103 **D4**
Smethport, PA 119 **E6**
Smíchov, 35 **E3**

Smith Wilderness Area, WY 181 **E4**
Smithfield, *Austral* 78 **C7**
Smithfield, NC 121 **G5**
Smiths Falls, 117 **E6**
Smithsonian Inst, DC 149 **D2**
Smoky Dome, ID 135 **E3**
Smoky Hill R, KS 127 **D2**
Smolensk, 15 **H2**, 52 **B5**
Smolyan, 25 **G5**
Smyrna, GA 152 **A6**
Smyrna, TN 120 **C6**
Snake R, 110 **C7**, 130 **A7**, 132 **E8**, 134 **D3**, 178 **B5**, 180 **C2**, 181 **G4**
Snelgrove, 104 **A7**
Snug Harbor, FL 154 **B4**
Snyder, TX 128 **D4**
So, 72 **A6**
So Kon Po, 75 **D2**
Soacha, 90 **B1**
Soborg, 36 **B6**
Sochi, 53 **A3**
Soch'o, 72 **D6**
Socialville, OH 151 **F4**
Socorro, NM 111 **D4**, 128
Socorro Isl, 94 **B3**
Socotra, 45 **H2**, 49 **G1**
Soda Springs, ID 135 **G2**
Sodaemun, 72 **C7**
Sodegaura, 68 **D6**
Soekarno-Hatta Intl Arpt, 64 **A3**
Sofia, 17 **G4**, 25 **F5**
Soho, NY 141 **F2**
Soho, *UK* 27 **B2**
Soignolles-en-Brie, 28 **E5**
Soissons, 23 **A3**
Soka, 68 **C8**
Söke, 25 **H3**
Sokol'niki, 56 **C4**
Sokoto, 44 **C2**
Soldier Field, IL 159 **E4**
Soldiers Delight Natural Environ Area, MD 147 **A4**

Soledad, CA 133 **B4**
Solingen, 34 **C5***
Sollentuna, 36 **E7**
Sollerod, 36 **B7**
Solley, MD 147 **D1**
Solna, 36 **E6**
Solntsevo, 56 **A3**
Solomon Isl, 77 **G6**, 80 **B4**
Solomon R, KS 127 **E3**
Solomon Sea, 76 **C1**
Solon, OH 150 **F6**
Solothurn, 37 **C3**
Solymár, 42 **A8**
Somali Pen, 45 **H1**
Somalia, 45 **H1**, 47 **H6**
Somerset, KY 118 **A1**, 120 **D6**, 125 **F2**
Somerset, MD 148 **C7**
Somerset, PA 119 **E4**
Somerset Isl, 100 **F7**
Somerton, AZ 131 **A3**, 133 **F2**,
Somerton, PA 145 **G6**
Somerville, MA 139 **C4**, 140 **A6**
Somerville, NJ 116 **A5**, 119 **H5**
Somes Pond, ME 186 **B5**
Somes Sd, ME 186 **B4**
Somesville, ME 186 **B5**
Sonarpur, 65 **F1**
Sonda de Vieques, 122 **D2**
Sønderborg, 22 **D5**
Songbuk, 72 **D7**
Songdong, 72 **D7**
Songea, 47 **G5**
Songhua R, 55 **F3**, 66 **B3**
Songnam, 72 **E6**
Songp'a, 72 **E6**
Sonora, CA 132 **C5**
Sonoran Desert, 96 **B6**
Sonoyta, 131 **A1**
Sopron, 23 **F2**, 24 **D6**
Sorae, 72 **B6**
Sorbonne, 29 **E1**
Sorel, 114 **A6**

Soria, 21 **C4**

Sorocaba, 86 **C6**

Soroksár, 42 **B6**

Sorong, 76 **A3**

Sorrento, FL 153 **F6**

Sossenhelm, 35 **A3**

Souk Ahras, 24 **A1**

Sousse, 24 **B1**

South Africa, 47 **E2**

South African Broadcasting Corp, 51 **F3**

South Apopka, FL 153 **F5**

South Australia, 76 **C3**

South Badger Creek, WY 181 **E4**

South Bend, IN 112 **C5**, 125 **E4**

South Bend, WA 134 **B5**

South Bitch Creek, WY 181 **E5**

South Boston, MA 139 **D3**, 140 **D2**

South Boston, VA 119 **E1**

South Byfield, MA 138 **F8**

South Canal, 88 **E7**

South Cape Beach SP, MA 185 **E2**

South Carolina, 113 **D4**, 121 **F4**, 179 **G3**

South Carver, MA 184 **A6**

South Chatham, MA 184 **D6**

South Chicago Hts, IL 159 **D1**

South China Sea, 61 **C3**, 67 **A1**

South Dakota, 101 **F1**, 110 **F6**, 126 **D6**, 178 **D5**

South Dennis, MA 184 **E5**

South Duxbury, MA 184 **A8**

South Entrance, WY 180 **B1**

South Euclid, OH 150 **F7**

South Fork Merced R, CA 182 **B1**

South Gate, CA 170 **C4**

South Georgetown, MA 138 **E8**

South Georgia, 83 **F4**, 87 **G2**

South Groveland, MA 138 **D8**

South Hamilton, MA 138 **F7**

South Harbor, 62 **B2**

South Holland, IL 159 **E2**

South Houston, TX 166 **C3**

South Isl, 77 **H1**, 80 **C1**

South Korea, 60 **D8**, 66 **D5**

South Lake Tahoe, CA 132 **C6**

South Lawrence, MA 138 **C8**

South Lehigh Creek, WY 181 **E4**

South Lincoln, MA 139 **A4**

South Lynnfield, MA 138 **D9**

South Mashpee, MA 185 **E2**

South Melbourne, 79 **B2**

South Miami, FL 155 **F1**

South Milwaukee, WI 157 **C1**

South Mtn Park, AZ 168 **B2**

South Natich, MA 139 **A3**

South Nation R, 117 **F6**

South Orange, NJ 142 **A4**

South Orkney Isl, 83 **E4**

South Orleans, MA 184 **F5**

South Park, PA 146 **C5**

South Pasadena, FL 154 **A3**

South Pass City, WY 130 **C6**

South Philadelphia, PA 145 **E2**

South Platte R, CO 127 **B3**

South St Paul, MN 161 **E1**

South San Francisco, CA 175 **B4**

South Sandwich Isl, 83 **F4**

South Shore Park, WI 157 **C2**

South Side Park, TX 163 **G1**

South Sioux City, IA 127 **E4**

South Sister, OR 134 **B3**

South Sta, MA 140 **D2**

South Street Seaport, NY 141 **F1**

South Truro, MA 184 **E7**

South Tucson, AZ 131 **C2**

South Valley Stream, NY 143 **G2**

South Wellfleet, MA 184 **F7**

South Weymouth, MA 139 **E1**

South Whittier, CA 170 **D4**

Southern Alps, 77 **G1**

Southern California, U of, CA 172 **D5**

Southern Methodist U, TX 165 **F4**

Southern Shores, NC 187 **C6**

Southern U at New Orleans, LA 163 **G6**

Southern Ute IR, CO 131 **D4**

Southfield, MI 156 **B8**

Southgate, KY 151 **D1**

Southgate, MI 156 **C5**

Southampton, NY 115 **B1**, 116 **D6**

Southampton, UK 19 **E2**, 20 **C7**

Southampton Isl, 102 **A5**

Southlake, TX 164 **D5**

Southold, NY 116 **C6**

Southport, Austral 77 **F4**

Southport, IN 157 **E1**

Southport, NY 116 **D2**

Southside Place, TX 166 **B3**

Southwark, 26 **D7**, 27 **E2**

Southwest Harbor, ME 186 **B3**

Southwest Mus, CA 172 **F7**

Southwest Research Inst, TX 163 **E2**

Southwestern College, CA 169 **G2**

Southworth, WA 176 **A4**

Sovetskaya Gavan, 55 **F4**, 66 **E8**

Sovong, 36 **C5**

Soweto, 51 **E2**

Spain, 16 **B3**, 21 **B3**, 44 **C5**

Spandau, 32 **B7**

Spanish Steps, 41 **D4**

Sparks, NV 132 **C6**

Sparrows Pt, MD 147 **E1**

Sparta, Greece 17 **G2**, 25 **F2**

Sparta, NJ 116 **A6**

Spartanburg, SC 113 **D4**, 121 **E5**

Spatsizi Plateau Wilderness Prov P, 136 **F6**

Spearfish, SD 126 **B6**, 130 **F8**

Specimen Ridge, WY 180 **C5**

Speedway, IN 157 **D2**

Spencer, ID 130 **B7**, 135 **F3**

Spencer, IA 124 **A5**

Spencer, MA 115 **B2**

Spencer, WV 118 **C3**

Spencer Gulf, Austral 76 **D3**

Spencerport, NY 116 **C3**

Sphinx, 50 **B1**

Spijkenisse, 30 **A1**

Spinaceto, 40 **C4**

Spitalfields, 27 **F3**

Split, 17 **F4**, 24 **D4**

Spokane, WA 101 **C2**, 110 **B7**, 134 **D5**, 178 **B6**

Spongeorama Exh Ctr, FL 154 **B6**

Sports Arena, 42 **B7**

Sportsforum Berlin, 32 **D7**

Spot, NC 187 **G6**

Spotsylvania, VA 119 **F2**

Spratly Isl, 61 **D3**

Spread Creek, WY 181 **H3**

Sprecher Brewery, WI 157 **C2**

Spreitenbach, 37 **D2**

Sprendlingen, 35 **B3**

Spring Creek, NV 130 **A6**, 132 **E7**

Spring Hill, FL 123 **E4**

Spring Hill, VA 148 B7

Spring Hills, IN 157 D3

Spring Lake, NC 121 G5

Spring Lake FP, IL 158 A6

Spring Valley, CA 169 G3

Spring Valley, TX 166 A4

Springbok, 47 E2

Springdale, AR 125 B1, 129 F6

Springdale, OH 151 D4

Springdale, OR 177 H5

Springdale, PA 146 E8

Springfield, FL 122 C5

Springfield, IL 112 B5, 125 C3, 179 E4

Springfield, ME 114 E6

Springfield, MA 112 E6, 115 B2

Springfield, MO 113 A4, 125 B2

Springfield, OH 118 B4, 125 F3

Springfield, PA 144 C2

Springfield, TN 120 C6

Springfield, VT 115 A3

Springfield, VA 148 B5

Springvale, 79 D1

Springville, NY 116 B2

Sprockhövel, 34 D6

Sproul SF, PA 119 F5

Spruce Knob, WV 118 D3

Spruce Woods Prov P, 126 D8

Squantum, MA 139 D3

Squaw Peak RA, AZ 168 C4

Sri Lanka, 59 C3

Srinagar, 58 C7

Staatsburg, NY 117 G1

Stade de France, 28 D7

Stafford, TX 166 A3

Staines, 26 B7

Stamford, CT 115 A1, 116 B6

Stammersdorf, 42 E8

Standing Rock IR, SD 126 C6, 130 F8

Stanford, CA 175 D2

Stanford, KY 118 A3

Stanford, MT 135 G5

Stanford le Hope, 26 F7

Stanford U, CA 175 C2

Stanislaus NF, CA 182 A6

Stanley, Falk Isl, 86 B2

Stanley, ID 130 A7, 135 E3

Stanley Park, 107 F3

Stanovoy Range, 55 D4

Stanton, CA 170 D3

Stanton, KY 118 B2

Staples Center, CA 170 C5

Star Ferry Pier, 75 C2

Stara Zagora, 17 H4, 25 G5

Staraya, 57 H2

Starbeyevo, 56 B6

Starke, FL 121 E1, 123 E5

Starkville, MS 120 B4

Starlight Theatre, MO 162 C4

State Administration Bldg, 99 F5

State Agricultural Park, 87 F2

State Capitol, IN 156 E2

State Fairgrounds, MI 156 D7

State Fairgrounds, WI 157 A3

State House, MA 140 C3

State Library & Mus of Victoria, 79 C3

Staten Isl, NY 116 B5, 142 B1

Staten Isl Zoo, NY 142 C2

Statenville, GA 123 E6

Statesboro, GA 121 F3

Statue of Liberty NM, NY 142 C3, 179 H4

Staunton, VA 119 E2

Stavanger, 14 D2, 22 B7

Stavropol, 53 A3

Steamboat Mt, AZ 183 D3

Steamboat Springs, CO 127 A3, 130 D6

Steele, 34 C7

Steelers Stadium, PA 146 C6

Steffisburg, 37 C1

Steglitz, 32 C6

Steinbach, Can 126 E8

Steinbach, Ger 35 A4

Steinberg, 35 C1

Stekene, 31 E6

Stendal, 23 D4

Stenhamra, 36 D6

Stenlose, 36 F4

Stephenville, TX 129 E4

Steppes, The, 53 D3

Sterling, CO 110 E5, 127 B3, 130 F6

Steuben, NY 177 F4

Steubenville, OH 118 D4

Stevens Pk, ID 135 E5

Stevens Pt, WI 124 D5

Stevenson Pt, NC 187 A6

Stewart Crossing, 136 E7

Stewart Isl, 77 G1, 80 C1

Stewart R, 136 E7

Stillwater, OK 127 E1, 129 E6

Stillwater Reservoir, NY 117 F4

Stinson Arpt, TX 163 G1

Stip, 25 F5

Stirling, 18 C5

Stock Isl, FL 188 A1

Stockbridge, MA 117 H2

Stockholm, 15 F2, 22 F8, 36 F6, 52 A6, 82 F7

Stockholm Train Sta, 36 E6

Stocksund, 36 E7

Stockton, CA 110 A5, 132 C5

Stockyards Natl Hist District, TX 164 B3

Stodulky, 35 D2

Stoke-on-Trent, 19 E3, 20 C8

Stoneham, MA 138 D5

Stony Brook, NY 116 C6

Stony Isl, NY 117 E4

Stoppenberg, 34 C7

Storm Lake, IA 125 A4, 126 F5

Stornoway, 18 C7

Stowe, VT 114 A5

Strafford, PA 144 B4

Strahov Stad, 35 E3

Strait of Dover, 19 F2, 20 D7

Strait of Gibraltar, 16 A3, 21 B1, 44 B5

Strait of Hormuz, 49 G4

Strait of Juan de Fuca, WA 134 A6

Strait of Magellan, 86 B6

Strait of Malacca, 61 A3

Strait of Sicily, 17 E2, 24 B1

Straits of Florida, 94 B5

Straits Pond, MA 139 F2

Stralsund, 22 E5

Strasbourg, 16 D5, 20 F6, 23 B2

Strasburg, CO 130 E5

Strasnice, 35 F3

Stratford, 23 E3

Stratford-upon-Avon, 19 E3

Strathfield, 78 D7

Streamwood, IL 158 A5

Streatham, 26 C7

Streetsville, 104 B5

Strel'na, 57 E1

Stresovice, 35 E3

String Lake, WY 181 F3

Stringtown, KY 151 B2

Strongsville, OH 150 B5

Stroudsburg, PA 119 G5

Strumica, 25 F5

Stuart, FL 123 F3

Stuart, VA 118 D1

Stubblefield Canyon, CA 182 B6

Stumpy Pt, NC 187 G4

Stumpy Pt Bay, NC 187 G4

Stupsk, 22 F5

Sturgeon Bay, WI 124 D5

Sturgis, SD 126 **B6**, 130 **F7**

Stuttgart, *Ger* 17 **E5**, 23 **C2**

Stuttgart, AR 120 **A5**

Suba, 90 **C2**

Subia, 90 **A1**

Sucre, 84 **D1**

Sudan, 45 **F2**, 48 **C2**

Sudbury, 103 **B2**, 112 **D7**

Suez, 48 **D4**

Suez Canal, 45 **F4**, 48 **D4**

Suffolk, VA 119 **G1**, 121 **H6**

Suffolk Downs Race Track, MA 139 **E4**

Sugandha, 65 **E4**

Sugar Creek, MO 162 **D5**

Sugarloaf, FL 188 **B2**

Sugarloaf Mt, 91 **E2**

Suhar, 49 **H3**

Suita, 70 **C6**

Suitland, MD 148 **E6**

Sukkur, 58 **B6**

Sullana, 84 **B3**

Sulu Sea, 61 **D3**

Sumatra, 59 **F2**, 61 **A3**

Sumba, 61 **E1**

Summer Palace, 57 **G2**, 73 **B4**

Summerland Key, FL 188 **B6**

Summerside, OH 151 **F2**

Summersville, WV 118 **D2**

Summerville, GA 120 **D4**

Summerville, SC 121 **F4**

Summit, CA 171 **G6**

Summit, IL 159 **C3**

Summit Lake IR, NV 132 **C7**

Summit, TX 166 **B3**

Sumner, WA 176 **C1**

Sumter, SC 121 **F4**

Sumter NF, SC 121 **E4**

Sun City, AZ 168 **A5**

Sun City, CA 171 **H2**

Sun City, FL 154 **C2**

Sun City Ctr, FL 154 **D3**

Sun Lakes, AZ 168 **D1**

Sun Valley, ID 135 **F3**

Sunbeam, ID 130 **A7**

Sunburst, MT 135 **F6**

Sunbury, PA 119 **F5**

Sundbyberg, 36 **E7**

Sundbyrester, 36 **C5**

Sunderland, 18 **E5**

Sundsvall, 15 **E3**

Sunfish Lake, MN 161 **E1**

Sunflower R, MS 120 **A4**

Sunken Gdns, FL 154 **B3**

Sunnyside, CA 169 **G2**

Sunnyvale, CA 132 **B5**, 175 **D2**

Sunnyvale, TX 165 **H3**

Sunol, CA 175 **F4**

Sunol Reg Wilderness, CA 175 **F3**

Sunset Beach, CA 170 **C2**

Sunshine, 79 **A3**

Sunshine West, 79 **A3**

Supai, AZ 183 **B2**

Superior, CO 167 **F5**

Superior, MI 112 **B7**

Superior, MT 135 **E5**

Superior, WI 124 **C6**

Superior NF, MN 124 **C7**

Supreme Court, 69 **B3**

Suquamish, WA 176 **A6**

Sur, 49 **H3**

Surabaya, 61 **D1**

Surakarta, 61 **C1**

Surat, 58 **B5**

Surco, 87 **G4**

Surfside, FL 155 **G2**

Surfside, MA 185 **H5**

Surgut, 53 **E4**

Suriname, 85 **E5**

Surquillo, 87 **G4**

Surrey, VA 121 **H6**

Surrey Hills, 26 **B5**

Suruí, 91 **E4**

Susanville, CA 132 **C7**

Susquehanna R, PA 117 **E1**, 119 **G6**

Susquehannock SF, PA 119 **E6**

Süssenbrunn, 42 **F8**

Sussex, NJ 116 **A6**

Susuman, 54 **E6**

Sutherland, 78 **D5**

Sutton, *UK* 26 **C6**

Sutton, WV 118 **D3**

Sutton Isl, ME 186 **C3**

Suva, 80 **C3**

Suwannee R, FL 121 **E2**

Suzano, 92 **D5**

Suzhou, 60 **D7**, 67 **C3**

Svalbard, 52 **E7**, 82 **E7**

Svinninge, 36 **F7**

Svishtov, 25 **G6**

Svobodnyy, 55 **E3**

Swainsboro, GA 121 **E3**

Swanley, 26 **E6**

Swampscott, MA 138 **E5**

Swan R, 101 **E2**

Swanquarter, NC 187 **E3**

Swanquarter NWR, NC 187 **E2**

Swans Isl, ME 186 **A1**

Swansea, 16 **B6**, 19 **C2**, 20 **C7**

Swanton, VT 114 **A5**

Swarthmore, PA 144 **B1**

Swarthmore College, PA 144 **C2**

Swaziland, 47 **G3**

Sweden, 22 **E7**

Sweeney Ridge, CA 175 **A4**

Sweetwater, FL 123 **F2**, 155 **E1**

Sweetwater, TX 128 **D4**

Sweetwine, OH 151 **E1**

Swift Current, 101 **D2**

Swindon, 19 **E2**

Swinoujscie, 22 **E5**

Swiss Natl Mus, 37 **E1**

Swissvale, PA 146 **D6**

Switzerland, 15 **D6**, 20 **F6**, 23 **C1**, 24 **A6**, 44 **D6**

Sydney, *Can* 103 **F3**

Sydney, *Austral* 77 **E3**, 78 **E7**, 80 **B2**

Sydney Centennial Park, 78 **F6**

Sydney Cricket Ground, 78 **E7**

Sydney Intl Arpt, 78 **E6**

Sydney Opera House, 78 **F7**

Syktyvkar, 52 **D5**

Sylacauga, AL 120 **C4**

Sylhet, 58 **F5**

Symphony Hall, CA 173 **C1**

Syracuse, NY 103 **D1**, 112 **E6**, 117 **E3**

Syria, 45 **G5**, 48 **D5**

Syrian Desert, 49 **E5**

Százhalombatta, 42 **A5**

Szczecin, 15 **F1**, 22 **E5**

Szczecinek, 22 **F5**

Szeged, 17 **F5**

Szekesfehervar, 24 **D6**

Szentendre, 42 **B8**

Szigetcsép, 42 **A5**

Szigetszentmiklós, 42 **B6**

Szigethalom, 42 **A5**

Szombathely, 23 **F2**, 24 **D6**

T

Tablada, 88 **D6**

Table Mt, WY 180 **D2**

Taboão da Serra, 92 **A4**

Tabora, 47 **F5**

Tabriz, 49 **F6**, 53 **A3**

Tabuk, 48 **D4**

Täby, 36 **E7**

Tachikawa, 68 **A7**

Tacloban, 61 **E4**

Tacna, 84 **C1**

Tacoma, WA 110 **B7**, 134 **B5**, 176 **B1**

Tacoma Dome, WA 176 **B1**

Tacony, PA 145 **F4**

Tadmur, 48 **D5**

Taegu, 55 **F1**, 60 **D8**, 66 **D5**

Taejon, 66 **C5**

Tafers, 37 **A1**

Taft, CA 133 **C3**

Taft, FL 153 G3
Taguig, 62 C2
Taguao, 90 A6
Tagus R, 16 A3, 21 B3
Tahiti, 81 E3
Tahlequah, WA 176 A3
Tahoe City, CA 132 C6
Taholah, WA 134 A5
Tai Hang, 75 D2
Tai Hu, 67 B4
Tai Kok Tsui, 75 C3
Tai Po Tsai, 75 F4
Tai Tam Country Park,
   75 D2
Taichung, 60 D6, 67 C2
Tainan, 67 C2
Taipei, 60 D6, 62 C5, 67 G3
Taipei Sung Shan Arpt,
   62 C5
Taishan, 62 B5
Taitao Pen, 86 A3
Taiwan, 60 D6, 67 C2
Taiwan Str, 60 D6, 67 B2
Taiyuan, 55 D1, 60 B7,
   66 A5
Taizz, 49 F1
Tajikistan, 58 B7
Takamatsu, 66 E5
Takarazuka, 70 B6
Takarazuka Theater, 69 D2
Takatsuki, 70 D7
Takeda, 71 E2
Takla Makan Desert, 53 F1,
   58 D7
Takoma Park, MD 148 D8
Takoradi, 44 C1
Taksony, 42 B5
Talara, 84 B3
Talca, 86 A5
Talcahuano, 86 A5
Taldyqorghan, 53 E2
Talent, OR 134 B2
Taliedo, 40 C1
Taliesin West, AZ 168 D5
Taling Chan, 63 E6
Talladega, AL 120 D4

Talladega NF, AL 120 C4
Tallahassee, FL 113 D3,
   120 D2, 122 D6, 179 G2
Tallasee, AL 120 C3
Tallinn, 15 G3, 52 B6
Tallulah, LA 120 A3
Tama, 68 A7
Tamale, 44 C1
Tamanrasset, 44 D3
Tamarac, FL 123 F2,
   155 F5
Tambov, 53 B4
Tampa, FL 97 G5, 113 D2,
   123 E3, 179 G1
Tampa Bay Downs
   Racetrack, FL 154 B5
Tampa Intl Arpt, FL 154 C5
Tampa Mus of Art, FL
   154 C5
Tampere, 15 F3, 52 B6
Tampico, 96 D4
Tampines, 63 H2
Tamworth, 77 E3
Tanabe, 70 E6
Tanana R, 100 B6
Tanga, 47 G5
Tangerang, 64 A7
Tangerine, FL 153 E6
Tangier, 16 A3, 21 B1,
   44 B5
Tangshan, 66 B5
Tanjiazhai, 74 D8
Tanjungkarang-
   Telukbetung, 61 B1
Tanjungpasir, 64 A8
Tanjungpriok, 64 B7
Tannan, 70 A8
Tanshi, 68 B7
Tanshui, 62 B6
Tanta, 45 F4, 48 C5
Tanzania, 47 G5
Taos, NM 127 A1, 131 E3
Taos IR, NM 128 B6
Taoyuan, 62 A4
Tapachula, 97 E2
Tapajós, 85 E3

Tappahannock, VA 119 F2
Taquara, 91 B2
Tara, 53 E3
Tara Hills, CA 174 B7
Tarakan, 61 D3
Taranto, 17 F3, 24 D3
Tarawa, 80 C4
Tarbaek, 36 C7
Taree, 77 F3
Target Center, MN 161 C3
Targhee NF, ID 180 A3, 181 E3
Tarija, 84 D1
Tarpon Springs, FL 154 A6
Tarragona, 16 C3, 21 D3
Tartu, 15 G2
Tashkent, 53 D1, 58 B8
Tasman Sea, 77 G2, 80 B2
Tasmania, 77 E1, 80 B1
Tastrup, 36 A5
Tatabanya, 24 D6
Tatar Str, 55 F4, 66 E8
Tate Gallery, 27 C1
Tatsfield, 26 D6
Tatshenshini-Alsek
   Wilderness Prov P, AK
   136 D6
Tatuapé, 92 C5
Taüffelen, 37 A3
Taunggyi, 58 F5
Taunton, MA 115 C2
Taunton, UK 19 D2
Tauranga, 77 H2
Taurus Mts, 48 D6
Tavannes, 37 A4
Tavares, FL 121 F1
Tavernier, FL 123 F1, 188 F3
Taverny, 28 C8
Tavoy, 59 F4
Tavros, 43 B2
Taylor, MI 156 B5
Taylor Mill, KY 151 D1
Taylors Creek, OH 151 B3
Taylorsport, KY 151 B2

Taylorville, IL 125 C3
Taymyr Pen, 54 A6, 82 C8
Taytay, 62 D2
Tazewell, TN 118 B1
Tbilisi, 45 G6, 53 A3
Teahwhit Head, WA 134 A6
Teaneck, NJ 142 C6
Teaticket, MA 185 E2
Tebessa, 44 D5
Tebet, 64 B7
Tecate, 133 E2
Technical U, 33 A3
Tecolote Canyon Natural
   Park, CA 169 F5
Tecomán, 96 C3
Tecuseh, 156 F6
Tegucigalpa, 84 A6, 97 F2
Tehachapi, CA 133 D3
Tehran, 45 H5, 49 F6,
   53 A1
Tel Aviv-Yafo, 48 D5,
   50 A6
Telegraph Creek, 101 B4
Telegraph Hill, CA 173 D3
Telford, 19 D3
Telluride, CO 131 D4
Telok Blangah, 63 F1
Teltow, 32 C6
Teluknaga, 64 A8
Tembisa, 51 H4
Temmangu Shrine, 71 B3
Tempe, AZ 131 B2, 168 C2
Tempe Park, AZ 168 C3
Tempelhof, 32 D6
Temple, TX 129 E3
Temple City, CA 170 D5
Temple Hill, MD 148 E5
Temple of Heaven, 73 E1
Temple of the Moon Park,
   73 C2
Temple of the Sun, 73 F2
Temple of 1000 Lights,
   63 F2
Temple Terrace, FL 154 D5

Temple U, PA 145 E3
Templestowe, 79 E3
Templeton, 105 C4
Temse, 31 F5
Temuco, 86 A4
10 Downing Street, 27 C2
Tena, 90 A3
Tenaya Lake, CA 182 C3
Tenjo, 90 C3
Tennant Creek, 76 C5
Tennessee, 113 C4, 120 C6, 179 F3
Tennessee R, 113 C4, 179 F3, 120 B5
Tennoji-Ku, 71 C1
Tenri, 70 F5
Tensas River NWR, LA 120 A3
Teófilo Otoni, 85 G1
Tepepan, 98 B1
Tepexpan, 98 D5
Tepie, 96 C4
Teramo, 24 C4
Teresina, 85 G3
Termini Sta, 41 E3
Termiz, 53 D1
Ternat, 31 F2
Ternate, 61 F3
Terni, 24 C4
Terra Bella, CA 133 D4
Terrace, 136 F5
Terrace Park, OH 151 F2
Terrassa, 38 D7
Terre Haute, IN 112 C5, 125 E3
Terrebonne, 106 C5
Terrytown, LA 163 G4
Teruel, 21 D3
Tervuren, 31 H2
Teslin, 136 E6
Tete, 47 F4
Teterboro Arpt, NJ 142 C5
Tetlin NWR, AK 136 D6
Teton Canyon Campground, WY 181 E3

Teton Creek, WY 181 E3
Teton Range, WY 181 E4
Teton Science School, WY 181 G2
Teton Village, WY 181 F2
Teton Wilderness Area, WY 180 C1, 181 H5
Tétouan, 21 B1, 44 B5
Tetuán, 39 C4
Tewksbury, MA 138 B7
Texarkana, AR 129 G5
Texarkana, TX 113 A3, 129 F5
Texas, 96 D6, 111 F3, 128 E4, 178 D2
Texas City, TX 129 F2
Texas Stad, TX 165 F4
Texas at Arlington, U of, TX 164 D3
Texas at Dallas, U of, TX 165 G5
Teyahualco, 98 B6
Thailand, 61 A4
Thailang Tobacco Monopoly, 63 G5
Thalwil, 37 E1
Thames Barrier, 26 D7
Thames R, 19 E2, 20 C7
Thane, 65 C3
Theatre of Marcellus, 41 D2
Theodore Roosevelt NP, ND 126 B7, 178 D5
Theodore Wirth RP, MN 161 B3
Thermalito, CA 132 B6
Thermopolis, WY 130 D7, 135 H3
Thessaloniki, 17 G3, 25 F4
Thetford, 114 C7
Thibodaux, LA 120 A3
Thief River Falls, MN 124 A7, 126 E8
Thiès, 44 A3
Thimphu, 58 E6
Thohoyandou, 47 F3

Thomas Isl, ME 186 B6
Thomaston, GA 120 D3
Thomastown, 79 C4
Thomasville, GA 120 D2
Thompson, Can 101 F3
Thompson, UT 130 C5
Thompson Falls, MT 135 E5
Thompson Isl Info Ctr, ME 186 A6
Thompsons, TX 166 A1
Thomson, GA 121 E4
Thon Buri, 63 F5
Thonon-les-Bains, 23 B1
Thonotosassa, FL 154 D6
Thornbury, 79 C3
Thornhill, 104 E8
Thornhill, 79 C3
Thousand Islands, 117 E5
3 Com Park, CA 174 B5
Three Rivers, NM 131 E2
Throgs Neck Brdg, NY 143 F5
Thun, 37 C1
Thunder Basin NG, WY 126 A5
Thunder Bay, 103 A3, 112 B7, 124 D7
Thunder Hole, ME 186 D4
Thunderbird Park, AZ 168 A6
Thunderer, The, WY 180 D5
Thurso, 14 C2, 18 D7
Thurston Isl, 83 C4
Tiananmen Sq, 73 D2
Tiancunzhen, 73 B2
Tiangizo, 73 D2
Tianjin, 55 E1, 60 C8, 66 B5
Tiber R, 17 E3, 24 B4
Tibesti, 45 E3
Tibet, 59 D6
Tiburon, CA 174 B6
Tiburon Angel Isl Ferry, CA 173 D4
Tiburtino, 40 C5
Ticoman, 98 B4

Ticonderoga, NY 115 A4, 117 H5
Tieling, 66 C3
Tien Shan, 53 F1, 58 D8
Tiergarten, 32 C7, 33 C3
Tierpark Berlin, 32 E7
Tierra Ceia, FL 154 C2
Tierra del Fuego, 86 B8
Tierra Verde, FL 154 B3
Tierrasanta, CA 169 G4
Tieton, WA 134 C5
Tieying, 73 E1
Tiffany & Co, NY 141 G5
Tiffin, OH 118 B5
Tifton, GA 121 E2
Tigaon, 64 F5
Tigard, OR 177 F4
Tigre, 88 C8
Tigris R, 45 G5, 49 E5, 53 A1
Tijuana, 96 A6, 111 A4, 133 E2, 169 F1
Tiksi, 54 C6, 82 B8
Tilbury, 26 F7
Tilden RP, CA 174 C6
Tillamook, OR 134 A4
Tillamook Head, OR 134 A4
Timaru, 77 G1
Times Square, NY 141 E4
Timisoara, 17 G5
Timmins, 103 B2
Timonium, MD 147 D4
Timor, 61 F1, 76 B6
Timor Sea, 61 F1, 76 B6
Timucuan Ecological & Hist Pres, FL 121 F2
Tinley Park, IL 159 C1
Tiny Town, CO 167 E4
Tioga Pass, CA 182 D4
Tioga R, PA 116 D1
Tioga SF, PA 119 F6
Tirana, 17 G3, 25 E5
Tirnavos, 25 F4
Tirosh, 50 B4
Tiruchchirappalli, 59 C3

Tisdale, 101 **E3**

Tisselt, 31 **G4**

Tisza R, 17 **G5**

Titagarh, 65 **F3**

Titusville, FL 121 **F1**, 123 **F4**

Titusville, PA 116 **A1**

Tivoli, 36 **C6**

Tizi Ouzou, 21 **E2**

Tláhuac, 98 **D1**

Tlajomulco de Zúñiga, 99 **F3**

Tlalnepantla, 98 **B5**

Tlalpan, 98 **B1**

Tlalpizahuac, 98 **D2**

Tlaquepaque, 99 **G5**

Tlemcen, 21 **C1**

Toapayoh, 63 **F2**

Toamasina, 47 **H4**

Tobago, 95 **H1**

Tobolsk, 53 **E4**

Tobong, 72 **D8**

Tobruk, 45 **E4**, 48 **B5**

Tocantins R, 85 **F2**

Toccoa, GA 121 **E5**

Toco Hills, GA 152 **C4**

Toda, 68 **B8**

Toffen, 31 **G4**

Toga, PA 145 **E3**

Togane, 68 **F6**

Togiak NWR, AK 136 **B6**

Togo, 44 **C1**

Tohono O'odham Nation IR, AZ 131 **B2**

Tokelau, 80 **D4**

Tokol, 42 **A5**

Tokorozawa, 68 **A8**

Tokoza, 51 **G1**

Tokyo, 60 **F8**, 66 **F5**, 68 **C7**, 69, 80 **A6**

Tokyo Central Wholesale Market, 69 **E1**

Tokyo Disneyland, 68 **D7**

Tokyo Metropolitan Govt Office, 69 **D2**

Tokyo Sta, 69 **D3**

Tokyo Stock Exchange, 69 **F3**

Tolanaro, 47 **H3**

Toledo, OH 103 **C1**, 112 **C5**

Toledo, *Spain* 16 **B3**, 21 **C3**

Toledo Bend Reservoir, TX 129 **F4**, 118 **B6**, 125 **F4**

Toliara, 47 **H3**

Tolleson, AZ 168 **A3**

Toluca, 96 **D3**

Toluquilla, 99 **F4**

Tolyatti, 53 **C4**

Tom Bass RP, TX 166 **C2**

Tom Price, 76 **A4**

Tombigbee NF, MS 120 **B4**

Tombouctou, 44 **C2**

Tombstone, AZ 131 **C1**

Tomilino, 56 **D3**

Tomisato, 68 **F7**

Tomkins Square, NY 141 **G2**

Toms R, NJ 119 **H4**

Tomsk, 53 **F3**

Tonalá, 99 **G4**

Tonasket, WA 134 **C6**

Tonbridge, 26 **E5**

Tone, 68 **E8**

Tong, 72 **A6**

Tonga, 80 **D3**

Tongass, AK 136 **E5**

Tongbu, 72 **E7**

Tongdae Mun, 72 **D7**

Tongjak, 72 **C6**

Tongliao, 66 **C2**

Tonopah, NV 132 **E5**

Tonto NF, AZ 130 **B2**

Tooele, UT 130 **B6**

Toongabbie, 78 **C8**

Toowoomba, 77 **E4**

Topanga, CA 170 **A5**

Topeka, KS 112 **A5**, 125 **A3**, 127 **F3**, 179 **E3**

Topkapi Palace, 43 **E2**

Topsfield, ME 114 **F6**

Topsfield, MA 138 **E7**

Tor de Cenci, 40 **C4**

Tor di Quinto, 40 **C6**

Tor Sapienza, 40 **D5**

Toranomon, 69 **B1**

Torignimmun, 72 **C7**

Törökbálint, 42 **A6**

Toronto, 103 **C1**, 104 **D6**, 112 **D6**, 116 **B4**

Toronto, U of, 104 **D6**

Toronto Island Park, 104 **D5**

Toronto Stock Exchange, 104 **E6**

Torrance, CA 170 **B3**

Torre Gaia, 40 **D5**

Torre Lupara, 40 **D6**

Torrenova, 40 **D5**

Torreón, 96 **C4**, 111 **E1**

Torres Str, 76 **B1**

Torresdale, PA 145 **G4**

Torrimpietra, 40 **A6**

Torrington, CT 115 **A3**, 117 **H1**

Torrington, WY 127 **B4**, 130 **E6**

Tórshavn, 14 **C3**

Tortosa, 21 **D3**

Tortuga Isl, 95 **F1**

Tortuguitas, 88 **B8**

Toshima-Ku, 68 **C7**

Totowa, NJ 142 **A6**

Totsuka-Ku, 68 **B5**

Tottenham, 26 **D8**

Touggourt, 44 **D4**

Toulon, 12 **D4**, 21 **F4**

Toulouse, 16 **C4**, 21 **D4**

Touraine, 105 **A4**

Tournament Players Club of Scottsdale, AZ 168 **D5**

Tournan-en-Brie, 28 **F6**

Tours, 16 **C5**, 20 **D6**

Towanda, PA 117 **E1**, 119 **F6**

Tower Fall, WY 180 **C5**

Tower Junction, WY 130 **C8**

Tower Lakes, IL 158 **A6**

Tower of London, 27 **F2**

Town & Country, FL 154 **C5**

Town & Country, MO 162 **A3**

Town Hill, ME 186 **B5**

Townsend, MT 135 **G4**

Townsville, 77 **E5**

Towson, MD 119 **G4**, 147 **D4**

Toyama, 66 **E5**

Toyonaka, 70 **C6**

Toyono, 70 **C7**

Trabrennbahn Volkspark, 32 **E6**

Trabuco Canyon, CA 171 **F2**

Trafalgar Sq, 27 **C2**

Trafaria, 38 **A6**

Tragliata, 40 **A6**

Trail, 101 **C2**

Traiskirchen, 42 **D5**

Trajan's Forum, 41 **D3**

Trakvista, 36 **D6**

Tralee, 19 **A3**, 20 **A8**

Transantarctic Mts, 83 **C3**

Transcona, 107 **H5**

Trapani, 24 **B2**

Trastevere, 41 **C2**

Traverse City, MI 112 **C6**, 124 **E5**

Treasure Isl, FL 154 **A3**

Trejos, 99 **H6**

Trelew, 86 **B4**

Trelleborg, 22 **E6**

Tremonton, UT 135 **F1**

Trent R, 19 **E3**

Trento, 23 **D1**, 24 **B6**

Trenton, FL 123 **E5**

Trenton, MO 125 **B3**

Trenton, NJ 112 **E6**, 119 **H4**

Treptow, 32 **E7**

Tres de Febrero, 88 **C7**

Trevi, The Fountains of 41 **D3**

Treviso, 24 **B5**

Trevose, PA 145 **G6**

Trezzano sul Naviglio, 40 **B1**

Tri-City, OR 132 **A8**

Triangle X Ranch, WY 181 **G3**

Triborough Brdg, NY 143 **E4**

Trident Thorofare Plateau, WY 180 **D1**

Triel-sur-Seine, 28 **B8**

Trier, 23 **B3**

Trieste, 17 **E4**, 23 **E1**, 24 **C5**, 40 **C6**

Trikala, 25 **E4**

Trincomalee, 59 **C3**

Trinidad, Bol 84 **D2**

Trinidad, CA 132 **A7**

Trinidad, CO 111 **E4**, 127 **B2**, 128 **C6**, 131 **E4**

Trinidad & Tobago, 85 **E6**, 95 **H1**

Trinity Islands, AK 136 **C5**

Trinity NF, CA 134 **B1**

Trinity River, TX 129 **F3**

Trinity River Greenbelt Park, TX 165 **F4**

Trionfale, 40 **B6**, 41 **A4**

Triple Creek Park, OH 151 **C4**

Triple Divide Pk, CA 182 **D2**

Tripoli, 44 **D4**, 48 **A5**

Trivandrum, 59 **B3**

Trois-Rivieres, 103 **D2**, 114 **A7**

Troitsk, 56 **A1**

Trolleyville USA, OH 150 **B6**

Trollhättan, 22 **D7**

Trombay, 65 **C2**

Tromsø, 15 **F5**, 52 **C7**, 82 **E7**

Trondheim, 15 **E4**

Trooper, PA 144 **B6**

Trophy Club, TX 164 **C6**

Tropicana, 30 **B2**

Tropicana Field, FL 154 **B3**

Troutdale, OR 177 **H5**

Troy, AL 120 **C3**

Troy, NH 115 **B3**

Troy, NY 115 **A3**, 117 **H3**

Troy, OH 118 **A4**

Troyes, 20 **E6**, 23 **A3**

Truckee, CA 132 **C6**

Trujillo, 84 **B3**

Trujillo Adobe HS, CA 171 **G4**

Trujillo Alto, 122 **C2**

Trumbull, CT 116 **B6**

Truro, MA 184 **E7**

Truro, UK 19 **C2**, 103 **E2**

Truth or Consequences, NM 128 **A4**, 131 **D2**

Tshikapa, 47 **E5**

Tsim Sha Tsui, 75 **C2**

Tsing Yi, 75 **A4**

Tsuen Wan, 75 **A4**

Tsukiji, 69 **E1**

Tsukuda, 69 **F1**

Tsumeb, 47 **E4**

Tsurumi-Ku, 68 **C6**

Tsz Wan Shan, 75 **D4**

Tualatin, OR 177 **F4**

Tuamotu Archipelago, 81 **E3**

Tuba City, AZ 131 **C3**

Tucheng, 62 **B4**

Tuchomerice, 35 **D3**

Tuckernuck Isl, MA 185 **G4**

Tucker, GA 152 **D5**

Tuckup Canyon, AZ 183 **B3**

Tucson, AZ 96 **B6**, 111 **C3**, 131 **C2**, 178 **B2**

Tucumcari, NM 111 **E4**, 128 **C5**, 131 **E3**

Tucuruvi, 92 **B5**

Tuktoyaktuk, 136 **E8**

Tukwila, WA 176 **C3**

Tula, 53 **B4**

Tulane U, LA 163 **F5**

Tulare, CA 133 **C4**

Tulelake, CA 132 **B7**

Tullamarine Intl Arpt, 79 **A4**

Tullamore, 19 **B3**, 104 **A7**

Tullinge, 36 **D5**

Tulsa, OK 113 **A4**, 125 **A1**, 127 **F1**, 129 **E6**, 179 **E3**

Tultepec, 98 **C6**

Tultitlán, 98 **B6**

Tulun, 55 **B3**

Tulyehualco, 98 **C1**

Tumba, 36 **D5**

Tumbes, 84 **B3**

Tune, 36 **A5**

Tunis, 17 **E2**, 24 **B1**, 44 **D5**

Tunisia, 17 **E1**, 24 **A1**, 44 **D5**

Tunja, 84 **C5**

Tunjuelito, 90 **C1**

Tunxi, 67 **B3**

Tuolumne Grove, CA 182 **A3**

Tuolumne Meadows, CA 182 **D4**

Tuolumne Pk, CA 182 **C4**

Tuolumne R, CA 182 **A4**

Tupelo, MS 113 **B4**, 120 **B4**, 129 **H5**

Tupper Lake, NY 117 **G5**

Tura, 50 **C1**, 55 **B4**

Turbat, 58 **A6**

Turgutlu, 25 **H3**

Turin, 16 **D4**, 20 **F5**, 24 **A5**

Turkey, 17 **H3**, 25 **H4**, 45 **F5**, 48 **D6**

Turkey Run Park, VA 148 **B7**

Turkmenbash, 53 **B2**

Turkmenistan, 45 **H5**, 45 **G6**, 49 **G6**, 58 **A8**

Turks & Caicos Islands, 95 **E5**

Turku, 15 **F3**

Turlock, CA 132 **C5**

Turner Field, GA 152 **B3**

Turner Ridge, CA 182 **B1**

Turnu Magurele, 25 **G6**

Turpan Depression, 58 **E8**

Turpin Hills, OH 151 **E2**

Turret Mt, WY 180 **D2**

Turtle Creek, PA 146 **E6**

Turtle MT Prov P, 126 **D8**

Turumo, 90 **D4**

Tusayan, AZ 183 **E1**

Tusayan Ruin & Mus, AZ 183 **F1**

Tuscaloosa, AL 113 **C3**, 120 **C4**

Tuscarora, NV 132 **E7**

Tuscolano, 40 **C5**

Tushino, 56 **B5**

Tuskegee, AL 120 **D3**

Tustin, CA 171 **E2**

Tuvalu, 80 **C4**

Tuxtla Gutiérrez, 97 **E2**

Tuz Golu, 48 **D6**

Tuzla, 24 **D5**

Tver, 15 **H2**, 52 **B5**

Tweed R, 18 **D5**

Tweedsmuir Prov P, 136 **F5**

Twentynine Palms, CA 133 **F3**

Twentynine Palms Marine Corps Base, CA 133 **E3**

Twickenham, 26 **B7**

Twin Bridges, MT 135 **F4**

Twin City Racetrack, FL 154 **B6**

Twin Falls, ID 110 **C6**, 130 **A7**, 132 **F8**, 135 **E4**

Twin Lakes, CA 182 **D6**

Twin Pks, CA 171 **H6**

Twinsburg, OH 150 **F5**

Two Ocean Lake, WY 181 **G5**

Two Ocean Plateau, WY 180 **C2**

Tyler, TX 113 **A3**, 129 **F4**

Tyler Arboretum, PA 144 **A3**

Tynda, 55 **D4**

Tyreso, 36 **F6**

Tyrrhenian Sea, 17 **E3**, 24 **C2**

Tysons Corner, VA 148 **A7**

Tyumen, 53 **D4**

U

Ubangi R, 45 **E1**

Ubaque, 90 **D1**

Uberlândia, 85 **F1**

Ucayali R, 84 **C2**

Uccle, 31 **G1**

Uchikanda, 69 **D4**

UCLA, CA 170 **B5**

Uddevalla, 22 **D7**

Udel'naya, 57 **G3**

Udine, 17 **E4**, 23 **E1**, 24 **C6**

Uelzen, 23 **D4**

Uetliberg, 37 **D1**

Ufa, 53 **D4**

Uganda, 45 **F1**, 47 **G6**

Uherské Hradiste, 23 **F2**

Uhrineves, 35 **F2**

Uijongbu, 72 **D8**

Uinkaret Plateau, AZ 183 **A4**

Uintah and Ouray IR, UT
130 **C5**

Uithoorn, 30 **D4**

Uiwang, 72 **D5**

Uji, 70 **F7**

Újpest, 42 **B8**

Ujungpandang, 61 **E2**

Ukhta, 52 **D5**

Ukiah, CA 132 **A6**

Ukraine, 17 **H6**, 45 **F6**

Ukyo-Ku, 71 **D3**

Ulaanbaatar, 55 **C2**

Ulan-Ude, 55 **C3**

Ullnasjon, 36 **E7**

Üllo, 42 **C6**

Ulm, 23 **C2**

Ulsan, 66 **D5**

Uluberia, 65 **D1**

Ulyanovsk, 53 **C4**

Ulysses, KS 127 **C2**

Umatilla, OR 134 **C4**

Umatilla NF, OR 134 **D4**

Umeå, 15 **F4**

Umeda-Koma Theater,
71 **A4**

Umnak Isl, AK 136 **A5**

Umpqua NF, OR 134 **B3**

Umraniye, 43 **F2**

Umtata, 47 **F2**

Unadilla R, NY 117 **F3**

Unalaska Isl, AK 136 **A5**

Underground Atlanta, GA
152 **B3**

Unga Isl, AK 136 **B5**

Ungava Bay, 103 **C4**

Ungava Pen, 102 **B5**

Unhos, 38 **B8**

Union, NJ 142 **A3**

Union, SC 121 **F5**

Union, WV 118 **D2**

Union City, CA 175 **D4**

Union City, NJ 141 **E6**,
142 **C4**

Union City, PA 116 **A1**

Union City, TN 120 **B6**

Union Park, FL 153 **H4**

Union Square, CA 173 **E2**

Union Square, NY 141 **F3**

Union Sta, CA 172 **E6**

Union Sta, Can 104 **E6**

Union Sta, DC 149 **F3**

Union Sta, IL 160 **B5**

Union Sta, MO 162 **C2**

Uniondale, NY 143 **H3**

Uniontown, PA 118 **D4**

Unionville, NV 132 **D7**

United Arab Emirates,
49 **G3**

United Ctr, IL 159 **D4**

United Kingdom, 16 **C6**

United Nations, NY 141 **G4**

United States, 81 **H6**,
96 **D6**

US Air Force Academy, CO
127 **B3**

US Customs, CA 169 **G1**

US Intl U, CA 169 **G5**

US Holocaust Mem Mus,
DC 149 **C2**

US Mint, CO 167 **G3**

US Supreme Court, DC
149 **F2**

USS Arizona N Mem, HI
177 **F3**, 178 **C1**

USS Constitution, MA
140 **D6**

Universal Studios, FL
153 **F3**

University City, MO
162 **B2**

University Hts, OH 150 **E7**

University Park, TX 165 **F4**

University Place, WA 176 **A1**

Unp'yong, 72 **C7**

Úpalota, 42 **B7**

Upington, 47 **E2**

Upland, CA 171 **F5**

Upland, PA 144 **B1**

Upolu Pt, HI 137 **E2**

Upper Darby, PA 144 **D3**

Upper Falls, MD 147 **F4**

Upper Hadlock Pond, ME
186 **C4**

Upper Klamath Lake, OR
132 **B4**

Upper/Lower Falls, WY
180 **B4**

Upper Matecumbe Key, FL
188 **F3**

Upper Montclair, NJ
142 **B5**

Upper Red Lake, MN
124 **B7**

Upper River Rouge, MI
156 **A8**

Upper Sandusky, OH
118 **B5**

Upper Saranac Lake, NY
117 **G5**

Upplands-Vasby, 36 **D7**

Uppsala, 15 **F3**, 22 **F8**

Ural Mts, 53 **D4**

Ural R, 53 **C3**

Uran, 65 **B1**

Uranium City, 101 **E4**

Urawa, 68 **B8**

Urayasu, 68 **D7**

Urbana, IL 125 **D3**

Urbana, OH 118 **B4**

Urench, 58 **A8**

Urganch, 53 **C2**

Uruapán, 96 **C3**

Uruguaiana, 86 **C5**

Uruguay, 86 **C5**

Uruguay R, 86 **B5**

Urumqi, 55 **A1**, 58 **E8**

Usak, 25 **H3**

Usaquén, 90 **C2**

Usera, 39 **C2**

Ushuaia, 86 **B2**

Uskudar, 43 **E2**

Uskumrukoy, 43 **E4**

Usme, 90 **C1**

Ussuriysk, 55 **F3**, 66 **C6**

Ust-Ilimsk, 55 **B3**

Ust'-Izora, 57 **H1**

Ust-Kut, 55 **C3**

Uster, 37 **F1**

Usti nad Labem, 23 **E3**

Ustyurt Plateau, 53 **C2**

Usumacinta R, 97 **E2**

Utah, 110 **C5**, 130 **B5**,
135 **F1**, 178 **B4**

Utan, 65 **A4**

Ute Mountain IR, CO
131 **D4**

Utica, NY 112 **E6**, 117 **F3**

Utrecht, 23 **B4**

Utsubo Park, 71 **A3**

Utsunomiya, 66 **F5**

Uttarpara, 65 **E2**

Utuado, 122 **B2**

Urukok R, AK 136 **C8**

Uvalde, TX 128 **D2**

Uwharrie NF, NC 121 **F5**

Uxbridge, 26 **B7**

Uzbekistan, 45 **G6**, 58 **A8**

Uzice, 25 **E6**

Uzumasa, 71 **D3**

Uzunkopru, 25 **G5**

V

Vaca Key, FL 188 D2

Vacaville, CA 132 B5

Vadnais Hts, MN 161 E4

Vadodara, 58 B5

Vaerlose, 36 B7

Vail, CO 127 A3, 130 E5

Val de Grace, 29 E1

Val-d'Or, 103 C2

Valby, 36 B6

Valdés Pen, 86 B4

Valdez, AK 100 A5, 136 D6

Valdez, FL 153 G6

Valdivia, 86 A4

Valdosta, GA 113 D3, 121 E2, 122 D6

Vale, OR 134 D3

Valence, 20 F5

Valencia, Spain 16 C3, 21 D3

Valencia, Venez 84 D6, 95 F1

Valentine, NE 126 D5

Valentine NWR, NE 127 D4

Valenzuela, 62 B3

Valera, 84 C5

Valhalla, 51 G5

Valjevo, 25 E6

Valladolid, 16 B3, 21 B3

Valladupar, 84 C5

Valle de Aragón, 98 C4

Vallejo, CA 132 B5, 174 C8

Vallentuna, 36 E8

Valleranello, 40 C4

Vallersville, MA 184 B6

Valletta, 17 F1,24 C1

Valley City, ND 126 E7

Valley Falls, OR 132 C8

Valley Forge, PA 144 A5

Valley Forge NHP, PA 144 A5, 179 H4

Valley Stream, NY 143 G3

Valley View, OH 150 E6

Valparaíso, Chile 86 A5

Valparaiso, FL 122 C6

Van Buren, ME 114 E8

Van Cortlandt Park, NY 143 E6

Van Dusen Botanical Gdns, 107 F2

Van Gogh Mus, 30 D6

Van Horn, TX 131 E1

Van Kleef Aquarium, 63 F1

Van Wert, OH 118 A5

Van Wyksrust, 51 E1

Vanceburg, KY 118 B3

Vancouver, Can 101 C2, 107 F2, 110 B8

Vancouver, WA 134 B4, 177 G6

Vancouver Intl Arpt, 107 F1

Vancouver Isl, 101 B2

Vandalia, IL 125 D3

Vandenberg Village, CA 133 B3

Vänern, 15 E2, 22 D7

Vanier, Can 105 B3

Vankaren, 136 A8

Vanuatu, 80 B3

Vanzago, 40 A3

Varanasi, 58 D5

Varazdin, 23 F1, 24 D6

Varberg, 22 D7

Vardø, 15 G6

Varedo, 40 B3

Varennes, 106 D4

Varese, 24 A5

Vari, 43 C1

Varimbombi, 43 C4

Varna, 17 H4, 25 H6

Värnamo, 22 E7

Varsta, 36 D5

Vasai, 65 B4

Vashon Hts, WA 176 B4

Vassa, 15 F4

Vasterås, 15 F4

Vasterhaninge, 36 E5

Vastervik, 22 F7

Vatican City, 17 E3, 24 B4, 40 C5, 41 A4

Vatican Mus, 41 B4

Vättern, 15 E2, 22 E7

Vaxholm, 36 F7

Växjö, 15 E2, 22 E6

Vecses, 42 C6

Vedbaek, 36 C7

Vega Baja, 122 B2

Vejle, 22 C6

Vekso, 36 A6

Velbert, 34 D6

Veld, 30 D6

Velen, 35 F3

Velké Prílepy, 35 D3

Velten, 32 C8

Vendelsö, 36 F5

Veneta, OR 134 B3

Venezuela, 84 D5, 95 F1

Venice, FL 123 E3

Venice, IL 162 C2

Venice, Italy 17 E4, 24 C5

Ventas, 39 D2

Ventspils, 15 F2

Ventura, CA 133 C3

Vénustiano Carranza, 98 B3

Veracruz, 96 D3

Verbania, 20 F5

Verdun, 106 C2

Vereeniging, 47 F3

Vereseghyáz, 42 C8

Vergennes, VT 117 H5

Veria, 25 F4

Verkhoyansk, 54 D5

Verkhoyansk Range, 54 D5, 82 B8

Vermillion, SD 126 E5

Vermillion R, 114 A8

Vermont, 103 D2, 112 E6, 115 A3, 179 H5

Vernal, UT 110 D5, 130 C6

Vernon, CA 172 F5

Vernon, NS 127 D2

Vernon Hills, IL 158 B6

Vero Beach, FL 123 F3

Verona, Italy 17 E4, 23 D1, 24 B5

Verona, NJ 142 A5

Verona, PA 146 E7

Verrazano Narrows Brdg, NY 142 C2

Versailles, Fr 28 C6

Versailles, KY 118 A3

Verwoerdburg, 51 H6

Vesuvius, 24 C3

Veszprem, 24 D6

Veterans Mem Coliseum, AZ 168 B3

Veterans Mem CP, MO 162 C3

Veterans Stad, PA 145 E2

Vialonga, 38 C8

Viareggio, 24 B4

Viborg, 22 C6

Vicálvaro, 39 E2

Vicente Guerrero, 133 F1

Vicente López, 88 D8

Vicenza, 24 B5

Vichy, 20 E5

Vicksburg, MS 120 A3, 129 H4

Vicksburg NMP MS 179 E2

Victoria, Austral 77 E2

Victoria, Can 101 B2, 110 A8, 134 B6

Victoria, Hong Kong 67 A3, 75 C2

Victoria, KS 127 D2

Victoria, TX 111 F2, 129 E2

Victoria Arts Ctr, 79 B2

Victoria Conv & Exh Ctr, 75 D2

Victoria de las Tunas, 94 C4

Victoria Gdns, 65 B2

Victoria Isl, 82 C5, 100 E6

Victoria Land, 83 B2

Victoria Pk, 75 B2

Victoria Rail Sta, 65 B1

Victoria Sta, 27 B1

Victoriaville, 114 B7

Victorville, CA 133 E3

Vidalia, GA 121 E3

Vidin, 25 F6

Vidnoye, 56 C2

Viedma, 86 B4

Vienna, *Aust* 17 F5, 23 F2, 42 E7

Vienna, VA 148 A6

Vienna-Schwechat Arpt, 42 F6

Vienne R, 20 D6

Vientiane, 61 A4

Vietnam, 61 B4

Vietnam Veterans Mem, DC 149 B2

View Bank, 79 D3

Vigentino, 40 C1

Vigny, 28 B8

Vigo, 16 A4, 21 A4

Vijayawada, 59 C4

Vila Formosa, 92 C4

Vila Madelena, 92 A5

Vila Maria, 92 B5

Vila Prudente, 92 C4

Viladecans, 38 D5

Villa Abemelek, 41 A3

Villa Ahumada, 96 C6, 128 A3

Villa Ballester, 88 C7

Villa Borghese, 40 C6, 41 D4

Villa Celimontana, 41 E2

Villa Coapa, 98 B1

Villa Crespo, 89 A3

Villa de Las Flores, 98 C6

Villa de Mayo, 88 B8

Villa Dominico, 88 E6

Villa Doria Pamphili, 41 A3

Villa Hills, KY 151 C1

Villa María del Triunfo, 87 H4

Villa Park, CA 171 E3

Villa Sciarra, 41 B3

Villach, 23 E1, 24 C6

Village Green, PA 144 A1

Village of Indian Hill, OH 151 F3

Villahermosa, 97 E3

Villanova, PA 144 B4

Villanova U, PA 144 C4

Villaverde, 39 C1

Villavicencio, 84 C4

Ville de Vallecas, 39 D2

Villeneuve le Comte, 28 F6

Villeneuve St-Georges, 28 D6

Vilnius, 15 G1, 52 A5

Vilvoorde, 31 G3

Vilyuy R, 55 C4

Vilyuysk, 54 D5

Vimodrone, 40 C2

Vimont, 106 B4

Viña del Mar, 86 A5

Vincennes, *Fr* 28 D7

Vincennes, IN 125 E2

Vincente Calderón Stad, 39 B2

Vincente de Carvalho, 92 D2

Vine Hill, CA 174 D7

Vineland, NJ 119 G4

Vineyard Haven, MA 185 G2

Vineyard Sd, MA 185 F1

Vinh, 61 B4

Vinings, GA 152 A5

Vinita, OK 127 F1

Vinkeveen, 30 D4

Vinnitsa, 17 H6

Vinnytsya, 53 A4

Vinor, 35 F3

Vinson Massif, 83 C4

Violet, LA 163 H4

Virden, 126 D8

Virgin Islands, 95 G4

Virginia, 112 E5, 119 F2, 179 G3

Virginia, MN 112 A7

Virginia Beach, VA 119 G1, 121 H6

Virginia Canyon, CA 182 C5

Virginia City, MT 135 G4

Virginia Gdns, FL 155 F2

Virginia Hills, VA 148 C5

Virginia Pk, CA 182 D5

Víron, 43 C2

Virum, 36 B7

Visalia, CA 133 D4

Visby, 22 F7

Viscount Melville Sd, 100 E7

Vishakhapatnam, 59 D4

Vishnu Temple, AZ 183 E2

Vista, CA 133 E2

Vista Encantada, AZ 183 E2

Vista Hermosa, 98 A4

Vistula R, 17 F6

Vitacura, 87 G3

Vitarte, 87 H5

Vitebsk, 15 H2, 52 B5

Viterbo, 24 B4

Vitim R, 55 D3

Vitinia, 40 B4

Vitória, *Bra* 85 G1

Vitoria-Gasteiz, *Spain* 16 B4, 21 C4

Vitoria da Conquista, 85 G2

Vittoria, 24 C1

Vlaardingen, 30 A3

Vladivostok, 55 F2, 66 C6

Vlorë, 17 G3, 25 E4

Vnukovo, 56 A3

Vnukovo Arpt, 56 A3

Voerde, 34 A8

Vol Irazú, 97 G1

Vol Tajumulco, 97 E2

Volga R, 45 G6, 53 B3, 53 C4

Volgograd, 53 B3

Volo, IL 158 A7

Volo Bog State Natural Area, IL 158 A7

Volodarskiy, 56 D1, 57 F1

Vologda, 52 C5

Volos, 17 G3, 25 F3

Volta Redonda, 86 C6

Volusia, 40 C6

Voorberg, 30 A3

Voorheesville, NY 117 G3

Voorschoten, 30 B4

Voortrekker Monument, 51 G6

Vorkuta, 52 E5

Voronezh, 53 B4

Vosendorf, 42 D6

Vosloorus, 51 G6

Vostochnyy, 56 D5

Voula, 43 B1

Vouliagmeni, 43 C1

Voyageurs NP, MN 124 B7, 179 E6

Vrane, 35 E1

Vranje, 25 F5

Vrasene, 31 F6

Vratsa, 25 F6

Vrsovice, 35 E3

Vsevolozhsk, 57 H3

Vulcans Throne, AZ 183 A3

Vyborg, 15 G3

Vysocany, 35 F3

W

Waarder, 30 C3

Waasmunster, 31 E5

Wabash R, IL 125 D2

Wabu, 72 E7

Waco, TX 111 F3, 129 E4, 178 D2

Wad Madani, 45 F2, 48 D1

Waddinxveen, 30 C3

Wade Park, OH 150 E5

Wadsworth, IL 158 C8

Wagga Wagga, 77 E3

Waggaman, LA 163 E5

Wagon Wheel Canyon Wilderness Park, CA 171 F1

Wah Fu, 75 B1

Wahiawa, HI 137 C3

Wahpeton, ND 124 A6, 126 E7

Waialeale, HI 137 A4

Waianae, HI 137 C3

Waidmannslust, 32 **C8**

Waikiki Beach, HI 177 **H1**

Wailing Wall, 50 **D4**

Wailuku, HI 137 **D3**

Waimalu, HI 177 **F3**

Waimea, HI 137 **E2**

Waingapu, 61 **E1**

Waipahu, HI 177 **E3**

Wakayama, 66 **E5**

Wake Isl, 80 **C5**

Wakeby, MA 184 **B5**

Wakefield, MA 138 **D5**

Wakkanai, 66 **E7**

Wako, 68 **B8**

Walbrzych, 17 **F6**, 23 **F3**

Walden, NY 117 **G1**

Walden Pond, MA 139 **A4**

Waldo, FL 123 **E5**

Waldoboro, ME 115 **D4**

Waldport, OR 134 **A3**

Wales, 16 **B6**, 19 **D3**, 20 **C8**

Walhalla Overlook, AZ 183 **E2**

Walker Art Ctr, MN 161 **C2**

Walker Lake, NV 132 **D6**

Walker Mill RP, MD 148 **F6**

Walkerville, 51 **F1**

Walla Walla, WA 134 **D4**

Wallace, ID 135 **E5**

Wallace, KS 127 **C2**

Walldorf, 35 **A1**

Wallington, NJ 142 **C5**

Wallis & Futuna, 80 **C3**

Wallisellen, 37 **F2**

Walnut, CA 171 **E4**

Walnut Creek, CA 174 **E6**

Walpole, MA 139 **B1**

Walsenburg, CO 127 **A3**

Walsum, 34 **C8**

Walt Disney World, FL 153 **F3**

Walterboro, SC 121 **F3**

Waltham, MA 115 **C3**, 139 **B4**

Waltham Forest, 26 **D7**

Walton, NY 117 **F2**

Walton, UK 26 **B6**

Walton Hills, OH 150 **E5**

Wambel, 34 **F8**

Wamesit, MA 138 **B7**

Wamsutter, WY 135 **H1**

Wan Chai, 75 **C2**

Wanchese, NC 187 **G5**

Wandsworth, 26 **C7**

Wanli, 62 **D6**

Wanne-Eicke, 34 **D8**

Wantirna, 79 **E2**

Wapato, WA 134 **C5**

Wappingers Falls, NY 117 **H1**

Waquoit Village, MA 185 **E2**

Warabi, 68 **B8**

Wards Chapel, MD 147 **A4**

Wareham, MA 184 **A5**

Warlingham, 26 **E8**

Warm Springs, NV 132 **E5**

Warm Springs IR, OR 134 **B3**

Warner Robins, GA 121 **E3**

Warnimont Park, WI 157 **C1**

Warrandyte, 79 **E3**

Warranwood, 79 **F3**

Warraq El Arab, 50 **B3**

Warren, MI 156 **E8**

Warren, OH 118 **D5**

Warren, PA 116 **B1**, 119 **E6**

Warren Park, IN 157 **F2**

Warrensburg, NY 117 **G4**

Warrensville Hts, OH 150 **E6**

Warrenton, VA 119 **F3**

Warrenville, IL 159 **A3**

Warrington, FL 122 **B6**

Warrnambool, 76 **D2**

Warsaw, IN 125 **E4**

Warsaw, NY 116 **C3**

Warsaw, Poland 17 **G6**, 52 **A5**

Warsaw, VA 119 **G2**

Warwick, NY 116 **A6**

Warwick, RI 115 **C2**

Wasatch NF, UT 130 **C6**

Wasco, CA 133 **C4**

Washakie Wilderness, WY 180 **D3**

Washburn Isl SP, MA 185 **E2**

Washington, 101 **C2**, 110 **A8**, 134 **B5**, 178 **B6**

Washington, DC 112 **E5**, 119 **F3**, 148 **D7**, 149, 179 **H4**

Washington, NC 121 **H5**

Washington, PA 118 **B4**

Washington, U of, WA 176 **C5**

Washington Mon, DC 149 **C2**

Washington Park, IL 162 **D2**

Washington Park, IN 157 **E2**

Washington Park, WI 157 **B3**

Washington Square, IL 160 **C8**

Washington Square Park, NY 141 **F3**

Washougal, WA 177 **H6**

Waskaganish, 103 **C3**

Wassaw NWR, GA 121 **F3**

Wassenaar, 30 **B4**

Watampone, 61 **E2**

Watauga, TX 164 **C4**

Watchtower, AZ 183 **F2**

Water Keys, FL 188 **B2**

Waterbury, CT 115 **A3**

Waterfalls, AZ 183 **B2**

Waterford, Ire 14 **B1**, 19 **B3**, 26 **B8**

Waterford, PA 116 **A1**

Watergate Complex, DC 149 **A3**

Wateringen, 30 **A3**

Waterloo, IA 125 **B4**

Waterloo, MD 147 **B1**

Waterloo, NY 116 **D3**

Waterloo Sta, 27 **D2**

Watertown, MA 139 **C3**

Watertown, NY 112 **E6**, 117 **E5**

Watertown, SD 110 **F6**, 126 **E6**

Waterville, ME 114 **D5**

Waterville, WA 134 **C5**

Waterworks Bldg, 89 **C3**

Watford, 26 **B8**

Watkins Glen, NY 116 **D2**, 119 **F6**

Watsoma, 79 **D4**

Watson Lake, 101 **C4**, 136 **F6**

Watsons Bay, 78 **F7**

Watsonville, CA 133 **B4**

Wattenberg, CO 167 **H6**

Wattenscheid, 34 **D7**

Wattenwil, 37 **C1**

Wattle Glen, 79 **E4**

Wauconda, IL 158 **A6**

Waukegan, IL 125 **D4**, 158 **C7**

Wausau, WI 112 **B6**, 124 **D6**

Wauseon, OH 118 **B6**

Wauwatosa, WI 157 **A3**

Wauwinet, MA 185 **G6**

Waverly, Austral 78 **F6**

Waverly, NY 117 **E2**

Waverly, OH 118 **B3**

Waves, NC 187 **H3**

Waw, 45 **F1**

Wawa, 103 **B2**

Wawona, CA 182 **B1**

Waxahachie, TX 129 **F4**

Waycross, GA 121 **E2**, 123 **E6**

Wayland, MA 139 **A3**

Wayne, MI 156 **A5**

Wayne, PA 144 **B4**

Wayne, NE 127 **E4**

Wayne, WV 118 C2
Wayne NF, OH 118 C4
Waynesboro, GA 121 E4
Waynesboro, MS 120 B3
Weald, The 26 E5
Weatherford, OK 127 E1
Weaverville, CA 132 B7, 134 B1
Webster Groves, MO 162 B1
Weddell Sea, 83 E4
Wedding, 32 C7
Weed, CA 132 B7, 134 B1
Weehawken, NJ 141 E6, 142 D4
Weesow, 32 F8
Wegendorf, 32 F8
Weiden, 23 D3
Weifang, 66 B5
Weigongcum, 73 C3
Weihai, 55 E1, 60 C8, 66 C5
Weikiva Springs, FL 153 G5
Weipa, 76 D6
Weiser, ID 134 D3
Weissensee, 32 D7
Wejherowo, 22 F5
Wekiwa Springs SP, FL 153 F5
Welch, WV 118 C2
Welkom, 47 F2
Welland, 116 B3
Wellesley, MA 139 A3
Wellesley College, MA 139 A3
Wellfleet, MA 184 F7
Wellfleet Bay Wilderness Sanctuary, MA 184 F6
Wellfleet Harbor, MA 184 F7
Wellington, KS 129 E6
Wellington, New Zealand 80 C2
Wells, ME 115 C4
Wells, NV 132 F7, 135 E1, 178 B4

Wells Fargo Mus, CA 172 E6
Wellsboro, PA 119 F6
Wellsville, NY 116 C2
Wels, 23 E2
Wembley, 26 C7
Wembley Stad/Conf Ctr, 26 C7
Wemmel, 31 F3
Wenatchee, WA 110 B7, 134 C5
Wenatchee NF, WA 134 C6
Wendover, NV 130 A6
Wendover, UT 132 F7
Wendover Range, UT 130 B6, 132 F7
Wengi, 37 B3
Wenham, MA 138 F6
Wenzhou, 60 D6, 67 C3
Werden, 34 C7
Werder, 32 A5
Werkendam, 30 D1
Werne, 34 E7
Werneuchen, 32 F8
Wernsdorf, 32 F5
Wersten, 34 B5
West Allis, WI 157 A3
West Bank, 48 D5
West Barnstable, MA 184 C5
West Bend, WI 124 D5
West Boxford, MA 138 D8
West Brewster, MA 184 E5
West Chester, OH 151 E4
West Chester, PA 119 G4
West Chicago, IL 159 A4
West Conshonoken, PA 144 C5
West Covina, CA 170 D4
West Dennis, MA 184 E5
West Entrance, MT 180 A4
West Falmouth, MA 185 E1
West Fargo, ND 126 E2
West Forks, ME 114 D6
West Grand Lake, ME 114 E6
West Harrison, IN 151 A3

West Haven, CT 115 A1, 116 C6
West Hempstead, NY 143 H3
West Hollywood, CA 170 B5, 172 A7
West Hoxton, 78 A6
West Ice Shelf, 83 D1
West Indies, 95 E4
West Kildonan, 107 F6
West Lake, FL 188 E4
West Linn, OR 177 G4
West Meadows, 79 B4
West Memphis, AR 120 A5, 129 H6
West Miami, FL 155 F1
West Mifflin, PA 146 D5
West Milwaukee, WI 157 B2
West New York, NJ 141 F6, 142 D4
West Orange, NJ 142 A5
West Palm Beach, FL 113 E2, 123 F2, 179 G1
West Paterson, NJ 142 B6
West Peabody, MA 138 D6
West Philadelphia, PA 144 D2
West Pittsburg, CA 174 E7
West Plains, MO 125 C1, 129 G6
West Point, MS 120 B4
West Point, NE 126 E4
West Point Military Academy, NY 119 H6
West Potomac Park, DC 149 B2
West Richland, WA 134 C4
West Roxbury, MA 139 C2
West St Paul, MN 161 E2
West Samoa, 80 D3
West Seneca, NY 116 B3
West Siberian Plain, 53 F4
West Slope, OR 177 F5
West Sommerville, MA 139 C4

West Springfield, VA 148 B5
West Tisbury, MA 185 G1
West Tremont, ME 186 A3
West Trenton, NJ 146 A6
West Union, OH 118 B3
West University Place, TX 166 B3
West Vancouver, 107 G3
West View, PA 146 B7
West Virginia, 112 D5, 118 D4, 179 G4
West Yarmouth, MA 184 D5
West Yellowstone, MT 130 B8, 135 G3, 180 A4
Westboro, 105 A3
Westbrook, ME 115 C4
Westbury, NY 143 H4
Westchester, IL 159 B4
Westerham, 26 D6
Western Addition, CA 173 B1
Western Australia, 76 B4
Western Bay, ME 186 A6
Western Desert, 48 C4
Western Ghats, 59 B4
Western Railway Mus, CA 174 F8
Western Sahara, 44 A4
Western Way, ME 186 C2
Westfalenhalle, 34 F7
Westfield, MA 115 A3
Westfield, NY 116 A3
Westfield, PA 116 D1
Westlake, OH 150 A7
Westlake, TX 164 C5
Westland, MI 156 A6
Westminster, 27 B1
Westminster, CA 170 D2
Westminster, CO 167 F5
Westminster, 26 C1
Westminster, MD 119 F4
Westminster Abbey, 27 C1
Westmont, NJ 145 F2
Westmorland, CA 133 E2

313

Weston, *Can* 104 **C6**

Weston, FL 155 **E4**

Weston, MA 139 **A3**

Westover Hills, TX 164 **B3**

Westview, MD 147 **B2**

Westville, NJ 145 **E1**

Westwago, LA 163 **F4**

Westwood, CA 132 **C6**

Westwood, *Can* 107 **F5**

Westwood, KS 162 **C4**

Westwood, MA 139 **B2**

Westwood Hills, KS 162 **C5**

Westwood Lakes, FL 155 **E1**

Westworth, TX 164 **A3**

Wetherill Park, 78 **B7**

Wetter, 34 **E6**

Wettingen, 37 **D2**

Wewahitchka, FL 122 **C5**

Wewak, 76 **C2**

Wexford, 19 **C3**

Weyburn, 126 **B8**

Weymouth, MA 139 **E2**

Whangarei, 77 **H2**

Wharton SF, NJ 119 **H4**

Wheat Ridge, CO 167 **F3**

Wheatland, WY 127 **A4**, 130 **E6**

Wheaton, IL 159 **A3**

Wheaton, MD 148 **D8**

Wheeler Pk, NV 130 **A5**

Wheeling, IL 158 **B5**

Wheeling, WV 112 **D5**, 118 **D4**

Whitby, 116 **B5**

White Bear Lake, MN 161 **F4**

White Bird, ID 135 **E4**

White Center, WA 176 **B4**

White Earth IR, MN 124 **A7**, 126 **F7**

White Horse, PA 144 **A3**

White Horse Beach, MA 184 **B2**

White House, DC 149 **C3**

White Marsh, MD 147 **F4**

White Missouri R, SD 126 **D5**

White Mountain NF, NH 115 **B4**

White Mountain Pk, CA 132 **D5**

White Mountains NRA, AK 136 **D7**

White Nile R, 45 **F2**, 48 **C1**

White Oak, MD 148 **E8**

White Plains, NY 116 **B6**, 119 **H5**

White Ranch CP, CO 167 **E4**

White R, 120 **A5**, 125 **B1**, 129 **G6**, 132 **F5**

White River NWR, AR 120 **A5**, 129 **H5**

White Rock Lake Park, TX 165 **G4**

White Sands Missile Range, NM 128 **B4**, 131 **D2**

White Sands NM, NM 128 **B4**, 131 **D2**, 178 **C2**

White Sea, 15 **H5**, 52 **D6**

White Settlement, TX 164 **A3**

White Sulphur Springs, MT 135 **G5**

Whitechapel, 27 **F3**

Whitecourt, 101 **D3**

Whitehall, NY 117 **H4**

Whitehall, PA 146 **C5**

Whitehorse, 100 **B5**, 136 **E6**

Whitesburg, KY 118 **B1**

Whitesnell PP, 124 **A8**

Whitestone, NY 143 **F5**

Whitestone Brdg, NY 143 **E5**

Whitewater Bay, FL 188 **D4**

Whiting, IN 159 **E2**

Whiting Ranch Wilderness Park, CA 171 **F2**

Whitley City, KY 118 **A1**

Whitnall Park, WI 157 **A1**

Whitney Mus, NY 141 **G6**

Whittier, CA 170 **D4**

Whyalla, 76 **D3**

Wichita, KS 111 **F4**, 127 **E2**, 178 **D3**

Wichita Falls, TX 111 **F3**, 129 **E5**, 178 **D2**

Wick, 18 **D7**

Wicked Pt, 116 **D4**

Wickliffe, OH 150 **F8**

Wiener Neustadt, 23 **F2**

Wierda Park, 51 **G5**

Wiesbaden, 16 **D6**, 23 **C3**

Wijnegem, 31 **H6**

Wild Water Kingdom, 104 **B7**

Wildau, 32 **E5**

Wildcat Canyon RP, CA 174 **C6**

Wilder, KY 151 **D1**

Wildfield, 104 **B8**

Wildomar, CA 171 **H1**

Wildwood Hills, MD 148 **B8**

Wilhelmshaven, 22 **C5**

Wilhemsdorf, 32 **A5**

Wilkes-Barre, PA 119 **G5**

Wilkes Land, 83 **C1**

Wilkins, PA 146 **E6**

Wilkinsburg, PA 146 **D6**

Willamette Falls, OR 177 **G4**

Willcox, AZ 131 **C2**

Willebroek, 31 **G4**

Willemstad, 95 **F1**

Willernie, MN 161 **F4**

Williams, AZ 131 **B3**

Williams Lake, 101 **C3**

Williamsburg, KY 118 **B1**, 125 **F2**

Williamsburg, NY 141 **H1**, 142 **D3**

Williamsburg, VA 119 **G2**

Williamson, WV 118 **C2**

Williamsport, PA 119 **F5**

Williamston, NC 121 **H6**

Williamstown, *Austral* 79 **B2**

Williamstown, KY 118 **A3**

Williamstown, MA 117 **H3**

Willimantic, CT 115 **B2**

Willingboro, PA 145 **H4**

Williston, FL 123 **E5**

Williston, ND 110 **E7**, 126 **B8**

Williston Park, NY 143 **H4**

Willits, CA 132 **A6**

Willmar, MN 126 **F6**

Willmersdorf, 32 **F8**

Willmore Park, MO 162 **B1**

Willoughby, 78 **E8**

Willoughby Hills, OH 150 **F8**

Willow, FL 154 **D2**

Willow Brook, CA 170 **C3**

Willow Creek, CA 132 **A7**

Willow Grove, PA 145, **E6**

Willowbrook, IL 159 **B3**

Willowdale, 104 **D7**

Willowdale SF, MA 138 **F7**

Willows, CA 132 **B6**

Wilmer, TX 165 **G1**

Wilmette, IL 158 **D5**

Wilmington, DE 112 **E5**, 119 **G4**, 179 **H4**

Wilmington, MA 138 **C6**

Wilmington, NC 113 **E4**, 121 **H4**, 179 **G3**

Wilmington, OH 118 **B4**

Wilrijk, 31 **G5**

Wilson, NC 121 **G5**

Wilson, WY 181 **E1**

Wilton Manors, FL 155 **G5**

Wimauma, FL 154 **D3**

Wimbledon, 26 **C7**

Winchester, IN 118 **A4**

Winchester, KY 118 **A3**

Winchester, MA 139 **C4**

Winchester, TN 120 **C5**

Winchester, VA 119 **E3**

Winchester Mystery House, CA 175 **E2**

Wind Cave NP, SD 130 E7, 178 D5

Wind River IR, WY 130 C7, 135 H2

Windcrest, TX 163 H3

Windermere, FL 153 F3

Windhoek, 47 E3

Winding Stair Mountain NRA, OK 129 F5

Window Rock, AZ 131 C3

Windsor, CA 132 A5

Windsor, Can 103 B1, 112 D6, 118 B6, 125 F4, 156 E6

Windsor, UK 26 A7

Windsor Castle, 26 A7

Windsor Intl Arpt, 156 E5

Windward Islands, 95 H2

Windward Passage, 94 C3

Winfield, IL 159 A4

Winfield, KS 127 E2, 129 E6

Winisk, 103 A3

Winkler, 126 E8

Winnemucca, NV 110 B6, 132 D7, 134 D1

Winnemucca Lake, NV 132 D6

Winner, SD 126 D5

Winnetka, IL 158 D5

Winnett, MT 135 H5

Winnfield, LA 129 G4

Winnipeg, 101 F2, 107 F4, 110 F7, 124 A8

Winnipeg Intl Arpt, 107 F5

Winnsboro, LA 129 G4

Winona, MN 112 A6, 124 C5

Winona, MS 120 B4, 129 H5

Winslow, AZ 111 C4, 131 C3

Winsted, CT 115 A3, 117 H1

Winston, OR 132 A8

Winston-Salem, NC 113 D4, 121 F6

Winter Garden, FL 153 E4

Winter Haven, FL 123 F4

Winter Park, FL 153 F4

Winter Springs, FL 153 H5

Winterthur, 37 F2

Winthrop, MA 139 E4

Winthrop Harbor, IL 158 C8

Winton Woods, OH 151 D4

Wiscassey, ME 115 D4

Wisconsin, 103 A1, 112 B6, 124 C5, 179 E5

Wisconsin R, WI 124 C5

Wisconsin, U of, at Milwaukee, WI 157 C3

Wismar, 22 D5

Witch Hole Pond, ME 186 C5

Witkoppen, 51 F4

Witten, 34 E7

Wittenberge, 23 D4

Wo Mei, 75 F4

Woburn, MA 138 C5

Woerden, 30 D3

Wohlen, 37 D1

Woking, 26 B6

Wolf Pt, MT 126 A8

Wolfe Isl, 117 E5

Wolfeboro, NH 115 C4

Wolfsberg, 23 E1

Wolfsburg, 23 C4

Wollochet, WA 176 A1

Wollongong, 77 F2

Wonga Park, 79 F3

Woltersdorf, 32 F6

Woluwe-St Pierre, 31 G2

Wolverhampton, 19 D3

Wolvertem, 31 F3

Wompatuck SP, MA 139 F1

Wondang, 72 B8

Wonsan, 66 D5

Wood Ridge, NJ 142 E4

Wood Village, OR 177 H5

Woodbine Race Track, 104 C6

Woodbridge, 104 C7

Woodbury, MN 161 F2

Woodbury, NJ 119 H4

Woodcrest, CA 171 H3

Woodhaven, NY 143 E4

Woodinville, WA 176 D6

Woodland, CA 132 B5

Woodland Mound Park, OH 151 F1

Woodlands, TX 129 F3

Woodlawn, MD 147 C3

Woodlawn, OH 151 D4

Woodlynne, NJ 145 F2

Woodmere, NY 143 G2

Woodmere, OH 150 F7

Woodmoor, MD 147 B3

Woodridge, IL 159 B3

Woodruff Arts Ctr, GA 152 B4

Woods Hole, MA 185 F1

Woodside, CA 175 C2

Woodside, NY 143 E4

Woodstock, Can 114 F7

Woodstock, MD 147 A3

Woodstock, NY 117 G2

Woodstock, VT 115 B4

Woodstock, VA 119 E3

Woodstream, NJ 145 H2

Woodsville, NH 115 B4

Woodville, FL 122 D6

Woodward, OK 127 D1, 128 D6

Woolen's Garden, IN 157 F3

Woollahara, 78 F7

Woolooware Bay, 78 E5

Woomera, 76 D3

Woonsocket, RI 115 B2

Wooster, OH 118 C5

Worb, 37 C2

Worcester, Afr 47 E2

Worcester, MA 112 F6, 115 B2

Worker's Stad, 73 E3

Worland, WY 130 D7, 135 H3

World Diamond Trading Ctr, 31 G6

World Trade Ctr, Austral 79 B2

World Trade Ctr Site, NY 141 E1

Worth, IL 159 C2

Worthington, MD 147 A3

Worthington, MN 126 F5

Wounded Knee, SD 126 C5, 130 F7

Wrangel Isl, 54 D8, 82 B6

Wrangell-St Elias NP & Pres, AK 136 D6, 178 B1

Wright Brothers Natl Mem, NC 187 G6

Wrigley, 136 F7

Wrigley Field, IL 159 D4

Wroclaw, 17 F6, 23 F4

Wuhan, 60 C6, 67 A3

Wuhu, 60 C7, 67 B3

Wujiaochang, 74 E8

Wuku, 62 B5

Wülfrath, 34 C6

Wupatki Natl Mon, AZ 131 B3, 178 B3

Wuppertal, 34 D5

Würzburg, 23 D3

Wutoschingen, 37 D4

Wuxi, 67 B4

Wuyi Shan, 67 B3

Wuzhou, 60 C5, 67 A3

Wyandotte, MI 156 C5

Wyandotte NWR, MI 156 C5

Wye R, 19 D3

Wylie, TX 165 H6

Wyndham, 76 B6

Wyndmoor, PA 144 D5

Wynndale, IN 157 E3

Wyoming, 101 D1, 110 D6, 130 D7, 135 H2, 178 C4

Wyoming, OH 151 D4

Wysocking Bay, NC 187 F3

Wytheville, VA 118 D1, 121 F6

X

Xai-Xai, 47 **G3**
Xalapa, 96 **D3**
Xenia, OH 118 **B4**
Xi R, 60 **B5**
Xiamen, 67 **B2**
Xian, 60 **B7**
Xiangfan, 60 **B7**, 67 **A4**
Xianghongoi, 73 **A4**
Xiangtan, 67 **A3**
Xiannongtan Stad, 73 **E1**
Xiao Hinggan Ling, 66 **C7**
Xiaotun, 73 **A4**
Xiaoqiaoli, 74 **E6**
Xichang, 60 **A6**
Xicheng District, 73 **C3**
Xigaze, 58 **E6**
Xingtai, 66 **A5**
Xingu R, 85 **F3**
Xining, 60 **A7**
Xinyang, 67 **A4**
Xiqiao Park & Zoo, 74 **A5**
Xiyuan, 73 **B4**
Xizhuang, 73 **D1**
Xochimilco, 98 **C1**
Xuanwu District, 73 **C1**
Xuhui District, 74 **C5**
Xuijiahui, 74 **C5**
Xujiazhai, 74 **C7**
Xuzhou, 55 **E1**, 60 **C7**, 67 **B4**

Y

Yablonovvy Range, 55 **D3**, 66 **A8**
Yabucoa, 122 **C1**
Yachats, OR 134 **A3**
Yachimata, 68 **F7**
Yachiyo, 68 **E7**
Yaesu, 69 **E3**
Yaki Pt, AZ 183 **E2**
Yakima, WA 110 **B7**, 134 **C5**
Yakima IR, WA 134 **C4**
Yakutat, AK 100 **A5**
Yakutsk, 54 **D5**, 82 **B8**
Yalova, 25 **H4**

Yalta, 53 **A3**
Yam, 56 **C1**
Yamagata, 66 **F6**
Yamal Pen, 52 **F5**
Yamashina-Ku, 71 **F2**
Yamashiro, 70 **F6**
Yamato, 68 **A6**
Yamato-Koriyama, 70 **F5**
Yambol, 25 **G5**
Yamenkou, 73 **A3**
Yamontovo, 56 **B2**
Yamoussoukro, 44 **B1**
Yamsay Mt, OR 132 **B8**, 134 **B2**
Yan Kit, 63 **H2**
Yan Nawn, 63 **G4**
Yanan, 55 **D1**, 60 **B7**
Yancheng, 67 **B4**
Yangch'on, 72 **C6**
Yangfangdian, 73 **C2**
Yangmingshan NP, 62 **C6**
Yangpu, 74 **F7**
Yangquan, 66 **A5**
Yangzhou, 67 **B4**
Yankee Stad, NY 143 **E5**
Yankton, SD 126 **E5**
Yantai, 66 **B5**
Yao, 70 **D5**
Yaojiazhai, 74 **F7**
Yaoundé, 44 **D1**
Yap Isl, 80 **A5**
Yaqui, 96 **B6**
Yaren, 80 **C4**
Yarmouth, Can 103 **E2**
Yarmouth, MA 184 **D5**
Yarmouth Port, MA 184 **D4**
Yaroslavl, 52 **C5**
Yarraville, 79 **B2**
Yarrow Pt, WA 176 **C5**
Yashio, 68 **C8**
Yau Tong, 75 **E2**
Yauco, 122 **B1**
Yavapai Pt, AZ 183 **E2**
Yavne, 50 **A5**
Yawata, 70 **E7**
Yazd, 49 **G5**

Yazoo City, MS 120 **A4**, 129 **H4**
Yazoo NWR, MS 120 **A4**
Yeadon, PA 144 **D2**
Yehod, 50 **B6**
Yekaterinburg, 53 **E4**
Yellow Sea, 55 **F1**, 60 **D8**, 66 **C5**
Yellowknife, 100 **D5**
Yellowstone Lake, WY 180 **D3**
Yellowstone NP, WY 130 **C7**, 135 **G3**, 178 **C5**, 180 **B4**
Yellowstone R, MT 126 **B7**, 135 **H4**, 180 **A6**
Yemen, 45 **H2**, 49 **F1**
Yenikoy, 43 **E3**
Yenisey R, 55 **A4**, 82 **D8**
Yeovil, 19 **D2**
Yerevan, 53 **A3**
Yesilkoy, 43 **D2**
Yesilkoy Arpt, 43 **D2**
Yichang, 60 **B6**, 67 **A3**
Yichun, 55 **E3**, 66 **C7**
Yinchuan, 55 **C1**, 60 **A7**
Yingko, 62 **A4**
Yingkou, 66 **B5**
Yining, 53 **F1**, 58 **D8**
Yogyakarta, 61 **C1**
Yokohama, 60 **F8**, 66 **F5**, 68 **B6**
Yokosuka, 68 **B5**
Yongsan, 72 **C6**
Yongzhou, 67 **A3**
Yonkers, NY 116 **B6**
Yorba Linda, CA 171 **E3**
York, Can 19 **E4**
York, PA 119 **F4**
York, UK 104 **D6**
York Factory, 103 **A3**
York Mills, 104 **E7**
Yorkton, 101 **E2**
Yorktowne Hts, NY 116 **B6**
Yosemite Falls, CA 182 **B3**
Yosemite NP, CA 132 **C5**, 178 **A4**, 182 **B4**

Yosemite Valley, CA 182 **B3**
Yosemite Village, CA 182 **B3**
Yosemite West, CA 182 **E2**
Yoshida, 71 **F4**
Yotsukaido, 68 **E7**
Young Heroes Mon, 99 **F5**
Youngstown, NY 116 **B3**
Youngstown, OH 112 **D5**, 118 **D5**
Yreka, CA 132 **B7**, 134 **B1**
Ystad, 22 **E6**
Yu Shan, 67 **C2**
Yu Yuan Gdn, 74 **E6**
Yuba City, CA 132 **B6**
Yucatan Chan, 97 **F4**
Yucatan Pen, 97 **F3**
Yueyang, 67 **A3**
Yugoslavia, 17 **G4**, 25 **E6**, 45 **E6**
Yukon-Charley Rivers Natural Pres, AK 136 **D7**, 178 **B2**
Yukon Delta NWR, AK 136 **B6**
Yukon Flats NWR, AK 136 **D7**
Yukon Plateau, 100 **B5**
Yukon R, 82 **B5**, 100 **A6**, 136 **C7**, 178 **A3**
Yukon Terr, 100 **B5**
Yulee, FL 123 **F6**
Yuma, AZ 131 **A3**, 133 **F2**
Yuma Proving Ground, AZ 131 **A3**
Yumen, 55 **B1**, 58 **F7**
Yungho, 62 **C5**
Yurakucho, 69 **D2**
Yurimaguas, 84 **C3**
Yurlovo, 56 **A5**
Yuzhno-Sakhalinsk, 66 **F8**

Z

Zaandam, 30 **C6**
Zabol, 49 **H5**
Zacatecas, 96 **C4**
Zadar, 24 **C5**

Zagreb, 17 **F4**, 23 **F1**,
   24 **D5**, 45 **E6**
Zagros Mts, 45 **H5**, 49 **F5**
Zahedan, 49 **H5**, 58 **A6**
Zaire, 45 **F1**, 47 **E6**
Zajecar, 25 **F6**
Zalaegerszeg, 23 **F1**, 24 **D6**
Zalatitán, 99 **G5**
Zama, 68 **A6**
Zambezi R, 47 **F4**
Zambia, 47 **F4**
Zamboanga, 61 **E3**
Zamora, 21 **B3**
Zandar, 17 **F4**
Zandvoort, 30 **B6**
Zanesville, OH 112 **D5**,
   118 **C4**
Zanzibar, 47 **G5**
Zanzibar Isl, 47 **G5**
Zapata, TX 128 **D1**
Zapopan, 99 **F5**
Zaporizhya, 53 **A4**
Zapote de Santa Cruz del
   Valle, 99 **G3**
Zapotitán de Hidalgo, 99 **E1**
Zapotitlán, 98 **C2**
Zaragoza, 16 **C3**, 21 **D4**

Zaria, 44 **D2**
Zdiby, 35 **E3**
Zehlendorf, 32 **C6**
Zelafon, 50 **B4**
Zele, 31 **E4**
Zellwood, FL 153 **E5**
Zemst, 31 **G3**
Zenica, 24 **D5**
Zepernick, 32 **E8**
Zephyrhills, FL 123 **E4**
Zeppelinheim, 35 **A1**
Zero Milestone, DC 149 **C3**
Zeuthen, 32 **E5**
Zeytinburnu, 43 **E2**
Zhabel District, 74 **D8**
Zhambyl, 53 **E1**
Zhangjiakou, 66 **A5**
Zhangjiazhai, 74 **A6**
Zhangye, 55 **C1**, 58 **F8**
Zhangzhou, 67 **B2**
Zhanjiang, 60 **C5**
Zhaojiahuayuan, 74 **C7**
Zhaojiajiao, 74 **B7**
Zheleznodorozhnyy, 56 **D4**
Zhengbaiqi, 73 **A4**
Zhengzhou, 60 **B7**, 67 **A4**
Zhenru, 74 **B7**

Zhezqarghan, 53 **E2**
Zhitomir, 17 **H6**
Zhongxinjingzhen, 74 **A6**
Zhoujiajiao, 74 **B6**
Zhoujiazhai, 74 **F7**
Zhoushenxiang, 74 **B5**
Zhuzhou, 67 **A3**
Ziamen, 60 **C6**
Zibo, 66 **B5**
Zielona Gora, 23 **F4**
Zigong, 60 **A6**
Zimbabwe, 47 **F4**
Zinder, 44 **D2**
Zinguinchor, 44 **A3**
Zion, IL 158 **C8**
Zion NP, UT 131 **B4**,
   178 **B3**
Zionsville, IN 157 **D4**
Zipacón, 90 **A3**
Ziyyon, 50 **D4**
Zizhuyuan, 73 **B3**
Znojmo, 23 **F2**
Zoetermeer, 30 **B3**
Zográfos, 43 **C3**
Zollikerberg, 37 **F1**
Zollikofen, 37 **B2**
Zollikon, 37 **F1**

Zoo, OR 177 **F5**
Zoological Gdns, Arg 89 **A4**
Zoological Gdns, Czech Rep
   35 **E3**
Zoological Gdns, Den 36 **C6**
Zoological Gdns, Ger 35 **B3**
Zoologischer Garten, Ger
   33 **B2**
Zuchwil, 37 **C4**
Zuglo, 42 **B7**
Zuid-Beijerland, 30 **A1**
Zuidland, 30 **A1**
Zuni IR, NM 128 **A6**,
   131 **C3**
Zuni Pueblo, NM 131 **C3**
Zunyi, 60 **B6**
Zuojiazhuang, 73 **F3**
Zürich, 16 **D5**, 20 **F6**,
   23 **C1**, 24 **A6**, 37 **E1**
Zurich-Kloten Arpt, 37 **E2**
Zurzach, 37 **D3**
Zushi, 68 **B5**
Zwickau, 23 **E3**
Zwijndrecht, 30 **C1**
Zyryanka, 54 **E6**

Record of Personal Data

Name:

Address:

E-mail:

Home Phone: Office Phone:

Cell Phone: Fax:

Social Security No.:   Passport No.:

Emergency Contact: Medical:

Legal: Frequent Flyer:

Other: